Using Software ...
Qualitative Research

Using Software in Qualitative Research

a step-by-step guide

Christina Silver
& Ann Lewins

second edition

Los Angeles | London | New Delhi
Singapore | Washington DC

Los Angeles | London | New Delhi
Singapore | Washington DC

SAGE Publications Ltd
1 Oliver's Yard
55 City Road
London EC1Y 1SP

SAGE Publications Inc.
2455 Teller Road
Thousand Oaks, California 91320

SAGE Publications India Pvt Ltd
B 1/I 1 Mohan Cooperative Industrial Area
Mathura Road
New Delhi 110 044

SAGE Publications Asia-Pacific Pte Ltd
3 Church Street
#10-04 Samsung Hub
Singapore 049483

Editor: Katie Metzler
Assistant editor: Lily Mehrbod
Production editor: Ian Antcliff
Copyeditor: Richard Leigh
Proofreader: Clare Weaver
Indexer: David Rudeforth
Marketing manager: Sally Ransom
Cover design: Francis Kenney
Typeset by: C&M Digitals (P) Ltd, Chennai, India
Printed and bound by CPI Group (UK) Ltd,
Croydon, CR0 4YY

Library of Congress Control Number: 2013954792

British Library Cataloguing in Publication data

A catalogue record for this book is available from
the British Library

MIX
Paper from
responsible sources
FSC® C013604

ISBN 978–1-4462-4972-7
ISBN 978–1-4462-4973-4 (pbk)

Contents

List of Figures

List of Tables

List of Boxes

Analytic notes boxes contain reflections on broad aspects relating to the nature of analysis. *Case notes* boxes provide case-study examples. *Functionality notes* boxes contain comments relating to specific analytic tasks enabled by software.

Companion Website

Using Software in Qualitative Research: A Step-by-Step Guide second edition is supported by a companion website. Visit http://www.uk.sagepub.com/silverlewins2e to take advantage of the learning resources for students and researchers, including:

- Full colour illustrations from the book
- Sample data to accompany case studies in the book
- Step-by-step instructions from software developers for the latest versions of the following packages:
  - ATLAS.ti
  - Dedoose
  - HyperRESEARCH
  - MAXQDA
  - NVivo
  - QDA Miner
  - Transana

Acknowledgements

We would like to thank the thousands of researchers and students we have met during our work with Computer Assisted Qualitative Data AnalysiS (CAQDAS) who have helped us to understand what works well in software, what they find easy to use, and what adapts well to their complex range of needs.

We are indebted to the early pioneers of the field and the many friends and colleagues who have contributed to our thinking, including Duncan Branley, Alan Bryman, Sarah Bulloch, Jeanine Evers, Graham Gibbs, Udo Kelle, Matthew Miles, Lyn Richards, Tom Richards, Christine Rivers, John Siedel, Renata Tesch, Eben Weitzman, Nick Woolf, and others mentioned below.

Historically, we have much to thank Ray Lee and Nigel Fielding for, particularly their inspirational creation of the CAQDAS Networking Project, but also for continually enabling us to draw on their experience and methodological expertise.

We thank Katie Meltzer at Sage Publications for her encouragement and feedback, and all who have contributed to the production of this book: for reading and commenting on early drafts, Jennifer Patashnick, whose scrutiny helped us flesh out ideas and avoid errors or omissions but was always provided in the best humour; Merete Watt Boolsen, whose theoretical eye has been invaluable; and Virginia Phillips, whose suggestions on writing style and feedback from a non-expert perspective helped us see the wood from the trees.

We particularly thank Jason Teal and Michael Strong for their patience, red wine, love and common sense. Also our wider families, especially parents (Christopher and Nelleke), children (Nathanael, Magdalena, Gregory and Emma) and grandchildren (Effie, Nell and Fred) with whom we are looking forward to spending more time now this book is finished.

Last, but not least, we would like to thank the ever responsive software developers and their support teams, without whom the companion website would not have been developed. Thomas Muhr, Susanne Friese and Scientific Software (ATLAS.ti), Eli Lieber and SCRC (Dedoose), Anne Dupuis and Researchware (HyperRESEARCH), Udo Kuckartz, Anne Kuckartz, Stefan Rädiker, Graham Hughes and Verbi (MAXQDA), Normand Peladeau and Provalis Research (QDA Miner), David Woods, Joseph Woods and the University of Wisconsin-Madison Center for Education Research (Transana).

Finally, we owe a debt of gratitude to our fabulous little laptops and … the comfy chair.

Christina Silver and Ann Lewins
October 2013

About the authors

Christina Silver became engaged with qualitative software from 1997 whilst studying for her MSc in Social Research Methods and shortly afterwards began working with Ann Lewins at the CAQDAS Networking Project. Christina has trained thousands of participants in the theory and practice of qualitative software, taught methods courses at universities across Europe and been involved in numerous qualitative and mixed methods research projects. In 2002 she co-founded with Ann Lewins Qualitative Data Analysis Services (QDAS), which provides bespoke consultancy, coaching and analysis for a range of clients. Since 2010 Christina has managed the CAQDAS Networking Project, leading it's capacity-building and training activities and she also co-directs Day Courses in Social Research, a programme of methods courses based in the Department of Sociology at the University of Surrey. She is particularly interested in the relationship between methodology and technology, software-supported visual analysis and the application of qualitative software outside of the academic social sciences.

Ann Lewins was a founding member of the ESRC (UK) funded CAQDAS Networking Project, which she managed until 2010. The project was created to provide a forum for debate around qualitative technology and to support those embarking on the use of qualitative software throughout the wider research community. Ann designed and led a vigorous programme of seminars and training events supporting a range of software applications and gained a unique level of knowledge in the field. Her work helped to establish the standing of the CAQDAS Networking Project as the leading international authority on qualitative software, a reputation that continues to this day.

Between 1994 and 2010 Ann trained thousands of participants at events held at the University of Surrey and many hundreds more at universities and research institutions within UK, Ireland and Europe. Recently she has specialised in supporting teams in their use of CAQDAS programs and has written detailed protocols to guide some of the planning and preparation of such research that are available from the website. She has advised many individual and collaborative research projects concerning both the preparation of complex datasets and the building of creative solutions to the challenges of working with software.

Introduction

The use of technology in qualitative research is not a new idea. Documentary film-making, the use of photographs and other visual documentary evidence are early examples. Subsequently, first analogue and now digital recording devices have been used to capture interactions and discussions. Bespoke technological support for analytic procedures, however, has a less lengthy and more controversial history. In many senses this is curious, given the role of technology in everyday life. The past 10 years, however, has seen a rise in published academic articles mentioning the use of Computer Assisted Qualitative Data AnalysiS (CAQDAS), a rise in demand for instruction in their use, and an increase in interest in them from those outside the academic social science disciplines within which they originally developed.

This book is the result of a collaboration that started in 1997 when Christina was studying for her MSc and Ann was running the CAQDAS Networking Project (CNP), which began in 1994. Our work together since then has shaped how we think about, use and teach qualitative software, and this book results from those experiences.

In this introduction, we summarise our working relationship, in order to contextualise our thinking about the role of qualitative software, explain why this book is needed, and frame the way that we have written it.

Some personal history

We first met during an overview about qualitative software that Ann gave to social research methods MSc students at the University of Surrey. Ann's engagement with qualitative research and software started during a period of struggle with a part-time history of politics research degree. She was collecting pilot interviews from Labour Party activists when she started her post with the CNP. She felt she had dropped from a great height, simultaneously into the world of social research methodology, technology and the demands of getting a new project off the ground in an innovative methodological area.

The CNP was funded by the UK Economic and Social Research Council (ESRC) but even so survived from the beginning on a shoestring budget which went up and down (mostly down) on seven successive hard-fought-for grants. Ann managed the CNP from 1994 to 2010. During that time she helped shape the project's role whilst great changes were occurring in researchers' expectations and needs of qualitative software and support in its use. The project was the brainchild of Nigel Fielding

(University of Surrey) and Ray Lee (Royal Holloway University of London) who, together with Ann, established its international reputation. Some of the packages, mostly begun as academic exercises amongst social researchers, gradually became commercial enterprises. Ann raised awareness about less well-known packages and delivered training for those establishing a significant place in the research world. The project was committed to balancing its main priorities – absolute absence of any commercial connection to any one piece of software, answering an increasing demand for training, and creating a forum for debate and a space where methodologists and researchers could meet developers face-to-face.

Christina had conducted qualitative analysis for her undergraduate dissertation using manual methods: cutting up photocopied printouts of interviews, marking them using coloured highlighter pens and sticking bits of cut-up transcripts on the bedroom wall in a matrix of themes (represented as columns) by respondents (as rows). Following Ann's overview, Christina, intrigued by the idea that there might be an easier way to manage quantities of data, asked Ann for a free copy of software to use for her MSc dissertation. Ann said no! At that time the department only had licences for software in the computer lab where training courses were run. Four packages were becoming prominent in the UK at that time – ATLAS.ti, WinMax (later MAXQDA), NUD*IST (later NVivo) and The Ethnograph. The picture was slightly different elsewhere – for example, in the Netherlands the locally developed Kwalitan was well used. Already in 1997 the CNP had become a national resource centre for qualitative software, with a website, created and maintained by Ann, providing information about software developments and forums for discussion between users and developers.

Ann's recommendation to the poverty-stricken student was to download a free trial version. NUD*IST fitted the bill as the trial version was fully functional (the only restriction being that you could not save your work). Christina duly transcribed her interviews and over a bank holiday weekend, set about importing them and began coding. Work started off very broadly, printing out bodies of initially coded data and working on those printouts with highlighter pens and scissors. The dissertation was on a knife edge! At any moment there could have been a power cut, a computer or software crash.

Ann was helpful and encouraging, showing Christina how to get as much done as possible within time constraints and concerns that her computer might overheat if left on for days on end. After working on exported hard-copy code reports and giving the computer a rest, Christina reimported them as new data files, recoded and interrogated them. It was thus a quasi-computer-assisted approach, but it got the job done and the degree was obtained. Later that year Christina started a PhD, and from 1998 began assisting Ann with software training courses, as the interest in qualitative software and thus participant numbers were rapidly increasing. That was 17 years ago. Christina is now running the CNP, since Ann retired from the university in 2010.

Via the CNP and our consultancy, QDA Services, we have trained more than 12,000 researchers in the use of qualitative software. We have taught on postgraduate methods programmes, consulted on the technical and methodological aspects of academic and applied research projects, conducted analysis on qualitative and mixed methods datasets, and troubleshooted for hundreds of researchers struggling with technical and conceptual aspects of using software. We have used different products in our own research. We have discussed, deliberated and disagreed amongst ourselves and with methodologists, students, researchers and software developers. We have, above all else, learnt from each other and those who have attended our training events and seminars.

Our thinking

When we teach, no two sessions are the same because participants arrive with different expectations and needs. Some are very methodologically oriented or experienced in specific manual analytic procedures. Such participants tend to know exactly what they want from software and either quickly succeed in finding it and leave satisfied, or feel frustrated because the software does not appear to live up to their expectations in some way. Others are much more practical in their thinking. Occasionally this manifests itself in a desire for short-cuts to speed up analysis. These participants often leave disappointed. More usually, participants are looking for systematic ways of managing large or complex sets of data. The virtues of CAQDAS packages in this respect come through quickly. The point for us has always been that software can be manipulated to suit a range of needs, that these needs vary from project to project, researcher to researcher, and change as projects progress. Contexts such as sector, discipline, methodology and computer 'savviness' all play their part in how individual researchers get on with CAQDAS packages. Many can teach themselves how to operate software, but what our workshops additionally do is to present packages in their entirety. Illustrating how to put the elements of software together so that you can exploit their potential fully is where we hope we add real value. Being methodologically aware adds an additional dimension when working in academic contexts. In applied contexts (e.g. public consultations, service evaluations), being clear about the practicality of required outcomes is fundamental to successful software use. PhD students fare better when they embark on software use with clearly specified analytic needs, have supportive and technologically knowledgeable supervisors and when they keep detailed notes about their software use so they can adequately justify their processes later on.

Using software is a creative process since qualitative software packages – in essence and design – are inherently flexible. There might well be an efficient way of proceeding, but there are multiple pathways to reaching a particular end-point and multiple purposes for doing so. Though key things need to be achieved in a workshop, the real driver for how it flows and the precise route we take are the participants. In the years we spent working and teaching closely together, we acted as a test-bed for ideas and applications for software use. There are challenges in reacting to the individual needs of participants. Finding solutions to a range of problems expanded our own understanding of the potential of software. We got to know developers and, together with many other software users, influenced the ways in which packages improved. Of course we cannot take too much credit for that! Although experienced users' feedback is critical, developers do know a thing or two about the potential of technology and how to make it work for analytic purposes!

The CNP is predicated upon the idea that there is no one 'best' software package. Each has a range of tools. There are general similarities, but each has different emphases and qualities. There are also tools in individual packages that are quite distinctive. We are impressed by some of these special aspects, and we hope this book will illustrate them.

Why a second edition?

The first edition of this book, published in 2007, resulted from a clear need for specific step-by-step support in the use of software. It was Ann's conceptualisation; Christina muscled in on it. The orientation was explicitly and intentionally practical. Many people do not read software manuals and find help menus confusing. Ann wanted to demystify the area in a practical way, and the first edition was firmly framed around that aim. Christina's current focus is to develop the teaching of technology within methodological frameworks. As software and research develop, the dialectic between them changes. So, in general terms, this second edition has been updated to account for some of the major developments that have occurred in the field since 2007. This has resulted in broadening the packages we continually illustrate and refer to. They do not all have the same focus, emphasising and excelling in different aspects of functionality. Some of the special elements within particular packages will appeal to different types of researcher.

The main issue with the first edition, as with most books about software, is that the specific technical information contained within it was quickly overtaken by software developments. We have therefore taken out most of the software-specific and step-by-step instruction from this edition, placing it on a **companion website** that we can keep up to date as new versions are released (www.uk.sagepub.com/silverlewins2e). Some of the software developers have been glad to contribute to the creation of these pages and we thank them for that.

The continued demand for CNP training in the full range of packages since the publication of our first edition is testament to a relative – and continued – failure of academic institutions to embed instruction in the technical aspects of CAQDAS packages into undergraduate and postgraduate curricula. More significantly, the questions still routinely asked at our training sessions indicate there to be a related lack of awareness of the methodological implications of using software to manage data and analyses. Therefore we have expanded this edition to offer more methodological contextualisation, including more detailed attention to visual analysis and mixed methods approaches. This is in response to increasing interest from outside academic social science disciplines and increasing requests for descriptions of how to undertake certain types of analysis using particular software packages. Both these trends speak to the breadth in potential for the use of CAQDAS packages, and the continued need for specific advice about how to use them.

To a certain extent this book is about highlighting excellence, both in the important routine tasks and in special or unique functions. We felt there was a need to point to particular strengths of software for particular research needs. Although it was not feasible in this book to do so systematically for all methodologies or practical eventualities, we provide suggestions about phases and tasks of analysis and information concerning the general and special provision of tools in these contexts.

Chapter overview

Chapter 1 provides the practical and analytic framework for the book and the way we think about and teach software. Broadly, it introduces qualitative data analysis in the context of CAQDAS use, discussing some of the main types of analysis that can be supported by them. It defines the term 'CAQDAS' and the way we understand and use it; discusses the practicalities of research in the software context; provides some historical contextualisation about the rise of qualitative software; and discusses selected analytic strategies in the context of software use. The chapter emphasises a critical yet flexible approach to the use of CAQDAS packages, considering analytic processes, levels of work and cuts through data, which resonate through the remainder of the book.

Chapter 2 outlines the key ways in which CAQDAS packages can support research projects. It illustrates their project management potential and discusses the implications of this for the ways in which tools can be used effectively and efficiently. The focus is a discussion of analytic activities that are common to many approaches (Figure 2.1; p. 45), describing our model for how these may intersect with software tools and the sense in which software projects can reflect research design. The chapter describes the three case studies that the illustrated processes contained throughout the book are based on: Case A, Young People's Perceptions; Case B, The Financial Downturn; and Case C, Coca-Cola Commercials. The chapter concludes by stressing that choosing the 'right tools for the job' depends on the nature of the project, and that software is inherently flexible, such that it always remains the researchers' decision what, when, why and how to use tools.

Chapter 3 summarises the CAQDAS packages featured in this book: ATLAS.ti, Dedoose, HyperRESEARCH, MAXQDA, NVivo, QDA Miner, and Transana. The descriptions provide a general overview of functionality, focusing on what is distinctive about each. Representatives of most of the software companies have contributed to this chapter, therefore summaries reflect the developmental thinking of each software as well as our assessment of their distinctiveness and particular benefits. In the chapters that follow we make reference to these software packages and their tools where we believe functionality supports an analytic need particularly well. This book is therefore not systematically comparative in its treatment of the packages. The purpose is to provide an overview of what these packages can do generally, but also to regularly focus attention on aspects of individual software that work particularly well for certain analytic tasks. We therefore do not cover every function in every software package. The fact that we have not illustrated a tool in a particular package does not mean that it is not present. You should refer to the product websites for a comprehensive list of software functionality.

Chapter 4 discusses data and their preparation for use in CAQDAS packages. This includes file formats and preparation for textual, multimedia and mixed data. The chapter is rather detailed and much of its content might not be relevant to your particular project, because it covers a whole range of possible data preparation considerations. Therefore, you may not need to read this chapter unless and until you are at the point of needing to prepare data for analysis. With respect to textual data, we include minimal transcription guidelines and make references to optimal, i.e. software specific, guidelines. These often concern inherent structures and units of recognisable context. For multimedia data we discuss early considerations, including distinctions between working 'directly' or 'indirectly', the use of social media content and assistance for transcribing. In considering mixed data we outline processes for descriptive and quantitative data import, pre-coding and auto-processing functions.

Chapter 5 outlines useful early steps in software, focusing on practical tasks for getting started and tools which are important to become familiar with early on. This includes setting up software projects and putting early organisational structures in place which reflect initial research design, yet maintaining the flexibility to grow ideas and alter placeholders as projects evolve. We introduce memos and other forms of writing and the importance of being transparent and reflexive in all you do.

Chapter 6 discusses exploration and data-level work, focusing on the key tools involved in becoming familiar with data once they are incorporated within a software project. This includes discussion of the universal utility of annotation tools, quick content-searching tools (including text-mining functionality), hyperlinking, and editing and marking textual data for emphasis. The focus is on experimentation such that if they are relevant to your analytic needs, you are able to develop a strategy for using them in the context of your own preferred ways of working, the nature of your data and the needs of your project.

Chapter 7 discusses principles and processes for qualitative coding in software. This involves a broad discussion of different approaches to coding (inductive, deductive, abductive) and possible strategies for using software when adopting code-based approaches. There is a separate section on coding visual data, and the chapter concludes with discussion concerning limits and cautions when using software coding tools.

Chapter 8 covers basic retrieval options for coded data. It discusses principles, purposes and types of simple retrieval, illustrating that a lot can be achieved without recourse to complex query tools. Although we discuss these tasks in a separate chapter, retrieval usually occurs in tandem with coding, as part of an iterative process. We present them separately only because of the constraints of the linear book format. The chapter ends by discussing reflexivity and rigour in the context of code and retrieve functionality.

Chapter 9 is the third chapter specifically covering coding tasks, discussing ways of working with coding schemes. We discuss the processes of breaking down data and building them back together; the differing structures of coding schemes in individual packages and their implications; how to escape the confines of the structures available and how to handle coding schemes that become too 'large'.

Chapter 10 discusses ways CAQDAS packages facilitate managing processes and interpretations through writing. This is one of the most important chapters in the book. We discuss the importance of writing in analysis, the forms, purposes and spaces for writing in software and considerations when doing so. This includes becoming aware of how you can integrate your writing with other aspects of work, and the benefits of doing so in eventually developing an evidenced and transparent account. We emphasise the flexibility provided by customised qualitative software in this respect.

Chapter 11 focuses on mapping tools where they are available in CAQDAS packages. It follows on from the discussion of managing processes and interpretations through writing as these are inherently related activities. We discuss and illustrate many different starting points and uses for maps, illustrating how they can be manipulated to suit various needs.

Chapter 12 discusses tools for organising data by known characteristics. This includes discussion of socio-demographic characteristics and other factual features in data, including those identified through the processes of analysis. We outline the importance of organisation and how this reflects research design. We discuss ways of organising whole and parts of documents, and illustrate the uses of working in each way.

Chapter 13 reiterates that interrogation happens throughout analysis, sometimes using simple tools in optimal ways (as discussed in Chapter 8). We build on this to outline more complex query tools designed to help you interrogate the dataset in a range of deeper ways. We discuss the role of interrogation in moving on with analysis, prioritising the incremental, iterative and repeatable nature of querying. We discuss ways to test theories, identify patterns and relationships, compare subsets and other interrogative options.

Chapter 14 concludes the book, presenting a brief round-up of our thinking. Entitled 'Convergence, Closeness, Choice', it discusses ways in which software functionality is coming together, but also how individual tools maintain their distinctiveness. We discuss the contentious issue of whether software acts as a barrier between researchers and their tactile relationship with data, or brings them closer to materials; we argue for the latter position. Above all, this chapter reinforces the threads common throughout: namely that you, as the researcher, remain in control of your methodological needs, your analytic strategies and your use of software. You have the choice of whether to use one of these customised tools in the first place; if you do, then which one; and once you have settled on a product, which tools within it to make use of, how, why and when.

CHAPTER EXERCISES AND THE COMPANION WEBSITE

All the task-based chapters (Chapters 4–13) include illustrations from our three case-study examples (described in Chapter 2). At the end of each chapter are exercises which can be followed using data from one of the case-study examples. Sample datasets can be downloaded from the companion website (www.uk.sagepub.com/silverlewins2e). The website includes step-by-step instructions for these exercises for most of the packages that we discuss in detail in the book. In most cases, these have been developed in partnership with the respective developers, for which we are very grateful. These are updated regularly to take account of functionality changes in new releases. The website also contains a section on teamworking in the context of CAQDAS use, which is not discussed within the book itself.

Our ultimate aim

In illustrating examples of software use in different contexts through three distinct case-study examples we hope to paint a picture of some common aspects of analysis in the context of software tools so that you can draw out ideas about what might be useful in your own particular research. We understand that your choice of software may be limited within the constraints of local provision, but our purpose is to enable ambitious yet secure use of *any* CAQDAS package and the moulding of its functions to your needs, while also adding to your awareness of what other tools work well for particular contexts. We believe that a broad understanding of software packages other than the one you happen to be using will open up your thinking about your own work.

Above all, we see ourselves as 'facilitators' rather than 'instructors'. The way we teach is informed by the belief that you are the expert about your project and your needs. We can show you tools, illustrate their benefits and caution against their potential limitations. We can make suggestions about their suitability (or not) for different approaches to data analysis. But you need to decide whether to use software at all – and if so, then which package. If you decide not to use software then you need to be able to justify this. If you decide to use software, you need to design a strategy for doing so within the parameters of your broader methodological context, specific analytic needs and any practical constraints within which you are working.

We hope this book will provide you with the context you need to frame your thinking about software, to give you insights into the way particular tools might be useful at various moments, and to heighten your reflection about the relationship between technology and methodology. More than anything else, we hope this book will inspire you to explore your data to greater depths, to experiment with software tools and to develop systematic and creative ways of conducting robust and well-evidenced analysis.

1

Qualitative Data Analysis and CAQDAS

This chapter introduces the eclectic field of Computer Assisted Qualitative Data AnalysiS (CAQDAS) in the context of qualitative research methodology and the techniques of analysis generally. We discuss the practicalities of research in the software context, outline some basic principles and distinctions which resonate throughout the book; discuss software developments, debates and functionality; and discuss selected qualitative approaches. The remaining chapters build from here, describing some core tasks you might undertake using CAQDAS packages, illustrated via three case-study examples (Chapter 2). Our overall emphasis is on the inherent fluidity between the processes involved in analysis and how customised CAQDAS packages reflect and reinforce them.

We discuss analysis in the context of technological possibilities. Table 1.1 lists common analytic tasks enabled by CAQDAS, but software itself does not dictate their sequencing, or whether certain tasks are undertaken or tools are used. These decisions rest entirely with you, informed by the interplay between methodology, analytic strategy, technology and practicality.

Table 1.1 Common tasks of analysis supported by CAQDAS packages

Task	Analytic rationale
Planning and managing your project	Keep together the different aspects of your work. Aid continuity, and build an audit trail. Later, illustrate your process and your rigour through transparent writing.
Writing analytic memos	Manage your developing interpretations by keeping track of ideas as they occur, and building on them as you progress.
Reading, marking and commenting on data	Discover and mark interesting aspects in the data as you see them. Note insights as they strike you, linked to the data that prompted them − enabling retrieval of thoughts together with data.

(Continued)

Table 1.1 (Continued)

Task	Analytic rationale
Searching (for strings, words, phrases etc.)	Explore data according to their content. Discover how content differs across data and considering how familiarising with content helps you understand what is 'going on'.
Developing a coding schema	Manage your ideas about your data by creating and applying codes (that represent themes, concepts, categories etc.). The structure and function of a coding scheme depends on methodology, analytic strategy and style of working.
Coding	Capture what is going on in your data. Bring together similar data according to themes, concepts etc. Generate codes from the data level (inductively) or according to existing ideas (deductively) as necessary; define the meaning and application of codes.
Retrieval of coded segments	Revisit coded data to assess similarity and difference, to consider how coding is helping your analysis, and prioritising 'where to go next'.
Recoding	Recode into broader or narrower themes or categories if appropriate and necessary. Perhaps bring data back together and think about them differently.
Organisation of data	Organise data according to known facts and descriptive features to allow consideration of how these aspects play a role in your understanding.
Hyperlinking	Link data to other data segments and/or to other files to track process, contradiction, association etc.
Searching the database and the coding schema	Test ideas, interrogate subsets for similarity and difference, identify anomalies, or generate another level of coding.
Mapping	Manage analytic processes by visualising connections, relationships, patterns, processes, ideas.
Generating output	Report on different aspects of your progress and the project at any stage. Save as files to capture status at an analytic stage, or to work in other applications. Print off to get away from the computer and think and work in more 'traditional' ways.

Qualitative research and data analysis

Qualitative research is a broad field that crosses disciplinary, methodological and sector-based boundaries, and it is important to acknowledge the variety contained within it. Different philosophical, theoretical and methodological traditions underpin the way researchers think about and do analysis. Much work has been done elsewhere to make sense of these – often competing and sometimes complementary – scientific principles. If you are new to the area we point you in the direction of the following in particular:

Bryman and Burgess (1994), Creswell (1998), Mason (2002), Bernard and Ryan (2010), Silverman (2010, 2011), Bazeley (2013) and Saldaña (2013). Neither the scientific and philosophical principles nor the disciplinary and methodological subtleties within approaches to qualitative research and analysis are the focus of discussion in this book. However, reflecting on your ontological and epistemological standpoints (i.e. how you understand the world to work and how you believe it can be investigated) is important in locating and justifying your research. In reading the literature you will come across many different terms used to define the context and manner of inquiry, including *perspective, framework, approach, strategy, methodology*, and *method*. There are no clear boundaries between or hierarchical structure to these terms; they overlap and are used differently in particular contexts. Categorisation of qualitative research in terms of data collection techniques has a long history, but detailed discussion concerning the *processes* and *procedures* involved in analysis (i.e. what we actually do) has only occurred more recently (Bryman and Burgess, 1994). This book discusses processes and procedures of analysis specifically in the context of customised software use.

The extent of diversity in the field is well illustrated by comparing the work of three authors, all of whom wrote during the 1990s yet conceptualised qualitative research rather differently. Tesch (1990) distinguished 27 *forms* of qualitative research (see Figure 1.1; p. 23). Woolcott (1994) differentiated qualitative research *strategies* according to six styles of collecting data (archival strategies, interview strategies, non-participant observation strategies, participant observation strategies, field study, ethnography). Miles and Huberman (1994: 7) argue that while a 'core' of recurring features exist across qualitative research, they are 'configured and used differently in any particular research tradition'. They distinguish between three traditions: *interpretivism* (including phenomenology, social interactionism, semiotics, deconstructionism, ethnomethodology and hermeneutics); *social anthropology* (including ethnography, life history, grounded theory, ecological psychology, narrative studies and case-study analysis; and *collaborative social research* (action research).

The range of ways used to describe qualitative research and analysis illustrates the difficulty of adequately reflecting the diversity in how general principles intersect to result in specific strategies. Most authors concede there to be much overlap between the distinctions they draw; there is often even blurring between understandings amongst different authors using the same terms. Researchers combine data collection methods in qualitative research design and borrow elements from various approaches in developing specific strategies for investigating new social problems or for using different forms of data.

Problems in categorisation systems are illustrated particularly clearly in contemporary writings about mixed methods. As more authors enter the debate, a tendency to generate increasingly specific categorical systems to reflect diversity ensues. Increasingly subtle differentiations complexify to such a degree that the area can become more difficult to access for novice researchers. Nevertheless, broad overviews and summaries are important in gaining entry to any field of scientific inquiry.

The use of customised software is not *required* in order to conduct robust analysis. But its use enables us to be more transparent in how we go about analysis because the tasks we engage in, their sequence, role and documentation can be more easily illustrated than when working manually.

The practicalities of research in the software context

The availability of customised qualitative software occurred within a diverse methodological field, which has only become more varied with digital technology, big data and the rise of applied, commercial and citizen-research. In addition there is increasing discussion of mixed methods approaches to research and analysis and the use of visual methods. Reflection about of the rise of qualitative software and the implications of its use must be done in the context of the practicalities of research, in which analysis is understood as a core activity throughout an iterative process.

Whatever the characteristics of a particular study, there are certain core elements involved in doing research. Planning is paramount (Box 1.1). Authors usually discuss several aspects in planning and conducting research. Mason (2002), for example, discusses 'questions of strategy', 'generating qualitative data', and 'analysing qualitative data'; Boolsen (2006) distinguishes between 'problem formulation', 'research design', 'data collection' and 'analysis'. In our experience researchers often plan data collection carefully, but neglect to put the same degree of effort into planning the analysis.

In the context of the use of software, much less has been written about research design than in relation to qualitative (and, increasingly, mixed methods) approaches more generally. Di Gregorio and Davidson (2008) wrote the first comprehensive discussion of research design in the specific context of software use that transcends individual products. In further opening up discussion about the role of software in designing and conducting research, we identify six key tasks in setting up a software project to reflect initial research design (Silver and Lewins, 2014). These tasks reflect the sense in which CAQDAS packages are essentially project management tools which can be used from the earliest moments of conceiving a research idea, through all the phases of planning and implementation of analysis to the tasks of writing up an account for publication, preparing for a conference presentation or organising a thesis (Chapter 2).

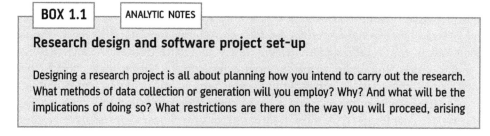

BOX 1.1 — ANALYTIC NOTES

Research design and software project set-up

Designing a research project is all about planning how you intend to carry out the research. What methods of data collection or generation will you employ? Why? And what will be the implications of doing so? What restrictions are there on the way you will proceed, arising from the circumstances in which you will work? What are the likely consequences of your design choices? What is your analytic focus likely to be? How will you handle changes in focus? These sorts of questions should guide the way you set up a software project. Although it is common to plan research, often this is done primarily in relation to data collection. It is just as important, however, to plan the analysis. Using software from the outset will help with integrating all types of planning into your work.

These tasks are: (i) managing and referencing literature; (ii) defining research topic and questions; (iii) representing theoretical frameworks; (iv) incorporating research materials; (v) defining factual features; (vi) developing analytical areas of interest. They are inherently interrelated, occurring in tandem rather than as discrete stages. One of the main benefits of using qualitative software is that flexibility can be built into analytic designs to reflect changes as projects evolve. This is a common thread through this book. This way of thinking about setting up a software project emphasises the importance of making explicit what you plan to do and how you plan to do it. Woolf (2014a) describes these essential elements as the *strategies* and *tactics* of analysis.

Managing and referencing literature

Reviewing existing literature concerning your broad topic is a fundamental early task. Technological developments mean that this process is changing rapidly and significantly. Many journals have electronic versions providing free or easy access to full-text articles. Bibliographic software has developed to the point that it is quick and easy to transfer reference lists and online material directly into libraries, along with associated metadata. CAQDAS packages have also developed significantly in this area, with several now enabling the direct importation of PDF files and references from bibliographic software. Conducting a literature review within qualitative software is not only feasible, but also incredibly useful. Chapter 5 distinguishes between *direct* and *indirect* handling of literature, via annotating and coding full-text articles and/or developing critical appraisals about and linking within and between them. However you chose to proceed, integrating literature with the rest of your work through a CAQDAS package enables you to later systematically compare existing literature with your analysis.

Formulating the research problem and defining the research questions

Formulating the research problem is more than just deciding on the topic. It is informed by your ontological and epistemological standpoint and your familiarisation with and critiquing of the literature, both of which help you rationalise why the area you are interested in requires further research. If you use software to facilitate the literature review, it makes sense also to write up your formulation of the research problem and define the initial research questions within the software project (Chapter 5). You can thus be explicit about your interest, assumptions, expectations and prejudices and link your writing to the literature that contributes to your problem formulation.

Representing theoretical frameworks

Whether your intention is to work within a clear theoretical framework, perhaps through applying existing theory or testing hypotheses on new bodies of data or areas of conceptual interest, or to develop theory from empirical data, you will never be working within a theoretical vacuum. Contrasting ways of working can broadly be distinguished according to the *direction* you are working in; whether *top-down* (deductive) or *bottom-up* (inductive). These approaches, and their combination (abduction), are discussed in the context of coding in Chapter 7. Whatever its role, it is important to relate your conceptualisation of the research problem to existing theory, to represent that within the software project at the outset and reflect how it evolves during the project. That might happen via memo-writing (Chapter 10) and/ or the visualisation of theoretical contexts in visual maps (Chapter 11). You will be able to refer back to these ideas at later stages and compare initial assumptions and expectations with the analysis as you proceed.

Incorporating research materials

Data collection is all about constructing the best possible dataset in order to investigate the research problem. Under ideal circumstances, what data are required to answer the research questions? What data are available? Could you construct a suitable dataset from existing sources and conduct secondary analysis, or do you need to collect new data? What instruments will you use to generate new data if required? How will you ensure data are of sufficient quality? In the context of setting up a software project, you can create locations for storing data and other research materials early on (Chapter 5). You do not yet need to have data ready to incorporate. You may even change your mind and work with different materials later on, but thinking about data, how they are related to one another and how they will be handled as soon as possible is an important part of research design and software project set-up.

Defining factual features

Factual features are known characteristics about data and respondents (Chapter 12). Depending on your design you may sample on this basis; for example, if conducting a comparative case study in which you are focusing on two or more organisations, settings or other entities. Alternatively, you may be interested in comparing how individuals with certain socio-demographic characteristics think about, experience or talk about an issue. One-case designs also include comparative elements, although these typically relate to features *within* cases rather than across multiple ones. In addition are analytic facts identified as salient through the processes of interpretation. Factual features often pertain to information which stays constant within a project. However, longitudinal designs include some such features which change over time, and these can constitute core comparative aspects. Either way, these aspects can be well handled in software.

Developing analytical areas of interest

There are many different approaches to qualitative data analysis, some of which we discuss in more detail below, and in Chapter 7. The main focus of this book is on how software packages specifically designed for the purpose may support *your* approach to analysis.[1] As such, this book will not tell you what your approach should be, or what the specific means are by which you will achieve them. Although this chapter discusses some common analytic strategies and the rest of the book discusses how analytic tasks can be supported by CAQDAS packages, this is done in broad terms. You should therefore read this book in tandem with the wider literature on qualitative research and data analysis, if you are not already familiar with it.

'Analysis' is often written about or conceived as a discrete *stage* in a research project. This is the result of having to separate phases of work or analytic processes in order to describe and discuss them without causing confusion. In many respects we are doing the same here, in this chapter, and throughout the book. However, conducting research is not a linear, one-directional task (see Figure 2.1; p. 45). The elements that comprise any project are interrelated and fluid. Analysis is not a *stage* of work with clear boundaries. You analyse from the first moments of conceiving the idea of a project, locating it within your 'world-view' and formulating the problem through design, data collection and into writing up. Doing a literature review is a form of analysis (Chapter 5). Deciding whether, how and what to transcribe is an analytic act (Chapter 7). Developing a coding scheme (Chapter 9) and linking data and concepts (Chapter 11) are analytic. Writing up an account is a form of analysis (Chapter 10). Designing a research project forces you to be explicit about what you want to analyse and how you intend to do so (see Silver and Lewins, 2014). You will get more out of your project and your use of software tools if you come to software clear in your mind what your analytic strategy is and what processes you need to go through in order to apply it and answer your research questions.

---

[1] There are many other software applications that may facilitate aspects of qualitative data analysis and qualitative research more generally but that were not specifically designed for the purpose. For an overview and discussion of such tools see Silver and Lewins (2013) and Paulus et al. (2013).

CAQDAS packages are project management tools which have potential benefits for all qualitative and mixed methods projects – far and beyond the ways they are most usually described, critiqued and reported. We discuss this further in Chapter 2, in describing our conceptualisation of their role in supporting the many phases of work.

Some basic principles and distinctions

Throughout this book we return to some central ideas which frame the way we perceive analysis and discuss and teach software. In preparing yourself for reading this book, and your general preparation for thinking about and engaging with software the most important of these are the following:

1. Analysis constitutes a series of processes which, although having distinct characteristics in their own right, are fluid and overlapping.
2. Analytic work can be distinguished according to levels of abstraction from data and directions of work, and these are reflected in the way you can work with software.
3. Approaches to analysis are usefully distinguished according to whether they are essentially code-based or non-code-based.
4. Analysis requires the ability to cut through data in different dimensions.

Making reference to the case-study examples (Chapter 2), we illustrate that the use of customised software significantly facilitates these aspects, allowing either the strict adherence to an established and documented analytic strategy, or the creation of one in relation to the specific needs of an individual project.

Analytic *processes*

Qualitative analysis, rather than being a linear set of procedures which follow on from one another in a logical, one-directional way, is better understood as a *process*. This is not a new idea. Bryman and Burgess noted in the mid-1990s, for example, that the previous decade had seen a number of 'shifts in emphasis' in the way research methodology was being discussed, including that 'stages of social investigation have been replaced with the idea of research as a social process which requires careful scrutiny' (1994: 1). Since then, many different qualitative approaches have been discussed in similar ways. Software explicitly designed for the purposes of qualitative data analysis reflects and reinforces its non-linear and fluid nature. We prioritise such fluidity in the way we discuss software tools and encourage you to think about and use them. The linear format of this book limits us somewhat in this regard. However, having the idea of *fluidity* in your mind from the outset is important. Refer to our conceptualisation of the 'core analytic activities' (Figure 2.1; p. 45) and the sense in which analytic tasks are carried out through the use of software tools iteratively and incrementally.. This view of software will set the foundation to enable you to make the most of your chosen package.

Something that has characterised qualitative data analysis generally, and the use of CAQDAS more particularly, is an absence of specific and detailed accounts of *how* analysis proceeds. There is much discussion about qualitative data analysis as a 'craft' which has resulted in a sense of *mystery* around what analysts actually do. We illustrate the role of software in 'opening up' qualitative data analysis, in making apparent both the *processes* involved, and the impact of technology on methodology. Whatever type of researcher you are, you have a responsibility to document and reflect on what you do, and the impact of your processes on the results. Using CAQDAS will not do this for you, or, in or of itself, make you a 'better' researcher. But it will provide you with tools that more directly and immediately allow you to illustrate and justify your analytic strategy. A theme of this book, then, is that CAQDAS provides the tools, but you, the researcher must use them wisely.

Levels and directions of work

Analysis happens at different 'levels'. In discussing the role of software in analysis we distinguish between four:

Sometimes you work at the *data* level, carefully viewing and reading relevant material and considering its importance in relation to the formulation of the research problem, the existing literature, and the adequacy of the data you have before you. You might make notes (usually called 'annotations') about what you see, which help you to identify and reflect upon interesting aspects of the data and decide what to do next, in order to move the analysis forward. You link data segments that appear to be associated.

Much (but not all) qualitative data analysis employs the mechanism of 'coding' to organise ideas about what is important in data, in relation to research questions. This might be thought of as the *indexing* level (depending on your analytic approach and methodological context). However described, it refers to the organisation of data according to what you, as the researcher, deem to be interesting in the materials you have before you. In some approaches, this level of work builds on work previously done at the 'data' level. Elements of work done at this level of work might also be conceptualised as 'thematic' if you consider codes to constitute themes.

If we think of coding (and other means of organising ideas such as linking) data segments as a process of indexing meaning or content; mapping out what is 'going on', it follows that at some point we need to 'move on' and work at a more *conceptual level*. This often proves challenging when using CAQDAS for the first time; regardless of how the terms 'codes', 'themes', 'concepts' and 'categories' are understood and conceived as operating within analysis. Difficulties can arise in doing so for several reasons, not least your confidence in analytic process and confidence in experimenting with software tools such that you can manipulate them to suit your needs. Issues in using the technology can be particularly challenging amongst researchers who are learning about software at the same time as learning about methodology, or amongst experienced analysts who are new to the use of technology for analytic purposes (Silver and Rivers, 2014). This is understandable and to be expected. Yet the tools that allow you to interrogate patterns, relationships and connections within and between data (Chapter 13) are where the significant potential power of using software, in comparison to working on paper, lie. We hope that this book will give you the confidence to experiment with software tools beyond those that appear most straightforward in the context of your methodological framework, analytic strategy, practical project demands and personal style of working.

The importance of stepping back from data and your developing analysis of them is a recurrent theme in this book. From a process point of view this entails working at a more *abstract* level. Whether your analysis is directly informed by theory (deductive), oriented around theory-building (inductive), or employing elements of both (abductive), creating connections between data, codes and your comments about them is an integral part of analysis. CAQDAS packages provide 'mapping', 'modelling' or 'networking' tools which enable you to interrogate connections according to earlier work, or to create connections according to you current thinking about (sub)sets. However you work, diagrammatic visualisations facilitate thinking in non-linear ways. We see the use of writing tools in tandem with mapping tools as integral to getting the most out of work at the abstract level specifically, and your use of software more generally.

Chapter 7 discusses different approaches to coding, distinguishing between *inductive, deductive* and *abductive*. This relates in part to the level at which you start and the direction of analysis. In broad terms, inductive approaches tend to be 'theory-building', starting at the data level and working up towards the abstract levels. Deductive approaches are often characterised as 'theory-testing' in which the project is driven or informed by an existing theoretical framework which is applied to, or tested on, a new body of data. Abductive approaches combine approaches. This is simplistic of course; rather than seeing different ways of working as mutually exclusive or distinct from one another, analysis often involves working in different ways, at different levels, in different directions, at different times. The use of software facilitates such flexible, iterative and incremental processes.

Code-based and non-code-based approaches

CAQDAS packages largely grew out of social science disciplines and are distinguished from other software tools by the sense in which they offer *qualitative* approaches to qualitative data (see below). Many now offer much more, but given their historical roots and the debates around their use, it is relevant to make some broad comments about their versatility in terms of analytic techniques generally. We do this in part by distinguishing between 'code-based' and 'non-code-based' approaches.

The packages we discuss in this book all have powerful and sophisticated coding tools. These can be used to facilitate a range of approaches to analysis (Chapter 7). Many methodologies employ coding as a means of organising ideas about data; therefore CAQDAS packages have wide appeal and are extensively used across sectors, disciplines, methodologies and analytic approaches. Amongst early criticisms were contentions that software served to homogenise qualitative data analysis because it prioritised coding, thereby encouraging code-based approaches at the expense of alternative ways of navigating data (Coffey et al., 1996; Lee and Fielding

1996). Although such criticisms have since been superseded by software developments, it is relevant to highlight the role of coding in analysis (whether supported by software or not).

The first point to make is that coding is not *in and of itself* analysis. Whether using software or not, coding is a device to organise ideas about data (Chapters 2 and 7). Coding is a common aspect of analysis and facilitates interpretive thinking. But it is essentially an indexing process, in which you catalogue that a particular segment of data is about, or a general instance of, something in which you are interested. Coding in software has a number of advantages over paper-based coding (Chapters 7–9), but technically a code is simply a position in a database system to which you link data segments. Codes need not, therefore, be conceived of, or used as, *interpretive* devices in the sense in which they are primarily discussed in the literature. They can be used in that way, of course. And many, perhaps most, who use software, do so. But you can use them for a whole range of purposes that transcend customary, methodological ways of working. Thinking about codes and the process of coding in narrow ways might be limiting and homogenising, but that is to do with the user, not the technique or the software itself.

However, some types of associations exist within data for which coding tools are inadequate. A classic example is when a respondent makes a comment which s/he later contradicts. The two statements might be about the same general topic, but they communicate something quite different. Associating them with the same code does not record that level of nuance. Or when reviewing literature, you read something which reminds you of a passage you read in a different article, and you want to note that association. Or in analysing the way a text builds an argument – perhaps in a political speech or other form of public discourse – you want to track how rhetorical or other linguistic devices are used to make a point. These are just some examples of instances in which coding fails to offer sufficient flexibility. Many CAQDAS packages include the additional ability to *hyperlink* between passages of data in addition to coding them (Chapter 6). These devices offer more flexibility in handling non-linear and non-thematic linkages such as those listed above (Silver and Fielding, 2008; Silver and Patashnick, 2011).

Cuts through data

The need to make comparisons *across*, and interrogate patterns and relationships *within* data is inherent to analysis. Distinguishing between the different *cuts* through the dataset you wish to make is a useful device in thinking about how tools might be employed for your analytic needs. Cutting through data 'horizontally' is typically about focusing on one area of interest across all data (or subsets). For example, you might focus on an individual code or theme and retrieve all data segments linked to it, regardless of the data files in which they occur. You are thus able to start thinking about how a particular topic or theme occurs across the whole dataset, to think more analytically and start interrogating more deeply. Cutting through data horizontally in this way allows you to ask questions like: Are the segments coded here equivalent, or do they need recoding in order to handle peculiarities, contradictions, nuances? Are there some segments which are not adequate instances of the code? Do they need uncoding, reconceptualising, disregarding? How does this sort of retrieval change the way you are thinking about the code? What further questions does cutting through the data in this way raise?

In addition, you may be interested in focusing attention on one particular data file, an interview transcript or set of field notes, for example, and visualising how multiple codes occur in relation to one another, 'vertically', throughout. This might be related to sequence, proximity or embeddedness. You might consider the relative occurrence of all codes, or selectively choose those that you envisage might be related, or will help you identify interesting patterns in the way you have coded. This can lead to further questioning of data, to ascertain, for example, whether a pattern in coding identified in one data file also occurs in other, related data. Language-oriented approaches can benefit in particular from this type of visualisation, or those in which the sequence of code application is of particular interest. For example, in analysing political discourse there may be a focus on how an argument is constructed. Considering the position of codes that capture particular linguistic devices according to the way sentences are structured, for example, would enable a comparison of how different politicians craft an argument. This type of coding can be combined with more content-based, descriptive or thematic types, in order to subsequently investigate whether arguments relating to particular topics are constructed differently. Consideration of the relative position of code occurrence in this way enables you to remain at the data level, although working in this way also allows you to combine the indexing and data levels.

Cutting through data horizontally and vertically need not be distinct activities. Some software packages allow you to visualise both dimensions at the same time. Such concurrent working offers means of 'playing' with data and the connections within in many different ways. You can also combine working with data and codes like this with interrogation on the basis of the factual characteristics pertaining to respondents and data. For example, having sampled for and interviewed respondents with different socio-demographic characteristics (e.g. gender, age, role), you can investigate the differences in how men and women think about, discuss and experience particular topics. This can be done both horizontally and vertically.

Throughout the book we illustrate how different ways of viewing data can facilitate your analysis. These are not restricted to vertical and horizontal cuts, but distinguishing on this basis offers a good starting point for considering how you intend to work with and compare data and explore the patterns and relationships between them.

The rise of qualitative software

Software programs supporting qualitative analysis have a relatively long history. The earliest handling of textual data developed on mainframe computers during the 1960s. These concordance-type tools provided quick listings of word usage, frequency and standardised measurements appropriate for certain types of quantitative content analysis and other language-oriented approaches. Basic data management systems geared around storing and indexing large volumes of textual information have also been available since the early days of personal computing. There are now many such software programs providing a variety of sophisticated management and linking tools that support the range of digitised information researchers collect to inform their work. The internet 'revolution' has broadened the range of possibilities almost infinitely. However, the tools we discuss in this book, categorised as CAQDAS, developed from the mid-1980s and share particular characteristics arising from their developmental origins.

What types of software do we categorise as CAQDAS?

Tesch (1990) began the process of relating analysis types and software tools. Weitzman and Miles (1995) built on her work, creating a taxonomy of qualitatively oriented software packages. The CAQDAS acronym is well understood across disciplines as broadly referring to software designed to assist the analysis of qualitative data. It was coined by Raymond Lee and Nigel Fielding following the 1989 Surrey Research Methods Conference which first brought together pioneers in the field. The subsequent CAQDAS Networking Project (established in 1994) had the effect of 'fixing' the acronym.[2]

However, there has been rather a fuzzy conception about which packages CAQDAS includes. We make a broad definition here. Software which falls under the CAQDAS 'umbrella' includes a wide range of packages, but their general principles are concerned with taking a *qualitative* approach to qualitative data. Qualitative data include text, visual and multimedia forms of non-numerical, or unstructured material (Chapter 4). A qualitative approach often includes a need to interpret data through the identification and possibly *coding* of themes, concepts, processes, contexts, etc., in order to build explanations or theories or to test or enlarge a theory (see below and Chapter 7). Qualitative data collection techniques include in-depth interviews, focus groups and participant observation. Approaches to qualitative research and analysis include action research, ethnography, ethnomethodology, hermeneutics and phenomenology. Qualitative analysis strategies include grounded theory, thematic analysis, Framework analysis, conversation and narrative analysis. Different approaches may employ a range of data types and analytic strategies, and the techniques employed and processes followed to undertake analysis cut across approaches and strategies.

The qualitative strategies we refer to are distinct from 'quantitative content analysis' or 'text mining' techniques, in which the statistics of word or phrase frequencies and their occurrence relative to other words or phrases are the basis of analytic work (see Holsti, 1969). We refer to tools that support such approaches in

---

[2]The acronym QDAS (qualitative data analysis software) is preferred by some (e.g. di Gregorio and Davidson 2008; Bazeley 2013) but we use CAQDAS because of its historical roots and more general use and acceptance in the field.

varying degrees. Where we include them it is because they have a focus on the qualitative as well. Chapter 3 provides an overview of the packages we are mainly concerned with in this book.

Which is the 'best' CAQDAS package?

This is perhaps the most frequently asked question, yet it is impossible to answer! All the packages we use and teach have tools in common, plus their own distinctive features (Chapter 3). The purpose of software is not to provide a methodological or analytic framework. The tools available support certain tasks differently, and there is some debate about whether individual packages may 'steer' the way analysis is performed. Users should take into account practicalities such as the way software programs are taught, and how much emphasis is placed on an 'ideal' way of using software. To promote only one way of using any package undervalues both the software and the methodological independence of the researcher. Creeping homogeneity helps no one in the long run except the person who is trying to sell you a method or product. As the researcher, you are the expert. You remain in control of the interpretive process and you decide which tools within a software package best facilitate *your* approach to analysis. You also have the responsibility for being transparent about your processes and ensuring the quality of your interpretation (Chapter 10).

Whichever package you choose, you will be able to utilise a selection of tools which will facilitate data management and analysis. Software developments and blurring boundaries mean that tools within a given package may not be appropriate for all qualitative approaches. Equally, just because a function is available does not mean you have to use it. We caution against choosing a package simply because it is the one you have the 'easiest' (e.g. immediate or free) access to, or that seems the most sophisticated. However, if you do not have a choice, you will usually be able to make a package work for you.

Analytic strategies in the context of software use

Methods of data collection cut across methodologies. Approaches may employ broadly interpretive techniques for analysis, but the respective sensitivities and beliefs about the nature of data and knowledge mean that the starting points of interpretation can be quite different. The significance (or not) of language and cultural contexts and also the purposes of research can be so divergent that a sentence of speech or an observed action will have different significance to an ethnographer compared with, for example, a conversation analyst, an ethnomethodologist or a grounded theorist.

Tesch (1990), in rationalising common and differentiating elements in the context of software, distinguished *types* of qualitative research according to where the research interest lies: (i) the characteristics of language; (ii) the discovery of regularities; (iii) the

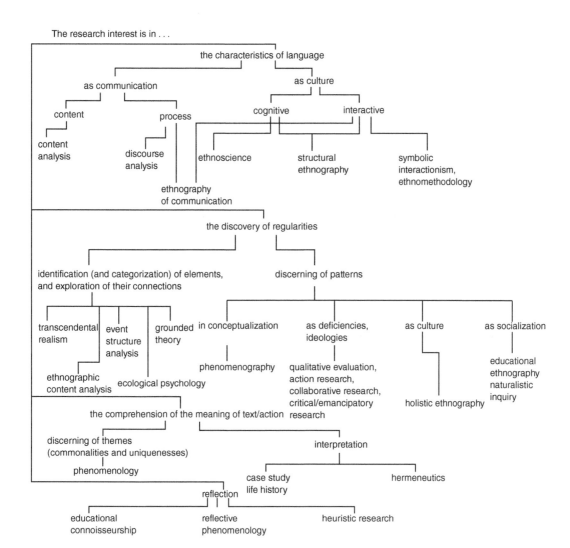

The research interest is in . . .

the characteristics of language

as communication

as culture

content

process

cognitive

interactive

content
analysis

discourse
analysis

ethnoscience

structural
ethnography

symbolic
interactionism,
ethnomethodology

ethnography
of communication

the discovery of regularities

identification (and categorization) of elements,
and exploration of their connections

discerning of patterns

transcendental
realism

event
structure
analysis

grounded
theory

in conceptualization

as deficiencies,
ideologies

as culture

as socialization

ethnographic
content analysis

ecological psychology

phenomenography

qualitative evaluation,
action research,
collaborative research,
critical/emancipatory
research

educational
ethnography
naturalistic
inquiry

holistic ethnography

the comprehension of the meaning of text/action

discerning of themes
(commonalities and uniquenesses)

interpretation

phenomenology

case study
life history

hermeneutics

reflection

educational
connoisseurship

reflective
phenomenology

heuristic research

Figure 1.1 Graphic overview of qualitative research types (Tesch, 1990: 72–73)

comprehension of the meaning of text/action; and (iv) reflection (see Figure 1.1). These distinctions reflect overarching philosophical stances and priorities. Although defining qualitative data as 'any information…that is not expressed in numbers' (1990: 55) Tesch explicitly focused on textual forms in her discussions.

Tesch herself acknowledged difficulties with these classifications, recognising that whilst some are representative of an epistemological stance, others are more about method. Thus at a conceptual level they are not equivalent. Much has changed since she was writing, but Tesch's work continues to have broad relevance to the intersection between qualitative methodology and technology. It is not within the scope of this book to discuss in detail the range of qualitative research types or systematically illustrate how software may support them. Indeed, our focus is on the qualitative strategies more specifically, and the way software tools can be employed to undertake them.

Therefore, as a lead-in to the task-based chapters that follow, we outline five strategies that can be well supported by CAQDAS packages. These are discourse analysis, narrative inquiry, Framework analysis, grounded theory and thematic analysis. In addition we discuss mixed methods research and visual analysis as broader approaches. Some are more commonly discussed in the context of software than others, and not all are included in Tesch's scheme. Our choices for discussing each in this chapter reflect our observations in one of three respects:

1. they are commonly used by researchers employing CAQDAS;
2. they are well supported by CAQDAS but are infrequently reported upon in the context of software use; and
3. there is significant potential growth areas for qualitative methodology and software in the future.

In discussing these strategies and approaches our aim is to provide a broad introduction. We do not claim to be presenting an exhaustive overview of qualitative research, approaches to analysis or the way software tools are used. However, we add comments regarding the history and context of software use; where appropriate, this includes packages which typically fall outside of the CAQDAS collection. We refer you to specific texts where you can gain more detailed information.

Analysis of discourse

Discourse analysis refers to a broad range of language-based approaches to the analysis of texts that consider the way knowledge is produced and used. This might entail a focus on particular types of discourse (e.g. medical, political, legal); the use of implicit theories to make sense of social action (e.g. economics, power, gender relations); or devices used to structure discourses and their intentions (e.g. rhetoric, linguistic devices, interaction) (Spencer et al., 2003; Silverman, 2001). Researchers across a wide range of disciplines employ variants of discourse analysis to study a multitude of aspects of social life, and in so doing have developed specific strategies. Conversation analysis, Foucauldian discourse analysis (Willig, 2001) and critical discourse analysis are frequently discussed derivatives, but there are many others (for an overview see Gee and Handford, 2012).

Hammersley (2002) in summarising the field, distinguishes between 'types' of discourse analysis in terms of their focus; the sorts of knowledge they claim to make; and in the kinds of technique they employ. Others distinguish more specifically between approaches. Glynos et al. (2009), for example, identify six, highlighting differences and similarities according to the dimensions of ontology, focus and purpose. Dick (2004) in contrast, discusses discourse analysis as a range of approaches, from descriptive variants that aim at understanding conventions such as 'turn-taking' to analytic variants that focus more on generating understandings of the use of language in specific social contexts. Wooffitt (2005) does a good job of demystifying the area, discussing conversation analysis as a key methodological approach to the analysis of verbal interaction, but also outlining distinctive features of various approaches to discourse analysis more generally, such as discursive psychology, rhetorical psychology, speech act theory, critical discourse analysis and Foucauldian forms of discourse analysis.

A discourse analysis can be conducted on data generated through various methods, including primary forms such as interviews, discussions, life histories and secondary forms such as policy documents, newspaper articles and speeches. Often, relatively small amounts of data and/or numbers of texts are utilised when conducting a discourse analysis, as they are analysed at a very fine level of detail, although with the support of software this need not be the case.

| **BOX 1.2** | FUNCTIONALITY NOTES |

Software tools for language-oriented approaches

Language-oriented approaches rely on close consideration of the presence or physical relation of the occurrence of words, phrases and structures. The text-mining type functionality provided by some CAQDAS packages (Chapters 3 and 6) enables such patterns in texts to be reliably found, coded (Chapter 7) and retrieved (Chapter 8), and these are particularly useful for derivatives of discourse analysis. The sophistication of these tools varies quite considerably, so consider options carefully if this type of functionality forms the basis of your work. You might simply need to locate occurrences, mark, write about and output them. You may not code them, but doing so will improve your repeated access to them. Getting the most out of the software might mean coding for certain linguistic devices and coding for the context in which they occur. You can then compare how certain devices are used differently in contextual discourses.

Narrative inquiry, in contrast, is characterised by a focus on the sequencing of textual characteristics rather than data fragmentation or reduction which is inherent in thematic (code-)based approaches. As such, preserving the natural features of texts, including both structural and sequential elements, is paramount and code-based tools may be seen as inappropriate for this task. Some CAQDAS packages provide two-dimensional spaces for 'mapping' connections. These could be useful for approaches needing to create graphic representations of relationships and structures revealed, for example, by conversations in a work or social setting. In narrative analysis, specific methods and formalised traditions vary in terms of how software might help in anything other than improved general management of and access to them. However, hyperlinking devices might provide ways of linking between structures within an account or across several (Chapters 5 and 11). For less structured approaches, for example to life history accounts or the observation of work, links between points in the data may be useful for tracking a chronology or a set of procedures (Chapter 6).

Narrative inquiry

Narrative inquiry is concerned with the structure of accounts, or stories, focusing on how they are constructed, including processes, sequences, intentions and meanings. It is used to investigate experiences, how they are known about, made sense of, and communicated. Narrative inquiry has increased in popularity in recent decades, frequently attributed to what has been termed the 'linguistic' or 'narrative' turn which is seen to have occurred during the 1990s (Atkinson, 1997; Lieblich et al., 1998; Fenton and Langley, 2011).

Authors differ in the ways they conceptualise the traditions, foci and processes of narrative inquiry and the practicalities of analysis. Bernard and Ryan (2010), for example, identify four major traditions: sociolinguistics, hermeneutics, phenomenology and grounded theory. Daiute and Lightfoot (2004), in contrast, in their edited volume organise the writings of authors from different disciplines according to 'literary readings', 'social-relational readings' and 'readings through the forces of history'. They see these as the three main ways of conceptualising narrative analysis, although they concede that they are neither discrete nor used in the same way by researchers. Lieblich et al. (1998) divide approaches to narrative analysis according to different ways of reading: 'the holistic-content reading'; 'the holistic-form reading'; the 'categorical-content reading'; and the 'categorical-form reading'. Riessman (2005) adds to these by further distinguishing between the performative or dialogical aspect of narrative and visual narratives. These examples of the range of ways of understanding narrative inquiry encapsulate the complexity of the field.

Rather than being a single or uniform approach or method, therefore, narrative analysis is characterised by diversity; not only is it utilised across disciplines and informed by a range of theoretical traditions, but also it constitutes a mix of methodological approaches. The 'texts' that are analysed may be 'naturally occurring' (such as documents generated for other purposes, for example, diaries) or collected through speaking with or interviewing research participants (often, but not exclusively, in the form of 'oral history' type interviewing). Its forms also utilise a variety of analytic strategies, including both quantitative and qualitative practices.

Framework analysis

Framework analysis is a specific method for analysing qualitative datasets. A matrix-based method for ordering and synthesising data, Framework analysis was originally developed during the 1980s at the UK-based National Centre for Social Research and is now a widely used method that supports case-based and thematic approaches to qualitative data analysis. At its core is the idea of a 'thematic framework' which is used to 'classify and organise data according to key themes, concepts and emergent categories' (Ritchie et al., 2003: 220). In contrast to other methods, Framework focuses on the *synthesis* of data, involving the creation of summaries of verbatim data rather than on data reduction activities through the use of coding. Fruber (2010) illustrates a five-phase process involved in undertaking an analysis of pregnant women suffering from mild to moderate psychological distress using the Framework method. This involved phases of (i) data immersion/familiarisation; (ii) developing a theoretical framework; (iii) indexing (coding); (iv) charting (using matrix charts); and (v) synthesising (summarising). Others break the process down slightly more. Whatever the exact processes involved, and how they progress, the development of summaries is achieved in such a way as to maintain context, language and meaning. Framework analysis has commonalities with other forms of qualitative analysis, including grounded theory and thematic analysis. It is distinct, however, in its focus on summarising and synthesising data and their display and analysis through the use of matrices, rather than on the use of coding as the main basis of analytic work.

BOX 1.3 — FUNCTIONALITY NOTES

Software tools for Framework analysis

Having developed it initially for in-house use, NatCen released the FrameWork software in 2009 for sale to the wider academic and applied research community. In 2011, NatCen formed a partnership with QSR International, its functionality was subsumed within NVivo, and FrameWork software taken off the market. There is not a wide literature concerning the framework method, or the degree to which it is facilitated by software applications, and that which does exist tends to originate from NatCen.

If using Framework analysis – or other matrix-based approaches – or indeed, simply needing to summarise or write about what is seen in a general sense, the bespoke summary-writing spaces provided by some packages will work well (Chapter 10). But you can always approximate the functionality through the use of standard memo-writing spaces where the specific tools are not available. You may do this before, after, or to the exclusion of coding. Comparison is likely inherent to these approaches, and factual data organisation (Chapter 12) will enable you to later interrogate writing and coding accordingly (Chapter 13).

Grounded theory

Originated by Glaser and Strauss (1967), grounded theory is a well-known and frequently discussed form of qualitative research. It comprises a methodological approach rather than simply being an analytic or coding strategy. Since the first descriptions there have been many adaptations. In *The Discovery of Grounded Theory* (1967), Glaser and Strauss created an organised and interactive approach to the collection and analysis of data, using what they called the 'constant comparative method'. The history of their co-operation is interesting and relevant to subsequent modifications. Strauss was instrumental in the development of the Doctorate of Nursing Science (DNS) at the University of California at San Francisco, and both he and Glaser had a shared research interest in chronic illness and dying. The development of grounded theory was in part pragmatic, arising from a need to create a text for DNS students that systematised a way of dealing with qualitative data. It was also a response to perceptions that qualitative data analysis had somehow lost its empirical connection to data in an over-preoccupation with theory. The text included in it new routines but also documented techniques already in use by the Chicago School. There was little writing of methodological texts up to that point (Morse et al., 2009). Personal descriptions in Morse et al. (2009) reveal how these creative moments in qualitative methodological history occurred and how a range of the 'second generation' of grounded theorists applied their own modifications to substantive research projects. Glaser continues to support and reinforce the original principles of the 1967 text and to stress inductive 'emergence' of codes and categories and theory-free starting points.

BOX 1.4 — ANALYTIC NOTES

Features of grounded theory (1967)

At the heart of the original grounded theory method was a basic principle, the 'constant comparative method'. Its main features are as follows:

- A coding process (later to become known as *open coding*) consists of annotations in the margin expressed as codes based on social constructs or on the respondent's own language (later labelled *in vivo* codes).
- Data segments are compared, thus refining ideas about this and subsequent categories.
- Memos are an important aspect, and should be kept updated about the development of each category.
- Collecting, coding and analysing data should occur concurrently; thus ongoing 'theoretical sampling' of data is performed to enable further comparisons to be made of different groups and settings.
- Categories are further refined and relationships among them identified.
- Categories are reduced to smaller set of more abstract higher-level concepts – allowing the possibility of generality or the production of formal theory.
- The collection of more data retains the principle of being grounded in the data and permits further incidents to be analysed in the light of these concepts – allowing the modification of these concepts.
- When concepts are not being modified any further, categories are said to be *theoretically saturated*. Theoretical saturation means that the analysis of more incidents is not adding further to ideas, it merely 'adds bulk to coded data and nothing to theory'.

Amongst the second generation who influenced later strands of grounded theory were several DNS students and associated postdoctoral researchers. We focus on two of these, since they possibly comprise the most influential developments. Firstly, Strauss with Juliet Corbin diverged from the original work and wrote *Basics of Qualitative Research* in 1990, developing grounded theory to such an extent that Glaser questioned whether it had any relationship to the original and suggested it was effectively another qualitative method. Corbin collaborated for 16 years with Anselm Strauss until his death, and continues to apply and adjust grounded theory to current substantive contexts and at a practical level to computer usage, having included reference to MAXQDA in the 3rd edition of *Basics of Qualitative Research,* published in 2008. Secondly, Kathy Charmaz, in many publications between 1975 and 2002 and with Anthony Bryant (Bryant and Charmaz, 2007) consolidated a constructivist version of grounded theory that accounts for beliefs about the relative, context-laden nature of interpretation. Although maintaining many of the features espoused by Glaser, Strauss and Corbin, constructivist grounded theory attends also to the active role of the researcher in research generally, and particularly in analytic processes; the interplay between researcher and data that results in the use of codes, development or categories and the theoretical account. Thus the effect of prior knowledge and existing literature, as well as the issue of reflexivity, are highlighted. Charmaz makes the point that grounded theory is primarily *a way of thinking about data* and, as such, cannot be standardised. Constructivist grounded theory attends to the ways in which theoretical development is tied to the engagement with epistemological issues, and as such illustrates the role of both deduction and induction in the analytic process (Charmaz, 2006).

BOX 1.5   FUNCTIONALITY NOTES

Software tools for theory-building approaches

Theory-building approaches are characterised by the need to move beyond description through writing (Chapters 6 and 10) and indexing of data through basic coding (Chapter 7) to generate themes, concepts or categories (Chapters 8 and 9). Grounded theory and thematic analysis are examples of theory-building approaches. CAQDAS packages support processes involved in generating theory very well, and you will find most of the tools discussed in this book useful at various moments.

Working deductively, you will likely have a theoretical framework at the outset which can be represented in the software as a map, model or network (Chapter 11). Working inductively, you will be working towards generating such a visual representation of your interpretation or theory. Software facilitates either approach or a combination of both (Chapter 7). You will need to record the factual features of data and respondents (Chapter 12) in order to make comparisons within and between cases (Chapter 13). You will need to write about your processes and analytic insights in identifying patterns and relationships and developing and testing theories.

Thematic analysis

Thematic analysis is a commonly used approach to the analysis of qualitative data, yet is relatively infrequently described or discussed in specific terms. Although those who write about it often understand it to constitute a method of analysis in and of itself (Braun and Clarke, 2013; Fereday and Muir Cochrane, 2006; Attride-Stirling, 2001), its techniques are used in many other approaches, and therefore its status is debated. Outside of these debates, it can be seen as constituting a set of analytic processes applicable in a variety of theoretical contexts, disciplines and topics of investigation (Boyatzis, 1998). This applicability is seen to relate to its inherent flexibility as well as its independence from theory and epistemology, as contrasted to other approaches such as conversation analysis, interpretive phenomenological analysis and grounded theory which have clear roots in particular traditions (Braun and Clarke, 2006). Indeed, elements inherent to thematic analysis are also evident in these approaches, and as such thematic analysis is applicable to theoretically driven research and more applied approaches. It might be argued that thematic analysis is the definitive 'code-based' approach in the sense that it entails a process of *encoding* qualitative information (Fereday and Muir Cochrane, 2006). In attending to an identified absence in the literature concerning specific procedures for conducting thematic analysis, Braun and Clarke (2006) propose a six-phase guide, involving (i) familiarising yourself with data; (ii) generating initial codes; (iii) searching for themes; (iv) reviewing themes; (v) defining and naming themes; and (vi) producing the report. They differentiate 'types' of thematic analysis in terms of its form and outcome, on a number of levels:

- Aim of the analysis: whether to develop a rich description of the dataset, or a detailed account of one particular aspect.
- Identification of themes: whether inductive or theoretical.
- 'Level' of themes: semantic and latent themes.
- Epistemological underpinnings: essentialist/realist vs constructionist.
- Types of questions being asked: research questions, questions asked of respondents where primary data are collected, questions which guide coding and analysis.

Mixed methods research

Mixed methods is a vast and varied field in social science methodology which, although with a long history in terms of the utilisation of more than one method within a given project (Hesse-Biber, 2010), has been much debated in recent years (Ivankova and Kawamura, 2010). Indeed, it is only seen to have *formally* existed as a field for 10–15 years (Teddlie and Tashakkori, 2012). Technological capabilities afforded by CAQDAS packages have the potential to play an important role in the continued growth of mixed methods, although the majority of discussions in the literature remain concerned with research design rather than the role of software (notable exceptions being Bazeley, 2006; 2011; Fielding, 2012; Kuckartz, 2012).

Mixed methods research involves the use of more than one type of method within a research project. That may involve mixing quantitative methods, mixing qualitative methods or mixing qualitative *and* quantitative methods. The latter type has come to the fore in methodological discussions and is often what is implied by the use of the general term. These approaches involve the collection, analysis and integration of both quantitative and qualitative data within a single study or as part of a longer-term strategy across multiple studies (Creswell, 2003; Kelle, 2006). In considering the appropriateness of employing a mixed methods approach, authors distinguish between paradigmatic, pragmatic and political (or transformative) rationales (Brannen, 2005; Creswell et al., 2011).

Mixed methods approaches are seen as transcending traditional paradigmatic debates between quantitative and qualitative approaches, and have thus been described as constituting a 'third paradigm' (Tashakkori and Teddlie, 2003). Indeed, one of the rationales for their use is the idea that employing and making explicit different philosophical positions is valuable to social science research (Greene, 2007). But there is huge variety in the way projects are designed, and importantly, what is being mixed, why and the stage(s) at which mixing occurs. Some authors therefore question the utility of conceptualising mixed methods in paradigmatic terms (Bazeley, 2009; Mertens and Hesse-Biber, 2012). Nevertheless, utilising both quantitative and qualitative methods is widely seen as enabling the benefits of each to be realised at the same time as minimising their limitations. More pragmatic rationales for the use of mixed methods are thereby discussed in terms of employing methods which best suit the nature of the problem under study. Giving primacy to the importance of the research question and valuing both objective and subjective knowledge are key aspects in employing methods according to 'what works' (Morgan, 2007). This may include the use of multiple researchers in collaborative projects as well as multiple methods. Political or transformative approaches emphasise the role of mixed methods research in improving society in some way (Brannen, 2005; Mertens, 2009; Mertens and Hesse-Biber 2013).

Whatever the rationale for employing mixed methods approaches, terminology is an issue in getting to grips with the literature. 'Mixed methods research' is perhaps the most widely used term to refer to the general field, but others are also employed, including 'mixed research' and 'multiple methods'. Once a close reading of the literature begins, it quickly becomes apparent that, similarly to qualitative research, particular terms are used in quite different ways across contexts. This can be confusing to the novice researcher. Authors develop increasingly specific and nuanced terms as they attempt to differentiate their conceptualisations from those of others. This is seen starkly amongst those who distinguish between types of mixed methods through developing research design categorisation systems, and several authors have called for more consistency in terms used (Bryman, 2008; Johnson, Onwuegbuzie, and Turner, 2007; Tashakkori and Teddlie, 2010). It is not within the scope of this book to discuss the field in detail or to make any further attempts to unravel its complexities; our focus is on the role of software in supporting analytic strategies rather than in rationales or designs *per se*.

BOX 1.6 — FUNCTIONALITY NOTES

Use of software for mixed methods

In the context of the use of CAQDAS packages, it is the task of mixing analytic techniques which is relevant, whatever the types of data or design being employed. This can mean employing a quantitative approach to qualitative data, a mixed approach to qualitative data, or a mixed approach to mixed data. Your analytic design will affect the software tools you use.

(Continued)

(Continued)

Software can enable quantitative information about qualitative materials to be imported and linked (Chapter 12). If you conduct coding in a particular way you can count the occurrence of certain features, thereby quantitising qualitative data (Chapters 7 and 8). You can import mixed data in the form of spreadsheets (Chapter 4). You can transform codes into categorical variables. You can export summary frequency information pertaining to qualitative coding to conduct statistical analyses (Chapter 13). Alongside these options you will use many of the other tools depending on the specific analytic design.

Whatever the emphasis, approach or design, conducting mixed methods research is much more than simply taking the 'best' from quantitative and qualitative methods and combining them; and the variety and debate in the literature is testament to this (Bergman, 2008). Indeed, as Bryman (2008) cautions, mixed methods projects are subject to methods-related shortcomings just like those originating within either paradigm, despite often being presented as a means of overcoming them. Considering the role of software in mixed methods research requires, however, moving away from the specifics of research design towards the practicalities and procedures involved in the analysis of data.

Visual analysis

The analysis of still and moving images has a long history, with their use in disciplines such as anthropology and management studies pre-dating the formalisation of visual sociology as a discipline, which occurred from the 1970s (see Schnettler and Raab, 2008, for a historical overview). The use of visual records in empirical research, however, has been advanced by the rise of digital technology and their use is now widespread across academic and applied disciplines. A range of specific theories concerning the use of visual records and strategies for their analysis have developed, although often in isolation from similar work in other disciplines (Hindmarsh, 2008). In addition, existing methodological approaches and analytic strategies have been applied to and adapted for the analysis of visual records. Examples include interaction analysis (Jordan and Henderson, 1995; Heath et al., 2010), visual ethnography (Pink, 2007), visual grounded theory (Konecki, 2011) and visual semiotics.

Approaches to visual analysis are informed by the role and analytic status of data within a given project as well as the methodological and disciplinary traditions which inform design (Silver and Patashnick, 2011). In considering visual analysis in the context of software use for supporting analysis it is useful to draw a number of distinctions:

- whether visual data are being used primarily for illustrative purposes or are construed as data sources in their own right;
- whether visual data are the only or primary data sources or are being used in combination with other data sources;

- whether still or moving images are being used, or both;
- whether the subject of analysis is the content of visual records, interaction contained within them, or indeed both;
- whether the approach to analysis is quantitative, qualitative, or mixed.

Making distinctions on these levels is not to say that approaches or techniques are, or need to be, mutually exclusive in this regard, just that considering these aspects at the outset of designing a project and in reading and evaluating research outputs is useful.

Notwithstanding these distinctions, the emphasis of visual research, where the focus is on some aspect of human behaviour or conduct, is frequently on the micro-analysis of sequences of interaction. This speaks to the affordances of the medium in capturing 'naturally occurring' behaviours, the complexity and multimodality of visual data, in particular video, and the work involved in analysing such material from a practical point of view. It also raises the issue of the means through which visual records are analysed, which necessitates the drawing of a further distinction: whether data are analysed directly, or indirectly through the use of a written transcript (Silver and Patashnick, 2011), leading to the consideration of the role of technology in visual analysis strategies in more detail.

BOX 1.7 — FUNCTIONALITY NOTES

Software tools for visual analysis

Working with visual data is very different from working with textual forms. You will first have to decide whether to work directly with the visual media, or indirectly via a written representation. Working directly, annotations, memos and codes are the key tools you will use to record your ideas about what is in the data. Working indirectly, the development of the transcript will constitute an intermediary analytic task. Visual analysis can employ various analytic strategies. Refer therefore to discussions about the other approaches discussed here in reflecting on which software tools will enable your analytic needs to be achieved, appropriately within your research design. That will also be affected by the status of the visual within the larger project; that is, whether it is the main or only form of data, or integrated with or supplementary to other forms.

Writing about and coding visual data may pertain to verbal content and/or non-verbal interaction. Where both are of analytic interest you will need to be particularly systematic in the use of tools for specific purposes. The amount of visual data you have and your analytic focus will affect the reliance on factual data organisation (Chapter 12) and interrogation tools (Chapter 13).

Concluding remarks: a critical yet flexible approach

We encourage the view that you as the researcher draw on elements of methodology and methods to provide the framework of your analytic strategy. You might be wedded to a particular approach and apply it through your use of software. You might draw on the principles and methods of more than one methodology, and, through your use of software, develop your own analytic strategy, specific to the needs of your project. However you work, throughout you must be thoughtful and transparent about your own role and beliefs (ontology and epistemology) and also be in tune with how working contexts impact on the way you analyse. 'Working contexts' include the use of software – a set of tools which at one level are just like the pencil or highlighter, simply enabling different ways of looking at, and cutting through, data. But software tools provide more potential for flexibility, access and thoroughness than their 'manual' or 'paper' counterparts. Nevertheless, they have to be used competently and appropriately.

You are responsible for ensuring the processes you go through are rigorous and the findings you report are true to your data. Never do something *just* because it is possible. The commercial context within which software packages are developed is worth remembering. Software companies need to make a profit, and although most are still true to their academic roots and the needs of researchers, commercial pressures mean that to a degree they all need to try and meet the needs of a range of researchers. Just like you do not need all the tools of your chosen word-processing application, you will not need all the tools of your chosen CAQDAS package for an individual analysis. We encourage experimentation, but always do so within the boundaries of your methodological requirements. Try to avoid being distracted by fancy or complex options unless they will actually help to achieve an analytic task. The impact of technology on methodology is exciting, but never let it distract you from the ultimate aim of your engagement with software: you need complete your project, therefore you need to focus on the means of achieving your ends. As such, consider how to adopt a critical yet flexible approach in planning for and actually using software.

2
The Nature of Software Support for Research Projects

This chapter builds on issues raised in Chapter 1 to present a practical discussion of the key ways in which CAQDAS packages can support qualitative research. We emphasise their project management potential, outlining starting points for your work with software and encouraging you to view the software project as a container for managing and organising your whole research project. We introduce three case-study examples used throughout the remainder of the book, outlining their research design, dataset components and possible analytic processes. Data for each case study can be downloaded from the companion website for use in the exercises at the end of Chapters 4–13. We discuss common qualitative activities of integration, exploration, organisation, reflection and interrogation (Figure 2.1; p. 45) and outline software tools which facilitate these tasks. Throughout, we emphasise the importance of being flexible in how you engage with software, selecting tools that are appropriate to your analytic strategy and being creative in the way you employ them.

The project management potential of CAQDAS packages

The project management potential of CAQDAS packages is fundamental to how they can support your research project and to the way you view their role. Much literature refers to the analytic support these tools provide and the term 'CAQDAS' itself implies the same. However, these packages neither 'do' analysis, nor is their potential use restricted to projects that involve analysis. If you are working in an academic research context, however, the way you use software to manage background project information, the materials you generate to inform it, and your ideas about them, is at the heart of your work and the potential benefits of using software. As outlined in Chapter 1, a software project can be set up to reflect initial research design in different respects: managing and referencing literature; defining research topic and questions; representing theoretical frameworks; incorporating research materials; defining factual features; and developing areas of analytic interest.

There is much you can do within a CAQDAS package at the earliest stages of conceptualising a research project. We encourage you to start using your chosen software as soon as possible (Chapter 5). Although it might feel quite early to set up structures and make decisions if you have not yet generated data, you can reorganise at any stage. Even if your project is explorative, the design emergent and the analysis inductive and iterative, being organised about what you intend to do is always productive. Being flexible and open in your approach, however, does not mean being inconsistent. Developing a systematic strategy is crucial to generating a robust analysis, whatever your methodological approach.

Starting points

There is no single set of processes for analysis. It is desirable to be clear about your intended analytic strategy and the tasks required to undertake it first, rather than seeing the software as being the architect of your analytic method. This is the ideal, of course, but in practice your chosen software will tend to modify the way you imagined you were going to work. Indeed, when you know a program well, you draw on your experiences with it in designing your next project. Using a customised CAQDAS package can open up additional possibilities of handling and analysing data. However, if you are employing a documented analytic approach and are clear from the outset about the tasks you need to employ, you can manipulate the software to suit those needs. The point is always that *you* are in control of what you do, when and why.

Familiarisation

It is noticeable when running software training that no two sessions are the same. Sometimes a methodologically motivated participant, with a clear idea of requirements, will vary the direction of the workshop. S/he will know what is needed at an interim stage of analysis, although the way to achieve the task within software may not be immediately obvious. Eventually, between us, we work out a strategy – often comprising several steps and the use of several different software tools – that produces the required outcome. Methodological and theoretical preparation will enrich the way you look at data. As you become more familiar with software, you will be able to mould its tools to serve your objectives and you will become more creative in combining tools to achieve complex outcomes. Your objectives and the conceptual progress you make, however, will come from *your* methodological underpinnings, *your* observations, *your* strategic decisions. The software will never do the thinking or the analysis for you.

The software project as a container for your work

One software 'project' should usually be created to represent one research project, i.e. not a separate project for each type of data, case or respondent. Having organised data into subsets (Chapter 12), representing the important aspects about which comparisons need to be made (e.g. data type, socio-demographic attributes of respondents, cases from which data derive), it will be possible to filter work to isolate these elements. If different aspects are in discrete software projects it will be more difficult to compare across them. Although separate software projects can be merged into one another (see Teamwork sections on the companion website) there is usually no need to separate elements when working as an individual. There may be situations in very large projects where starting off by separating cases into individual projects is useful, but this needs careful thought and management in order that they can subsequently be brought together efficiently.

Case-study examples

We use three case-study examples to illustrate analytic tasks, their execution in CAQDAS packages and the potentials of different products. Here we summarise the datasets, list the research questions and outline possible processes for analysis.

The case-study examples are drawn from real research projects and/or reflect contemporary sociological issues. We use them to illustrate common analytic activities and tasks encountered in a range of methodologies and to enable discussion of efficient and robust analytic strategies. Our intention is not to promote any particular method of analysis, nor to suggest that there is necessarily an 'ideal' way of using a particular software program. Rather, we offer *ideas* for analysis in relation to different data types and methodological and practical contexts.

Table 2.1 lists in overview format *suggested* analytic processes for each case study. The individual elements of each phase are expanded upon in the relevant chapters. These processes illustrate that customised CAQDAS packages can support a range of approaches and highlight how different forms of data and analyses of them may be integrated. A note of caution here: use quantitative summaries of qualitative data and the other mixed methods analytic tools (Chapter 13), where provided, sensitively. The field of mixed methods is growing (Chapter 1), but that does not mean your project *should* incorporate such elements. We discuss these tools because they have a place in many projects; but always use them appropriately and avoid extrapolating beyond the relevance of your dataset.

We use the case-study examples to illustrate three broad approaches:

(i) a 'theory-driven abductive approach' (Case Study A, Young People's Perceptions);
(ii) a 'theory-informed abductive approach' (Case Study B, The Financial Downturn);
(iii) a 'theory-building inductive approach' (Case Study C, Coca-Cola Commercials).

We refer to the case studies in these broad ways because we want to avoid being prescriptive about them in strict terms. Specifically, we are not in the business in this book, to outline step-by-step processes for conducting grounded theory or narrative analysis, or critical discourse analysis, or IPA, or whatever, using software. Partly because the way these approaches are understood are varied; also because our remit is to discuss a range of CAQDAS packages, and there simply is not scope to look in detail at multiple analytic approaches as well as multiple software packages and tools. The purpose of the case-study examples is to highlight that the processes you go through and the tools you use are determined by the needs and characteristics of each project.

Chapter 1 introduced the broadly contrasting techniques of induction, deduction and abduction. Chapter 7 discusses them in more detail in the context of strategies for coding. The processes outlined in Table 2.1 are just examples of possible ways of proceeding; it would be equally valid to proceed differently Some processes are unique to a particular case-study example, others occur across all three. Some processes happen at different stages in each example. You can use sample data with the support of step-by-step instructions to follow them through using your chosen software (see the companion website). Alternatively, you can choose to experiment with alternative ways of working. Your purpose in working with our sample data may be to familiarise with and compare particular software packages. Or you may use them as a means of experimenting with different tools in order to inform the development of your own software-supported analytic strategy. Whatever your purpose, be creative and experimental. The processes we present are not the only ways of proceeding with these types of data. You will get more out of software and data analysis if you try out different tools and processes and reflect on how they will suit the needs of your data and your preferred ways of working.

Pick and choose from across the case-study examples and, most importantly, reflect on all that you do. As always, we encourage *you* to be the architect of *your* method and to manipulate software tools as *you* see fit. Our role is to provide you with a range of ideas for how you might proceed in different circumstances. Your role is to make informed decisions based on your own needs. In reading about our case-study examples and the tools provided by software, reflect upon the needs of your own work; your overarching epistemological and ontological standpoint, your methodological approach, your research questions, your analytic approach, the tasks you need to achieve and the way you like to work.

Case study A: Young People's Perceptions

Case Study A comprises a sub-sample of data drawn from Silver's (2002) PhD project which comprised a comparative exploration of the historical development, provision and experience of school-based sex education in England and Wales and the Netherlands. The original project involved large amounts of several forms of primary and secondary data. The sub-sample discussed throughout this book – and

Table 2.1 Suggested processes for case-study example projects: An Overview

Case A, *Young People's Perceptions* **Suggested processes for theory-driven abductive analysis**	Case B, *The Financial Downturn* **Suggested processes for a theory-informed abductive analysis**	Case C, *Coca-Cola Commercials* **Suggested processes for a theory-building inductive analysis**
PHASE ONE: Data preparation and project set-up • Data preparation • Software project set-up to reflect research design • Incorporate project materials and data PHASE TWO : Review the literature: identify theoretical focus • Familiarise with the articles • Plan your approach to handling literature • Generate and organise critical appraisals of literature • Create a theoretical model arising from literature appraisal PHASE THREE: First wave coding: deductive, broad brush coding across the dataset • Read-through and content-based data familiarisation • Analytic writing: dynamic between literature and data • Topic based auto-coding for repeated data structures • Content based auto-coding for key words and phrases • Process and analytic writing: integrating materials and ideas	PHASE ONE: Data preparation and project set-up • Data preparation • Software project set-up to reflect research design • Incorporate project materials and data • Plan team-working protocols PHASE TWO: Factual data organisation • Group data according to type • Group data according to known characteristics PHASE THREE: Survey data-analysis & media familiarisation • Read-through and content-based data familiarisation • Broad-brush coding of survey data • Basic code-retrieval – preliminary data interrogation PHASE FOUR: Inductive analysis of focus-group data • Read-through and content-based data familiarisation • Content-based searches (based on survey and media finds) • Initial inductive coding – and code retrieval • Refinement of coding scheme structure • Continued data interrogation – integration of primary data analysis	PHASE ONE: Project set-up • Data preparation • Software project set-up to reflect research design • Incorporate project materials and data PHASE TWO: Exploration and identification of analytic focus • Familiarise with commercials • Make analytic notes • Map your expectations • Transcription PHASE THREE: Initial coding: inductive indexing • Indirect inductive coding (via transcript) • Direct inductive coding (without transcripts)

(Continued)

Table 2.1 (Continued)

Case A, *Young People's Perceptions* Suggested processes for theory-driven abductive analysis	Case B, *The Financial Downturn* Suggested processes for a theory-informed abductive analysis	Case C, *Coca-Cola Commercials* Suggested processes for a theory-building inductive analysis
PHASE FOUR: Inductive recoding of broad-brush codes • Identify broad codes relating to each research question • Inductively recode broad codes • Refine coding scheme • Build on analytic and process writing	PHASE FIVE: Deductive analysis of media content • Deductive coding possible in light of themes identified in primary data analysis • Basic code retrieval • Process writing: integrating materials via coding procedures	PHASE FOUR: Basic code retrieval and provisional analytic commentary • Broad overview via basic quantitative retrievals • In-context qualitative retrieval • Outputting for reflection out-of-context • Visualise coding scheme in a map
PHASE FIVE: Factual data organisation • Group data according to type • Group respondents' contributions according to socio-demographics	PHASE SIX: Integration and comparison of coding across data types • Qualitative and quantitative code retrieval • Analytic writing: dynamic between sensitising topics and primary data	PHASE FIVE: Secondary analytic coding: developing themes, concepts, categories • Review and explore previous work visually • Revisit broad codes and recode them into more detailed (sub)codes • Refine codes and their position in the coding scheme
PHASE SIX: Code retrieval, theoretical refinement, analytic reflection • Qualitative and quantitative code retrieval • Analytic writing: dynamic between theoretical model and primary data • Refinement of the coding scheme	PHASE SEVEN: Interrogate data to establish findings • Interrogate connections and illustrate structures using visual tools • Compare coding across the whole (or subsets of) the dataset • Identify patterns in coding within data files (or subsets) • Add variables or short-cut groupings to handle analytic facts as they become apparent	• Generate alternative code groupings to consider relationships • Write up preliminary analysis PHASE SIX: Factual data organisation • Record meta-data about commercials • Integrate analytic facts derived from earlier work

Case A, *Young People's Perceptions* Suggested processes for theory-driven abductive analysis	Case B, *The Financial Downturn* Suggested processes for a theory-informed abductive analysis	Case C, *Coca-Cola Commercials* Suggested processes for a theory-building inductive analysis
PHASE SEVEN: Interrogate data to establish findings	PHASE EIGHT: Building the interpretation and writing up	PHASE SEVEN: Integration of analysis of publicity materials
• Interrogate connections and illustrate structures using visual tools	• Write-up the research design and analytic process	• Add materials to software project
• Compare coding across the whole (or subsets of) the dataset	• Write authoritative and evidenced accounts	• Focused reading, exploration and coding
• Identify patterns in coding within data files (or subsets)	• Report and output for illustration	• Comparative retrieval, cross-referencing and concept refinement
• Add variables or short-cut groupings to handle analytic facts as they become apparent		PHASE EIGHT: Interrogating data to identify findings
PHASE EIGHT: Theoretical reconsideration in light of primary data analysis		• Map based interrogations
		• Link data and concepts and visualise the connections
• Integration of analytical results with literature		• Querying data to make comparisons
• Develop theoretical models		• Querying data to identify patterns
PHASE NINE: Building the interpretation and writing up		PHASE NINE: Building the interpretation and writing up
• Write-up the research design and analytic process		• Write-up the research design and analytic process
• Write authoritative and evidenced accounts		• Writing authoritative and evidenced accounts
• Report and output for illustration		• Report and output for illustration

available for use in the exercises from the companion website – includes interview transcripts, vignettes, discussions arising from visual prompts, images, documents and literature.

The interview transcripts have been significantly reduced in size and heavily edited in order to provide a manageable dataset for the current purpose and to ensure complete anonymity. Data concerning sensitive topics have been removed completely. In some instances content has been changed. Therefore, although data reflect the real experiences of young people living in England and Wales and in the Netherlands at the time the original research was conducted, individual respondents cannot be identified.[1]

The interview data comprise semi-structured questions around five key topics. Within these sections similar issues were broadly discussed, although the level of detail and specific content differ between respondents. Depending on the flow of the conversation, some topics were discussed in more detail by individual respondents. Data files have been formatted such that these broad sections can be auto-coded within software (where possible), allowing all respondents' discussion of each topic to be viewed together (see Chapter 12).

At the end of each interview respondents were shown four textual vignettes describing fictional situations and were asked to respond to them in terms of general opinions and how they would react if they found themselves in similar situations. This was followed by showing respondents two images which they were also asked to discuss.

BOX 2.1 —— CASE STUDY A

Young people's perceptions: Broad research questions

- To what extent do young people living in England and Wales and the Netherlands have similar experiences of learning about sex and relationships?
- How do the socio-sexual attitudes of young women and young men differ? Can these differences be related to aspects of their family background?
- To what extent do the attitudes of this sample of young people reflect other research findings?

The vignettes and photo prompts provide additional insights into the socio-sexual attitudes of this sub-sample of young people and augment the interview data. They are separated from the interview transcripts in order to make it more straightforward to analyse them independently within qualitative software (see Box 2.4; p. 47). There are therefore three sources of data deriving from each of the eight respondents in the sub-sample.

---

[1]The Dutch data have been translated into English using Google Translate for the purposes of this book.

Case study B: The Financial Downturn

Case Study B is a mixed methods socio-political project about the global financial crisis, considering how its effects are experienced and expressed by communities in the UK. This dataset was generated for the purposes of this book and we chiefly treat it as a relatively small regionally-based project. However, the case itself could easily be part of a wider cross-regional or cross-national study, and we use it in part to make reference to how geographically dispersed research teams may collaborate using qualitative software (see the companion website). The study consists of three elements:

- a subset of five focus groups consisting of retired professionals, mixed employed, recently redundant, rural employed and urban employed (collected within one region in the UK during late 2011 and early 2012);
- 191 responses on a subset of questions containing quantitative, descriptive and open-ended comments (sent out to 520 respondents);
- a subset of 70 different media releases derived from relevant local media, global finance/business, national popular press, and national broadsheet publications over 4 years (2008–2012).

The sample survey data include a number of closed questions concerning respondents' attitudes towards the causes and impacts of the global financial crisis and open-ended questions designed to elicit a fuller understanding of how they feel they have been personally affected. Socio-demographic characteristics of respondents, such as their employment status and age group, are included. The raw data are held in a spreadsheet and can be downloaded from the companion website together with the original survey questions.

BOX 2.2 — CASE STUDY B

The financial downturn: Broad research questions

- In what contexts are the implications of the financial downturn expressed by the focus-group respondents? Do their experiences reflect the wider sample in the survey in terms of the major impacts on lives?
- What are respondents' understandings of the causes of the downturn and how are these expressed?
- How are the issues constructed in media reporting and to what extent are respondents' understandings reflected by them?

The inclusion of media content allows the contextualisation of the media back-story, principally at a local level, but background national and global releases additionally provide the opportunity to compare the experiences of the public with media representations. Focus-group data are structured according to speaker sections and discussion topics, for auto-coding (see Chapter 12). Some focus-group respondents also appear in the survey data, allowing for a link between the two forms, and a comparison of how respondents speak about issues in response to different types of questioning.

Case study C: Coca-Cola Commercials

Case Study C is a multimedia dataset with the primary focus on the analysis of visual content, concerning the mechanisms used to advertise Coca-Cola over the past 50 years and the extent to which advertising commercials can be seen to reflect the gendered social relations of their time. The dataset was generated for the purposes of this book and comprises a subset of publically available materials, downloaded from the internet.

The Coca-Cola case constitutes two elements: 15 Coca-Cola advertisements aired between 1960 and the present, each between 30 seconds and 2 minutes in length; and official Coca-Cola company material concerning the history of the company and product and its mission, vision and values.

BOX 2.3 —— CASE STUDY C

Coca-Cola commercials: Broad research questions

- How do Coca-Cola commercials reflect the gendered stereotypes of their time?
- What are the cinematic and advertising mechanisms used to promote Coca-Cola as a brand, and how have these changed over time?
- To what extent do the content of the commercials reflect the company's stated mission, vision and values and its history?

The Coca-Cola advertisements are short video files in MP4 format. The visual elements are variously accompanied by musical soundtracks and voiceovers. Some have been transcribed and timestamped such that they can be incorporated into a software project and synchronised with the accompanying MP4 file. By following the exercises in Chapters 4 and 5 you will be able to experiment with generating your own accompanying time-stamped transcripts for some of the others. Where your chosen software allows, you can also experiment with working directly with the audiovisual data without an accompanying written transcript, although we point you to the discussion in Chapter 7 about the role of transcripts as analytic vehicles through which the visual is accessed. Alongside the audiovisual data are text documents comprising official Coca-Cola company material which have been copied from the Coca-Cola website (www.thecoca-colacompany.com).

Qualitative activities and software tools

CAQDAS packages provide a range of tools to choose from. The software project is the container for your study, providing means of linking different aspects of your work into a coherent and structured unit and facilitating continuity in your thinking and processes. Since none of these things happen automatically, your role as analyst and software user is crucial.

The activities of integrating, organising, exploring, reflecting upon and interrogating data are common amongst qualitative and mixed methods approaches, although the extent, order and manner in which they occur and and in which software tools are

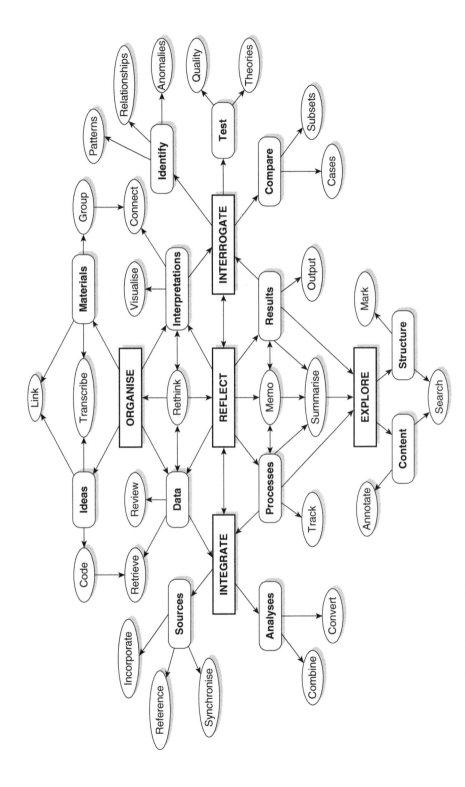

Figure 2.1 Analytic activities and CAQDAS tools

employed vary. This is illustrated in Figure 2.1. It is unlikely that a given research project will need to make use of all the tools provided by an individual CAQDAS package; it is up to you, as the researcher, to pick and choose the tools which suit your research questions, dataset and analytic strategy. Silver and Lewins (2010) provides a detailed description of a simplified version of Figure 2.1 (first published in Lewins and Silver, 2007). Silver and Lewins (2014) follows the logic of the version of the model shown in Figure 2.1 through, focusing in particular on the way in which reflection is core to analytic work and the means by which quality can be illustrated and assessed. Here we provide a practically-oriented and tools-focused overview, illustrating how analytic activities and software tools are relevant to the three case-study examples.

Integration of sources and analyses

Many research projects comprise several types of information and data. CAQDAS packages support data management and the integration of materials which can facilitate holistic analysis. Three aspects of data integration in particular are illustrated through the case-study examples:

(i) simple incorporation of multiple data sources for independent or sequential analysis;
(ii) the time-based synchronisation of multiple representations of the same phenomena, to view and analyse concurrently;
(iii) complex integration of analyses – through combining qualitative and quantitative approaches and/or converting select qualitative data into numeric summary information, for use in a statistical analysis.

Incorporating and referencing data sources

Different sources and forms of data can be incorporated within or referenced from the software project in order to be handled together or separately. Not all materials relating to the project need be analysed; some – for example, the research proposal and other background documents – may simply be available in order to view and refer to. Others, such as literature files, may be referenced and summarised (see Chapter 5). Sources can be stored within or accessed from different folder-type locations within the software project, enabling work to be focused on groups of materials.

Once work begins, access to directly incorporated or referenced sources, together with the notes you make about them, becomes almost instantaneous. This enables seamless flicking between materials otherwise only accessible through different programs. Such basic organisational tools facilitate continuity, keeping you in reliable contact with everything relevant to your project.

Synchronising multiple representations

Visual data offer access to alternative perspectives and interactions. Software varies according to how still and moving images can be handled, a key aspect being whether it is possible to work 'directly' – that is, without the need for a textual representation of visual content in the form of a transcript (Silver and Patashnick, 2011). Direct analysis involves marking, annotating and coding segments of still images or clips of audio or video files. Indirect analysis involves these tasks happening via a written log or transcript that may be synchronised with the corresponding media file. The appropriateness of strategies depends on the status of data and methodological approach; the technical and practical implications of each option affecting what can subsequently be achieved.

Integration of analyses: combining and converting

Mixed methods projects are commonly undertaken and can be greatly facilitated by the use of CAQDAS packages. Products are increasingly providing new ways of linking qualitative and quantitative data and representing qualitative analyses quantitatively. There are different types of methodological integration, the more sophisticated forms requiring the transformation of qualitative data into variables (Bazeley, 2006, 2013). CAQDAS packages facilitate this type of work in several ways. Numeric data in the form of tables and matrices can be outputted for further statistical analysis, assuming the sample to which they refer is suitably large (Chapters 8 and 13). Some CAQDAS packages were developed specifically to support mixed methods analysis and incorporate specific tools for these purposes (Chapter 3).

Quantitative information derived from spreadsheets can be imported and linked to qualitative records. This might constitute factual information about respondents – such as socio-demographic characteristics – numeric information generated from survey responses, or other measures (Chapter 13).

BOX 2.4 — CASE NOTES

Integration of sources and analyses

Case Study A, Young People's Perceptions and Case Study B, The Financial Downturn, are both examples of projects which constitute several different data types, all pertaining to the same general topic. These need to be treated independently as their roles in answering the research questions differ. Yet bringing them together within a single software project also allows their comparison to establish commonalities and linkages. Thus, within- and cross-case analysis is enabled.

In the Young People's Perceptions project sample data were initially collected together but are split for the purposes of analysis in order to make it straight-forward to treat each form independently. The interviews involved direct questioning concerning respondents' experiences and evaluations of different modes of learning and other relevant issues. The vignettes and photo-prompt parts had the specific purpose of uncovering more subtle attitudes than might be expected to elicit from direct questioning. It is therefore relevant to

(Continued)

(Continued)

treat them independently of the main interview transcripts, as well as being able to consider all three concurrently.

The Financial Downturn project, in which a sub-sample of survey respondents subsequently took part in focus-group discussions, provides an example of how qualitative and quantitative data and analyses may be integrated. The original survey data held in a spreadsheet can be imported such that responses to the open-ended questions are treated as qualitative textual records, and the numeric responses to the closed questions linked with them, and treated as quantitative variables. The transcripts of the focus-group discussions can be considered in relation to the survey data in two ways: firstly, in terms of providing a more in-depth understanding of the issues captured through the survey; and secondly, by combining the responses from individuals who took part in both the survey and a focus group. The factual characteristics of respondents are used as socio-demographic variables and linked with survey and focus-group speaker sections (Chapters 4 and 12).

Exploration of content and structure

Becoming familiar with volumes of data is fundamental to analysis. Whether generating data by interviewing and producing verbatim transcripts, observing respondents and developing field notes, using secondary data to inform a documentary analysis, working with audiovisual recordings or in a mixed methods context, the process of data familiarisation starts well before work with data inside a software package. Indeed, becoming aware of what is interesting and rationalising significance is a process that begins during the first moments of project design as well as occurring during the more formal analytic phases of annotating, coding, retrieving, interrogating, etc. Chapters 5 and 6 encourage you to become familiar with software tools in tandem with data, illustrating how experimentation can lead to important early insights as well as helping you to develop a clear strategy for how your chosen software will support your analytic approach.

We discuss annotation and searching tools as means of exploration at different analytic levels (Chapter 1). However, searching the content of textual files for key words, phrases or character strings may have several purposes. It may be a simple explorative task, form part of a closer analytical reading, or be an essential component of a quantitative content analysis. The same is true when working with non-textual data forms, such as still and moving images or audiovisual recordings which may not be transcribed. Exploring the content of data as well as your own notes in the form of memos or annotations is an iterative process, and consideration of content and structure as well as meaning can help reflect on them from different perspectives (see below and Chapter 10).

Marking and annotating data

In exploring data you may mark or highlight interesting segments in order to return to them later to consider in more detail. Working with textual data within

CAQDAS packages, this is usually easily possible by editing data using standard formatting functions such as bold, italics and colour. Working in this way, however, usually only constitutes a cosmetic marking device, in that data cannot be retrieved accordingly. Some packages do offer functional marking devices in terms of options for retrieval on the basis of their existence, but even where this is not the case, coding tools (see below) can always be used in a preliminary fashion to effect a similar result.

Annotations are writing spaces where you can describe and reflect upon marked data segments. They are directly linked to the data segments which they are about and can usually be retrieved independently. In textual documents they act similarly to footnote functions in word-processors and can usually be outputted in this way at the level of the whole data source, or along with coded data. Depending on methodology, researchers may rely more or less heavily on these tools, some wishing to use them to the exclusion of coding tools (Chapter 1). CAQDAS packages differ, however, in the way that they enable annotation and the extent to which these tools can be used independently from coding tools. Nevertheless, marking and annotation are flexible ways of managing data and provide retrievable connections between data and the researcher's thoughts about them.

Searching for content and structure

It may additionally be useful to explore textual data for content and/or structure more quickly and at a 'broader' or 'higher' level. Word frequency, text search and auto-coding tools enable this sort of exploration based on the occurrence of individual words, collections of words, phrases or inherent structures. Although there are some important limitations to the resultant coding of data according to 'hits' found in this way for certain types of project (Chapter 6), exploration of this kind can provide a general overview of content which may not be achievable otherwise.

Word frequency tools Most CAQDAS packages include some basic data mining tools such as word frequency counts which list hits in tabular format, providing counts across the whole – or parts – of the dataset. With roots in the quantitative content analysis tradition, such tools may be considered crude and irrelevant in uncovering meaning. As mentioned above, quantitative summaries of qualitative data should rightly be treated with caution. For example, one of their limitations is their failure, in the tabular view, to discriminate between the origins of words (e.g. who used certain words in an interview file). However, there are often stepped workarounds where such origin is important, and these tools offer alternative ways of viewing and accessing textual data which are particularly useful when analysing documentary evidence or using software to facilitate a literature review. This is particularly true where Key Word In Context (KWIC) functionality is enabled, such that quick access is present from key word lists to surrounding source data (Figures 6.4; p. 148 and 6.5; p. 149).

Text search tools   Text search tools allow you to specify which strings, words or phrases to look up, and therefore provide additional flexibility in searching for similarity. They usually not only provide access to the searched-for key words or phrases within source data but also for specified context around each hit to be auto-coded (e.g. sentence, paragraph or other meaningful unit). Most CAQDAS packages enable the use of wildcards to find alternative endings or prefixes. Boolean operators and other functions refine instances for retrieval. Caution again needs to be applied as these tools will only locate searched-for words, and will miss instances where texts refer to the topic without using them. Absence is often as analytically meaningful as presence, yet projects with extensive data corpora will find the ability to quickly and automatically code data according to the presence of a selection of similar key words or meaningful phrases a useful way of initial exploration, or to ensure important passages are not missed. These tools might also be a useful basis upon which to initiate broad-brush coding (Chapter 7); however, CAQDAS packages vary quite significantly in the sophistication of these text-mining type tools (Chapters 3 and 6).

Auto-coding repeated structures   Some forms of data contain structure, such as repeated sections within and/or across data files. Structured interview transcripts for example, contain repeated structures based on the questions asked, where each section contains responses of an individual respondent. Even where interview schedules are semi-structured, similar general topics will have guided discussions, and these broader topic areas may constitute meaningful repeated structures. Certain types of documentary evidence may also contain repeated structures across multiple data files. Other types of data, such as focus-group transcripts and field notes, often contain repeated structures *within* them; speaker sections in the former, and observed settings in the latter. Where such structures constitute meaningful units of analysis in their own right, once the correct transcription or formatting protocol has been followed for the software being used, these can be searched for and auto-coded (data preparation and formatting is discussed in Chapter 4). Thus in a structured interview dataset, each repeated question can be auto-coded such that all respondents' answers to each question are accessible independently.

BOX 2.5    CASE NOTES

Exploring data

Case study B, The Financial Downturn, includes extensive material derived from media discussions of the topic. Auto-coding large volumes of data based on the presence of key words (or phrases) is likely to be methodologically more justifiable than doing so with smaller volumes of data, providing the first step towards a quantitative content analysis of terms used by the various publications. Comparison of the use of value-laden and jargon terms in different data records is facilitated by text searching. Phrase finder tools in some packages are of particular use for this type of work (Chapter 6). In projects where large volumes of data are involved, and/or where the use of language is an analytic focus, the frequency information generated by this sort of work is as valuable to the analysis as any resultant coding of the context surrounding each hit. Most CAQDAS packages do not enable statistical analyses of numeric data,[2] but all provide means to export information in tabular format for subsequent analysis in other applications.

Case study C, Coca-Cola Commercials, includes official company material concerning its history, mission, vision and values. An exploration of the terms used to promote the product in these materials may reveal an additional dimension to the interpretation of the advertisements. If the commercials are analysed indirectly, via written transcripts, these could also be searched for the occurrence of repeated words or phrases as a means of, for example, identifying the frequency of use of certain slogans in advertising. In order to be able to rely on such findings, however, verbatim transcriptions would need to be consistently developed. In addition, segments of the commercials themselves, where the soundtrack, voiceover or visual content was seen to illustrate aspects of the company vision, could be marked and annotated. In software packages which support linking of marked or coded data segments (see below), video clips can also be linked to related textual segments, thus enabling 'data-level' association. Both annotating and linking in this way would help the process of tracking the nature of association identified across diverse data records.

Organising materials and ideas

Organisation is a key aspect of handling and analysing qualitative data. CAQDAS packages provide a range of ways in which to do so. We distinguish between these by categorising them into three types: grouping, coding and linking. Grouping according to the characteristics of materials, cases or respondents, and structurally coding parts of files according to who is speaking (as discussed above) are closely connected. More conceptually, coding is often the means by which researchers organise their ideas about data. Related to this conceptual work might be the linking of data segments to track processes or interactions. As with any other analytic task, the manner, extent, stage and sequence of organisation largely depend on the methodological approach and forms of data involved (Chapter 1).

Grouping

Organising materials into groups enables parts of a dataset to be isolated in order to focus on (combinations of) subsets of data and/or respondents. It is usually possible to group *whole* files which represent a unit of analysis (e.g. a case or individual respondent – such as interview transcripts, published reports or video files), or *parts* of files where, for example, several cases or respondents occur within a file (such as in focus-group, survey, or

---

[2]QDA Miner – when used in conjunction with the SimStat module – is the exception, although we do not discuss SimStat in this volume.

field data). Whatever the situation, known characteristics, often conceptualised as socio-demographic attributes or variables, can be used for grouping purposes. This enables subsequent filtering, retrieval and interrogation based on individual or combinations of groups. A tabular view is typical, and the information can either be inputted manually, or through the importation of a file which originated in a spreadsheet or statistical application (e.g. Excel or SPSS). Chapter 12 discusses the factual grouping of data in more detail, and Chapter 13 the interrogation of data on this basis.

BOX 2.6 — CASE NOTES

Organising data

Case study A, Young People's Perceptions, contains data in different sources derived from the same respondents. Grouping tools are thus important in order to gather together all the contributions from each respondent so that they can be interrogated according to the socio-demographic characteristics of individual respondents. The way this can be achieved differs in subtle but important ways among software packages, but all allow it to be done. The coding of their responses to the interview topics, the vignettes and visual prompts, is key to the way respondent data are conceptually organised, and this case study is used in the book to illustrate a combined deductive–inductive (or abductive) approach to coding (Chapter 7).

Case study C, Coca-Cola Commercials, might use grouping devices to track the longitudinal aspects of the dataset. A key aspect of the analysis pertains to how advertising techniques and gendered stereotypes have changed over time within the commercials, and therefore this aspect of time is the key factual organisation driver (Chapter 12). With respect to the conceptual organisation of ideas about this dataset, however, the situation is less clear-cut, and the approach taken will depend, in particular, on whether data are to be analysed directly or indirectly (Chapter 7). This is affected quite heavily by the functionality of the chosen CAQDAS package, however, with some offering more choices in approach than others.

Coding

Many qualitative analyses involve organising data by way of conceptually or thematically indexing them. In this sense, coding is usually a key aspect of managing interpretation. There are many different approaches to qualitative coding, some of which are discussed in Chapter 7. In general terms, coding is the process by which segments of data are identified as relating to, or being an example of, a more general idea, instance, theme or category. As such, coding is a means of organising your ideas about what is interesting in the data, in relation to your research questions.

Qualitative researchers may take inductive, deductive or combined (abductive) approaches to generating and applying codes, each of which is usually well supported by software. From a technological point of view, all CAQDAS packages provide flexible coding tools. For example, codes can be generated at the data level, or independently of it. The same code can be applied to any number of data segments derived from any data source. In most of the packages designed originally for textual analysis the same or overlapping or embedded data segment can be coded by any number of relevant codes. The amount of data coded can be increased or decreased. Codes can be merged or grouped; previously coded data can be recoded or uncoded. Codes can be defined, renamed, listed, printed or exported. Coded data can be easily retrieved and outputted.

The coding functionality of most CAQDAS packages is similar, although there are some subtle variations which may be important to researchers working within certain methodological paradigms. One example is the way in which coding schemas are visually presented. Researchers vary in their expectations of these structures, some preferring visually hierarchical systems, others feeling constrained by perceived notions of hierarchy. What is more useful than any set structure is that you can often regroup, reorder and visualise codes in alternative ways. This reflects the need, having broken data down by initial coding processes, to combine codes and their data differently simply in order to output these new permutations of data for re-examination. Sometimes this can be part of a necessary stepping back from data after having been immersed closely in them for a long time.

Hyperlinking

Some approaches to qualitative data analysis view coding as limiting. This is often because it is perceived as fragmenting and reducing data to an extent that obscures the dialectic relationship between reading text (or viewing multimedia data) and writing. Rather than abstracting from the 'data level' through the collecting together of similar segments – the essential process of coding – researchers may wish to create associative trails through material at the level of data themselves. Where the analytic focus is on the relationship between instances rather than concepts, hyperlinking and annotation tools may best support work.

Hyperlinking is a free association approach to building up an analytic chain of reasoning embedded in data. It facilitates an unstructured, non-linear, 'data-level' approach to identifying, writing about and linking ideas, whereby multi-directional associative trails can be created. Hyperlinking tools may be used to track processes as diverse as narrative, sequence, time and interaction.

Among the software packages discussed in this book, ATLAS.ti provides the most advanced and flexible tools for hyperlinking between segments of data (termed 'quotations' in ATLAS.ti) across or within data records – to the extent that, using this package, it is possible to analyse qualitative data without using coding tools at all (see Chapters 3 and 6).

Reflecting upon data, interpretations, processes and results

The ability to 'step back' from raw data and ideas about them and reflect at a 'higher', more 'conceptual' or 'abstract' level about your growing interpretation is an important aspect of working qualitatively. Iterative processes of flicking backwards and forwards between analytic tasks and software tools are the core business of analysis. Reflection is the analytic task that occurs throughout analysis, hence its centrality within our model (Figure 2.1; p. 45). Interpretive processes take different forms according to philosophical context, methodological approach, research questions, analytic strategy, practical dynamics, required outcomes and researchers' working styles. Whilst we reiterate that software does not analyse or interpret data in itself, it does provide a range of tools which can facilitate these processes. As well as various ways of interrogating the dataset discussed below, retrieving and reviewing, writing, connecting and visualising are major analytic processes, and the tools developed to facilitate them are key to the benefits of using customised CAQDAS packages.

Retrieve, review and rethink data and ideas about them

Retrieval of coded or hyperlinked data provides a means of reviewing progress across the whole dataset in order to reconsider a body of data, reconceptualise a theme, and move a 'higher', more conceptual or abstract level of work. It is usually possible to retrieve data for these purposes without needing to create complex queries (Chapter 8). Coded data can be viewed in context or lifted out of context to consider in isolation, either within software, or by generating output (e.g. to view in a word-processing or spreadsheet application or in a web browser). This facilitates general consideration of all instances of a theme or concept, *horizontally* across all data files.

Filtering options, though enabled with varied degrees of complexity, allow horizontal retrieval across limited parts of the database; some software packages enable this in very simple ways, others via more complex query options (Chapter 13). It is often also analytically useful to consider one data file at a time, for example where it contains an individual interview transcript or field notes about a particular setting. Viewing an individual data file *vertically* in this way – by all or selected codes – provides a way of considering a case or situation as an independent entity. This can be achieved visually within the software, using a margin view illustrating where particular codes (co-)occur, or by generating output which lifts out all the segments within that file coded by each code.

Whatever the approach to coding qualitative data, it will often be necessary to recode. If coding in a broad-brush or deductive way, this can be facilitated by most CAQDAS packages by first retrieving data coded with a broad-brush code, and then recoding into more detailed codes. This process adds additional codes to the original data, thereby allowing analysis of the theme in more depth.

Most packages also provide quantitative overviews of how data have been coded in various respects (Chapter 8). Tables showing, for example, frequency of code application by data file, by number of words in textual data or duration of coded clip in an audio-video file, coded across the dataset, are usually either provided automatically or can be generated very easily. Such tables are often fully interactive within the software; that is, each cell of a table provides a direct link to the data regardless of the way it is counted in the table. Additionally, these tables can be exported to spreadsheet applications for more complex statistical analysis (where appropriate).

Memo, summarise, track, output

Taking informal notes, making annotations and writing longer, more formal, summaries or explanations about what is seen in data are analytic activities which are undertaken throughout the process of qualitative and mixed methods research. In many senses writing *is* analysis.

In addition to annotation tools as discussed above, memo systems provide larger and more central writing spaces which can be used for a range of purposes. These might include recording the research progress, writing an analytic description about a code or concept, fleshing out a theoretical idea as it is illustrated in the data, summarising what seems important about a particular respondent, and referring back to research questions. A well-designed system needs to be created to store these insights. Even a literature review can be undertaken within the software (Chapter 5), and the final written report begun as separate memos. The benefit of using integrated memo systems rather than keeping memos outside of the CAQDAS project relates to the systematic management and retrieval of writing. Most packages allow you to treat memos as data by means of coding your own writing and linking it with other material. This enables you to integrate ideas with the data that prompt them, or to link your interpretations with the evidence that supports them. Writing spaces within CAQDAS packages are discussed further in Chapter 10.

Connecting and visualising interpretations

Many CAQDAS packages include integrated mapping, modelling or networking tools enabling visual representations of aspects of work. The way these tools function varies considerably among packages, which therefore offer quite different ways of working. Nevertheless, there are several ways in which mapping tools can be particularly useful when undertaking analysis. For example, graphically representing hypotheses, hunches or theoretical models at the outset of a more deductive analysis; or when working more inductively, the ability to represent the linkages which seem to exist in the project, based on the tasks already undertaken. There are many bespoke packages exclusively developed to 'map' processes and connections. Some of them are freely available. However, mapping tools in CAQDAS packages usually provide dynamic interactivity back to the source data.

As well as mapping tools providing means of visualising connections between data, concepts and ideas, other types of qualitative and quantitative visualisations are provided in many CAQDAS packages. These include margin views of applications of codes vertically through data files (Chapter 8), charts and matrices (Chapter 13). This is an area of significant development and the growing number of visualisations provide increasingly complex ways of accessing findings and reflecting on their significance.

Interrogating to identify, compare and test

CAQDAS packages offer various means to interrogate the dataset based on earlier work, and these tools are the power-house of moving from description to interpretation. This involves going beyond code and retrieve tasks which characterise much qualitative work. Functionality ranges from simple to complex, and the range of possibilities varies somewhat between packages. Chapter 8 illustrates the role of simple retrieval functionality within the iterative design of the case-study examples. Chapter 13 discusses software query tools in detail in the context of their role in moving analytic thinking on, and interrogating data and coding to establish findings.

Identifying patterns, relationships and anomalies

Mapping tools can provide visual ways of making connections or viewing patterns and relationships in the data at an abstract level (Chapter 11). However, query tools provide more sophisticated ways to interrogate the dataset according to the presence and absence of codes as they have been applied. Boolean and proximity query operators are common to many CAQDAS packages, allowing the identification of where two or more codes occur together or separately in data. They may be run at early stages of work in order to test a hunch, or generate a general overview of the current situation. The way queries are built can usually be saved and rerun at a later stage. Doing so is a way of creating reminders of interesting aspects which deserve revisiting, or ensuring the same questions are asked of multiple phases of data in a longitudinal design. In this way queries may be used as hypotheses. They can also contribute to the iterative and incremental coding process. It may be at the latter stages, however, when you are confident that main coding process has been completed consistently, that the results of queries are used as the basis for establishing findings.

Comparing subsets and cases

All research projects include a comparative element. This is often explicit in the research design in terms of the populations or corpora from which respondents and sampled or data are gathered. Within case-study or other comparative designs it is necessary to compare how different cases or types of respondent discuss, experience or perceive certain aspects. Having grouped data according to known characteristics (Chapter 12), comparative queries are enabled (Chapter 13). The ease with which query results, sometimes viewed as matrices, can be generated varies, but many CAQDAS packages provide the facility to compare groups of codes by socio-demographic characteristics, such as gender, age, teacher, pupil, or parent. Alternatively, it may be useful to create a qualitative cross-tabulation of codes by codes in order to see where particular codes occur together in the data.

Where the comparative element occurs within cases, settings or over time, the organisational basis for enabling the comparisons is different, as are the tools used within CAQDAS packages. This has much to do with the distinction between *vertical* and *horizontal* cuts (Chapter 1): comparison can happen on the basis of how applied codes relate to one another, as well as how certain types of respondent or data sources contain particular codes.

BOX 2.8 —— CASE NOTES

Interrogating data

Case Study A, Young People's Perceptions, is used to illustrate some different ways in which simple retrieval and more complex querying can be combined to make comparisons (Chapters 8 and 13). Queries are used to compare how themes discussed in the literature occur within primary data; to pick out similarities and differences in how individual respondents talk about particular issues across the three types of primary data; and to compare respondents' experiences and opinions according to their factual characteristics, such as gender and nationality (Chapter 12).

Case Study B, The Financial Downturn, is used to illustrate how quantitative and qualitative interrogations and visualisations offer different analytic insights and means of representing data and findings. Comparisons are made between how themes identified in open-ended responses to the survey questions are reflected by discussion amongst focus-group participants (Chapter 4). This includes the direct comparison of a sub-sample of

(Continued)

(Continued)

respondents who contributed to both. Themes identified in the primary data are contrasted with those evident in media content, and the utility of various quantitative representations of query results and findings is explored (Chapter 13).

Case Study C, Coca-Cola Commercials, as an example of a 'theory-building inductive' analysis, illustrates the role of simple retrieval and more complex querying in the iterative process. The role of basic retrieval options in developing themes that are evidenced across the dataset and moving the analysis on from the descriptive indexing level to a more conceptual and thematic level of analysis is a key focus (Chapters 7 and 8). In addition, this case study illustrates the value of considering individual data files *vertically*, such that patterns in coding sequentially throughout a transcript can be used to reveal relationships of analytic interest. This will relate in part to the use of repetition in visual representation and verbal content in the commercials.

Testing theories and assessing quality

Some projects apply existing theories to new or alternative bodies of data, with the explicit intention of testing hypotheses. Others are concerned with generating new theory. The former is often broadly be conceptualised as 'deductive' and the latter 'inductive'. In practice, in terms of the strategies employed to conduct a given analysis, it is common to combine inductive and deductive processes. This is discussed in particular relation to coding in Chapter 7. Whether working *down* from theory, or *up* towards it, software tools – in particular retrieval and query tools – can be employed to check the relevance and applicability of a given theory across the dataset.

Another aspect of *testing* relates to assessing the quality of your work. Perhaps one of the most important advantages of using customised CAQDAS packages is the ability software provides to quickly and reliably access data and earlier work (Chapters 8 and 13). There are several bases upon which you might assess and prove the quality of your work, but there are no universally accepted criteria for doing so in the field of qualitative research because of the variety in standpoints that underpin the ways researchers work. The 'criteriology debate' refers to the relevance and possibility of developing, universally applicable or consensually agreed criteria for assessing qualitative research. Some have developed criteria or guidelines for assessing quality (including Guba and Lincoln, 1981; Goodwin and Goodwinn, 1984; Lincoln and Guba, 1985; Shaw, 1999; Angen, 2000; Bryman, 2001; Sparkes, 2001) whereas others have questioned (Seale, 1999) or disputed (Smith, 1984, 1990) the ability to do so. Despite issues in developing and using criteria across divergent approaches, Bazeley (2013) provides a useful discussion of the topic, raising questions to consider around the quality of data, process, product and outcome. We touch on these issues throughout this book, in particular in Chapters 8, 10 and 13, and provide a more explicit discussion in Silver and Lewins (2014).

The right tools for the job

The tasks of qualitative analysis can be used selectively. You remain in control of the analysis and choose which software tools are useful at which moments. CAQDAS packages are developing at great pace and most now offer a broad array of tools. It is useful in your early consideration of products to keep the commercial context in mind. Most are competing for custom, and this has an effect on the range and nature of the tools on offer. It is unlikely that you will need all the tools provided by any one package for a particular research project. Some tools are designed specifically to support certain types of analysis, and it is important to use them because they support *your* approach, not simply because they are there! In this book we introduce many of the tools available and provide guidance about how they can be valuable. But it is *your* task to decide which are appropriate to your particular needs. The next chapter is designed to help more specifically with your choice between packages, as it provides a more detailed overview of each of the products we discuss in the book.

Several factors vary the way software is used. Practical issues concerning resources, expertise or time available will often determine the number of different functions used, and the extent of reliance on the software. Silverman (2000: 42–43) reminds us that once you have chosen a methodological approach you can 'treat it as a "toolbox" providing a set of methods and concepts to select your data and illuminate your analysis'. That methodological toolbox starts at a conceptual level. The CAQDAS package acts as another toolbox at a more practical level. Be selective and sceptical about tools and the 'results' provided.

Concluding remarks: flexibility in the sequencing of tasks

Although software does not dictate the order in which you perform various tasks, it might influence you in terms of the number and complexity of the tasks you undertake, or your readiness to perform them. It is a paradox of this type of software that, while systematising the management and storage of data and your ideas about them, it in fact frees you from having to be quite so systematic in the order in which you do things. Using software liberates you from clerical constraints which may prejudice flexibility using more traditional 'craft' methods. Although the chapters that follow occur in a certain order, this is not done in order to recommend one sequence or one process. One of the principal benefits of using software is that you can revisit tasks and rethink areas of interest as you go. As illustrated in Figure 2.1, analysis is cyclical and iterative rather than linear, and CAQDAS packages have been designed to reflect and reinforce this.

The bits in between

Reducing work that is done with data to a set of tasks inevitably misses those parts of the process that change your account from a straightforward description to something at an analytically higher level of abstraction – an interpretation. However you proceed, different aspects of your work will need to come together to form a coherent whole. We emphasise two main aspects that facilitate this:

- *Become thoroughly familiar with writing/memo tools* early in your use of software and constantly build on your earlier writing. Use tools to help you to retain insights and remind you of small impromptu action plans that might bear fruit later. This will help you feel less isolated within coding or linking devices. Chapter 5 discusses the role of a centralised 'research process journal' and the utility of creating a structural framework for your more analytical memo writing. Start thinking about this as soon as possible.
- *Come out of the software when you want to.* To do that, we encourage printing of output on a regular basis. Print important memos. Print reports of coded data. Go back to basics: use coloured highlighters and pens to deconstruct coded data reports. Print tabular summaries of code frequencies; look especially for gaps, investigate them and read whole files where these gaps exist. Print code lists; draw connections or mark codes you think belong together in some way. While we believe that software can help with most projects, there will always be exceptions. Even when it can help, using software does not mean you need to become a slave to your computer.

3
Software Summaries

This chapter summarises the CAQDAS packages featured in this book and for which there are step-by-step materials on the companion website (www.uk.sagepub.com/silverlewins2e). Most of these summaries have been developed in conjunction with the software developers themselves. They therefore reflect the philosophy behind each package and also developers' own views of what is exceptional about their products. We are grateful for their input. We wanted to avoid this chapter becoming a 'sales pitch', so we have edited developers' summaries and added our own contributions.

Information contained here was correct at the time of writing (autumn 2013). However, software develops quickly and neither this chapter nor the book as a whole describes all the functions available. You should therefore consult the software websites for additional and up-to-date information.

The variety in histories, rationale and functionality means the summaries concentrate on different aspects. Some tell the story behind the software because an appreciation of the underlying developmental philosophy is important in understanding the tools. Some concentrate on distinctive tools and the 'personality' of the software. In any case, there is relatively scant reference in this chapter to the fundamental tools for qualitative data analysis that they all provide: coding, organising and searching data (Chapter 2). We present the summaries in alphabetical order.

ATLAS.ti

ATLAS.ti[1] was developed from the late 1980s in the Psychology Department at the Technical University of Berlin, led by Heiner Legewie, Erhardt Conrad, Thomas Muhr and a team of computer scientists and linguists. It is now developed and supported by Scientific Software Development GmbH. Inspired by Anselm Strauss's work and the field of hermeneutic text interpretation, the aim was to support the data-level work inherent to qualitative data analysis. The quotation architecture

---

[1]http://www.atlasti.com/index.html. With thanks to Thomas Muhr for his contribution.

and integrality of the networking functionality in making connections, expressing ideas and moving on to more abstract analyses are at the heart of the design and workflow. Working with ATLAS.ti is characterised by oscillating between the data level of segmenting, coding and memoing and the conceptual level of linking and building theories. The idea is that such a de-linearisation fosters a deeper understanding of the researched phenomena, supporting the building up of a 'context of discovery'. Projects, documents, codes, memos, and groups of these entities are ingredients of virtually any kind of qualitative data analysis software. Particular to ATLAS.ti and capturing the essential aims in the origins of the program is the explicit representation of relationships between concepts. ATLAS.ti supports describable and functional links between codes and/or data segments. Sets of relations can define associations on many different levels: for example, relations between codes in a grounded theory project; and the structures, flow and connections in a narrative analysis of speech.

ATLAS.ti supports code-based approaches to qualitative data analysis very well, but also approaches that prioritise the tracking of non-linear and non-thematic associations (e.g. forms of narrative, discourse and linguistic analysis). In particular, its emphasis on in-context navigation and retrieval, the level of integration of memo-writing tools with other aspects of work and the flexibility of the networking tool are distinctive. Both Windows and Mac platforms are supported.

Data

Many kinds of documents are supported: plain and rich text, native PDF, images, audio, video and geo data. Documents can be associated in pairs (e.g. an audio file and its synchronised transcript). Data are added to a project by selecting files, or via imports (surveys (Excel), transcriptions (F4), or iPad projects). Visual data can be handled directly or indirectly (Chapters 1 and 5).

'Quotation' architecture

Quite distinctive in ATLAS.ti is the 'quotation' structure. These data segments can remain independent of anything else, coded, linked to other quotations or memos. Hyperlinks between quotations can represent rhetoric structure (e.g. 'statement A <supports> statement B'), track a story or process or any other relevant data-level association (see Figures 6.1; p. 137 and 11.2; p. 265). Quotations derived from different types of data can be linked; for example, a video clip and a geo-location to an observation in the text.

User interface

ATLAS.ti's margin display, showing codes, memos and hyperlinks between quotes, mimics traditional ways of 'interacting' with a text, but goes beyond 'paper and pencil' scribbling and annotating. Items in the margin can be manipulated in many ways, including filtering devices for codes and traversal of hyperlinks between quotes. The margin operates consistently across different data types, making it easy to transfer 'know-how' between media (Figure 7.5; p. 178). Up to four documents can be displayed side by side, especially useful for related documents such as transcripts and their source media, working with literature and navigating hyperlinks without losing the context (Figure 5.3; p. 118).

The Network Editor

Networks provide a central workspace for building and revising models and displaying spatially clustered items. They can be used for many purposes, for example, gathering quotes or codes together (Figure 11.2; p. 265); recoding broadly specified themes; linking codes to other objects (memos, codes or quotes) (Figure 10.6; p. 247); creating rational connections between quotations; creating subset groupings ('families') of codes, documents or memos; and interrogating connections between codes (Figure 11.7; p. 275).

Analytic functions

Various tools facilitate generation of overviews and development of relationships, including interactive code co-occurrence tables, word frequency (lists and tag cloud) (Figure 6.4; p. 148), and document-code tables. The query tool allows interrogation based on semantic ('transitive') connections between codes as well as the more common ways of identifying co-occurrence and proximity. The unique 'super-code' function enables the building, running and incorporation of queries as if they were codes.

Embedded visualisations

Amongst the most effective visualisations are those directly available within routinely used tools. Object managers offer a variety of 'embedded' visualisations, including frequency bar statistics, cloud view for code 'groundedness' (number of quotations), and connectivity with other codes. Documents, networks and memos can be displayed as previews in the managers.

Interoperability

The import and export of project data using a standardised format (XML) avoids being locked in a proprietary framework. Projects can be populated from survey Excel data, and word counts sent to Excel for display and further processing. SPSS export bridges the gap to quantitative approaches.

Mobile app

The ATLAS.ti mobile app can be used as a field recorder to support data collection and data reduction phases. Text, audio, video, image and PDF can be assigned to iPad projects, and the interface with the main software is good.

Dedoose

Dedoose[2] is web-based, platform independent software. Its founders, Eli Lieber and Tom Weisner, are innovators in the contemporary evolution of mixed methods approaches and have been providing qualitative and mixed methods research consultation to domestic and international research teams for over 15 years. They felt there were no tools to efficiently meet the needs of most of the researchers they were working with. Teams were geographically distributed, working on varying platforms, and team members had varying levels of experience and training. At the same time, internet technology and data visualisation development were booming. Many at the time were abandoning more complex software due to high purchase and training costs and were resorting to cobbling things together with more familiar solutions such as SPSS, Word, and Excel. The challenge was how to work efficiently and effectively and generate evidence to serve the requirements of high-level scientific research and the production of manuscripts, reports, and presentations, as well as how to best serve the new, rapidly increasing frequency of truly mixed methods cross-disciplinary research. Dedoose is developed by SocioCultural Research Consultants, LLC (SCRC) and was first released commercially in 2010. Dedoose is a well-developed code-based system which can be manipulated for a range of methodologies. It has a much shorter history than the other packages summarised here, and that is reflected in the range of tools currently on offer. Development is ongoing, however, and new features are being added all the time. Apart from being web-based, it is distinctive for a number of reasons, including its focus on concurrent teamworking, provision for mixed qualitative and quantitative displays in the form of its chart selector and use of coloured highlighting in the excerpting process.

Web-based architecture

Being web-based and rentable on a monthly basis, Dedoose (formerly Ethno Notes) is fundamentally different from the traditional standalone software researchers were using for qualitative data analysis at the time of its release. Dedoose is natively collaborative, platform independent, inexpensive, and optimised for mixed methods while offering a shallow learning curve, without install, upgrade, or maintenance issues. Operating online means team members

---

[2]https://app.dedoose.com. With thanks to Eli Lieber for his contribution.

are free from reliance on single machines and the burdens of sending files back and forth. Instead teams access the same projects from any internet-connected device in real time. Team leaders can control costs, providing access to any number of team members on a short-term basis, as needed. Similarly, individual users benefit from the same features being able to log on to their project from any work station in any internet-enabled environment without long-term commitments to purchase.

User interface

A series of screens or workspaces provide alternative foci. Dedoose's complexity can be thought of as a sliding scale with the interface intentionally designed accordingly. For example, it is easy to learn the basics (uploading media, excerpting, coding, making memos, and generating reports). Therefore, activities often tasked to less experienced assistants can be accomplished with simplicity and transparency (Figure 10.8; p. 253). An example of its visual accessibility is illustrated by the process of coding excerpts. Different coloured highlighting of text is achieved automatically as coding proceeds. This is difficult to illustrate in a black and white hard copy (see the companion website for colour illustrations), but it appeals since it resonates so well with manual highlighting using highlighter pens to indicate different types of significance. Additional features are accessed via other workspaces (windows), so more complex analytics can be carried out by those with greater experience and training (Figure 8.2; p. 194). Using workspaces to separate sets of features keeps the Dedoose interface clean and accessible. In order to move into more advanced workspaces, systematised training modules accompany the web-based resource to provide support at every stage of work.

The mixed methods emphasis

The focus on mixed methods data integration and analysis in Dedoose's architecture is another major distinguishing characteristic. Fundamental to its design is the ability to easily import demographic, survey, rating, and other quantitative data. Further, the simple links between these data and associated qualitative media drives many of its interactive data visualisations (Figures 8.2; p. 194 and 13.5; p. 319). Early creation of excerpts and their subsequent coding can produce visualisations that allow exploration in different dimensions that contribute to discovering and presenting patterns. The Chart Selector (Figure 13.5; p. 319) provides a range of ways to visually interrogate the project. The starting points for working exploring data via charts are easy to access. The resulting visualised graphs and charts are fully integrated, easily customised, exportable, and dynamically linked for immediate access to all associated qualitative excerpting and coding. Finally, the flexible Dedoose code weight system allows researchers to include code ratings/weights for individual code applications to bring an additional dimension to analysis.

HyperRESEARCH

HyperRESEARCH[3] was originally created by Sharlene Hesse-Biber and her partners at Boston College, Massachusetts, and is now developed by Researchware, Inc. Underlying its development is the belief that less time should be spent on the mechanics of research, and more time spent on the research itself. Researchware's analytical tools are designed accordingly, and HyperRESEARCH is intended to work flexibly with a wide range of qualitative research methods. It is a well-developed code-based system, emphasising case-based analysis and providing some unique features, but the range of tools on offer is not as diverse as some of the other packages we summarise here. Since the outset it has been developed dual-platform and therefore until recently has been one of few options for Mac users. Used alongside Hyper-TRANSCRIBE™, Researchware offers a bundle of tools to support researchers from transcription through analysis.

Case-based architecture

HyperRESEARCH supports a case-based structure for comparative analysis that is unique amongst the packages summarised in this chapter. Although use of the case structure is optional, cases can consist of any grouping the researcher wishes to compare: individual study subjects (e.g. individual respondents), institutions, time periods, or any other categorisation. Individual data sources (e.g. interview transcripts, observational field notes, newspaper articles) can be used in multiple cases, and any number of sources can be used in an individual case; therefore cases need not be linked to a particular source. Relevant data segments from sources can be used in multiple cases. This is ideal for analysing group interactions and conversations that include more than one respondent or any other form of data in which more than one entity or unit of analysis (case) occurs across multiple data sources.

User interface

The case card is architecturally central and the means through which coding actions are registered. Whatever the case represents (e.g. an individual respondent, several respondents, or a dimension of analysis) the case card lists the relevant codes and where they apply to data (Figure 12.3; p. 293). Clicking on each code reference opens up the highlighted section of the document in its full context. The codebook and the interactive source window alongside comprise the basic coding environment.

Data

Source data for use in HyperRESEARCH can include images, audio, video, or text (DOCX, ODF, HTML, RTF, TXT, or PDF). It supports world languages and character

---

[3]http://researchware.com. With thanks to Anne Dupuis for her contribution.

sets (such as Chinese and Arabic). Transcripts created in the companion HyperTRAN-SCRIBE software can also be used. Audio and video files can be viewed simultaneously with related transcripts. Coding can be performed either directly on audio and video sources, or indirectly via transcripts. Teamwork is supported via the ability to merge several researchers' data into one study. Researchers can share standardised code books or combine them as needed.

Analysis and interrogation

Coding is as simple as clicking and dragging to select material and applying one or more codes from the code book. Automated coding, based on a search for key terms, provides a quick start.

Code and case filters create subsets of coded data, allowing the researcher to restrict analysis to specific codes and cases, cross-correlate codes, and look for relationships between coded segments within source material. Analysis and reporting are performed on filtered sets of codes and cases, so researchers can quickly create 'slices' of their data for analysis. Filters can easily be removed when the need is to interrogate across the whole dataset. The simple **Report Builder** offers easy options to vary the display, output and sorting of finds.

The **Theory Builder** provides an additional route to interrogation from which researchers can scan for and verify themes 'emerging' from their data. This is a built-in inference engine that analyses code relationships and looks for correlations (see Figure 13.2; p. 308). The hypothesis or query can be built up in several stages, at each of which a code (or theme) can be applied to all the cases which satisfy the criteria. All types of filtering, analysis and reporting can be done at any stage. Generally, researchers can work iteratively by doing initial coding, then analysing, and letting the results guide further examination and coding of the source data.

Visualisation

HyperRESEARCH has an unusual code-map device which, as well as illustrating meaningful connections, can for example be used as a code selection device to reveal cases containing certain codes.

Cross-platform working

HyperRESEARCH is cross-platform, working natively with Mac and Windows. Files are easily moved between platforms, so researchers can use a mix of computer types. A USB stick drive can hold working Mac and Windows versions plus the study data, allowing researchers to plug in and start working immediately on any computer that is accessible to them, even if HyperRESEARCH is not installed on it.

Modular add-ons

A modular tool architecture enables new tools to be plugged in as they become available. Researchers can easily add the tools they need from Researchware's growing suite. Currently available and planned tools include such functions as importing data from other software packages, inter-rater reliability, word frequency analysis, examining survey data for mixed methods analysis, and more.

MAXQDA

MAXQDA[4] is the latest in a series of software packages (including Winmax) which were originally named after sociologist Max Weber. Development began in the late 1980s. The original author and continuing inspiration behind the software, Udo Kuckartz, developed the software to handle his own work on political discourse about the environment. MAXQDA is now developed by Verbi GmbH. MAXQDA supports the analysis of qualitative and mixed data using a variety of approaches including grounded theory, thematic analysis, discourse analysis, phenomenology, ethnography, content analysis and more. MAXQDA focuses on the idea of coding, memoing and working with a framework of categories iteratively developed during the research process. It is a code-based system which offers sophisticated and flexible tools and a range of visualisations which are unique amongst the packages summarised in this chapter. In particular, its use of colour is striking and versatile; its memo tools powerful for integrating different levels of writing with data; its pre-processing and survey import tools streamlined; and its recent developmental focus on mixed methods analytic tools distinctive. Both Windows and Mac platforms are supported.

Data

As well as handling text documents (including PDF, Word and rich text), there are functions for coding pictures, audio and video files (including synchronicity between transcript and media), and direct import from Excel (including auto-processing and auto-coding of both the qualitative and quantitative fields during the import process (Figure 4.4; p. 102)).

User interface

From the outset of development, MAXQDA put its emphasis on user-friendliness, particularly on a clear and uncluttered user interface comprising a quadrant of rearrangeable and interactively connected main windows. This architecture continues and supports quick and easy work flow (Figure 5.3; p. 118). Many elements of MAXQDA's concept – such as using colours to identify codes – are now used in other packages, but for a variety of functions MAXQDA offers fast, intuitive and unique solutions to get

---

[4]http://www.maxqda.com. With thanks to Udo Kuckartz for his contribution.

complex things done. These often rely on a range of effective visualisations and dynamic lists. Other key distinctions include the ability to *activate* or switch on any selection of codes for retrieval and visualisation purposes, and the provision of many instant tabular retrievals offering interactive views of coded data with associated memos, co-occurrences and frequencies (Figures 8.3; p. 196 and 9.5; p. 225).

Visualisations

There are several unique tools in MAXQDA. Some of the complex visual tools and functions that support mixed methods analysis are easy to generate. Visual tools such as the Code Relation Browser, the Code Matrix Browser and the Cross-tabs tools display respectively code co-occurrences or proximity, a document-by-codes matrix, and codes by attributes (e.g. socio-demographics), all of which are interactive with original documents. Other more unusual diagrams like the Codeline, Document Portrait and Text Comparison Chart match up with the colours assigned to codes to offer new cross-sectional perspectives on the text (Figure 13.9; p. 327). Most of these functions bypass more complex query processes. The MAXMaps mapping tool allows the production of different kinds of concept maps visualising theoretical and empirical relations and dependencies in the data. All elements of a map, such as symbols for codes, memos, and coded segments, can be determined by the user, thus helping to create unique and optionally layered illustrations or even posters (Figure 11.3; p. 268).

Mixed methods development

The simplicity with which both document and code variables can be created provides easy data management for the quantitative part of a mixed methods study. The software also allows the direct import and auto-processing of survey data from spreadsheet applications (Figure 4.4; p. 102). A special focus in MAXQDA's development, however, is given on *joint displays* that bring together qualitative and quantitative results in one integrated table. These include the Quote Matrix, Crosstabs and Typology Table. In addition, the Summary Tables and Summary Grid bring a different level to the systematisation of analysis. The ability to create an interactive table where summaries of each theme can be written up in the Summary Grid is based on a document-by-codes matrix (Figure 10.3; p. 241). The Summary Grid is a dynamic function connected to the coded data, allowing the user to modify and aggregate summaries at any time and to display an overview of selected parts together with socio-demographic information as Summary Tables.

Report publishing

A Smart Publisher produces a user-defined ready-for-print report of a whole study containing all the relevant coded segments sorted by categories and subcategories.

Mobile app

MAXQDA has a mobile companion, MAXApp, that allows the use of smart phones to gather, code and memo data and then transfer everything directly to MAXQDA for further analysis. An emoticode function (available also in the main software), provides more than 300 different icons for coding providing new options for concept coding, attitudinal coding and transverbal coding, for example in international researcher teams.

NVivo

NVivo,[5] and before it NUD*IST, were designed by university researchers Lyn and Tom Richards. They brought complementary academic experiences of qualitative social research and computer science to the conception and coding of NUD*IST in the 1980s and 1990s, then the development of NVivo. NUD*IST was developed on a Mac platform, but later versions were only on PCs; NVivo recently returned to both Windows and Mac platforms. QSR, the current commercial developers, are based in Doncaster, near Melbourne. NVivo is a code-based system which offers sophisticated and flexible tools. It is particularly well developed in its support for structured qualitative data and the incorporation of materials from other applications (such as bibliographic, social media and note-taking tools).

Architecture

The two main structures within the database are sources (data files) and 'nodes'. A range of materials can be incorporated directly as sources, or referenced from within the software, and thus handled indirectly. Nodes act as holders of information and sources. They may act as thematic codes and/or reference more structural catchments of data. In complex research designs nodes are required to enable the application of attributes (e.g. socio-demographics, metadata) to data contributed by respondents (or other entities). This happens via a link made between these structural nodes and 'classification' nodes (of which there are two types).

User interface

NVivo provides an environment similar to Outlook for moving around its main functions and windows and is thus familiar to many. The Navigation pane provides access to the different main functional areas of the software (e.g. *Sources, Node, Classifications, Models, Queries*). Each function has a set of folders associated with it. Some folders are predefined, some created by the user as required. When a folder is selected, the objects within it are listed alongside and available to open in a Detail pane (Figure 5.2; p. 116).

---

[5]http://www.qsrinternational.com

Data

As well as the more established qualitative data types such as transcripts and field notes and audiovisual data, recent developments in NVivo have focused on enabling imports from specialist environments. New ways of handling social media data and related profile-style metadata from Facebook, Twitter and LinkedIn have become possible using NCapture (an add-on tool for Internet Explorer). In addition, direct import from Survey Monkey is possible.

Qualitative functionality

The focus is on providing places to manage analysis in terms of the systematic handling of codes, centrally located memos, dispersed annotations linked to data, and simple links made possible between memos and data. The latter helps to integrate and connect analysis and writing processes with key, illustrative sections of data or literature. In addition to thematic nodes (codes), special combination nodes, called 'relationship nodes', offer ways to express relationships between concepts or respondents and allow the evidence for those relationships to be coded at them. This is rather different functionality from linking tools in other packages. Figure 11.5 illustrates how particular relationship nodes can be visualised in a model.

In addition, the unique *Externals* folder stores proxy files which can be created and compiled to represent data entities which cannot be physically imported. Externals are then treated as actual data with all associated functionality (Figure 5.2; p. 116). Some of these functions reinforce the tailor-made tools for supporting literature management in the software. These do not seek to provide all the listing and formatting functions available in customised bibliographic software; rather, they provide an environment in which a literature review can be managed. The management of literature is offered in routines which result from exported (and then imported) libraries from bibliographic software. Figure 5.6 shows metadata that can be imported from, for example, Zotero, EndNote, RefWorks and Mendeley. With the inclusion of full-content PDFs, literature can be treated in similar ways to primary data and integrated with substantive work if it seems useful (Figures 5.7; p. 129 and 10.7; p. 247).

Visualisations and analysis

Supplementing the range of code, retrieve and query functions within NVivo are multiple ways to arrange panes and views to optimise particular needs and to visualise coded data (Figures 7.1; p. 159 and 9.1; p. 208). A variety of easily generated visualisations using dynamic charts provide quantitative overviews of content and coding across selections of data.

The modelling tool can be used in multiple ways. A model comprises a way to reveal graphic illustrations of connections which already exist in the data, subsequent, for example, to coding actions, or to scribble in new connections which may, for instance, only be relevant in the current model. The use of colour at codes and proactive steps to differentiate parts of a model can produce switchable layers (Figure 11.4; p. 269).

QDA Miner

QDA Miner[6] was designed as qualitative software for mixed methods research. It was built to share the format of Simstat, statistical software, and WordStat, text mining software, both also developed by Provalis, thus enabling the storage and analysis of qualitative and quantitative data within one file. From its first version QDA Miner has integrated statistical and visualisation tools such as clustering, multidimensional scaling, heatmaps, correspondence analysis and sequence analysis, as well as offering ways to compute common statistical tests such as chi-square and Pearson correlation. The idea driving development is to offer ways to consider dimensions of qualitative data from different epistemological standpoints and also to quickly visualise coding patterns and trends, explore relationships in coding applications and test hypotheses without the need to export to a separate statistical program. QDA Miner is a code-based tool offering the range of qualitative analysis tools expected of CAQDAS packages. It lacks some tools that other packages excel in, such as mapping functionality, but takes options significantly further with respect to mixed methods analytic support. With the WordStat and Simstat add-ons, this is even further extended in terms of text mining and statistical analysis, respectively.

Data

Data types include most textual formats including PDF. Image formats are well supported (Figure 8.6; p. 202) and a range of specialist geo-tagging tools (with time coordinates) enables analytic integration with Google Earth, ArcView and other similar GIS programs. Database formats including Access and dBase, and projects from other qualitative software can be converted and imported. Data can be imported at any time, but QDA Miner is unusual in that the entire project file can be initiated from scratch by the selection of multiple files in a folder or from a spreadsheet containing survey data.

User interface

The qualitative aspects of QDA Miner are contained within its main interface, showing the selected source file, the codes listing alongside and a coding margin flagging codes applied to data linked memos. Interrogations are accessed from main menus. Subsequent retrievals and analytic results are viewed initially in tabular format, interactively connected to source data. A range of alternative displays and functions are available via icons in retrieval windows (e.g. 'append table to report',

---

[6]http://provalisresearch.com. With thanks to Normand Peladeau for his contribution.

'delete code', 'define new code'). When WordStat is utilised further menu items are made available enabling additional analyses (including cross-tabulations and frequencies). Within results panes a wide variety of quantitatively oriented results and further analyses are instantly selectable.

Large datasets – fast processing

QDA Miner was designed in order to easily manage large projects consisting of hundreds or thousands of documents. It offers computer assistance in coding large corpora quickly and reliably via advanced text search and retrieval tools such as the Keyword Retrieval tool (which searches in a single pass hundreds of key words and phrases) and the Section Retrieval tool (which enables automatic retrieval and then tagging of sections in structured documents).

Unique to QDA Miner in relation to other packages summarised in this chapter are its pattern matching tools. The Query by Example tool, for example, utilises artificial intelligence to retrieve text segments similar to an example of text selected by the user, which can then be coded. The tool 'learns' from the rejections and acceptations of the user, such that increasingly refined and accurately matched segments are offered (Figure 6.7; p. 153). The Cluster Extraction tool, in contrast, applies artificial intelligence to group similar sentences or paragraphs into clusters, also enabling quick, selective coding based on the results. The Code Similarity search tool retrieves uncoded text segments similar to those that have already been coded in a particular way. All these tools add to the ability for researchers to ensure coding is consistent.

Report writing

QDA Miner provides assistance for both the compiling and the formatting of the report writing process in a way unique to the packages covered here. Presentation-quality graphics can be created, but more importantly, the Report Manager can store all relevant queries and analysis results, tables and graphs, as well as research notes and quotes, in a single location (Figure 5.4; p. 121). Its outliner design allows the organisation and formatting of findings into chapters and sections, and then the exportation of everything to Microsoft Word, RTF or HTML for final editing.

Add-on text-mining functionality

QDA Miner can be integrated with the add-on module, WordStat, adding the major dimension of quantitative content analysis and text mining. This enables the automatic extraction of themes in the qualitative database to identify trends and patterns (Figure 13.1; p. 306). WordStat offers a dictionary-based approach to content analysis, allowing the use of existing dictionaries or the creation of bespoke dictionaries for particular studies. WordStat also offers an artificial intelligence module to develop automatic document classification models based either on naive Bayes or *k*-nearest neighbour algorithms. Qualitative codings achieved in QDA Miner may be used to restrict text analysis performed using WordStat to specific coded segments. Because all Provalis Research tools share the same file format, users can integrate numerical and textual data into a single project, perform qualitative coding on stored documents using QDA Miner, apply content analysis and text mining features on those same documents with WordStat, and perform statistical analysis on numerical and categorical data using Simstat.

Transana

Transana[7] is a sophisticated software program for the transcription and qualitative analysis of video, audio data and still images. Originally created by Chris Fassnacht, Transana is now developed and maintained by David K. Woods at the Wisconsin Center for Education Research, University of Wisconsin-Madison. The relatively low cost of this open source non-profit software supports continued software enhancement and a professional level of technical support. Transana is a code-based system offering many flexible features for making sense of data. The ability to synchronise media files and create multiple transcripts is unique and offers additional dimensions for analysing visual data. Noteworthy are its tools for visually annotating still images. Although lacking some tools offered by CAQDAS packages developed initially for the analysis of textual data, when visual materials make up a significant proportion of a dataset, Transana is a good choice.

User interface and architecture

Transana is cross-platform (PC and Mac). The main screen is divided into four parts: a transcript area (up to four transcripts per media file); a video window (up to four videos can be synchronised with one another); the waveform visualisation (which can by shown with or without code applications); and the database view (showing hierarchical listings of series, episodes, clips, collections and keywords (codes)). This is the central architecture which enables the management and analysis of data. Various other panes can be opened to visualise aspects of work, such as Keyword Map and Series Keyword Sequence Map (see below). Working collaboratively using Transana Multi allows concurrent analysis of visual data by researchers working at different sites.

Single or multiple synchronised transcripts

Underlying Transana's architecture is the principle that transcripts serve as important tools for navigating audiovisual data and segmenting them into meaningful sections. For some researchers, transcripts are simple maps that describe and index

---

[7]http://transana.org. With thanks to David Woods for his contribution.

material in a convenient, searchable form, while for others, transcripts are mechanisms for analysis. Individual researchers transcribe very differently, ranging from including just enough text to allow easy navigation and segmentation of the media files, through verbatim, descriptive or analytic transcripts, to conversation-analytic transcripts using Jeffersonian notation, and beyond.

Transana's flexible transcript window allows the creation of up to four different textual representations (transcripts) associated with each media file (Figure 4.3; p. 99). This allows concurrent analysis at several levels and for different dimensions of the media file (episode) in question. Transcripts are flexible and dynamic; they can be added to as analysis progresses; multiple translations can be merged, or individual transcripts split; transcripts can be linked, in order to integrate the data segments (clips) created across them; they can be formatted to illustrate different nuances with them; and they can be outputted – either independent of or associated with coded clips.

Qualitative coding

Transana allows researchers to easily select, categorise, and code portions of their visual and auditory data as part of the analytic process (Figure 7.2; p. 162). This is done via transcripts. Small or large portions of video, audio files image files can be selected. Analytic significance can be identified in several different ways, depending on their theoretical orientation and analytic style. The process of annotation or marking can be a coding action (Figure 7.6; p. 179).

Visualisations

Transana provides a number of text-based and visual reports, maps, and graphs for making sense of the coding and categorising researchers do. For example, the Keyword Map shows coding across the timeline of a media file, and the Series Keyword Sequence Map applies this same layout standardised across media files, allowing researchers to explore changes in patterns of coding across files (Figure 8.4; p. 199). The Search function allows the exploration of relationships between codes applied to segments of media files and still images. The Collection Report presents important visual and textual information about portions of the data that have been grouped together by the researcher. In these reports, Transana keeps researchers as close to their original data as possible; source video, audio, or image files are usually only a click or two away.

Innovation in multimedia analysis

Transana facilitates analysis of complex, multimodal data in a variety of unique and innovative ways. The software allows the synchronisation and simultaneous display of multiple video files to facilitate understanding in data-rich environments, such as classrooms, which cannot be adequately captured with a single video stream. Transana facilitates using multiple simultaneous transcripts to allow researchers to look at several analytic layers within their data simultaneously. Its ability to visually annotate and code still images (Figures 6.3; p. 144 and 7.6; p. 179) is unique amongst the CAQDAS packages discussed in this book and offers more precise ways to work with still images. Transana also pioneered collaborative analysis, allowing multiple collaborators to share the same data at the same time, seeing each other's work in real time, even over a distance and between Windows and Mac computers.

Resources

Based on extensive experience of using and teaching with the software applications that we feature in this book, we can reliably say that they are all well supported, frequently updated and widely used. Table 3.1 lists some useful additional resources we recommend and have helped to create. There are many more, and we include some of those on the companion website.

Table 3.2 lists other software applications of which we have less experience. Some of them are free or low-cost. Mainly they are about qualitative data processing or they concentrate on developing further a particular dimension of analysis, data handling or visualisation. This list is also augmented on the companion website.

Our advice is to make your own inquiries with respect to your own needs. Platform and operating system requirements change, so we have not included this information here. Before you start using any package try to get an idea of how well it is supported; for example, when it was last updated, what is the user base, whether there is a user forum, etc. In Tables 3.1 and 3.2 we have included just one URL to access each software package, but in some cases this might be the URL of one distributor, and there may be other distributors to investigate.

Table 3.1 General resources for qualitative methodology and technology

RESOURCES	DETAILS
CAQDAS Networking Project	On-going project to support research community at large in the use of qualitative software; guidance working papers to support particular aspects of using software, with previous input from QUIC project, based at University of Surrey, UK http://www.surrey.ac.uk/sociology/research/researchcentres/caqd as/
Qual-software	Academic internet JISCmail discussion list enabling researchers, teachers, methodologists and software developers to communicate about qualitative technologies.
Online QDA	Online QDA is a set of learning materials which address common issues of undertaking qualitative data analysis (QDA). http://onlineqda.hud.c.uk
Methodspace	Online community for anyone interested in social science methodology. Hosted by Sage.

Table 3.2   Additional software applications for handling qualitative data

SOFTWARE APPLICATIONS	DETAILS
FOR DATA PROCESSING	
Evernote	DOCUMENT MANAGEMENT / NOTE TAKING Manage and write notes, web clips, files and images; share between devices http://evernote.com/evernote/
InfoRapid Cardfile	DOCUMENT MANAGEMENT Electronic database system for managing text and image documents. http://www.inforapid.de/html/cardfile.htm
F4/F5	TRANSCRIPTION Keyboard (or optional foot pedal) controlled aid to digital transcription of audio/visual files http://www.audiotranskription.de/english/f4.htm
ExpressScribe	TRANCRIPTION Foot pedal controlled digital transcription audio player software – assist the synched transcription of audio recordings. http://www.nch.com.au/scribe/index.html
Transcriber AG	TRANCRIPTION Annotation of speech signals http://transag.sourceforge.net/
WITH ANALYTIC TOOLS	
Coding Analysis Toolkit	CAQDAS category application Textual data analysis, with additional tools for calculating inter-coder reliability. ATLAS.ti coded datasets can be uploaded for calculating coder statistics. http://cat.ucsur.pitt.edu
Concordance	CONCORDANCES Instant lists of words in immediate context texts of any size – wordlists, frequency. Web Concordances – one click turn concordance into linked HTML files, ready for publishing on the Web, www.concordancesoftware.co.uk/
Digital Replay System	CAQDAS category application Developed at the University of Nottingham. Large heterogeneous datasets, synchronised playback of related multimedia file types. http://sourceforge.net/projects/thedrs/
QUALRUS	CAQDAS category application Manages qualitative textual, multimedia, web pages. Analysis, code & retrieve, annotate, organise, map, interrogate. Option to use machine learning based on previous coding actions pattern recognition. http://www.qualrus.com
TAMS Analyser	CAQDAS category application Ethnographic and discourse research, Text Analysis Markup System to assign codes in texts (web pages, interviews, field notes). http://tamsys.sourceforge.net/

(Continued)

Table 3.2 (Continued)

SOFTWARE APPLICATIONS	DETAILS
MAPPING	
Cmap Tools	MAPPING Construct, navigate, share, criticise knowledge models represented as concept map. http://cmap.ihmc.us/
iMindMap	MAPPING From inventor of mind maps – mapping, notes, organising, illustrating ideas. http://www.thinkbuzan.com/
Inspiration	MAPPING Visual learning strategies using images and mapping helps students organise and analyse information, integrate new knowledge and think critically. Graphic Organisers, diagrams and outlines are just some strategies of visual learning. http://www.inspiration.com/
MULTIMEDIA – capture or processing	
Audacity	Cross platform: AUDIO PROCESSING, records live sound, edit, splice, improve sound quality, convert to digital formats etc. http://audacity.sourceforge.net/
Videodub	PC: Video editing: delete unwanted parts from video files without re-encoding – program preserves original quality of the input video files. http://www.dvdvideosoft.com/products/dvd/free-video-dub.htm

4

Data and their Preparation for CAQDAS Packages

Many types of data are acceptable to CAQDAS packages. These are summarised in Table 4.1. We think of software 'projects' as containers for, or connectors to, all the materials pertaining to a research study. We thus broadly emphasise their project management potential (Chapter 2). Different combinations of material (data and other information) are relevant to particular projects. Some may be fully *integrated* (e.g. for triangulation purposes); others may simply be *incorporated* to provide background context or maintain a balanced view; still others may be *referenced* from within a software project, but held in raw format outside.

This chapter spotlights certain aspects of data preparation in general terms and also in specific relation to the case-study examples. If considered early, such aspects make the clerical burden of data preparation less onerous and more controlled. We focus on no-fuss, *minimal* starting points for transcription that enable subsequent *optimal* formats, where necessary. The latter are on the companion website, in reference to individual software requirements.

Other technological developments mean that digital recordings and transcription tools increase the possibilities for data conversion. Related are potentials for retaining synchronicity between media files and dimensions logged in written transcripts. Such synchronicity can enrich analysis, although it is not a pre-requisite. We cover preparation of mixed data, survey import functionality and pre-processing possibilities as well as processes enabling more complex organisational structures, discussing how integrating descriptive or quantitative data can facilitate later processes of filtering and interrogation (Chapters 8 and 13).

Data types

A basic benefit of using CAQDAS packages is that any material that can be converted into an appropriate format can be treated as 'data'. You may incorporate some materials but not perform any analysis on them. That they are listed alongside other relevant materials helps keep various strands of work together, aiding continuity and cross-referencing. Working in this way maximises the *project management* potential of these software programs (Silver and Lewins, 2014).

In considering forms of data, their role, management and analysis, it is useful to distinguish between primary, secondary and tertiary forms. Although most can be treated similarly, you may wish to treat dissimilar data types differently. Basic data management tools such as folders facilitate handling materials separately and/or together (Chapter 5). An understanding of how software tools support analytic tasks at the outset of a project may affect how certain data are formatted before being incorporated.

- Primary data are observed or directly collected by you, specifically for the purposes of the research – i.e. through interviews, focus-group discussions, surveys, etc. These are examples of data gathered from 'artificial' interactions occurring specifically for the specific research purposes. Some forms, however, capture naturally occurring events or phenomena, such as video recordings of classroom interactions, and observational field notes.
- Secondary data are materials generated by others. This might include data generated by others for previous research studies, or material that is generated for other purposes and would be in existence irrespective of any research project. For example, documentary evidence (e.g. policy documents, parliamentary debates, newspaper articles); internet-harvested data, such as those derived from social media, such as Facebook or Twitter threads, LinkedIn exchanges, blog entries or forum discussions.
- Tertiary data are background materials that contribute to the broad context of your research. These might include sources which summarise, reference or compile other sources (e.g. encyclopaedia and dictionary entries), but also any material which generally provides background context to your study.

In addition to considering how you intend to *treat* different types of data, consider the broad distinction between *direct* and *indirect* data handling. Any material incorporated into a software project can be treated directly, in that software tools can be manipulated to manage and interpret them. The range of data formats directly analysable is considerable. Table 4.1 lists data types differentiated according to whether they are computer-readable (and therefore *directly* analysable) or not. It is not always practicable to convert or digitise material. In such circumstances, consider using 'proxy' files that represent the original, thus enabling their partial incorporation. These might be embodied as lists, summaries or spaces for your ongoing appraisal of them (Chapters 5 and 10). Materials usefully treated in this way are numerous, including archival film material or television programmes; handwritten diaries and other historical documents; websites, literature and other online records. Such proxy files can be treated in the same way as any other material, improving cross-referencing and management across the whole study. We discuss working *indirectly* with respect to conducting a literature review in Chapter 5 and with respect to visual material in Chapter 7.

There are also many tools for converting data (see Resources area of the website). Text, HTML and images on web pages can often be selected, copied and pasted. Web pages can be captured and converted to PDF. CAQDAS packages handle PDF better now than ever before. Optical character recognition (OCR) technology enables the conversion of handwritten, typewritten or printed text into electronic format.

Table 4.1 Types of data

Computer readable – directly analysable without conversion (Transcribed text or digital formats)	Not computer readable[c] unless converted or incorporated indirectly
Interview/focus-group transcripts (structured, semi-structured, unstructured)	Handwritten archival material (diaries, letters, official documentation etc.)
Observational field notes	Analogue film, photography, audio etc.
Narrative accounts (life history, diaries etc.)	Artifacts, ambient experiences, environmental contexts
Survey data (open-ended questions and answers)	Hard-copy books
Discourse (political, journalistic, conversation etc.)	
Archival material (e.g. Mass observation archive)	
Bibliographic material[a] (reference lists, online abstracts)	
Online material (email exchanges, chatroom/social-network discussions, websites)	
Multimedia data:[b] graphics (e.g. .bmp), digitised photos (e.g. .jpg), video (e.g. .avi, .mov), audio (.wav, .mp3) etc.	

Notes:

[a] Bibliographic material can now be integrated more directly in some packages. Workarounds can be found for others e.g. exporting reference lists or abstracts and importing into the software project for coding/annotating (Chapter 5).

[b] The ranges of acceptable multimedia data types differ in each software. At the time of publication ATLAS.ti, Dedoose, HyperRESEARCH, MAXQDA, NVivo, Transana directly handle whole sound or video files though levels of functionality vary. All handle graphics. Any package which can handle pdf formats can potentially capture web pages and incorporate them (but not all handle pdf). Qualrus and TAMS Analyser also advertise multimedia and web page analysis. Check the developer web pages for up-to-date list of acceptable formats.

[c] Data not machine readable can be incorporated via machine readable lists of offline data sources or abstract notes. The lists can be imported as data, and integrated into the analysis and cross-referencing processes. Some non-computer readable can be digitised (e.g. audio) or scanned as images (e.g. handwritten diaries). Alternatively proxy files for entities (which are not in their totality able to be rendered in digital format) can be incorporated and commentary and analysis can be accumulated. Embedded hyperlinks to files or resources held within or outside the software project can enrich understanding and conceptions of the abstract.

File formats

CAQDAS development has occurred in tandem with technological developments more generally. As such, the range of file formats directly acceptable has mushroomed in recent years. Check developer websites for up-to-date information. Tables 4.2, 4.3 and 4.4 illustrate divers data preparation considerations in the context of the case-study examples.

Textual formats

Most packages accept textual data saved with the .doc or .docx file extensions. Earlier versions often required Rich Text Format and some will still convert into RTF upon importation.[1] Saving directly into RTF avoids the added complication of in-software conversion. Web pages are written in scripting languages such as Hypertext Preprocessor (PHP) or Hypertext Markup Language (HTML). Simple web page content can be copied into a word processor, sometimes taking along the graphics, sometimes not. There are many unpredictable results based on how web pages are created. Having saved as Word or RTF, they are acceptable to most CAQDAS packages, although how they display can be unpredictable.

Most packages also handle PDF files. However, different types of PDF format are not manipulable to the same degree. Key reasons for working with PDF files include doing a literature review (Chapter 5) or working with forms of documentary evidence, where the original layout is important to preserve for analytic reasons. Background project material (tertiary data) may well be harvested from the internet. Using CAQDAS packages not supporting direct incorporation of PDF files, it will be possible to work indirectly with them through the creation of 'proxy' files and hyperlinking devices. You can still, of course, cross-reference literature by integrating and annotating imported reference lists.

BOX 4.1 ——— FUNCTIONALITY NOTES

Options when working with PDF

- Fully manipulate-able PDFs. Some PDF formats enable the selection and searching of text contained within them as if they were RTF files. Typically these were saved from original machine readable formats, like Word.
- Manipulate freely as above: (though possibly less beautiful) are PDFs which have been generated where OCR has been used to convert text identified in places from a scanned image, for example (the technologies for doing this are improving all the time). Some conversions of large volumes to PDF format can be a bit slippery when it comes to text selection in some CAQDAS packages, although they are searchable, which is of great benefit.

  o Scanning: when you scan a document using, for instance, the scanning component in Microsoft® Office Document Imaging, OCR is automatically performed on your document. OCR does not interfere with the scanning process, but it does take additional time.
  o When you scan a document on a fairly basic home printer without using special software to initiate it, you are probably not using OCR.

- PDF files which have not had the OCR process applied are viewable but you cannot select or search text – these are in effect just scanned images of the original.

---

[1]This is because RTF is the common transferable format.

- **Generate PDFs based on web pages:** use Web2PDF for Mozilla Firefox, NCapture for Internet Explorer, and the File/Print/PDF menu option in Safari, to convert web pages to PDF. This process in most cases produces text which can be manipulated.

  o You may not get exactly quite what you expected, or the full contents of the page you were looking at.
  o The links and bookmarks within the page which sometimes remain in the PDF may not work as you expect them to. Experiment with individual software's treatment of these. The coding processes might be slightly different, but the text is usually searchable.

Multimedia formats

Multimedia data – still images, audio and video – can be incorporated into most CAQ-DAS packages. Original formats are numerous, so you may need to convert source data. Tools available for analysing multimedia data vary quite significantly (see below and Chapter 7), so this is the principle deciding factor for how to prepare data. Technical issues with hearing or viewing files are usually because you do not have the correct codecs installed on your computer; rectifying this usually solves the issue.

Quantitative formats

CAQDAS packages enable the integration of quantitative information with qualitative data. This might take the form of linking descriptive information (e.g. socio-demographic variables) with qualitative records, or importing survey-type data directly from statistical or spreadsheet packages (e.g. SPSS, Excel). Some packages require very little special formatting of such data, others quite a lot. Requirements usually depend on the nature of data and how you want them to appear within the CAQDAS package. We discuss options for preparing such material later in this chapter. Chapter 13 illustrates how quantitative data can be used for analytic purposes.

Table 4.2 Data and their preparation for CAQDAS packages: some suggestions in the context of case study A, Young People's Perceptions

Tasks from PHASE ONE: Data preparation and project set-up	

Data preparation	• Transcribe primary data (verbatim transcriptions can be downloaded from the companion website)
	• Format structured data according to the requirements of your chosen CAQDAS package, to enable auto-coding on the basis of:
	
	   o Interview data: according to topics in the interview guide
	   o Vignette data: according to the hypothetical vignette scenarios
	   o Photo prompt data: according to the photos shown

Textual data preparation

There are certain considerations when preparing textual files for use within CAQ-DAS packages. These vary according to whether data are primary, secondary or tertiary and the structures inherent within them. Generating materials that constitute primary data for direct analysis often happens by transcribing audio or video recordings. Although some CAQDAS packages allow audiovisual data to be handled directly (see below), and despite the time required to transcribe, this way of working remains dominant. Textual formats usually provide easier ways for managing, searching and retrieving data. This is particularly true when the content of what is being said is the analytic focus.

For the purpose of generating transcripts, an initial decision concerns whether to maintain synchronicity with the original media, or to disassociate and handle them independently. Synchronicity between transcript and audio or video are advantageous where physical dynamics or non-verbal interactions are under scrutiny, opening up additional layers of meaning. Such linkages usually happen via time-based synchronisation. In relation to your research design, consider whether direct analysis or synchronicity with original media adds anything. In practical terms, the inclusion of audiovisual material increases the logistical challenges of moving work from computer to computer. When analysing data collected via audio recordings of interviews, focus groups and the like, most researchers disassociate the original recording and the resultant written transcript. We consider disassociated transcriptions first. Below we discuss raw multimedia data preparation, for direct and indirect analysis.

It is important to remember that transcription itself is not a neutral process. There are different transcript conventions. Epistemological concerns about the 'partial' nature of transcripts and recordings are important, relating to fundamental questions about what constitutes data. They are affected by but not resolved with technology. The trend to create 'verbatim' transcripts of interviews only became possible with the development of the tape recorder. In a sense, observational note-taking is even more subject to bias. Decisions concerning what to include or omit are subject to the interpretation of the researcher; the accuracy of recall can compromise data. Mason (2002) cautions against 'overestimat[ing] the representational and reflective qualities of interview transcripts'. Not only is a transcript prone to subjective translation, it may neglect significant non-verbal interaction. Being aware of the debate and reflexive about your own limitations and preferences as you transcribe is a significant step towards being proactively transparent in the generation and processing of data.

Data structures

Although qualitative data is often referred to as 'unstructured', some qualitative data have levels of structure inherent within them. It is therefore useful to distinguish between structured data and structures *in* otherwise unstructured data. Structured data are those that are pre-organised into numeric categories; typically quantitative data ready for statistical analysis (Woolf 2014b). Data that have levels of structure inherent within them are qualitative materials that contain within them repeated structures. Such repeated structures may exist within individual data files or across multiple ones – for example, repeated speaker sections *within* focus-group discussions; actor- or setting- based observations *within* field notes; or repeated questions *within* (semi-)structured interviews or survey data.

In addition are smaller inherent structures within textual material; for example, sentences, paragraphs, chapter or section headings. Interjections by the convener or interviewer or just the respondents' speech may be useful to isolate. Although not always relevant to your analytic needs, it is useful to know that some software can exclude or exclusively *include* these structures in certain searches. For example, if interested in the language used by respondents in referring to certain topics, being able to search for specific words or phrases *only* in the speech of certain respondents will be useful. Doing so quickly and accurately is reliant on informative and consistent speaker identifiers and the preparation of data according to the requirements of the software being used (Figure 4.1; p. 87). For example:

- Case Study A, Young People's Perceptions
    - *002-ENG-F-15* for interview data (respondent 2, English, female, 15 years old)
- Case Study B, The Financial Downturn
    - *N1-FG2-R09* for focus group data (northern region 1, focus group 2, respondent 9)

In both cases the original transcript started off with a simple respondent identifier (R- and R09, respectively). Editing tools in Word such as Find and Replace can isolate the use of R- or R09 in the text, so you can always quickly add further identifying information, such as region identifier and focus-group number in Case Study B (see Box 4.2). The ability to use certain short-cut identifiers in this way has relevance to all types of textual data (see Table 4.5; p. 100).

BOX 4.2 ──── FUNCTIONALITY NOTES ────

Minimal but useful formatting

Useful devices contained within textual transcripts to enable fast and consistent changes in Word, include:

(A) if required, every occurrence of the prefix R- can be globally (found and) replaced with additional useful information such as R-RUR-, R-FG4- or N1-RUR-FG4. The latter indicates in a collaborative project which team is responsible for these data (e.g. Northern region 1).

(B) If 481- is a farmer, all of his contributions could be replaced in the same way with 481-Fmr – so the complete speaker identifier could very quickly end up being

(Continued)

(Continued)

R-RUR–FG4–481–Fmr, providing on-the-spot information about the background of the speaker.

(C) The –X identifier used below might allow the use of Find and Replace in Word to put it on its own line via the insertion of paragraph marks after the –X (only useful if wanting to convert speaker identifiers into heading levels – NVivo makes use of these for auto-coding). For most software this is not necessary.

(D) A text search or auto-coding process can find and code all paragraphs beginning with R-, thus creating one batch of coded data containing all respondents' data in this file.

(E) Sentences do not always occur naturally – but they will form useful units of context to include when/if using text search tools in all packages (except NVivo which does not recognise the sentence). So consider adding full stops after the first go at transcription (the first attempt is always full of mistakes – so use the cleaning up process to insert these).

R-481-X Well actually I'd like to talk about them both, I mean cost of petrol and insurance as well? Sorry I'm Jack. I'm a tenant farmer – my son has actually found a job – chuffed to bits about that because he's been biding his time on the farm... but he doesn't really want that. Now he's got this job... but can he get to work? We're taking him when he can't get a lift.

MOD-X Has he got a car?

R-481-X Well he has but he can't afford to insure it. I mean we'll sort something out we've got to see about putting him on our insurance – but his own quote was well over 2000. We can't afford that – it's not actually money down the drain but it's close. He certainly can't afford that. Don't know the answer. And I know it's not just about the value of the car – about 1200 I'd say – it's his mam's but she's given it to him and wouldn't it be great if he could get some time on his own insurance to bring the costs down.

MOD-X So can you see it improving –this car business?

R-481-X It gets me down it does ...let's see man – it gets him down as well.......yes. I hate to see that. You want them to get on with life don't you? And it's not just about work it's about just getting around and being independent of your da a bit. I'll say this for him – he's not about to be a farmer but he gets around with the Young Farmers ....

MOD-X And how about public transport then?

R-02-X Well it's the cost of petrol too isn't it? We pay more to drive ourselves where we've got to go, and now there's even less public transport since Arriva cut their services. 3 times a day instead of 5 – not that I get the bus..well you don't do you if you've got a car. But they've cut the earlier service which my lad needs to get.

Units of recognisable contexts

The units of text that are (semi-)automatically recognised by software are important because they constitute the basic unit of context which can be isolated for analytic purposes. Software packages differ in the units which are easily (i.e. semi-automatically) identifiable. This is closely related to auto-coding (Box 4.3; p. 90 and Chapter 12) and text searching (Chapters 6 and 13). If you intend to use these tools, become familiar with the units of recognisable context of your chosen software when preparing textual data. The degree of automation possible with regard to auto-coding structures varies. This is also relevant to pre-coding (see below).

- Sentences (indicated by full stops, exclamation marks, question marks) are not always recognised by CAQDAS packages. If your chosen software does recognise sentences and you intend to make use of auto-coding tools, consider adding extra full stops (and/or hard returns to create paragraphs) into otherwise unstructured data, to create meaningful units of text.
- Paragraphs are always recognised (most frequently by one hard return). Find out what indicates a paragraph in your chosen software and consider how they may be useful to you. ATLAS.ti, for instance, recognises two types – or levels – of paragraph; those separated by one hard return (Enter) and those separated by more than one hard return. Auto-coding can therefore include several smaller paragraphs, extended to the parameters of a broader 'section' at the larger 'divide' of two or more hard returns. Most other software packages simply define one level of paragraph via one or more hard returns.
- IMPORTANT: Often Shift+Enter is used to insert 'soft' line breaks. Although this is space saving and looks similar to a new paragraph start, most software programs do not recognise this type of break as a paragraph identifier.

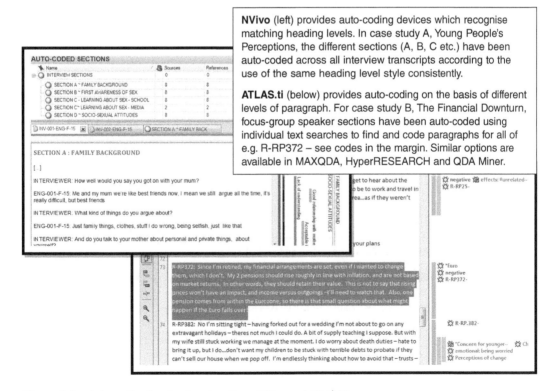

NVivo (left) provides auto-coding devices which recognise matching heading levels. In case study A, Young People's Perceptions, the different sections (A, B, C etc.) have been auto-coded across all interview transcripts according to the use of the same heading level style consistently.

ATLAS.ti (below) provides auto-coding on the basis of different levels of paragraph. For case study B, The Financial Downturn, focus-group speaker sections have been auto-coded using individual text searches to find and code paragraphs for all of e.g. R-RP372 – see codes in the margin. Similar options are available in MAXQDA, HyperRESEARCH and QDA Miner.

Figure 4.1   Auto-coding for structured sections (NVivo and ATLAS.ti)

- Sections are only recognised in some software packages (where a section may contain several paragraphs, e.g. in ATLAS.ti as discussed above). NVivo also enables the recognition and fast auto-coding of matching sections through the use of MS Word styles. Both consistent heading style formatting (up to nine levels) and consistent text at the section headers are necessary to make this work.

Transcription guidelines for textual data

We now focus on practical issues and provide a little more detail regarding useful general formatting for textual data. We divide the practical advice concerning transcription into three sections:

(i)   basic starting points (relevant to all types of textual data);
(ii) minimal (but useful) protocols relevant to semi-structured and some structured datasets;
(iii) optimal guidelines for structured data (provided on the companion website; they are different for each package).

The principle is that attending to basic and minimal protocols will enable fast changes to an optimal format later. You may never need to handle textual data in the optimal ways possible, but preparing transcripts according to the minimal guidelines keeps your options open, should it become clear later that inherent structures are more important than you had first imagined.

Technological support for transcription has developed considerably in recent years and can assist in achieving the recommended minimal protocols. Adopt basic guidelines initially, at transcription stage, then apply minimal protocols as part of the cleaning-up process. To a large extent basic starting points are common sense and do not place too much burden on sub-contracted transcribers, not familiar with the context of your project. You can of course adapt the list your own needs. If you have a transcriber, a much shorter set of firm pointers can be provided to them. Transcribers often have their own procedures and layouts; it is important that there

Table 4.3 Data and their preparation for CAQDAS packages: some suggestions in the context of case study B, The Financial Downturn

Tasks from PHASE ONE: Data preparation and project set-up	
Data preparation	• Transcribe primary data (verbatim transcriptions can be downloaded from the companion website)
	• Format structured data according to the chosen CAQDAS package, to enable auto-coding on the basis of
	○ Focus group speaker identifiers and speaker sections
	○ Survey data – software related format for 'survey import'
	• Download media content
	○ Experiment with saving in different formats (e.g. Word, PDF)

be no room for doubt about what is required, so that you, as the researcher, receive files that can be further formatted if required.

Basic starting points

No special format may need to be imposed to prepare completely *unstructured* data, assuming they are in electronic format. However, a few aspects are worth considering, irrespective of data type.

(a) *Anonymise as early as possible.* The later this is left, the more burdensome the process becomes and the less 'secure' the data. Consider all the ways data will be shared with others, either in collaborative projects or simply via written publications and oral presentations. If you need to remember the real names of respondents, perhaps so you can contact them for a follow-up interview, keep this information in a spreadsheet or memo, not in the file name or speaker identifier.

(b) *Create an efficient naming protocol for files.* Systematic file names that codify important information are very useful for various reasons later on, particularly when retrieving coded or linked data (Chapter 8). Think about the four or five most important factual characteristics of each file and add short identifiers accordingly. For example, R33-F-CR-PH2 (respondent 33, who is female, a carer, and this file is the second-phase interview with her). If you have an interview respondent who also took part in a focus group or completed a questionnaire, make sure the speaker ID in the focus-group transcript has the same elements as the file name for the interview transcript.

(c) *Consider the wider role of speaker identifiers.* Even if data are completely unstructured, there may be elements you wish to treat differently or leave out from various searching or retrieval tasks. The use of consistent identifiers will enable this.

(d) *Avoid importing double-spaced texts into software* unless you have considered this carefully first and experimented in your chosen software with the implications. Some software packages leave you short of space in the default view (especially those that do not line-wrap, such as NVivo). The less redundant space between lines, the more data you can see without scrolling.

(e) *Avoid transcribing into tables* (even simple ones). Tables were useful devices before CAQDAS became commonly used, providing a column for the speaker, a column for the speech and a column for a comment. Such formats may be acceptable to software in terms of display, but they often restrict manipulation for analytic purposes later. Avoid them unless the layout is analytically imperative.

(f) *Consider whether you will need to edit, correct or change text* after import. Some software allow editing, some do not.

(g) *Consider whether the potential to insert images or links to a web resource might be of use.* Packages which enable editing usually allow embedded files and hyperlinks to be inserted after import. This can be particularly useful when working with literature (Chapter 5).

(h) *Think about the analytic tools you might use* (Tables 1.1; p. 9 and 2.1; p. 39). For example, will you use text searching tools to find identifiers, words, synonyms and/or phrases? If working with software that recognises sentences you consider the placement of full stops, exclamation or question marks during transcription. These define useful 'chunks' (units of analysis), providing contexts to which to code/index around the 'hits'. The same applies to the way your chosen software identifies paragraphs.

(i) *Remember that working with PDF will allow you to code, annotate and make memos* but not to edit them.

(j) *Use quickly inserted but easily replaceable speaker identifiers.* For example, for one-to-one interviews, use R... for the respondent and or I... for the interviewer. Never use just R or just I as they appear in other places within the text and therefore cannot be replaced quickly using find and replace tools.

Minimal (but useful) protocols

Much useful formatting can be achieved quickly in word-processing applications. Having followed the basic starting-point recommendations, a few additional guidelines can be useful. We use the 'minimal (but useful)' label to emphasise that: even though minimal, such identifiers can immediately (in most software packages) be useful 'flags' in the data for which to search; and such identifiers, when consistently applied, can always be converted to auto-codable structures by fast find and replace, should this need arise.

(a) *Speaker identifiers and question numbering.* Always accompany identifiers with a short exclusive and consistently entered *text* or *syntax* prefix, and preferably also a suffix. In the example below, the exclusive prefix is Q.. or Q-, and the exclusive suffix could be :: or .. It does not really matter what the prefix/suffix is as long as it is unlikely to be found anywhere else in normal spoken or prose data. 'Q' on its own would not do, '1' on its own would not do. The rule is: think about maximising the benefit of using find and replace to change format, style or text throughout the file on at least one standard prefix or suffix (and preferably allow for both) (see Box 4.2). An easily replaceable suffix might be required for inserting headers, speaker IDs, question numbers, etc. on a separate line (most important for software that recognises heading level styles). A global find and replace of the suffix (and replacing it with the 'special' paragraph mark character) will enable this.

(b) *Consistency.* Find and replace tools, text search and auto-coding tools will only work reliably if identifiers which refer to the same structure across or within files, are indeed entered exactly and consistently the same.

BOX 4.3 ——— CASE NOTES

Narrative-driven auto-coding of one respondent's contributions from a focus group transcript (Case Study B, The Financial Downturn)

Scanning through the answers to Q.3A 'Fault-Comments' – concerning how blame for the financial downturn is attributed – highlighted that Respondent 382 had strong feelings of a political nature. This respondent also took part in a focus group. In his recent working life he held a middle management post in an EU agency. It was interesting to extract all his focus-group contributions and compare them with the comments he gave in answer to the survey questions. In most software packages it is possible to make use of the fact that the speaker identifier is attached to the paragraph of his/her speech for this purpose. A text search or auto-coding task can find all those occurrences and save the paragraph attached to those positions.

Such tasks are generally very quick to execute. They can be focused on one file or performed across all files where an identifier occurs. We were thus able to get a clear narrative from this respondent – even though his contributions were spread across data files. For example, we identified that he had strong views as a 'victim' of the downturn; a beneficiary of the EU entity but also a critical onlooker. It would have been more difficult to compare his contributions and consider him as an entity without gathering all his contributions together.

Keeping speaker identifiers adjacent to the paragraph of the subsequent speaker section (as shown below), enables this quick auto-coding task in most packages. Clear paragraph breaks are in place (i.e. hard return at the end of the speaker section).

R-RP382-X Can I start? – I've never been convinced about the viability of the euro. Well actually – it was wonderful in theory, it has always struck me as an enormous act of faith. I mean nations were required to sign up to a set of rules about level of debt to within a certain percentage of GDP. Was it 3%?

R-RP382-X Well it seems now there was never any obvious attempt to get them to rein in their spendthrift ways, nor any regulator or central authority to sound a warning, even when it was obvious to the rest of us.

R-RP382-X I don't know whether you can because the gravy train or whatever you want to call it that Greece and Spain etc got so much of well it encouraged spendthriftness – money without the pain. Look at Ireland as well. Spend spend but balancing the books should have been regulated by Europe surely – the euro was a European thing – not a national thing. I mean OK there was national responsibility but Europe shouldn't have just sat back and watched.

R-RP382-X Well.... as for me – the financial mess cost me the final 3 years of my working life. I worked for a European inter-governmental organisation. It got income from airlines and other stakeholders ... that was reducing significantly. I mean commercial aviation was just contracting in the wake of the downturn – fewer passengers. The scope of its work had to be cut. My contract came to an end in July last year. In normal circumstances I would have expected to have been kept on for another 3 years, to take me up to 65. Those 3 years would have made all the difference to – I don't know just feeling comfortable – able to do things I have to be careful about now.

Optimal (software-specific) protocols

Optimal protocols are not necessarily something you should aim for at the outset. Basic transcription is hard enough without worrying about fiddly and time-consuming tweaking during transcription. Optimal guidelines are in fact more necessary for NVivo than any other package, and then only if you want to use its special section-based auto-coding devices (see below and Chapter 12). For most packages the minimal guidelines are usually sufficient unless you need to see more information at speaker identifiers or change text at identifiers later on (e.g. to quickly anonymise data). Optimal formatting might simply mean knowing that for most packages it is better to start off keeping speaker identifiers on the same line as the beginning of the corresponding speech section, whereas for others it might be important in certain circumstances to keep them on separate lines (e.g. NVivo). Some of this detail is built into our minimal guidelines, but there are subtle variations; if it matters to you (especially where you have data with significant and meaningful structures inherent), consult the optimal guidelines for your chosen software on the companion website.

BOX 4.4 | FUNCTIONALITY NOTES

Auto-coding possibilities relevant to data formatting

Primary data are often inherently structured. For example, interview transcripts might be structured according to the broad topics framing the interview guide. Sometimes data are structured at more than one level. For example, focus-group discussions contain speaker-section structures as well as those based on broad topics.

Auto-coding functionality across multiple levels is more powerful in NVivo than other packages because it recognises up to nine levels of heading style within texts; auto-coding captures matching heading styles (with matching text) in whatever data sources you have scoped to (Chapter 12).

Figure 4.1 illustrates data captured by NVivo through auto-coding all material related to *Section A: Family Background* (from Case Study A, Young People's Perceptions) formatted using heading level 2. Thus a review of all interviewees' discussion relating to the topic of 'Family Background' is enabled. In addition, later on, patterns concerning how 'carefully applied' thematic, conceptual or topic-based codes occur within Section A is possible (see margin display).

Similar applications of auto-coding functionality are available via slightly less automated tools in other packages. Usually paragraphs are the useful structures rather than heading level sections. This is illustrated in ATLAS.ti with focus-group data derived from Case Study B, The Financial Downturn (Figure 4.1; p. 87). In this example, repeated focus-group speaker sections co-occur with the broad topic-based discussion about financial security. The speaker-based coding has been achieved via auto-coding (using the paragraph as the contextual unit). The topic-based coding has been done carefully by the researcher.

Figure 4.2 illustrates the result of auto-coding for an individual respondent's speaker sections in QDA Miner, for the purposes discussed in Box 4.3. The Section Retrieval dialogue has various tools within it to interrogate the results in more detail, such that the narrative of this speaker's contributions can be interpreted in isolation from the broader discussion – as well as within that context.

Are special formatting considerations really necessary?

For semi-structured and unstructured data, there is often no point in aiming for optimal data formatting because auto-coding tools will not be appropriate. In fact the ability to auto-code only becomes *essential* where hundreds of structured records need time-saving structural coding because doing so in a step-by-step way would take many hours. In other words, though the basic starting points for textual data are always worth consideration, you can make a judgement about whether to avoid the bother of special, software-specific, 'optimal' formats. For certain data even the 'minimal' guidelines will be unnecessary. In Case Study B, for instance, the sample dataset is relatively small but we have formatted the focus-group speaker identifiers to illustrate auto-coding as an exercise (see Box 4.2; p. 85). There is always a balance to be reached between expending extra effort applying auto-codable formats before importing data or instead simply assigning the relevant codes in a step-by-step way in imperfectly formatted data. It is always useful to experiment with auto-coding (if you think it might be a useful function) in a small subset of data to ensure it works the way you expect. The Case Study B survey data are a small subset of the whole but with it we can demonstrate (and experiment with) the pre-coding element and see clearly whether the auto-processing has worked as expected upon data import.

In the case of completely unstructured or semi-structured data, one of the reasons for wanting to use at least minimal formatting might be to do with the idea that, in various searches, you wish to be able to filter out the interviewer's speech. The auto-coding process could enable speedy coding of all respondents' speech at one special code if suitable speaker identifiers and the right units of context have been used. Filtered text searching would then be enabled since in some packages, notably MAXQDA, NVivo and QDA Miner, you can choose to only search for text in data coded in a particular way. The example described in Box 4.3 is an illustration of just one analytic utility of this kind.

With focus-group data you may not be interested in the socio-demographic characteristics (Chapter 12) of individual respondents. Indeed, you may not know anything specific about participants, other than that they have some generic similarity in background or experience. For example, in a project about health service provision, you may run one focus group with consultant registrars and another with ward-based nursing staff. In this type of design, it would be the general *group* view that you were interested in analysing – for example, do doctors and nurses have different opinions relating to local services and how can their experiences be drawn upon to improve patient satisfaction? The socio-demographic characteristics of the individual focus-group contributors are thus largely irrelevant. In Case Study B, we do know various characteristics about the individual focus-group respondents (such as their age, gender and marital status), and the groups were compiled based on the geographical location of their residence (whether rural or urban) and their current employment status (whether employed, retired or recently redundant). Being able quickly to gather up (via auto-coding devices) the responses of an individual participant offers a very different way of thinking about respondents' contributions. As long as you are able to track who said what from the transcript (and in reality this is not always possible) then this sort of *narrative-driven* auto-coding will be useful in accessing and thereby easily analysing the entirety of individual participants' views. As the case notes in both Boxes 4.3 and 4.4 illustrate, there are powerful ways to compare contributions, track associations, develop typologies and establish connections, based at the level of textual responses (these issues are discussed in further detail in Chapter 6).

Table 4.4 Data and their preparation for CAQDAS packages: some suggestions in the context of case study C, Coca-Cola Commercials

Tasks from PHASE ONE: Data preparation and project set-up	
Data preparation	• Convert the media files to an appropriate format for the chosen software • Name the media files meaningfully and consistently
Tasks from PHASE TWO: Exploration, transcription and identification of analytic focus	
Familiarise with commercials	• Watch each commercial through several times
Make analytic notes	• Create a memo for each commercial noting initial thoughts about visual content in relation to research questions

Transcription	These steps assuming you have decided to work indirectly
	
	EITHER
	
	• Develop multiple transcripts (where software allows), creating a separate transcript for each of the different elements of analytic interest
	  o 'descriptive log': constituting content-based description of what is happening
	  o visually within each commercial 'soundtrack': containing information about any music being played, including lyrics, where present
	  o 'voiceover': verbatim transcript of what is said by the commentator
	
	OR
	
	• Develop one transcript per commercial which combines all analytic elements
	  o Use text formatting structures or other features to identify different analytic elements in the combined transcripts
	
	FOR BOTH APROACHES
	
	• Experiment with associating transcripts with source media concurrently (i.e. at the same time as writing them) and as a secondary step
	• Experiment with different placement of time codes/stamp placement and consider the implications on subsequent analysis by the units of analysis that result

Structural coding without auto-coding
(no special formatting)

Some datasets are inherently structured and respond well to auto-coding treatment. Box 4.3 illustrates one example. Figures 4.1 and 4.2 illustrate how further actions and searches can often take place on similarly structural coding.

It is important to be aware of such functionality, but it would be a mistake to design a whole interview around what can be achieved quickly by auto-coding. It is rarely enough just to auto-code. Structural coding does not have to happen using

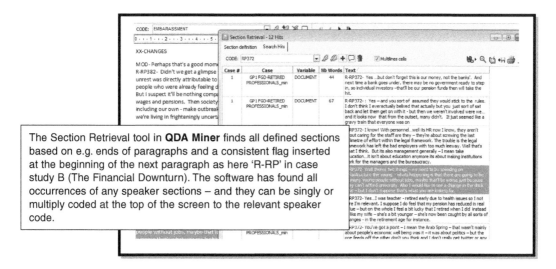

The Section Retrieval tool in **QDA Miner** finds all defined sections based on e.g. ends of paragraphs and a consistent flag inserted at the beginning of the next paragraph as here 'R-RP' in case study B (The Financial Downturn). The software has found all occurrences of any speaker sections – and they can be singly or multiply coded at the top of the screen to the relevant speaker code.

Figure 4.2 Section retrieval enabling auto-coding (QDA Miner)

auto-coding tools. If the right formats are not present in a file to enable auto-coding, step-by-step structural coding can achieve a similar result, albeit more slowly. Much step-by-step coding can anyway be rather structural in nature. In Case Study B it was necessary to code for the context in which discussion happened as well as the topics, attitudes and concepts; for example, when a respondent talked despairingly about local access to transport, was he talking about family welfare or work-related matters (or both)? There is more on this in Chapters 7–9.

We raise these issues now since they explain the rationale for efficient transcription protocols for all data, however structured. The role of structural auto-coding is not usually directly analytical in the first place. But having conducted more careful analytic coding (Chapter 7), those aspects can be compared across the structural auto-coded sections (see Chapter 13).

Formal transcription conventions

It is unusual for conversation analysts to use CAQDAS packages because the micro-examination of patterns of talk they are concerned with often involves very small datasets. However, the formalised notation convention, devised by Gail Jefferson and discussed by various proponents of the methodology (Atkinson and Heritage, 1984; Hutchby and Wooffitt, 1998; ten Have, 1999), is relevant to consider. Jeffersonian notation consists of symbols and words which codify pauses, overlaps, hesitation, rise in pitch, etc. There are many slight variations on the original convention; indeed, you could devise your own version if it is useful to record particular non-verbal occurrences. In this book we stick mainly to more general transcription, since datasets analysed using CAQDAS programs are often much larger than those employed in conversation analysis. Transana, however, has certain short-cut tools for inserting symbols that indicate aspects such as whispered speech, audible breath, rising and falling intonation, thus providing short-cut means to developing the detailed transcriptions characteristic of the needs of conversation analysis.

Multimedia data preparation

Working with multimedia data (still images, audio recordings and video files) is very different from working with textual formats. How you prepare them will depend on a number of factors, including their role and status in the study, the number and duration of files, your approach to their analysis, and what you need to be able to do with results in terms of output and representation. Of particular relevance is the debate around whether to work directly (without an associated transcript) or indirectly (via a written transcript which is synchronised with the source media file) (Silver and Patashnick, 2011). Sound and video recordings necessarily leave out information and unrecorded circumstances. Mason (2002) suggests that the 'debate should not be about what technology can do but what it is about the visual that interests us and how we are doing the visualizing'. Clearly analysis of visual materials is guided by ontological and epistemological assumptions, just as are the analysis of other forms of data. However, technological awareness generally, and functionality possibilities specifically, affect how we can gain access to the aspects of the visual that interest us. It is naive to divorce discussion of analysis from technology. Part of what Mason implies is that there has to be something about the visual dimension that is of analytical interest in order to work with it. Choosing to incorporate the visual dimension without good reason, just because you can, will not add anything. Indeed, this is one area in which the relationship between technology and methodology is in tension, with technological developments lagging behind methodological discussions and analytic requirements (Silver and Patashnick, 2011; Silver and Lewins, 2014). There will always be tensions between the nature of research, the fundamental nature of data, the new forms of data and new methods of data handling enabled by technology. It is important therefore to be aware of and critical about the value and limitations of data and the way they are collected.

An example of how technology can drive methodology is apparent with Transana. Allowing up to four separate transcripts per media elevates the role of the written transcript as the vehicle through which we gain analytic access to data (Box 4.5). Understanding this level of technological functionality and considering its analytical implications are fundamental to debates about the relationship between technology and methodology and the practical issues of choosing software, preparing data and designing analysis. Other packages, such as ATLAS.ti, NVivo and MAXQDA, allow you to work either directly or indirectly. Transana requires there to be an associated transcript in order to code audiovisual material. Technological subtleties can be very important analytically and if you are working predominantly with audiovisual data because it is central to the requirements of the research design. It is essential to experiment with software tools and consider the implications of functionality on analytic capabilities before committing to a particular tool. These issues are discussed further in Chapter 7.

Social media

Social media, smart phones and associated applications are changing the research landscape in terms of how communication happens, the effects of social communications, how data are collected and create the context of research (see Paulus et al., 2013). CAQDAS packages have responded to these environments. Several have created 'lite' versions, or as apps for mobile or tablet devices, and some enable the import of data generated by social media, including blogs, Twitter feeds, EverNote collections and YouTube data. We do not describe the processes of preparing to use these data formats here since they are very software-specific and diverse. Indeed, once such material are produced in file format, most of the software packages we feature which have a mixed methods or multimedia capacity will be able to handle it. It is enough to say that if you are 'media-savvy', access to such data and the processes of transferring them will be well supported in help menus.

Direct or indirect handling

Some software packages enable you to work *directly* with still or moving images and audio files. This means that sections of graphics or clips in audio and video recordings can be marked, annotated and coded without the need for an associated textual transcript. Such functionality can be quite seductive, with some researchers becoming excited about the idea that they therefore need not transcribe audio recordings of interviews, for example. They somehow believe this will save time. In fact, it rarely does, merely moving the time investment from the early stages of a project to the latter ones as you slowly replay coded video segments in real time, one at a time. More importantly, adopting this sort of attitude is usually lazy in analytic terms. Qualitative data analysis is time-consuming. There is no getting away from that, nor should there be in most contexts. Transcription is an analytic act because of the nuances involved in deciding what, how, when and why to transcribe. Working with multimedia data compounds the analytic importance of developing transcripts because of the multidimensional nature of data.

BOX 4.5 — CASE NOTES

Planning the use of transcripts (Case Study C, Coca-Cola Commercials)

Working with visual data in CAQDAS packages necessitates thinking about whether to work directly or indirectly. This was introduced in Chapter 1 (Box 1.7; p. 33) and is discussed in more detail in Chapter 7. Packages vary according to whether and how different ways of working with visual data are enabled (Chapter 3). For the Coca-Cola project we felt that as a minimum the voiceover and soundtrack should be transcribed as they constitute powerful ways in which messages are conveyed as a mechanism of advertising.

(Continued)

(Continued)

Transana requires at least one written transcript associated with each media file. This is the medium through which access is gained to visual material. Transcripts can be as full or brief as required, and up to four separate transcripts can be created per media (Figure 4.3; p. 99). Other packages that provide support for video analysis typically allow one transcript per media (Figure 7.4; p. 175), or allow them to be annotated and coded directly (Figure 7.5; p. 178).

In relation to the creation and use of transcripts, synchronised with the Coca-Cola commercials, we discuss two options:

A. Using a minimal transcript merely as a means of logging time sequences – based on scene changes.

   o If working with Transana, this would replicate a process similar to what might be achieved when analysing visual data directly in other packages.
   o Using other packages, this would enable quick access to parts of the media which are of particular analytic interest – whether the main intention is to work directly or indirectly.

B. Creating multiple transcripts to track and synchronise notes about different dimensions of the recorded session (only possible in Transana at the time of publication).

   o This allows you to focus in on particular aspects in isolation as well as in combination.

We experimented with different approaches to the development and use of transcripts in order to illustrate some of the implications of working in different ways. For some, we developed three transcripts for each video: descriptive log; soundtrack; and voiceover. Figure 4.3 shows the three transcripts associated with commercial loaded in the media window. These are synchronised so that they can be played concurrently. Alternatively, transcript windows can be closed so that a particular aspect can be focused upon in isolation.

For other transcripts we used option A above, and this relatively empty file became the medium by which we could create short notes where it was necessary or add key words or codes (see Chapter 7).

Having cautioned against naively working with multimedia data directly, it often depends on whether you are interested in the content of what is happening, the non-verbal interactions, or both. The processes of working indirectly with the transcript of the video, but retaining the video synchronised and visible at all times alongside the transcript, will anyway seem much like direct analysis but have the advantages of allowing fast access to coded or annotated collections of text passages from multiple other transcripts at the same time. The decision to use video directly should first and foremost be considered at the research design stage and ethical considerations are a crucial aspect of any decision relating to the use of images of real people.

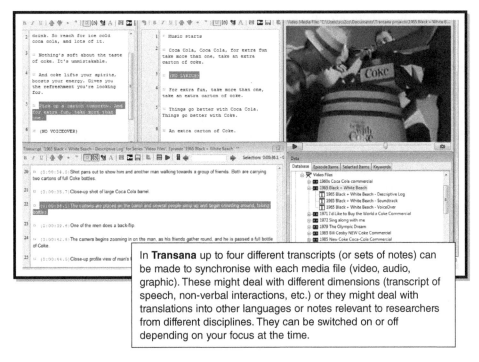

In **Transana** up to four different transcripts (or sets of notes) can be made to synchronise with each media file (video, audio, graphic). These might deal with different dimensions (transcript of speech, non-verbal interactions, etc.) or they might deal with translations into other languages or notes relevant to researchers from different disciplines. They can be switched on or off depending on your focus at the time.

Figure 4.3 Multiple synchronised transcripts for one media file (Transana)

Assistance for transcribing – and developing synchronised transcripts

The insertion of speaker identifiers can be aided by the use of particular transcription technologies. There are a number, mostly free or low-cost, which assist the routine processes of generating textual transcriptions of digitised sound or video files. Transana, Transcriber, HyperTRANSCRIBE and F4/F5 are all specifically designed to assist in this process. They do not transcribe automatically, but provide keyboard shortcuts and auto-structuring of textual transcriptions. For example, Transcriber provides easy ways to enter speaker identifiers at turn-taking in a discussion. With some of these packages the written transcript can remain linked to – or synchronised with – the associated media file, thus enabling the subsequent analysis of the audio/video concurrently with the written version. Files generated in F4/F5 can retain this synchronised relationship in MAXQDA and ATLAS.ti; transcriptions generated in HyperTRANSCRIBE perform the same function in HyperRESEARCH. A key aspect of Transana is transcription. Some CAQDAS packages provide internal but rather more basic functions to transcribe audio/video and thereby to generate synchronised transcripts. NVivo allows the addition of a transcription in a table alongside the video or sound file. Bespoke transcription tools offer more advanced support (keyboard shortcuts, insertion of regular text structures) so it is usually preferable to transcribe first and subsequently import transcripts into the chosen CAQDAS package, unless your analytic strategy is such that it is desirable to be annotating and/or coding while transcribing – or you are using Transana.

In addition, there are several voice recognition packages that enable you to dictate text into a machine-readable format. Many computer users who have wrist and hand problems which affect their ability to use a mouse make use of voice recognition software. However, such software only recognises speech by the person who has trained it. Accents, pitch and cadences of personal speech vary significantly, so the recognition of multiple voices with sound quality affected by the interview environment may be unsuccessful. A cumbersome workaround would be to listen to sections of the recording and then read back the sections in your own voice. Additionally the user has to become familiar with a number of voice-activated editing commands to correct mistakes made by the software during inputting. Software options include Dragon Naturally Speaking, Talking Desktop and Express Scribe, although their reliability in terms of generating accurate and usable transcripts for analysis, without further editing, may be variable.

Mixed data

'Pre-coding' devices differ from auto-coding functions. Both vary in terms of how software packages enable them. Pre-coding is about adding particular text annotations to raw data or using special formats to enable auto-processing and auto-coding of marked structures at the same time as data are imported. Not all CAQDAS packages enable this. Auto-coding, however, is available in most and is usually instigated *after* data import. As discussed above, auto-coding tools can make use of recurring and matching structures throughout data, so for semi-structured or structured data these tools have a particular value. Auto-coding can happen on various bases, however. Searching for the occurrence of particular words or phrases in the content of text is a form of auto-coding (see Chapter 5). Useful context surrounding the 'hits' can be included in the coding (Table 4.5). There are recognisable and often naturally occurring structures even in unstructured data. The degree to which these structures need consideration is related to the type and amount of data and the methodological underpinning of the project.

Table 4.5 Text formats, auto-codeable structures and pre-coding facilities

Software program	Units of auto-codeable context (enables the matching text/ matching formats and codes to specified units of text)	Pre-coding facility (enables the auto-coding of sections simultaneously with data import)
ATLAS.ti Word, Rich Text Format, Plain text, pdf.	Word/String, Sentence, Paragraph, Sections (defined by more than one hard return)	**Excel spreadsheet import:** e.g. for open-ended responses to survey data. A) turns each spread sheet row (representing a respondent) and relevant qualitative answers into documents. B) creates and applies question-based codes to qualitative answers. C) adds factual characteristics (e.g. socio-demographics) as document families.

HyperRESEARCH Word, Rich Text Format, Open Office Files	Words (+/- any number of words), Paragraphs	n/a
MAXQDA Word, Rich Text Format, Plain text, pdf files	Word/String, Sentences, Paragraphs	1. **Textual documents**: pre-codes consist of text and syntax used for any number of data sections. Auto-coding happens simultaneously on the import of the document/s into 'project' 2. **Excel spreadsheets** (functions the same as described above for ATLAS.ti).
Dedoose	n/a	n/a
NVivo	Word/String (+/- any number of words), Paragraphs, Sections (defined by 'heading levels')	n/a
QDA Miner	Paragraphs or Sections defined by syntax or text	Any Excel or dbase file is naturally pre-coded for QDA Miner. This means that a whole project and some of its structures can be initiated on the basis of one tabular file (e.g. Survey). Variables, and question-based chunking of qualitative text by case are processed at project creation.

Just as the units of text recognised by software vary, so the auto-coding tools in each package vary in their functioning. NVivo has a greater degree of automation, since multiple different sets of headings, each respectively with matching text and matching heading levels, can be searched for, recognised and coded in one task (see Box 4.2; p. 85). Though auto-coding is more automated in NVivo, more effort is required at transcription since the formatting processes are more detailed in terms of using heading styles. In other software auto-coding tools have more in common with text search tools – particular strings of characters are searched for one at a time, and subsequent coding is done on the results of each (see Figure 4.1; p. 87).

Descriptive or quantitative data import

The incorporation of quantitative descriptive data – such as socio-demographic variables pertaining to respondents, or any other factual characteristics – enables the subsequent interrogation of data based on complex comparisons. Linking up variable-type numeric information with the corresponding qualitative data can be done in a step-by-step way inside software or via the import of a table or spreadsheet. It is useful to understand how to do this first in a step-by-step way in order to appreciate the logic of what it will do for you analytically, before undertaking the import of quantitative data in a spreadsheet (see the illustration in Figure 4.4). These functions are discussed more fully in Chapter 12 and instructions provided where appropriate on the companion website. For now it is just useful to know that MAXQDA, ATLAS.ti, NVivo, QDA Miner and Dedoose enable descriptive data import for categorising qualitative data already present. It is usually best to prepare the quantitative information in Excel, but data originating in SPSS or other databases can also be rendered acceptable for direct importation. Data formatting and importation processes are relatively simple as long as software-specific protocols are understood (i.e. to determine how the rows and columns match up and apply to the correct bits of qualitative data).

Pre-coding – survey data import and auto-processing

Pre-coding is slightly different to auto-coding since it relies on pre-annotating or pre-formatting work on data before importation. MAXQDA unusually offers pre-coding ('pre-processing') mark-up routines which can be used on any textual data, whether structured or unstructured. Strategically placed text labels with syntax flag up the codes and the text to be assigned by the software. Such

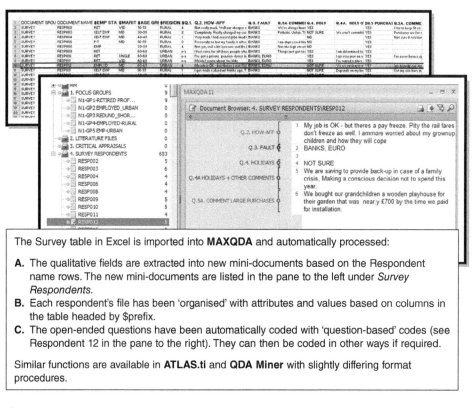

The Survey table in Excel is imported into **MAXQDA** and automatically processed:

A. The qualitative fields are extracted into new mini-documents based on the Respondent name rows. The new mini-documents are listed in the pane to the left under *Survey Respondents*.

B. Each respondent's file has been 'organised' with attributes and values based on columns in the table headed by $prefix.

C. The open-ended questions have been automatically coded with 'question-based' codes (see Respondent 12 in the pane to the right). They can then be coded in other ways if required.

Similar functions are available in **ATLAS.ti** and **QDA Miner** with slightly differing format procedures.

Figure 4.4 Importing survey data from an MS Excel file (MAXQDA)

pre-coding is particularly suitable where volumes of data are imported (e.g. mass observational data, newspaper articles, collections of short essays) that would benefit from some automatic coding or indexing upon importation. Data preparation in this respect can be automated using find and replace tools. The time saved can be very beneficial, especially where large quantities of data have repeated structures. The software auto-processes data as they are imported and structural or topic based coding of the relevant passages happens without expending too much effort.

More often, however, pre-coding is relevant to very structured data – often originating in tables (see Figure 4.4; p. 102). Although the term 'pre-coding' is not used explicitly by any of the developers, we use it to clearly differentiate the auto-processing functions (arising from pre-coding) from 'normal' auto-coding which is proactively instigated after data import. Most software packages offer the latter, fewer the former. ATLAS.ti, MAXQDA and QDA Miner make use of such pre-coding for open-ended questions when presented alongside more quantitative data in spreadsheets. Column header information in the spreadsheet tell the software that some columns are quantitative not qualitative and should be treated as such using different functions to organise the qualitative open-ended questions. Usually what happens upon importation is that the open-ended answers formerly in a table are reformatted and re-presented as document-based texts. The **correct textual or syntax have to be present** at the relevant column headers. The results are as follows:

- Textual data from open-ended questions are lifted out of the table to create continuous text (for each respondent).
- The same text is coded according to column headers (effectively the pre-coded elements) – so in the margin display codes representing, for example, the question numbers will appear against the text.
- The respondents are categorised into subsets based on quantitative or descriptive information in the other columns (dependent on correct syntax at column headers).
- MAXQDA and ATLAS.ti create mini-respondent based documents combining all indicated fields so that respondents' fuller answers can be read as narrative, uninterrupted by other more quantitative columns. QDA Miner is unusual in that it can start an entire project out of a large spreadsheet or dBase file, where all the open-ended questions are represented as text fields and all the quantitative fields are used to organise the cases. We refer here only to the ability of some software to process pre-coded data automatically on import.[2] Chapter 12 discusses how quantitative information in tabular format can classify qualitative data already imported. Dedoose was devised as a mixed method software package so that, once the quantitative data are imported, charts and tables will instantly be made available, breaking down the sample, providing statistics which compare the occurrence of codes with subsets, etc. (see Figure 13.5; p. 319).

---

[2]NVivo enables the import of spreadsheet data which can include open-ended questions, but nothing much happens automatically at the time of the import; they have to be further coded or auto-coded using additional multiple functions in sequence once inside the software.

Questions to ask yourself when preparing data

- To what extent are the different forms of data you intend to work with inherently structured? If they are, to what end might you be able to make use of these structures within your chosen software?
- If you have already transcribed data, will you really gain anything analytically, or save any time, by reformatting in order to enable auto-coding?
- If working with visual data, what are your analytic aims and how will this affect the ways you choose to work?

Concluding remarks: laying the groundwork

This chapter covered issues relating to data and their preparation for management and analysis in CAQDAS packages. We have discussed these broadly in terms of data types (primary, secondary, and background or tertiary material) and data formats (textual, multimedia, mixed). The discussion reflects the changes in capacity to handle diverse media, and this in turn reflects technology changes in the wider world. The three case-study examples used throughout this book and for which we provide step-by-step instruction in different software packages on the companion website illustrate some of the different options. The level of detail provided is rather high. But in most situations, with qualitative data to prepare you will be able to get started with using your chosen software quickly if you simply attend to the issues highlighted in relation to our *minimal (but useful)* guidelines. Thinking ahead about data, their inherent structures and what you need to achieve analytically lays the groundwork for systematic analysis. Preparing data to optimise subsequent possibilities will enhance your potential to cut across the dataset in various ways. The next chapter discusses some of the early steps involved in using qualitative software in relation to the practical tasks of getting a project ready to manage data and thinking effectively.

The following exercises are designed to help you familiarise yourself with your chosen case-study example or to think about your own data in the context of these exercises. The exercises are focused on ensuring that data structures are consistent (Case Studies A and B) and to enable you to experiment with transcribing video data (Case Study C). For your own research project, there may be quite a lot of preparatory work required before you get started with using a software package. When using software to help analyse a qualitative dataset, it is often said that the first project turns out to be the learning ground for the next project (because of missed opportunities and mistakes made the first time round). So, it is a good idea to spend the time on this now – even if it feels like you are delaying the 'interesting' work – as it is usually more difficult and time-consuming to alter data formats later.

1. Download the sample data for the case study (or use your own).
2. Extract the case-study data files from the zipped folder and save them somewhere sensible. The exercises throughout the book assume you save the data and the software project in the Documents folder (when using a PC), but you can save them elsewhere if you prefer.
3. Open the Case Study Project notes file.

    (a) Become familiar with the naming protocol for each data file – think of ways you could replicate this with your own data.
    (b) Gain a sense of the type of data they are, the way they been formatted – also refer to the notes about the formatting decisions that were made. See also the case-study boxes in this chapter that refer to these decisions.

4. Familiarise yourself with the structures of the data files in the case study you are using or consider your own data.

    (a) Are there repeated structures which provide important ways to search or to group equivalent sections in the same file or across other files?
    (b) In Case Study B, the repeated speaker identifiers are useful structures – auto-coding speaker sections (or identical questions in structured interviews) helps to gather similar data together very quickly (see Chapter 6 for more on these processes).

5. Use Find and Replace tools in Word.

    (a) Experiment with these tools to alter the formatting of speaker identifiers from 'minimal' to 'optimal' (Case Studies A and B only).

6. Working with video or sound files – making decisions about how you will work. If you are using Case Study C, Coca-Cola Commercials, you will possibly need to install the software (see Exercises 1–3 and, importantly, Exercise 9 at the end of Chapter 5) before conducting the following data preparation and transcription tasks. In fact it will be very important to read the software-specific information relevant to audio/sound on the companion website before making decisions about how you will approach transcription.

    (a) Having explored the options available, if working with your own data, decide on the status of the multimedia files in your project – evaluate the role of the video/sound file for your research purposes. We assume you will not consider importing video or sound data unless at some level your analysis relies on identifying interactions, dynamics or happenings which would otherwise be missed.
    (b) Will you mainly code and explore/search the transcripts, with the multimedia file as a background? Or (as with Case Study C) is the visual/sound data the crucial resource?
    (c) Decide whether you intend to make full transcripts or partial transcripts or just notes here and there; also refer to discussions about direct and indirect data in the chapter.

7. Test the format. Having made decisions, eventually you will need to create a project in the software, and import one multimedia file just to make sure the format is acceptable to the software (see also Chapter 5 exercises).

5

Early Steps in Software: Practical Tasks and Familiarisation

This chapter focuses on getting software projects ready for serious work. There is much that can be done to gain familiarity through experimentation. The more you experiment to test the logic and implications of simple organisational structures, the more confident you will become in applying them to reflect research design and the needs of later interrogation. Getting started usefully involves integrating literature, contributing to understanding how project management can be tackled in a rounded way. Certain steps can be taken to plan work, creating initial signposts for where you need to go in terms of process and analysis. Working as part of a team additionally requires working in ways that complement others' tasks and that are agreed with research partners (see the companion website for specific considerations when preparing for teamwork). Tables 5.1, 5.2 and 5.3 list processes relevant to each respective Case Study.

Chapter 2 emphasised that increased familiarisation with software enables more confidence to experiment and determine how to achieve complicated outcomes within particular methodological contexts. We outlined how software projects can be set up to reflect initial research design (managing and referencing literature; defining research topic and questions; representing theoretical frameworks; incorporating research materials; defining factual features; developing areas of analytic interest). Having a well-thought-out research design before you embark on using a software package will maximise your focused use of tools. We discuss this in more detail in Silver and Lewins (2014). In this chapter, we take a slightly less prescriptive stance, because, for many researchers, early engagement with software happens before research design is fully formulated, or the two might occur in tandem. Individual packages provide particular ways to set up and reflect design and early thinking. What follows, therefore, is a practically oriented discussion about starting off a software project such that you can understand the implications of using technology in certain key aspects. We discuss four aspects: (i) basic software familiarisation and project set-up; (ii) getting the software project and interface shipshape; (iii) creating a framework of memos; and (iv) scoping the topic area and critiquing the literature.

The way work can happen

Qualitative data analysis is an iterative process, whether or not you are using software. CAQDAS packages provide inherently flexible workspaces. However, working without customised software requires a degree of linearity in processes because certain tasks tend to be one-off or happen at a particular stage only; changing direction in even small ways can pose major challenges. The interconnected elements of data analysis (Figure 2.1; p. 45) are supported by software. At the heart of our model is reflection. Everything leads towards that; and reflection occurs throughout the process as well (Chapter 10). Data do not have to be transcribed before a coding scheme is created; materials do not have to be imported before memos are written; coding does not have to wait until all data are imported; organising materials can happen early on, or can wait until complex interrogating and searching; the coding scheme can be in place at the outset, if working within a theoretical framework, or iteratively created and refined as data are coded in a more emergent design. Tasks can happen 'now and then', when it seems logical or necessary to move on in certain ways. Within these freedoms, and given the great variety in software functions, you need to remain systematic and in control. Your research questions, analytic strategy and outcome requirements inform the particular ways you use tools.

Gain familiarity with software by setting up a project

Note-making and tracking the development of ideas occurs throughout analysis; indeed, it begins during project design. So, a software project can be created long before primary data are 'ready' to be imported. This might involve integrating notes, background material and literature references. It might involve setting up a structural framework that represents your research design (see Chapter 2). However you start off, working within software will spur your thinking about how to store different elements of information relevant to the project as a whole, including, but not limited to, actual 'data'. Indeed, technically, anything you can incorporate into your software project can be treated as 'data'. Thus, the use of software can open up thinking about the status and role of different materials and how they might be combined to produce a holistic and well-evidenced interpretation and written account. Bedding in and tweaking the structures you create early on will improve your confidence to proceed in a flexible but systematic way. By the time primary data are ready to work with inside the software project, the technology will feel like a comfort blanket with various pockets safely sorting and enclosing your data and ideas, providing quick access to various elements underpinning your work.

Creating the project

CAQDAS packages offer different ways of starting projects. Most commonly, you simply open the software and choose to 'create a new project' (as with ATLAS.ti,

NVivo and MAXQDA, for example). Transana, in contrast, requires you to specify a database (project) name to initialise. However you start off the project, become familiar with the default location for saving projects. You might want to change this, but wait until you are confident about the software's needs in this respect. The project file will contain, or link to, everything you subsequently add or import. In most packages, this file remains empty until you incorporate data or create other entities within the project. The internal File menu usually pertains to the project as a whole, so unless saving happens automatically, save the project as soon as you have made it.

Transparency

Start thinking immediately about transparency and how to consciously maintain reflexivity over the project's course, right through to your final report, article or dissertation write-up. Doing so from the early moments has numerous effects. It helps you keep in mind that quality is a priority. The need for transparent account-ability imposes its own discipline. Software can encourage good record-keeping, creation of logs, audit trails and spaces to reflect on all you are doing (Chapter 10). Though it requires significant effort to create an authoritative account, begin to take advantage of the spaces provided by your chosen software in which to write. We introduce memos and some other writing tools below, but there may be additional mechanical ways to create an audit trail of actions that can assist the recall of pro-cesses. In NVivo, for instance, checking a box upon the creation of the software project enables a log of actions to be created automatically.

BOX 5.1	FUNCTIONALITY NOTES

Planning for software use

We are strongly of the opinion that researchers should approach the use of software in a critical and aware way. This is important when you are choosing a package, but also when you start planning for and using a particular product. You need to build an awareness of certain principles and structures inherent in the way your chosen package works. We call this the 'flavour' of software. This is a simple list of aspects to feel confident about as soon as possible:

- Have a clear purposeful idea about the way you intend to work with your data (your analytic strategy) based on problem formulation, research design, methodological concerns, etc. Get clear about this as soon as possible – preferably before you start using software in earnest.
- Always remember that software does not do the thinking – the reflection and inter-pretive analysis is all done by you. Quality rests with you.
- Regarding project design, research questions and analytic strategy – be aware how the software can reflect these elements.

- Remember the project management aspect of software; think about whether integrating literature and other supplementary materials might enable your analysis to be more grounded and holistic.
- You can organise data for later interrogation in the software project any point.
- You can code data and structure codes in the way you want (if coding processes are relevant to the way you will work).
- If your approach is not code-based – understand where you can 'write' in the software project – are the annotation tools adequate? Will you also need linking tools?
- If you will be using coding devices – understand how the code structures provide you with satisfactory way of organising ideas.
- Facilitate how you will work either as an individual or as a team. (If you are working in a team, make early plans for how you will share work – get advice if you need it.)

Naming and backing-up routines

Lay the groundwork for protecting your project. Mistakes can be made. There is sometimes an Undo button, although not always. However, individual tasks can be undone or reverted.

Become familiar with saving and backing-up instructions (see the companion website). Once you start serious work, you must frequently make duplicate versions as back-ups. When working on different computers, this is important so you can move projects around easily and efficiently. Plan for bringing projects back to your original computer, adequately named, so that they do not get confused with earlier versions. Also plan ahead to back-up before you change analytic direction; for example, when about to modify a coding scheme (Chapter 9). If things go wrong at this stage you might accidentally undo weeks of work, so intentional back-ups are important. Slightly different are system back-ups that some packages provide. ATLAS.ti, MAXQDA and QDA Miner remind you from time to time that you have not created a recent system back-up. These usually overwrite earlier system back-ups, providing an immediate safeguard, but they cannot be relied upon in procedural terms like your own proactively created back-ups that serve as a record of your progress more generally.

Establish a project naming convention immediately. Keep it simple. The first time our case-study project called 'Downturn' was backed up we called it Downturn-11–08–23 (indicating the date, 23 August 2011). This dating convention will sort the file listing by the whole date rather than by the day of the month, i.e. in YY-MM-DD order. You can then more easily track the chronology of change in the project title itself. Additionally, when working for a prolonged period, make back-ups throughout the day, noting in the back-up file name the time at which you created it as well as the date (e.g. Coca-cola 11–05–04am, and Coca-cola 11–05–04pm). Experience has taught us that paranoia is safer than complacency in terms of your important analytic work! Most packages are stable, but crashes sometimes occur, and it is better to have back-ups that you subsequently delete than to lose several hours of work.

Table 5.1 Early steps in software: some suggestions in the context of case study A, Young People's Perceptions

---

Tasks from PHASE ONE: Data preparation and project set-up

Software project set-up	Create and save a software project
	Create a basic structural framework representing initial research design (can be added to/changed later if required)

- ...for different types of data

  o Literature
  o Interviews
  o Vignettes
  o Photo prompts

- ...for different types of writing

  o Process memos
  o Critical appraisals of literature
  o Analytic memos
  o Respondent memos

- ...for different types of coding

  o Thematic codes
  o Topic codes

Incorporate project materials and data	Import/add data files into relevant places within the structural framework

---

Tasks from PHASE TWO: Review the literature: identify theoretical focus

Familiarise with the articles	Read through literature files
	Experiment with annotation tools for making contextual notes
	Experiment with content searching to gain broad overview
Plan your approach to handling literature	Consider how you will handle the synthesis of

- Definitions and origins of work
- Key concepts and theories
- Main debates raised by literature
- Political standpoints taken

Consider how to manage this in your chosen software

- Direct work – coding/annotating/memoing
- Indirect work – generating critical appraisals

Consider the relevance of important information from bibliographic software

- Control process in bibliographic software by creating small, key 'collections' or libraries – for exporting in report form or RIS / XML format
- Import into software project where enabled. Either use special software functions for handling imports or devise workarounds

Generate and organise critical appraisals of literature	Make notes about your critical reading of each literature file in the context of the research questions

- Structure appraisals consistently using formatting functions
- Link your appraisals to the full text articles (where possible)
- Consider how it will be useful to code your appraisals

---

	o Practical codes (references to get; points to follow-up)
	o Critical codes (unsubstantiated claims; methodological implications)
	o Thematic codes (being young; gendered experiences)
Create a theoretical model arising from literature appraisal	Represent in a map the core aspects identified in the literature review, in the context of the research questions
	Make notes in analytic and process memos throughout

Each time you move your project to another location, ensure the name is such that you do not accidentally overwrite an earlier version (if you are not ready to delete it!). Follow the procedures in each software package. With most this is an easy process. However, large multimedia files are usually left outside the project database file, so there is a little more to think about when moving projects around. Ways of moving projects between computers are different in each package and so the safeguards required are slightly different also. The point is, if you know you will need to move projects around, become familiar with efficient means of doing so before it matters too much. Make your mistakes early on so that you can correct them.

Incorporating research materials

Having created a software project, try incorporating some material, to practise the process and experiment with the choices. Functions for varying project settings and other options are often located in the File or Project menu, but getting data into the project usually starts off somewhere completely different. This is an early common stumbling block for those who are uncertain of how things fit together in the software architecture. Usually importing data happens from a menu or icon listing options for 'Documents' or 'Sources'. With Transana, however, in which audiovisual material is the basis upon which you start off, the process is somewhat different, necessitating the creation of 'Episodes' into which you add media files. QDA Miner offers several different ways of proceeding (see Figure 5.1; p. 112 and Box 5.2; p. 113).

Most software handle Word, rich text, plain text or PDF formats of textual material (see Chapter 4 on preparing data for import – particularly if materials are structured). If you do not yet have textual material (transcripts, etc.) to work with, import a literature list, the project proposal or any other background material. Having found the right menu option, browse to find and select the files you want. Note that your chosen software will probably not even list files at this point if they are in an unacceptable format. If you choose the wrong option when starting off the import function you can hit problems. If you have material saved in unacceptable formats for your chosen software, there are usually workarounds to incorporate them. For example, you can convert website material from HTML to PDF or from PDF to Word or rich text format using

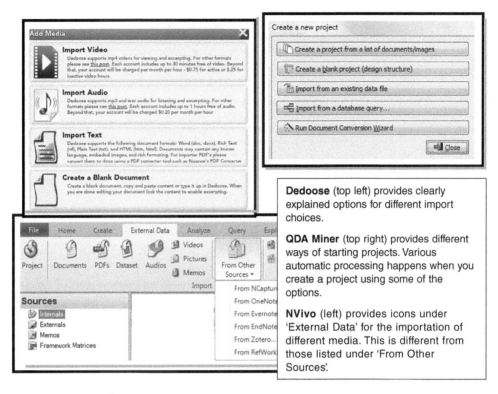

Figure 5.1 Importing research materials and starting projects (Dedoose, QDA Miner, NVivo)

bespoke (often freely available) converters. Media files can also be converted into different formats.[1]

It is important to understand that the 'import' process usually creates a copy of the file inside the software project.[2] Once incorporated, check where they appear within the software project and open them. Are they listed and does the content display as you expected? Experiment with renaming or even deleting (or removing) files; you will not be altering or deleting the original versions. In some packages you can create new empty files (i.e. empty sources or documents) for writing notes, pasting clipboard material from other applications, or directly transcribing audio-visual data. This can serve many functions, not least as an additional way to integrate 'occasional' material from elsewhere. Now consider the benefits of organising a mixture of different files. Even if you have named your data files thoughtfully and consistently (Chapter 4), storing them within the CAQDAS project in different

---

[1]See the CAQDAS Networking Project website for information on multimedia converters: http://www.surrey.ac.uk/sociology/research/researchcentres/caqdas/support/analysingvisual/ preparing_video_data_for_use_with_caqdas_packages.htm

[2]This is not always the case, however, especially when working with multimedia (audio or video) files. You must, therefore, check the way your chosen software package handles data (see the companion website step-by-step instructions).

locations ('folders' and/or 'sets') can reflect your research design in terms of data collection and enable later interrogation on these bases. We discuss the early creation of these 'placeholders' below, ways of manipulating them in Chapter 9 and ways of interrogating them in Chapter 13.

BOX 5.2   FUNCTIONALITY NOTES

Alternative ways of starting off software projects

Although most of the packages we feature allow straightforward importing of textual files, there are exceptions. In Transana media files (audio, video or still images) are the anchor for analytic work. Media files are added as Episodes first, after which an empty transcript can be created, or one that has already been written can be imported. Transcripts are synchronised with media files through the insertion of 'timecodes' (see Chapter 2 and 7), thereby becoming the vehicle through which the audiovisual material is accessed. The Coca-Cola case includes transcripts for importation and other commercials which require a transcript to be created.

Many packages additionally allow for types of data import which rely on special formats. QDA Miner, for example, offers options for starting projects from a folder of documents, a spreadsheet or a database, as well as initially creating an empty project (Figure 5.1; p. 112). As such data import can happen simultaneously with project creation. Case study B, The Financial Downturn, includes an Excel spreadsheet comprising a sub-sample of a survey, a mixture of qualitative comments and more descriptive quantitative information. The companion website include instructions for starting a QDA Miner project on that basis, simultaneously creating the project, importing qualitative data and creating Variables and Cases on the basis of the columns and rows of the spreadsheet.

However you start off a project, many things can be done before dealing directly with data. In our case studies we began by creating certain entities as 'placeholders' for types of work we knew we would need to engage in late on. We now go on to discuss some of these.

Getting the software project and the interface shipshape

Your first software project might just be an experiment. Alternatively, it could be a serious effort to set up a container for analysis. In the latter situation, think about the framework you create as a reflection of your research design (Chapter 2). Simple things can set up fundamental structures and create signposts for further work. We focus here on folders and short-cut groupings (sets, families or collections) and spaces for writing and tracking processes. Setting up any organisational structures, putting things in them and moving them around, can be very helpful in the familiarisation processes.

The software's flexibility supports trial and error in setting up in satisfactory ways; your confidence with software and how it can best support your work will increase. Equally, experiment with the interface to optimise its layout to suit the way you work. ATLAS.ti, for example, provides easy ways for several data files to be viewed side by side. This is useful for various purposes, including visual comparison of answers between respondents in (semi-)structured interview data (or indeed, the interviewer's questions!), comparing literature files and your written critiques about them (Figure 5.3; p. 118), and tracking the contributions of an individual respondent

Table 5.2 Early steps in software: some suggestions in the context of case study B, The Financial Downturn

Tasks from PHASE ONE: Data preparation and project set-up	

Software project set-up	Create and save a software project
	Create a basic structural framework representing initial research design (can be added to/changed later if required)
	
	• ...for different types of data
	
	   o Local media
	   o National media
	   o Focus-groups
	   o Survey data
	
	• ...for different types of writing
	
	   o Process memos
	   o Analytic memos
	   o Respondent memos
	   o Group memos
	
	• ...for different types of coding
	
	   o Thematic codes
	   o Topic codes

Incorporate project materials and data	Import/add data files into relevant places within structural framework • For survey data take advantage of any special import processes enabled by chosen software (e.g. import Survey data with simultaneous auto-coding – where possible)
Plan team-working protocols (see companion website)	Initial project meeting i) Familiarise with how your chosen software handles team-working ii) Make decisions about how to exchange information (2 other regions will have similar focus group data) iii) Make decisions about how memos will be written up so that all team-members are producing similar sets of material for comparison. iv) Make small sub-set of 3 transcripts for team members to code up independently. Next meeting i) Discuss progress ii) Confirm policy on coding scheme development and use iii) Discuss what needs to be included in attribute organisation of the respondents. Discuss recommendations for increasing depth of later focus groups...more probes etc.

to multiple data types (Box 4.3; p. 90). NVivo and MAXQDA allow 'browser' windows to be 'undocked', thus enabling a similar comparative presentation. Transana enables up to four transcripts to be associated with each media file (Figure 4.3; p. 99) and for different presentations of some associated visualisations (e.g. the Keyword and Waveform views). NVivo and MAXQDA allow the interface to be reoriented according to preference.

Project design

Project design involves many aspects. Overarching philosophical and methodological contexts, problem formulation, research questions, methods and rationales for generating data, the different origins, descriptors and demographics of respondents' or other data all form the basis of inquiries, comparisons and, not least, the strategies employed in conducting analysis (Chapters 1 and 2). However, not all infrastructure need be set up from the outset. Some packages provide easy ways to organise which enable limited filtering and scoping, and we focus on these first. However, there are more complex and powerful ways to draw out relationships and comparisons across and within different cases and subsets (Chapters 12 and 13). It is important to have an understanding of such longer-term potential as soon as possible, so that, when you are ready, you can do the necessary organisation. Although you could set up these structures early on, by adding factual characteristics for data and respondents straight away (as illustrated for Case Study B), it might be worth waiting until you are more familiar with the steps needed to achieve it. There is usually no requirement to achieve the more complex organisation early on. We will deal with the easy aspects first. A lot can be achieved in the simple creation of folders.

Early organisational structures for data

MAXQDA and NVivo provide both *folders* (called *groups* in MAXQDA) and *sets* for the storage of data. Transana uses *episodes* (equivalent to folders) for storing media files. ATLAS.ti provides sets (called *families*) that act as short-cuts. In other software, folders are not relevant because other ways of organising are more prominent (e.g. *cases* and *variables* in QDA Miner, and *descriptor sets* in Dedoose).

Folders, groups or *episodes* are user-created and source material can usually be added to or moved between them at any time. They should contain exclusive sets of data files; you would not normally have the same file in two folders, because the folders contain the actual files, and you must avoid having duplicate versions of the same file. Sets or families, conversely, contain short-cuts to files – therefore one file can belong to multiple sets. The two types of entity are complementary. Folders are 'clerical' places to store data, while sets or families are places to rearrange groups of data files for various analytical purposes without upsetting the clerical order of things.

Usually, primary and/or secondary data are incorporated into the project in order to 'directly' analyse. Additionally, we refer to 'tertiary data' which might be spaces

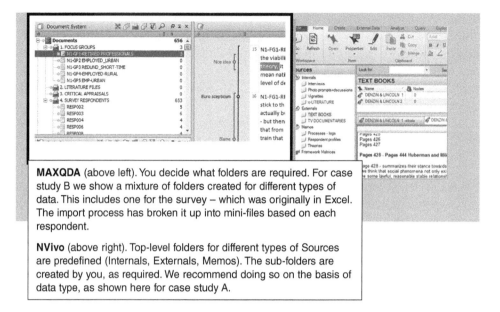

MAXQDA (above left). You decide what folders are required. For case study B we show a mixture of folders created for different types of data. This includes one for the survey – which was originally in Excel. The import process has broken it up into mini-files based on each respondent.

NVivo (above right). Top-level folders for different types of Sources are predefined (Internals, Externals, Memos). The sub-folders are created by you, as required. We recommend doing so on the basis of data type, as shown here for case study A.

Figure 5.2   Folders for storing project data (MAXQDA and NVivo)

created within projects to accommodate notes and analyses concerning background material, files or objects that you cannot – or do not want to – physically incorporate (Chapter 1). Where you are working with different types of material in this way, it will always be useful to separate them according to type, because there will be many occasions when you want to focus your attention on just one type, or a combination (e.g. just the primary data, or just the literature files).

Within the requirements of your chosen software, you can create these basic storage locations and import individual data files into them, or bring data files in first, and then move them into storage locations later on. Where folders (or equivalent devices) are present, files can be moved around; so if you make a mistake to start with it does not matter – you can fix it. The two main benefits of folders are tidying up and filtering. Being tidy will pay off many times over during your working processes. Being able to filter searches so that the software only looks in particular places will be analytically useful and save time (Chapters 8 and 13).

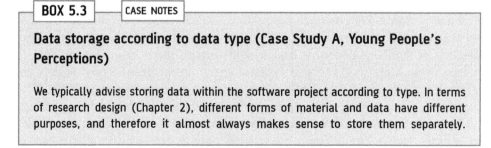

BOX 5.3   **CASE NOTES**

Data storage according to data type (Case Study A, Young People's Perceptions)

We typically advise storing data within the software project according to type. In terms of research design (Chapter 2), different forms of material and data have different purposes, and therefore it almost always makes sense to store them separately.

Usually, in complex designs, there will be a need to isolate material in terms of type later on, regardless of other factual features inherent in them (Chapter 12). Storing according to type makes the scoping of queries on this basis much easier, and the use of attributes/variables will additionally allow for queries (Chapter 13) on a whole host of other bases.

In Case Study A, Young People's Perceptions, primary data were originally collected together. They were split for the purposes of analysis because of their differing contribution to the project. The main interview transcripts are relevant to the first two research questions (Box 2.1; p. 42). Data contributed by the same respondents in response to the photo prompts and hypothetical vignette scenarios were designed to unpack respondents' socio-sexual attitudes and therefore are particularly important to the second research question. It is therefore important to be able to consider the three types of primary data in isolation, as well as together. As such, we created the main folder structures on the basis of data type (Figure 5.2; p. 112).

A key part of the 'theory-driven abductive' project design, and reflected in the third research question, concerns the consideration of primary data with existing literature; to what extent do these data reflect existing knowledge and open up new understandings? It is important to be able to bring the results of the literature review (see below) together with analysis of primary data. However, integrating the diverse materials may not be beneficial from the outset. For example, in terms of searching for content (Chapter 6), respondents talk about communicating with different people about sensitive matters repeatedly in the three forms of primary data. Although results of a close analysis of this theme would need to be considered in light of existing literature, we did not necessarily want to do so straight away. Searching all the data for "talk to" or "talk" or "tell" or "confide" would produce much irrelevant and time-wasting material if performed concurrently on the literature and primary data. Scoping the search to just primary data contained within bespoke folders ensures the relevance of the search results, in the first instance. Later, the literature could be revisited in light of preliminary results, and integrated with them.

Dilemmas about folders – they cannot serve every purpose

You are likely to face dilemmas about folder structures for data storage. It is typical to want to reflect key comparative elements in the basic folder structure. For instance, Case Study A, Young People's Perceptions, includes the national comparative dimension – the Netherlands and England and Wales. It is tempting to create separate folders for *Netherlands Vignettes* and *English Vignettes*, *Netherlands Interviews* and *English Interviews*, etc. This makes intuitive sense because cross-national comparison is a key aspect of the research design. However, there are additional important comparative features: respondents who were 15 (under the UK age of consent) and those who were 16 years of age, those living with both parents and those living with one parent, etc. You cannot reflect all these dimensions using folders, so where do you call a halt to folder complexity?

There is no hard-and-fast rule about this, but we generally advise keeping data storage as simple as possible. There are other structural functions – principally attributes/variables – that are much more powerful (irrespective of folders) in enabling complex filtering and interrogation. For example, a query scoping to attributes/variables would allow you to look code(s) in female English data only – or in female English 15-year-olds. Attribute/variable values can be combined in various ways. Chapter 13 covers many potential interrogation options, bringing together attributes/variables (Chapter 12) with coding and conceptual work (Chapters 7–9).

Queries can be scoped to individual or multiple folders, but they will not be clearly differentiated on the basis of folder origin in the results. So, folders for the storage of data are in essence simple things. We should not be too didactic about this – if you are clear about the utility of variables/attributes you can cut down on folders. If the software makes it difficult to work out the most efficient way to apply variables/attributes – then folders are a good fall-back for more 'focused' interrogations (see also the use of *sets* below). NVivo enables the creation of sub- and sub-sub-folders (and so on), apparently allowing a more complex structure. This can be useful for scoping queries, but only to a limited extent. Though it is useful with a large dataset to be able to hide documents away on occasions, it is not helpful to bury them so completely that revealing them takes more than one or two mouse clicks. However, NVivo's architecture concerning the application of variables can be a little convoluted, and it can therefore be difficult at the outset to see the bigger picture of what is possible and how best to achieve it. Generally, therefore, it is best to keep things simple at the beginning; you can always complexify things later on when you are more comfortable with the workings of the software.

Using folders to separate different phases and types of work

Folders might be created to manage different 'writing' locations. In most packages there is a separate memo or note-taking function, while in NVivo memos have status and functionality equivalent to other data sources and are stored in a predefined Memos folder (Figure 5.2; p. 112). When creating spaces for writing about material that is not directly incorporated into the software project (see below with respect to literature) it makes good sense to separate these using folders. In NVivo a special area is predefined specifically for the handling of links to externally held materials. Sources created within the Externals folder are empty writing spaces linked to externally held files or web pages. If appropriate, they can have structures (page numbers, chapter numbers, etc.) embedded within them, that reflect the characteristics of the external material they represent. Where such specific functionality is not provided by your chosen software, similar tasks can be approximated.

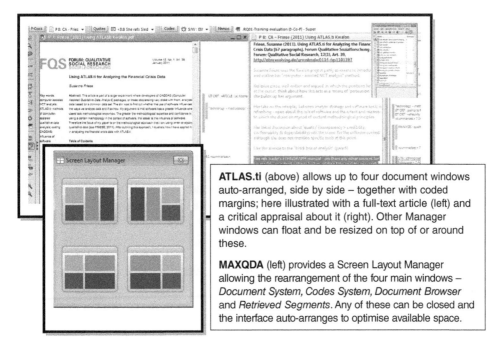

ATLAS.ti (above) allows up to four document windows auto-arranged, side by side – together with coded margins; here illustrated with a full-text article (left) and a critical appraisal about it (right). Other Manager windows can float and be resized on top of or around these.

MAXQDA (left) provides a Screen Layout Manager allowing the rearrangement of the four main windows – *Document System*, *Codes System*, *Document Browser* and *Retrieved Segments*. Any of these can be closed and the interface auto-arranges to optimise available space.

Figure 5.3 Optimising the user interface (ATLAS.ti and MAXQDA)

The virtue of empty places for thinking and growing

Think of your 'software project' as offering not only places for storing actual material, but also places to *grow* things. Gradually you put the analysis together in those places and your control over all strands of the project will become more manageable. Short-cut groupings (sets, families), where enabled, are endlessly useful and flexible structures. They are a bit like large empty plant pots – you know roughly the mixture and types of flowers going in them but you do not quite know how it will turn out, what the exact appearance will be, which plants will do well and which will be submerged by other stronger plants or, as in our case, *ideas*. Making places to store evidence and examples of things and to gather notes about them is a valuable first step in growing the analysis. It does not matter if you have not yet got material to fill them and you will likely change your mind about them later on anyway, but creating the spaces for ideas to grow is motivating.

Therefore, we consider *sets* as places to think. At the outset, these 'signposts' might be related to research questions, theoretical frameworks, ideas generated from literature, or hypotheses to test. As analysis progresses you might create additional sets that represent 'hunches', emerging interpretations, tentative conclusions, or, more practically, the different articles you want to write, or the various materials you need to gather for each chapter of your eventual dissertation.

It is important to make a distinction between short-cut groupings for data and codes. Packages differ in this respect. ATLAS.ti and MAXQDA respectively provide *families* and *sets* for documents and codes separately. Transana provides *collections* which enable the grouping of *clips* (data segments which may or may not be coded). HyperRESEARCH uses a case-based structure (Chapter 3) which can work similarly for data files. NVivo has only one type of short-cut grouping (sets) which can contain multiple project items (including sources, codes and other items), which offers the greatest flexibility.

In relation to the storage of and access to source data files, the principle advantage of sets over folders is that one item can belong in many sets. You can create them for almost any circumstance. Adding something to a set only creates a 'short-cut', so the members of each set are 'virtual'. However, because they are short-cuts, you can access content and analytic functionality from within them (Figures 10.7; p. 247 and 13.4; p. 313). They can be procedural, practical or serve a real analytic purpose. In Case Study A, Young People's Perceptions, sets were created to remind us which documents had been through the first pass coding process. More analytically, a set of documents was produced to group all the young people demonstrating a high degree of self-awareness and a set of all who seemed to experience severe communication difficulties within their family. In projects where several interviews with one person, or with different members of the same family, have been conducted, the individual transcripts need to be seen as part of the whole dataset as well as in relation to each other. It would be awkward and limiting to permanently isolate related transcripts in a folder for each individual or family in the main document listing. However, a *set* for each such grouping would work well, enabling occasional scoping or filtering based on the individual or family groups. In NVivo, MAXQDA and ATLAS.ti sets can be produced as a result of a complex combination of variables previously assigned to data (Chapter 12). Figure 13.4 illustrates this in ATLAS.ti and MAXQDA, where the process of making sets in this way is particularly simple.

The important thing to remember is that sets can be created and left empty, acting as 'signposts' for later work. It is not that you know exactly which direction

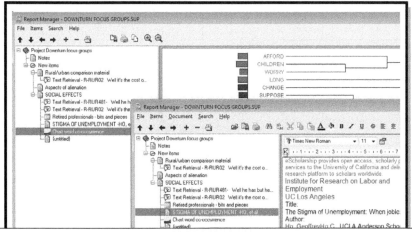

The **QDA Miner** Report Manager (case study B, The Financial Downturn) showing various report headings (top left): *Rural/urban comparison material; Aspects of alienation; SOCIAL EFFECTS*). Within the 'SOCIAL EFFECTS' report area various materials are being gathered: coded data, charts, parts of literature, etc. Selecting items under the report shows their content on the right (see also Chapter 10).

Figure 5.4   The Report Manager for gathering materials (QDA Miner)

work will take you, but creating structures early keeps ideas or targets in mind from the outset.

In QDA Miner neither sets nor folders feature, though something quite original in the shape of its *Report Manager* provides successful 'collection points' which provide similar markers for future attention (Figure 5.4). The results of searches and explorations can be selectively collected in organised slots which can have analytic or procedural headings. In most other packages such output has to be gathered somewhere outside the software, but the continued integration into project work enabled by the QDA Miner Report Manager encourages a natural organisation that is more flexible than storing versions of reports or other output outside the software project. In addition, material being gathered in Word files can be imported into the relevant Report area.

We discuss sets further in relation to the grouping of codes and manipulation of coding schemes in Chapter 9 and in relation to interrogation in Chapter 13.

Creating a framework of memos

Just as sets can be created and left empty as markers, so memos can be created as signposts for procedural or analytic directions. Ongoing reflections about your project can be recorded in memos representing different aspects of the research design. How you manage your writing within the software project will depend on your needs in terms of outcome and the ways you like to write. The functionality of your

Table 5.3 Early steps in software: some suggestions in the context of case study C, Coca-Cola Commercials

Tasks from PHASE ONE: Data preparation and project set-up	
Software project set-up	Create and save a software project
	Create a basic structural framework representing initial research design (can be added to/changed later if required)
	• ...for different types of data
	○ Commercials
	○ Background documents
	• ...for different types of writing
	○ Process memos
	○ Analytic memos
	○ Commercial memos
	• ...for different types of coding
	○ Inductive codes
Incorporate project materials and data	Import/add data files into relevant places within structural framework of the software project

chosen software can be adapted to your needs. Usually there is an explicit 'memo' or 'notes' tool. How this is enabled differs enormously between packages (Chapters 6 and 10). Some provide separate spaces for writing annotations (smaller comments about particular data segments) and memos (larger writing about any aspect of analysis). In some programs comments exist where codes are attached to data. In others, they exist linked to other items. Some allow freestanding memos, which have their own independent listing, and though they can sometimes be linked to other objects (codes, data files, text passages, clips), they do not have to be attached to anything.

The first memo

It makes sense to have at least one memo from the outset. This could serve as a central 'project process journal' for recording day-to-day tasks and the questions arising from them. At the end of a work session, summarising the day's progress and noting follow-up actions will improve continuity next time you work in the project. Even where memos are not freestanding, you will be able to find a place which acts as the location for this central project journal. Some packages provide a specific place for this type of writing, in others you have to create it yourself. You might create an empty document which serves the purpose, or a special code, 'project management', could have the project journal memo attached to it. One way or another, mould the software to make a location for this very important process-oriented writing. Keeping this record up to date will foster your ability to be transparent about your processes later on.

The dispersal of notes around the project

Investigate memo functionality, and think early on about how you intend to organise your writing. Researchers must always have in mind how important fragments of writing will be retrieved, collated and eventually integrated into the main writing-up process. Think also about the difference between annotation tools (discussed below) and memos in your chosen software. Always be systematic about the management of memos. Though rather different in scale than the challenges of retrieving the right bits of data to exemplify important arguments (via coding or linking), insightful analytic thoughts logged in memos can be as difficult to collate at the appropriate moments. Software packages which 'list' memos as objects in their own right (e.g. ATLAS.ti, MAXQDA and NVivo) are more easily organised.

Ideas for naming memos effectively

Good naming protocols will allow you to track down the important notes you have made. Linking devices associated with memos may help to connect writing to important other entities, segments of data, codes, documents, other memos, etc., thereby providing ongoing reminders of important notes and connections in your thinking. Freestanding memos can usually be named. As an early task, create your own protocols for naming things. For instance, make titles revealing about the subject matter contained within them. You may additionally categorise memos by a system of prefixing. Some ideas:

- All memos containing summaries of individual respondents could be prefixed by PROFILE-...
- All theoretical memos could prefixed by TH-...
- All procedural memos prefixed by Log-...
- All memos about data collection or conduct of focus groups or interviews DC-...
- All team memos, prefixed by TeamA-..., TeamB-..., etc.

Memos – like anything else – can be renamed, so if you start working in a slightly disorganised way a system can be imposed later as you realise that the volume of your writing makes it difficult to recover valuable thinking moments! You can thus begin feeling in control of where you are going without predetermining what you might discover. Inevitably it is almost impossible to be sure that your notes are going in the right place; as you write something in one memo you think of another memo that the same note should go in. Your memo system will never be perfect so, paradoxically, the need to cater for complexity means that the mantra 'keep things simple' with regard to memos, their number and organisation, will help you find detailed work later.

Overt reflections and reflexivity: thinking out loud; telling the story

Generating a constant reflective log of ideas and dilemmas creates a resource which improves transparency for its own sake, thus contributing to validity. Keep in mind the potential to produce a methods paper explaining the nitty-gritty processes of analysis using software. While substantive findings of research usually take priority in terms of outputs, keeping track of the progression of decision making and actions is valuable in recalling the subtle evolution of analysis. Each project and each researcher is different. The true nature of the dilemmas, turning points and eureka moments are often lost in the drive to produce findings, yet it is how all these things fit together in the narrative of analysis that might provide the colourful and revealing 'documentary' of the process for each project. One of the many useful aspects about recording the conversations you have (with yourself or others) is that the detail, whether or not it became useful, is not lost. Apparently low-level decision making in terms of analysis suddenly gains more importance when putting together a commentary about the nuts and bolts of processes (Box 5.6).

BOX 5.6 | CASE NOTES

Tracking the processes of analysis in a project process journal (Case Study A, Young People's Perceptions)

In Case Study A there was initial uncertainty concerning where to write down thoughts about each respondent: whether to keep notes about interview, vignette and photo-prompt data derived from each respondent separate, or bring all writing about each respondent together. This is an extract from the process journal:

Originally wanted to keep the three separate – in case different types of coding and different treatment of them was necessary. Now I think incorporate the three elements in one memo for each person – but keep the commentaries quite separate within each memo. This way we can quickly collect all the writing done about the vignettes into one memo about 'all vignettes' if needed – yet will also be able to get a whole sense of the person from the one memo.

Memos attached to other entities

Some locations for writing notes depend on other entities being in place. For instance, data-level work in the form of *annotations* anchored to data segments enables much work to be done close to the data (Chapter 6). These tools suit most methodological approaches and offer possible departures from, or supplements to, code-based strategies. It is worth investigating such devices to evaluate their fit with your analytic needs and also to consider how they can be useful in practical terms. Some packages only have memo devices which depend on other entities (e.g. Transana, QDA Miner), and so these act like annotations anyway. The issue of where to write and how to hang on to subtle ideas prompted by passages or clips of data is not trivial. Some methods, such as interpretive phenomenological analysis, are heavily dependent on note-making in the right places. Using software means that you can not only link writing to points in data, but also retrieve it on that basis. This type of note-making is illustrated in MAXQDA and ATLAS.ti at Figure 5.5; these two packages

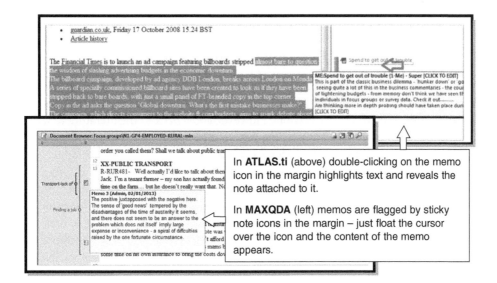

In **ATLAS.ti** (above) double-clicking on the memo icon in the margin highlights text and reveals the note attached to it.

In **MAXQDA** (left) memos are flagged by sticky note icons in the margin – just float the cursor over the icon and the content of the memo appears.

FIGURE 5.5 Interactivity of memos/annotations at text level (ATLAS.ti and MAXQDA)

are particularly effective in their layout and level of interactivity with the data with respect to annotations.

Standalone memos – as project management devices

It is impossible to over-emphasise the value of memos. They can operate in a relatively simple way and still be valuable. Whatever your methodology, the cycling between familiarising, rereading and making notes about data will be indispensable. Since software enhances the contact between data and notes, it is important to optimise the different benefits of memo tools. The logic of functioning of some packages (e.g. NVivo) is such that memos have the same status as other project materials (e.g. data files) and thus can be treated like primary data. Other packages (e.g. ATLAS.ti and MAXQDA) provide easy ways to convert memos into data files and thus treat them in this way. Independently existing memos therefore have a life of their own and can be worked on before data are imported or even collected. This might be particularly important where the processes of working on a literature review (see below) precede the collection of data, as in Case Study A. The production of multiple memos to chart existing contributions in your chosen field of study might be the end in itself for your work in software. If you chose later to add primary data to the same software project you then remain closely connected to key concepts, questions and issues addressed by existing literature. Whatever the particular memo functionality of your chosen software, realise that your own writing is a valuable source of material that can be integrated with other work in various ways. Experiment, therefore, with the options and think about their potential implications for your analytic needs and preferred style of working.

Scoping the topic area and critiquing the literature

A systematic review of relevant literature is part of the process of refining the research topic and generating research questions. However, going back to the literature to reflect anew in light of your data and finding new useful references is likely to continue throughout analysis. While CAQDAS packages are not designed as bibliographic tools, there are elements which they have in common. The disadvantages of using CAQDAS packages as the only means of 'managing' bibliographic support in a research project are that the sorting, exporting and formatting of bibliographic material according to various conventions for publication are just not there. However, there are several ways in which they can be used to facilitate a literature review. Material generated and organised in bibliographic software can be integrated in some form or other inside a CAQDAS project to improve the cross-referencing and continuing awareness of the literature's contribution to your subject area (Figure 5.6; p. 128 and Box 5.7; p. 127).

Ways of integrating literature with your work

- Exported bibliographies (essentially lists) from any package such as Endnote, RefWorks or Zotero can be imported into a CAQDAS project, in the same way as primary data. They can be annotated and written about in memos created for the purpose.
- Downloaded PDFs of full-text articles, conference papers, seminal works, etc. can be incorporated into the software project as full 'data' files in most CAQDAS packages. They can then be treated just like any other source material.
- Spaces for generating your own notes about the literature (whether as freestanding memos or full-ranking data sources) enable you to summarise and critique literature within the software. These 'critical appraisals' can sometimes be linked to the source literature (where they exist electronically and you have them saved on your computer). Where this is not possible or relevant, you can always reference source literature via the use of consistent naming protocols. The creation of individual appraisals about the important contributions might house your discussion of topics such as:

  o Epistemological and ontological underpinnings of the discipline/subject area
  o Definitions and origins of work, key concepts and theories
  o Main debates and issues raised by literature
  o How knowledge of your subject is structured
  o Political standpoints taken on the subject (adapted from Hart, 1998).

Exports from customised literature management tools

Most bibliographic software packages enable various exports which can then be integrated at some level into a CAQDAS project. These include:

- A report which very quickly collates the contents of a library or collection into a list
- A bibliography – a list of references in your chosen citation style (American Psychological Association, Harvard, etc.)
- A collection or library export – an **RIS** file containing all the information laid out in a systematic way that can act as an exchange file between other applications.

Many CAQDAS packages can be used creatively to manage one or several of these exports. Even where there are no explicit functions for integrating literature, work-arounds can easily be devised. An illustration of how a 'report' from Zotero has been handled in ATLAS.ti shows the use of methodological and substantive codes in Figure 5.6. When the code 'Vulnerability of weakest' is retrieved later, reminders of both primary data and where you have identified literature in the same context, will be seen. The illustration of MAXQDA at the top of Figure 7.1 shows a coded critical appraisal of a literature file.

In **ATLAS.ti** (above) a 'report' of literature references generated in Zotero has been imported (any similar bibliographic software will do). Memos and codes based on substantive and methodological themes have been assigned directly to it (see Figure 7.1; p. 159 for similar illustration in **MAXQDA**).

In **NVivo** (below) there is a special import function for RIS files exported from most bibliographic software. This import creates 'proxy' *external sources* for each reference and imports the metadata about the references as Source Classifications (lower section). An XML export/import from EndNote will also bring in any full-text PDFs attached to the references.

Figure 5.6 Integrating literature (ATLAS.ti and NVivo)

Some packages have explicit tools oriented to managing literature in more sophisticated ways. They have different ways of doing so. QDA Miner, for instance, can initiate a whole project from an RIS file which then forms the structure of further work. This can include the creation of critical appraisals of key works and the importation of the relevant PDFs to link with the references. Metadata about each reference is added, although you can select which to include. NVivo supports the importation of similar libraries but additionally creates empty writing spaces in the Externals folder, for each reference listed in the RIS file. Using the XML export from EndNote (instead of the RIS file) enables the simultaneous import into NVivo of the full-text PDFs attached to a library or collection in the bibliographic software. What distinguishes the options in QDA Miner and NVivo from other CAQDAS packages is that the import process provides customised support for integrating metadata (author, date, publication, type of publication, ISBN, etc.) into existing variable/attributes. However, it might be sufficient to do without all that information within the CAQDAS package (you have it in the bibliographic resource after all). Much of it is anyway superfluous to your needs when doing a literature review. You can achieve a good degree of integration in many software packages whether or not a specific function is available. Figure 5.2 provides a glimpse of a proxy External file in NVivo created to gather summaries of important sections of the Denzin and Lincoln (2002) edited essays on qualitative research methodologies. This involved no import at all. It is up to you to create a system which works for your needs.

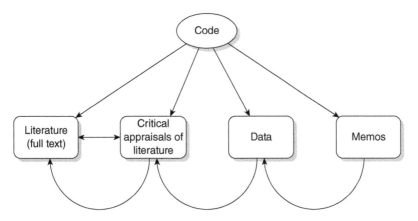

Figure 5.7 The potential of codes as collection devices for tracking ideas from literature through a study

Optimising tools for literature management

Experiment with the exchange of data. Results vary according to the type of export available from the bibliographic package as well as the import enabled into the CAQDAS package. There are associated dilemmas. You have to evolve personal systems to deal with these which will differ depending on the tools within each package. Even those that customise more support for literature management do not resolve all the issues (Box 5.8).

BOX 5.8 FUNCTIONALITY NOTES

Benefits and associated pitfalls of working with literature in CAQDAS packages

Overall, there may be varied ability to integrate between bibliographic software and CAQDAS:

- Having imported bibliographic data, there is no dynamic connection between further work in the bibliographic tool and what you do in the CAQDAS program. You need to evolve personal systems for later updating work in the CAQDAS program as you do more in the bibliographic software.

Overall, you can integrate full-text literature files, e.g. in PDF, and search, annotate or code them:

- This may foster a tendency to place more emphasis on working with 'available' literature while neglecting off-line but key resources. This will negatively impact on the consistency of the synthesis of work in your research area.

(Continued)

(Continued)

In particular, you can text-mine or search the full-text PDFs:

- Because you cannot search papers, books, etc. for which you do not have full text integrated into the CAQDAS project, important work might be marginalised.
- An over-reliance on the frequency of 'mentions' will miss nuanced content and the need to make notes as you read.

Customised tools in software bring in all category and information elements of references (date, author, journal, volume, etc):

- There may be just too much of this metadata.
- More complication can mean more cleaning up when, for example, duplications occur or when updated work is ported between bibliographic software and CAQDAS.

'Less might be more' when managing literature since it is less important to be concerned about the effectiveness of the technology and more important to concentrate on the quality of the review. You might decide to take less meta-information into the CAQDAS package, especially if you have the choice or if you are adapting other tools to integrate literature. With customised tools, especially while getting used to processes, import small but important collections. Examine the import dialogue boxes carefully to make sure you are not importing redundant or duplicated information. Try to be discriminating about the selection of PDFs to be included. You will thus stay in control as you design an efficient system for managing the review process. It probably is not helpful to import hundreds of full-text PDFs straight away and imagine that you will be able to treat them all equally. You may already be developing ways not mentioned here to integrate these different elements of the research process. More and more researchers are attempting to use CAQDAS, looking for ways to improve the process and the end results of literature reviews. Hart (1998) discusses the variable quality of literature reviews, implying that some are little more than 'thinly disguised annotated bibliographies' and that 'quality means appropriate breadth and depth, rigour and consistency, clarity and brevity, and effective analysis and synthesis'. Do not fall into that trap by being seduced by the ease with which some packages allow large bibliographic libraries and associated literature files to be imported. It is important to be discriminating.

Finally, be sure in your own mind why you are integrating literature. If you are simply seeking to improve cross-referencing between substantive analysis and work done by others in the field, a more minimal approach could be taken and the annotation, linking and coding of a reference list (as complete as possible) or numbers of lists will be of great help.

Concluding remarks: groundwork for efficient analysis

Whatever your methodological approach, there are simple steps you can take to manage your software workspace efficiently from the outset. This chapter has been about some of those steps. The process of understanding why you might do certain things, familiarising yourself with creating structures to contain different types of material, putting up metaphorical and physical signposts in the project and providing spaces to write, will increase your confidence in the flexibility and 'safe-keeping' of your work. The next chapter takes this a bit further, suggesting that working at data level is valuable at various moments.

EXERCISES: GETTING STARTED

The following exercises are designed to help you set up your software project to create a logical structural framework which represents your research design. In your own work, these tasks can be started as soon as you have decided upon which CAQDAS package to use, even before you have collected primary and/or secondary data for analysis. See the companion website for step-by-step instructions, and to download the data files. If you prefer to use your own data to experiment with, you will be able to follow the relevant exercises below together with the website instructions within your chosen software package. Remember, you need not necessarily do these tasks in the order we present them here. In any case, depending on the software you are experimenting with, not all exercises are relevant or enabled.

1. Install the software you have decided to experiment with.

    (a) The trial version will be sufficient for the purposes of the exercises, although you should note the restrictions as these differ according to package.
    (b) There are links on the companion website to the software websites where you can access trial versions or purchase software.
    (c) Check whether your institution has a site licence for the package you wish to use. If they do you may be able to get free access to it.

2. Create a project in your chosen software and save it somewhere sensible.

    (a) Notice while you are doing this where the software suggests saving.
    (b) Become aware how much space you have allocated in the default saving location. If you are a student working on an institutional server this is sometimes restricted and can be a reason for things going wrong later. Software project files can grow to be quite large. Decide if the default location works for you – if not, choose to save it somewhere else.

3. Create the empty structural framework within which to start working.

    (a) This could reflect the project research design in terms of data collection, sampling and factual characteristics of data/respondents (Chapter 12), research questions, any theoretical framework or model (Chapter 11) that guides work.
    (b) If relevant to the software create simple folder structures to house different types of source data, e.g. interviews, field notes.

4. Think about the key aspects of the project you will need to keep notes about.

   (a) Create a research process journal to keep notes about your procedures.
   (b) Create a memo for each research question.
   (c) Consider whether you will summarise each respondent (or other entity or analytic unit) at a corresponding memo. Create a memo each for the first few cases or interviews you will analyse.
   (d) Create a memo for any other analytic or theoretical aspects you envisage will be written about later on – each memo can remain empty until you are ready to add ideas and insights.

5. If it is relevant for you, begin generating critical appraisals of key literature files.

   (a) Consider using memos or new documents to create spaces to do this.
   (b) Experiment with textual formatting functionality such as colour, bold, italic, etc. to visually structure your writing and to emphasise important types of writing.

6. Experiment with backing up and moving your software project.

   (a) This will include coming up with a systematic protocol for naming back-ups so you can easily see when they were created chronologically, but also at what analytic stage.
   (b) If you will regularly need to work on more than one computer, becoming confident with moving the software project file and any of its associated data files around will be very important.

7. Experiment with creating and defining codes (see specific exercises in Chapter 7).
8. Import data files into your new software project.

   (a) Perhaps you have created folders in the software project that you can import into. If not, you can rearrange files at any time.
   (b) If folders are not enabled or relevant in the software, remember that good naming of your primary data files will help to keep them organised and identified within a list.
   (c) Use short, informative codified labels for each data file. If working in a team, remember to include a team or site identifier in the file name (see Chapter 4).
   (d) The data files imported into your project will be copies of the originals, and any changes you make inside the software project do not affect the originals and vice versa.

9. Getting started with video/sound files (see also Chapter 6).

   (a) Read any software-specific step-by-step information on companion websites – important since functionality varies.
   (b) Experiment with varying relevant options on one multimedia file (not all available in each software) including:
      (i) Importing video files first.
      (ii) Creating new empty files to create and associate full transcripts with/alongside video in the software project.
      (iii) As above, but transcribing partially, only where content or interaction is identified as analytically significant.
      (iv) Importing ready-made transcripts then associating with video files manually.
      (v) Using specific transcription software – importing both transcript and video/sound files together to synchronise association between the two 'automatically'.

10. Organising data using other devices. Depending on the software and your familiarity, you might also create (or import from other applications) a framework of attributes and values concerning, for example, descriptive or socio-demographic information about your data files. If this is not done now it does not matter. All such work can be accomplished later (see Chapter 12 – these procedures vary significantly).

6

Exploration and Data-level Work

This chapter discusses working at data level in order to help you situate your analytic work. Within our model (Figure 2.1; p. 45), exploration covers many of the tasks discussed here, including marking and annotating, searching content (for words and phrases), and linking between points in data. We discuss searching for structure and auto-coding on that basis, aspects of exploration, in Chapters 4 and 12. Linking materials and ideas about them is illustrated as an aspect of organisation in the model, but similarly contributes to the processes of exploration and data-level work that we discuss in this chapter. The ordering of our discussion about analytic activities and software tools does not imply any linearity, sequencing or process that *has* to be followed. We are not prescribing what you should do, merely suggesting what you might do. We stay clear of coding tasks in this chapter (these are discussed in detail in Chapter 7). However, we suggest that you can, at times, use coding functionality just to mark interesting data in a relatively *non-committal* way.

This is one of the most important chapters of the book, since the use of software itself can tend to conventionalise data and expectations and assumptions about conducting analysis. We encourage independent application, critical and flexible use of tools. Our aim is to raise an awareness of options for working at the data level and the uses to which tools can be put, particularly at an early stage of work, but also as you continue with analysis. The tools we discuss here have relevance to a broad range of data types, research designs and analytic strategies. Their appropriateness to your particular needs is for you to judge; experiment to design an efficient and effective way of using them, or dismiss them – being fully aware of why.

The possibilities discussed in this chapter do not represent a discrete *stage* of analysis, nor are they specific to any methodological approach. We contextualise them with our Case Studies. In each example different varieties of code-based approaches (Chapter 1) are used. However, multiple phases of analysis (see Table 2.1; p. 39) and parts of the datasets benefit from data-level working for different purposes. Coding implies a movement away from data (Chapter 7). Whatever your approach, the tools we refer to in this chapter have the potential to keep you within touching distance of the fundamentals of information and data throughout analysis, embedding your handling and thinking at the data level (Chapter 1). Some tools provide quick ways of exploring and marking text, and perhaps (auto-)coding as a result; others facilitate slower and more careful consideration of small data segments. Tables 6.1, 6.2 and 6.3 provide some suggestions for exploration and data-level work in the three case-study examples.

Early exploration of data

The process of becoming aware of what is interesting and significant in the materials you generate starts during the first moments of any study. Reflection happens during and after data gathering, and continuously throughout analysis (Chapter 10). Some of the practicalities and processes of collecting and processing data will vary

Table 6.1 Exploration and data-level work: some suggestions in the context of case study A, Young People's Perceptions

---

Tasks from PHASE TWO: Review of the literature and identification of theoretical focus

Familiarise with literature articles	• Familiarise with literature through content-based searching (no resultant coding)
	    ○ Mark interesting passages
	    ○ Identify areas of theoretical interest
	• Read each article in depth
	    ○ Annotate in relation to research questions

Generate and organise critical appraisals	• Generate a critical appraisal of each literature file ○ Use colour and other formatting devices to structure your writing systematically • Link significant passages in articles with corresponding comments in critical appraisals • Output annotated articles and associated memos • Generate lists of possible codes in relation to theoretical focus

---

Tasks from PHASE THREE: First wave coding – deductive, broad-brush coding across the data set

Read through and content-based familiarisation	• Read through each primary data file, focusing on developing an understanding of the personality and opinions of each individual respondent • Mark passages that resonate or challenge areas of analytic focus as embodied in the initial coding scheme
Content-based searching for keywords and phrases	• Use word frequency tools to gain a broad overview of the frequency with which individual keywords occur ○ Summarise your early impressions about each respondent in a memo, reflecting on their use of language as well as their experiences and opinions (chapter 10)
Deductive coding of primary data (see also chapter 7)	• Use text searching tools to locate specific terms identified in the literature as relating to theoretical focus ○ Code contextual passages around each occurrence of keywords and phrases

---

according to the media used (Chapter 4). Once they are incorporated into the software project, however, you will begin the more systematic and structured processes of exploring research materials for specific analytic ends. This might initially take the form of unstructured familiarisation, leading on to more focused and analytic exploration.

Familiarisation during early handling

The use of software provides different options for whether, how and when to transcribe digital audio/video files (Chapters 4 and 7). Raw data come in different forms, including audio recordings of interview or focus-group discussions, videos of naturally occurring interactions, open-ended responses to surveys, and internet-harvested multimedia content. You might decide to view, explore and think about audiovisual data 'directly', perhaps as a means of deciding whether and how to transcribe. You can do this in a standard media player, but the annotation devices provided by CAQDAS packages offer more options for capturing your thinking whilst doing so. However you start off, it is still quite customary to transcribe in some form, certainly when working with primary data generated specifically for the purposes of research. Working directly with multimedia, there are fewer intervening 'handling' processes. The fact that it is possible to code audio and video files directly can make it tempting to side-step the labour-intensive processes of transcription. However, transcription may form part of the overall process of exploration and reflection, and usually this is in itself an important phase of analysis. One of the advantages of text is that as summaries or transcripts develop, your access to the raw data improves; as the files are incorporated within a CAQDAS package, access continues to improve. Now you need only open a single file (the CAQDAS project file) to have immediate access to all data or any individual source. Everything waits to be navigated, explored, thought about, searched and annotated.

We differentiate between direct and indirect analysis of multimedia data (Chapters 2 and 7). Where media files are analysed directly, contact with them is in real time. There may have been little 'handling' prior to their import into the software project, in which case watching or listening to them once incorporated into your chosen CAQDAS package will constitute an important initial familiarisation process. Particularly relevant here are annotation tools since there is usually no ability to mark or change multimedia data from within the CAQDAS packages (they are not editing tools[1]). The slowness of real-time playback means that each opportunity to annotate (and code if relevant) must be taken advantage of 'in the moment'. Putting off linking a thought to the relevant clip may mean it never happens and thus the idea and the subtle visualised moment are lost. In ATLAS. ti and Transana, the ability to mark quotes or clips for later playback and attention

---

[1]Note that you can export clips from Transana as new media files.

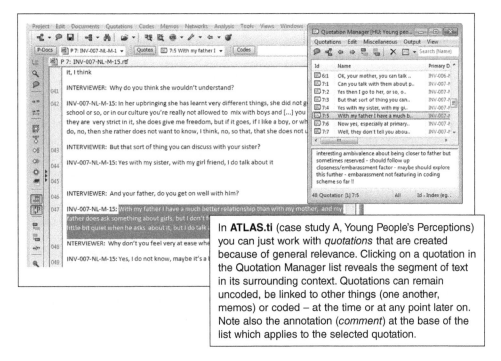

Figure 6.1   Data reduction: list of 'quotations' created for later attention (ATLAS.ti)

(without the extra task of coding) is a particularly quick and easily performed action (see Figures 6.2; p. 142, 7.5; p. 178 and 7.6; p. 179). ATLAS.ti provides the additional option to hyperlink those quotes together to record the nature of an association (see below). Transana also allows 'snapshotting' of video data to create stills which can be visually annotated (Figures 6.3; p. 144 and 7.6; p. 179).

Marking data for relevance and significance

Studies involving interaction with respondents (interviews, observations, group discussions, etc.) always benefit from a read-through or viewing of data files in their entirety as an initial step. This facilitates gaining an overview of the content and processes inherent in the session and the main respondents/actors involved. A read-, watch- or listen-through may be advisable anyway before entering into more detailed reflection of what is going on since an overall picture may helpfully qualify how you interpret detailed statements or actions. The 'big picture' is always relevant to your consideration of the detailed nuances. Part of this process could include marking individual data segments for relevance or particular attention. Most packages that we reference allow the use of editing tools to highlight, colour or underline textual data segments. If the software you are using does not have an editing facility you can use annotation tools instead (see below).

Literature familiarisation as means of focusing subsequent analytic work (Case Study A, Young People's Perceptions)

In Case Study A, early work in software involved detailed reading of literature and the development of critical appraisals (Chapter 5). This contributed to the formulation of the research problem, the framing of the research questions and the development of the initial coding frame, designed in the lead-up to handling the primary data. Once primary data were imported – and before coding commenced – reading through transcripts began to throw up nuanced ideas about the role of certain types of talk which were not yet included in the coding frame. In relation to the interview transcripts, this included identifying what appeared important discussion about family dynamics, early awareness about sex(uality) and the importance of informal modes of learning. It was useful to mark data segments which threw up unexpected ideas that needed further attention. When engaging in depth with data for the first time you are often struck by something, but are not always sure why, or what to do with it. The ability to mark data segments in CAQDAS packages offers a way of remembering that something seems significant, without letting your concerns about why distract you from getting on with the task at hand. Doing so enabled us to later consider the importance of those ideas, to build them into the coding frame, and ensure we later considered their relevance across other forms of data.

Simple data reduction devices and workarounds

Qualitative analysis is sometimes described in terms of data reduction (Miles and Huberman, 1994). There are many ways this can happen in CAQDAS packages. Coding (Chapter 7) is usually seen as the core process although other software tools also provide alternative means. Organising your ideas about data is the essence of analytic work whatever your methodology; coding, linking and writing (transcribing, annotating, memoing, summarising) are amongst the tools at your disposal to do so in software (Figure 2.1; p. 45). All CAQDAS packages have well-developed, sophisticated and flexible coding tools, but the architecture of some packages lends itself more readily to data-level work. We highlight the quotation architecture of ATLAS. ti in this respect (Box 6.2; p. 139 and Figure 6.1; p. 137).

In any software, at the most basic level, you could simply reduce data down to what immediately strikes you as relevant by applying a code such as 'Relevant' or 'Interesting' to segments that seem pertinent in some sense (Figure 9.3; p. 212). Even if your analytic approach does not include a code-based process, such a simple indexing action will enable you to pull out just those 'relevant' or 'interesting' data segments for further attention. The colour highlighting of coded data segments in Dedoose and MAXQDA provides good visualisation and functionality for this type of initial work. The result provides visual highlighting quicker than you could achieve through simple editing, but also enables you subsequently to focus in on just the data segments marked for this particular reason. Such highlighting is not just a visual marker, but, by virtue of being coded, is retrievable. Open up your mind to the idea of using software coding tools for purposes outside of customary, methodological ways of thinking of 'coding'. Even where your chosen software does not do colour highlighting on the basis of coding, coding tools can be used for these exploratory purposes since a margin display of such simplistic codes will be useful because they point to relevance.

BOX 6.2 — FUNCTIONALITY NOTES

Software architecture and flexible working at data level

ATLAS.ti has its own distinct architecture, developed around the notion that you start work at data level and work towards more abstract ideas – progressively coding, linking ideas and testing relationships to build up an analysis. Quotations (sometimes referred to as 'quotes') can be created but remain unassociated with codes (until and unless you are ready to associate them). Quotations have their own listing and are thus independent 'objects' in their own right. They thus have equal status in the project with other objects, such as data files (documents), codes, memos and networks. Selecting a quotation immediately opens the source data file it exists within and highlights the passage in its surrounding context (Figure 6.1; p. 137). Each quote can be annotated with a comment to enrich work at data level. These notes are retrievable from multiple places, reminding you of insights, whenever those quotes are viewed or exported. Later we talk about hyperlinking – and any number of 'quotes' in ATLAS.ti can be hyperlinked together to form clickable paths through the data (Figure 11.2; p. 265).

You might feel it is yet too early to determine what is 'relevant'. This is a justifiable argument, pointing to the need to use such tools appropriately and flexibly. Working in this way is just an option. No data are lost. It is just one example of a creative use of software tools in simple and timely ways to help manage a bulky dataset. You will develop your own ideas on adapting tools for your specified analytic needs. The same devices are designed for use during the more thoughtful coding processes, whether working inductively, deductively or abductively (Chapter 7).

Annotation tools – their universal utility

Annotation involves applying a note or comment to segments of material. Software enables this in various ways, although programs do not always call them 'annotations'. They may simply be called 'comments', 'notes' or 'memos' (Figures 6.1; p. 137 and 5.5; p. 125). Such tools can be useful when managing any mass of qualitative information, to record spontaneous thinking processes and maintain connection to the material that instigated the thoughts. Insights might be prompted by the read-through or indeed searching for content (see below).

Note-taking is a routine necessity in all types of research and approaches to analysis (Chapters 2 and 10). Other functions such as coding, text searching, auto-coding and modelling may be well used to facilitate particular approaches, but the annotation of data, documents and supporting material is indivisible from analytic tasks and, often, the general management of information within wider areas of work. To that end, we see uses of CAQDAS packages, and in particular annotation tools, for *any* type of research or day-to-day work which generates or collects *any* textual or multimedia material that would benefit from being stored in one manageable project file.

A crucial element of managing analysis is the development of a transparent audit trail comprising a log of all the processes followed, describing the small analytic leaps contributing to the analysis as a whole (Chapter 10). Whether these notes become annotations anchored to data segments, new parallel files or memos, the benefits come in exploiting the interactive links from notes to the passages and clips of data to which they refer.

Any researcher from any disciplinary background can make use of the potential of CAQDAS. The management of any collection of essays, abstracts, notes, lists, articles, etc. would be enhanced by the ability to search for key words or phrases across a number of files. Seale (2000), for instance, describes his use of NUD*IST (predecessor to NVivo) to manage book writing by supporting the process of collating and searching his notes and accumulated records on literature. The addition of annotation tools in NVivo means that notes are interactively linked with data within the software project and print out as numbered endnotes in an exported electronic or hard-copy report. You can use most CAQDAS packages like this. You just need to be clear about what you need to achieve, know what tools are available and then adapt them to your own needs. Some software packages have developed interactivity between writing tools and other functions to a greater extent. Therefore, if annotation is at least as important as coding within your methodology, experiment with these tools in trial software versions in order to assess whether they will work for you. Subtle differences in software functionality in this regard can have quite significant analytic implications.

Using Case Study A, Young People's Perceptions, as an example, we discuss ways of doing a literature review using CAQDAS packages (Chapter 5). The suggested analytic process for this example (Table 2.1; p. 39), as we discuss it in this book, is theory-driven and the coding scheme originates to a large degree from the literature (Chapter 2). Working like this, developing critical appraisals of key works within the software project will be central to your formulation of the research problem and the development of the research questions as well as your thinking about and representation of theoretical frameworks which guide your analysis. All of this informs the ongoing decisions you make about a coding frame. In searching and reading literature – if you have full-text sources integrated into the software project – the use of annotation and other tools will be similar to their use with primary data. They will assist in the building of ideas towards each critical appraisal. If you are using a CAQDAS package to manage the entire literature review, it is up to you whether to keep this work in a separate project from the substantive data or to integrate them (Chapters 5

Table 6.2 Exploration and data-level work: some suggestions in the context of case study B, The Financial Downturn

Tasks from PHASE THREE: Media familiarisation and deductive analysis of survey data & PHASE FIVE: Deductive analysis of media content	

Read through and content-based familiarisation	• Familiarise with media content and survey data using content-based searches
	
	   ○ Focus on the identification of trends references to lifestyle choices and the literature more broadly (sensitising concepts)
	   ○ Consider the role of word frequency counts in contributing to your understandings
	   ○ Consider the contexts within which terms are used and the way opinions are expressed
	
	• Link passages in media content which explicitly relate to or build upon one another
	• Link passages in survey responses where respondents make contradictory statements
	• Annotate significance of what is seen
	
	   ○ E.g. how language use evokes opinion etc.
	
	• Prioritise keywords and phrases that would be useful basis for coding
	
	   ○ Write about why in memos
	
	• Code contextual passages according to key terms and phrases

Tasks from Phase FOUR: Inductive analysis of focus-group data	
Read through and content-based familiarisation	• Use word frequency and text searches to ○ check context within which topics identified as important in phase 3 are discussed in focus groups; to throw up possible areas for inductive coding • Make list of possible codes, definitions and potential uses (see chapter 7) • Read through focus-group transcripts and make notes about each general discussion • Mark or annotate text for further attention

and 10). The decision may have something to do with when the literature review gets done; is it going on in parallel with the analysis of primary data – or, as in Case Study A – is the literature review mostly achieved prior to further work? If they are integrated in one project then all the notes about both forms of material are together and the potential for tracking literature through the study is increased (Figure 5.7; p. 129), but your project will be bigger and needs careful managing.

It is useful to distinguish between a 'full' literature review and the need to cross-reference. At a simple level, annotation in the form of adding comments to a simple list of references could be the means of registering the significance of key volumes. A partial list of references, or indeed a series of lists, may together represent a more complete compilation of relevant literature. You could use CAQDAS annotation tools to make notes about the relevance or content of references, or edit the lists to create annotated bibliographies. This would work well where you do not have all the relevant literature as full-text PDF files within – or accessible from – the project, ensuring nothing of significance is entirely left out. Such minimal use of annotations of reference lists (in terms of what other functions are enabled for literature) works as one way of incorporating and cross-referencing literature with substantive work. If such annotations were then to be hyperlinked (see below) to more central analytic writing locations (embodied perhaps in memos) or later coded to substantive or methodological codes, then the cross-referencing between substantive work and literature is further improved. A similar idea is illustrated in Figure 5.6.

Multimedia data: annotations and data reduction

We briefly discussed the direct and indirect handling of multimedia in Chapters 2 and 4. In Chapters 7 and 8 this comes up again with respect to direct application of codes to pictures, sound and video files. Notes can be attached directly to whole multimedia files, or parts of them, selected areas of a picture, selected clips of sound or video files, or indirectly to the associated transcript. Clicking on the note may display or play back the relevant part of the multimedia file. This functionality varies since there may be several different writing spaces within a package that can be used for the purposes of annotation. Where this is the case you need to devise a rationale for how you use them (bearing in mind that you need not use them all) and be systematic in doing so (Chapter 10). Some are displayed as interactive icons or footnotes sitting close to the data; their content may not be fully revealed until you click on them. Other tactics might be to create notes (or a full transcript) in a synchronised, parallel file which can then, in turn, be annotated

In **Transana** (case study C, Coca-Cola Commercials) three transcripts are synchronised with one video. Two of them contain 'snapshots', i.e. stills taken from the video to add context to the transcripts. Transcripts can be exported with snapshots embedded. One of these transcripts (centre) contains text and snapshots.

In **NVivo** the transcript can be created alongside the video and will be synchronised if created in the right 'transcript mode' (via the *Timespan* column). You can also create 'annotations' either linked to selections/clips of video *directly*, or *indirectly* via the transcript.

Figure 6.2 Textual annotation of video (Transana and NVivo)

(and/or coded). It is advisable to experiment with the different methods in your chosen software and use what suits your needs with respect to reconnecting with contextual thoughts as the video or sound file is playing. In Transana, the creation of the parallel transcript is the necessary step to enable further work since codes are applied to the media via the transcript (Figure 6.2).

In NVivo we illustrate a similar way of working (Figure 6.2). Each multimedia file can have a parallel file associated with it (although it need not). Where transcripts are generated, they are represented in adjacent tabular format. When in the correct 'transcript' mode you can directly make notes against selected areas or clips (represented as rows). With still images, the display is similar. There might be many purposes and uses for working in this way, including generating a narrative about each source. The adjacent display is useful, and each row of notes is interactively connected to the relevant coordinates in the picture (or clip in an audiovisual file). Most packages that handle visual material can be used in this sort of way.

There is yet another way in which annotation of multimedia data can be initiated. MAXQDA and ATLAS.ti have close links to the transcription software F4. When a transcript, having been generated in F4, is imported, the accompanying media file is also imported and will become automatically synchronised with the transcript. HyperRESEARCH has its own transcription partner software, HyperTRANSCRIBE. Such tools beg the very important question: when is transcription appropriate? We raised this issue in Chapters 4 and 5. Several factors determine this, not least what you want to get out of the data, whether you need to be able to search the text in the transcript, as well as research design, analytic strategy and ethical considerations (Box 6.3). We touch on these issues further in Chapters 4, 5 and 7.

| BOX 6.3 | ANALYTIC NOTES |

Debating the need for transcripts of video data

In designing the analytic strategy for Case Study C, Coca-Cola Commercials, we debated the various ways to handle video. As may be the case with many other visual projects, our analytic needs did not seem to fit the development of a 'transcript' in the way these are typically understood. Indeed, the very nature of the commercials renders the development of 'verbatim' transcripts, in the customary sense, redundant. There is no 'speech' or 'interaction' present akin to what might be seen if video had been shot of a naturally occurring event (e.g. a classroom interaction or patient–doctor consultation). In deciding how to proceed, we took a balanced view, taking into consideration the needs of our broad 'theory-building inductive' approach (Chapter 2), the nature of the raw data (short commercials developed for the purposes of advertising), the analytic strategy we were adopting and the availability and flexibility of various tools within the different software packages (we principally illustrate Case Study C in the book using Transana, ATLAS.ti, MAXQDA and NVivo). As such we developed the specific detailed plan as a result of a trialectic between data, methodology and technology.

(Continued)

(Continued)

One reason for working directly relates to the essential power of visual data. Some commercials contain limited or no voiceover; thus the visual stimuli are prioritised. This can be difficult to translate well in a transcript, given that non-verbal action within them is quite different from what is typically captured by established protocols for transcribing interactions for research purposes. In fact, in these commercials it is often the soundtracks that are particularly evocative. From an advertising perspective this is well evidenced in the fact that the 1994 'Diet Coke Break' advert and the 2013 'remake', the 'Gardener', use the same soundtrack, thereby utilising nostalgia to evoke memories of the iconic earlier commercial amongst a particular demographic of potential customers. The use of evocative tunes or jingles is a characteristic of the advertising branding of Coca-Cola. The power of sound is reflected in the fact that at least one of the songs used became a popular standard: 'I'd Like to Teach the World to Sing' by The New Seekers and The Hillside Singers actually started off as 'I'd Like to Buy the World a Coke" in 1971.

However, as soon as you are interested in the content of what is going on in visual material as well as non-verbal interactions, some form of transcript becomes useful. This is not just because the act of deciding what and how to transcribe is a form of analysis, but also because words are searchable and therefore generating even a simple log or summary of visual content has benefits for the quick navigation to parts of a visual record that are of interest. In addition, the ability to organise videos, to locate and access them easily is infinitely enhanced by what you can do directly to the video: the ability to go through a data reduction process to improve access to just the relevant clips, to annotate the clips and reconnect with all your insights.

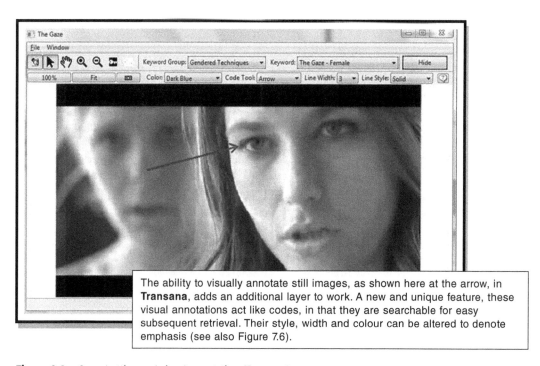

The ability to visually annotate still images, as shown here at the arrow, in **Transana**, adds an additional layer to work. A new and unique feature, these visual annotations act like codes, in that they are searchable for easy subsequent retrieval. Their style, width and colour can be altered to denote emphasis (see also Figure 7.6).

Figure 6.3   Snapshotting and visual annotation (Transana)

Annotating data – to aid continuity, reflexivity and openness

As discussed above, marking data for future attention is part of the continuum of analysis. Taking time to additionally annotate, based on reflections and insights, is also invaluable in retaining contact with thought processes as you read through and review data. Annotation tools allow you to connect spontaneous ideas with the data that produced the thought, and, later in your iterative work, to be reminded of earlier thoughts and reasoning. Processes of exploration highlight that your role as researcher is not neutral. Managing the accrual of ideas that contribute to analysis should be consciously reflexive. The tools discussed here provide convenient places for you to remain explicit about any such influences on the data (including the way they were generated) and analysis. A thought can come and go, but still, tacitly, influence later work. Once a fleeting thought is written down you become more accountable for it; more aware and responsible for where it came from, its place here, connected to this particular bit of data, and its role in developing interpretation. This helps increase the transparency and continuity of the analysis. The act of writing an annotation about specific statements or clips encourages a reflexive consciousness

Table 6.3 Exploration and data-level work: some suggestions in the context of case study C, Coca-Cola Commercials

Tasks from PHASE TWO: Exploration and identification of analytic focus	
Familiarise with the commercials	• Watch each commercial several times • Create a memo for each commercial and make notes about first impressions generally, and in relation to each research question • Informed by the capabilities of your chosen software, decide whether to work directly or indirectly
Working directly	• Rationalise and justify the decision not to generate transcripts; what might you gain or lose in adopting the direct approach? • Experiment with creating clips and annotating them (where this is possible to the exclusion of coding)
Working indirectly – transcript development	• Use software transcription tools to develop synchronised transcripts for each commercial (experimenting with developing multiple transcripts where this is possible) • Consider the importance of the placement of timestamps (time codes) in terms of subsequent qualitative retrieval and quantitisation (the implications differ depending on the software) • Be clear in your mind about the different role of annotations and transcripts in terms of your methodology and the capabilities of the software you are using.
Tasks from PHASE SEVEN: Integration and analysis of publicity materials	
	• In light of the write-up of the preliminary primary data analysis (Phase Five), explore publicity materials • Use text searching tools to quickly locate passages indicative of the themes you previously generated • In memos write about the connections seen between the commercials and the publicity materials

about the thinking processes. This theme continues to resonate when we look at the broader topic of memo tools and managing the processes of writing and analysis in Chapter 10.

Quick content searching tools

One key advantage of bringing all material broadly pertaining to a research project together into one software project is the ability to switch from the careful vertical or sequential analysis, top to bottom, through an individual data file, to a horizontal process of flicking quickly through all (or some of) the project materials in order to discover recurrent words or phrases (Chapter 1). The content searching tools discussed in this chapter are closely related to the 'auto-coding' tools discussed in Chapters 4 and 12 as a way of interrogating data and saving the 'finds' or 'hits'. We deal with them separately since we distinguish the processes in several ways. Physically and philosophically, fast searching of content, *without* automatically coding the results, serves multiple purposes. It constitutes a close level of work in data that appeals to many categories of analysis. Auto-coding, by contrast, simply because you are saving the results with surrounding context, implies a greater level of analytic reliance on possibly limited catchments of data. By implication, doing so potentially lowers the status of text which fits the meaning but is left out of the auto-coding process (because the terms used do not match). This is not to say this *will* be the effect of auto-coding or that using these tools results in lazy inferences; it simply makes the use of the auto-coding tools more debatable and subject to careful consideration. The auto-coding of repeated formal structures within otherwise unstructured data (questions, sections, etc.) is discussed in Chapter 4. Here we position the utility of text searching and word frequency tools within the context of more careful exploratory work, giving contact with some, but not all, appropriate bits of text. Chapter 1 mentioned constructionist language-based approaches to analysis, and so we additionally touch on particular functions where pattern recognition in text produces automatic examples of similar text passages.

BOX 6.4 — CASE NOTES

Content searching for generic and contextual familiarisation (Case Study B, The Financial Downturn)

It is usually the case when conducting your own primary data collection for the purposes of a dissertation or thesis that you also transcribe data. This is a good idea simply because the act of transcription constitutes a significant moment of contact with data; in itself it is a form of analysis (Chapter 10). There are different protocols and traditions for developing transcripts, depending on methodological context (Chapter 5). There are also analytic implications related to working with audiovisual data directly or indirectly (Box 4.5).

Sometimes, however, you may be working with data you have not collected and transcribed yourself, or indeed with materials not generated for the specific purposes of the particular study you are working on. It is useful in such circumstances to use content searching tools as a means of gaining some initial overview of and familiarity with the breadth and depth of the textual material.

In Case Study B, The Financial Downturn, there is much media content derived from various sources that provide the contextual backdrop for the project. In addition, one of the project aims was to investigate how the issues are constructed in media reporting and to what extent the survey and focus-group respondents' understandings and attitudes are reflected by them (Box 2.2). An early task therefore, (Phase Three, Table 6.1) involved exploring terms used by respondents and within media content to express the notion of the financial downturn. We needed to identify key terms and consider the frequency with which they were used by different respondents (retired, recently redundant, unemployed, male, female, etc.) and within different types of media content (print media, internet media, international media, local media, etc.). However, additionally we needed to be able to examine the context within which these terms were used. For example, were negative terms or experiences broadly referred to concerning personal or familial circumstances, or were they more general comments about the economy? We used a selection of word frequency and pattern matching tools, depending on the software being used. Later we focused attention on specific collections of words using text search tools to home in on topics in as thorough a way as possible. The different visualisations resulting from these searches (Figures 6.5; p. 149 and 6.6; p. 151) offer various ways to reflect upon and further interrogate the use of individual key words, collections of similar terms, and evocative phrases.

For instance, exploration via text searching looked for cut*|slash*| reduction*|tighten belt*|belt |tighten* (in this case the asterisks allowed the software to look for variations in endings to these words, e.g. *belts* or *tightening*). Figure 5.5 shows the annotation (in this case a 'memo') attached to one of the resultant quotes found by the search (shown in ATLAS.ti).

Word frequency tools in CAQDAS packages

Word frequency tools are exploratory. They allow the quick production of a comprehensive overview of the physical content of data broken down by individual words in one, several or all textual files. Most CAQDAS packages provide such tools, although there are different advantages in the subtle differences of functionality. Often there is a way to go from the counted list of words to where particular words appear in the text; at that point there may be the capacity to select surrounding text and code the 'hits' as in MAXQDA, NVivo, QDA Miner (with the text mining module WordStat). The latter package includes functions which provide more sophisticated ways to view, differentiate and analyse such information. NVivo provides useful extras such as the ability show the word frequency table in groups of stemmed (different word endings or beginnings) or synonymous words and various visualisations which offer ways viewing the proportionate occurrence of words. It lacks, however, the ability to build an explicit dictionary of words upon which to base the search, as found in MAXQDA and QDA Miner.

In a sense simple word frequency tools are inductive. They just tell you what words are in the data in an exhaustive and inclusive way. Some packages can differentiate the word count across documents, so you have an instant comparative dimension. Some types of research will place much importance on such tools; you must evaluate their relevance to how you need to work and make sure the particular range of functionality suits what you will want to do. Generally, in interpretive analysis, you will be less interested in counting occurrences than accessing the surrounding context. Whatever the particular options provided by your chosen software package, there is a real sense that quick initial exploration is made easy and accessible by such tools, and the more data you have, the more valuable they will be.

Text or lexical searching – the practicalities

Generally, text search tools are used in more proactive ways, allowing you to search for specific key words or phrases that you have a particular interest in. It can be useful to look for terms within certain forms of textual data separately, or indeed

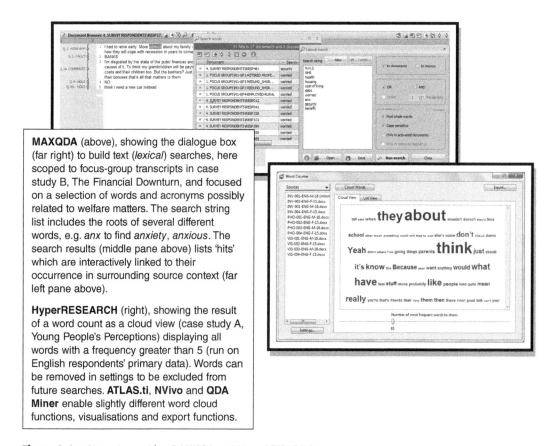

MAXQDA (above), showing the dialogue box (far right) to build text (*lexical*) searches, here scoped to focus-group transcripts in case study B, The Financial Downturn, and focused on a selection of words and acronyms possibly related to welfare matters. The search string list includes the roots of several different words, e.g. *anx* to find *anxiety, anxious*. The search results (middle pane above) lists 'hits' which are interactively linked to their occurrence in surrounding source context (far left pane above).

HyperRESEARCH (right), showing the result of a word count as a cloud view (case study A, Young People's Perceptions) displaying all words with a frequency greater than 5 (run on English respondents' primary data). Words can be removed in settings to be excluded from future searches. **ATLAS.ti**, **NVivo** and **QDA Miner** enable slightly different word cloud functions, visualisations and export functions.

Figure 6.4 Content searching (MAXQDA and HyperRESEARCH)

across all forms concurrently, as a means of making direct comparisons concerning their use in different contexts or by different 'authors'. Consider, therefore, literature and other supplementary documents you have integrated into the project and how text or lexical searching might gain access to significant passages (see also Chapter 5). In addition, you may use these tools to search for words or phrases used in your own writing – in annotations or memos, for example.

There are two important general points to make about text search tools. First, software fairly consistently allows viewing of all or some of the surrounding context in which key words or phrases are found, though the ease with which this happens varies. Second, keep in mind that the use of the tool is initially deductive, based as it usually is on your choice of words to search for. Progressively such searches can become more inductive as you spot other words or phrases in the first result to include in further investigations. In this sense your use of these tools can be iterative. Most CAQDAS packages allow for fairly complex search expressions which might include a good range of possible combinations of words (Box 6.4). A typical but fairly simple text search might look something like the illustration from MAXQDA (Figure 6.4) which provides a Lexical Analysis tool allowing you to search all data files, selections of them, or only in data previously coded in a particular way. Typically software programs expect you to create lists or a string of words or roots of words.

The point about such fast text exploration tools is that they have benefits throughout analytic work. They may fit early on, contributing to your familiarisation. They may fit later on, as a means of checking that all data around a particular topic or issue have been captured. They can be used at any point, for quickly finding material you want to view again or writing you want to append. Dip in and out of other tasks as

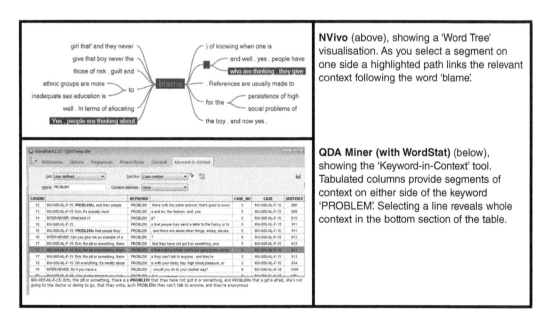

NVivo (above), showing a 'Word Tree' visualisation. As you select a segment on one side a highlighted path links the relevant context following the word 'blame'.

QDA Miner (with WordStat) (below), showing the 'Keyword-in-Context' tool. Tabulated columns provide segments of context on either side of the keyword 'PROBLEM'. Selecting a line reveals whole context in the bottom section of the table.

Figure 6.5 Contextual visualisations of text search finds (NVivo and QDA Miner)

you catch sight of an interesting word or phrase and then use the text search tool to find out where else it occurs and in what context. This type of work uses the power of the software to enrich contact with all of the data, albeit within the natural limits imposed by variations in the ways respondents describe things. A range of different visualisations are available; several applications include word cloud views, as illustrated in ATLAS.ti (Figure 6.4; p. 148); see also the Word Tree in NVivo (Figure 6.5; p. 149).

Text-mining tools and complex pattern searching

Some CAQDAS packages have additional text-mining tools that allow more complex searching based on patterns in textual data and the use of language more generally.[2] Where present, these tools can be used in early exploratory ways, to double-check, confirm or disconfirm relevance or salience, or as the core means by which texts are analysed. They are particularly useful when adopting a language-based approach but can also add an additional layer to analyses stemming from more interpretive traditions (Chapter 1). However, they may not be appropriate for some approaches simply because the work of much qualitative research is about unpacking the meaning of texts in terms of respondents' experiences, attitudes and beliefs rather than concentrating explicitly on the language used. The overuse of these tools in an interpretive approach may be a red herring, perhaps over-simplifying or skirting over complex undercurrents and nuance. Typically, they may have more relevance for the larger data corpora, although they can have uses in smaller datasets. They are a good example of why it is so important to be clear about what you need to achieve analytically before embarking on serious software-use.

Working with large volumes of data, material that you have not generated yourself, or when taking a language-based approach, text-mining type tools can be very effective. Case Study B, The Financial Downturn, includes media content in which a focus was on finding trends in terms of the use of particular 'evocative' or resonate terms. Several CAQDAS packages incorporate tools informed by text-mining traditions. NVivo, for instance, provides further help with cluster analysis type display of word frequency queries. This is in some ways similar to QDA Miner, although content-based analysis is taken much further in QDA Miner, especially when coupled with WordStat. Indeed, although we hope a human has better interpretive powers, a

---

[2]Researchers who engage in the type of content analysis which involves less of an interpretive element may use the text-mining style of software for much larger data corpora or for the summarisation of text for more constructionist approaches to analysis, or to discover and break down the physical content of a corpus of literature. They might need a simpler function set which concentrates on the single dimension of content and the provision of additional variations of functionality within that dimension, etc. Some such tools have been around since the mainframe computers of the 1960s and were not at the time considered appropriate for sociological research. Concordance, TextQuest, Word Smith or Textworld are present-day low-cost or free examples, although they do not provide parallel functions allowing thematic interpretation and annotation. They might be used in literature and linguistics, translation and language engineering, corpus linguistics, and forensic science.

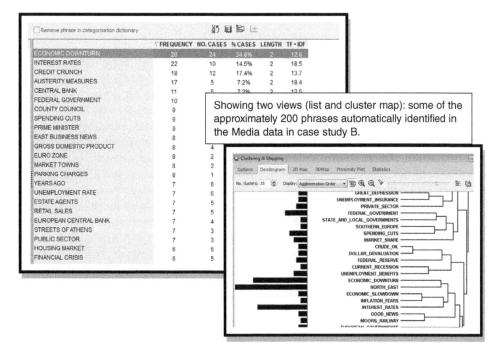

	FREQUENCY	NO. CASES	% CASES	LENGTH	TF • IDF
☐ Remove phrase in categorization dictionary					
ECONOMIC DOWNTURN	28	24	34.8%	2	12.8
INTEREST RATES	22	10	14.5%	2	18.5
CREDIT CRUNCH	18	12	17.4%	2	13.7
AUSTERITY MEASURES	17	5	7.2%	2	19.4
CENTRAL BANK	11	5	7.2%	2	12.5
FEDERAL GOVERNMENT	10				
COUNTY COUNCIL	9				
SPENDING CUTS	9				
PRIME MINISTER	9				
EAST BUSINESS NEWS	8				
GROSS DOMESTIC PRODUCT	8	4			
EURO ZONE	8	2			
MARKET TOWNS	8	2			
PARKING CHARGES	8	1			
YEARS AGO	7	6			
UNEMPLOYMENT RATE	7	6			
ESTATE AGENTS	7	5			
RETAIL SALES	7	5			
EUROPEAN CENTRAL BANK	7	4			
STREETS OF ATHENS	7	3			
PUBLIC SECTOR	7	3			
HOUSING MARKET	6	6			
FINANCIAL CRISIS	6	5			

Showing two views (list and cluster map): some of the approximately 200 phrases automatically identified in the Media data in case study B.

Figure 6.6 The Phrase Finder (QDA Miner/WordStat)

computer can identify patterns in ways a human would find hard to even begin to achieve systematically. This was the rationale behind the development of exploratory tools such as clustering, sequence analysis, proximity plots, and correspondence analysis. QDA Miner is the qualitative analysis arm of a suite of software which can be put together in different combinations. QDA Miner (without any add-on modules) has extra ways of visualising and accessing the data (including the Phrase Finder and Query by Example tools as discussed in Box 6.5 and illustrated in Figures 6.6 and 6.7). QDA Miner in conjunction with WordStat provides far more ways of finding, framing and outputting quantitative measures of content and pattern matching (see Chapter 3). Qualrus includes similar 'natural language pattern matching' that operates as one means of suggesting codes to the user (see Chapter 7).

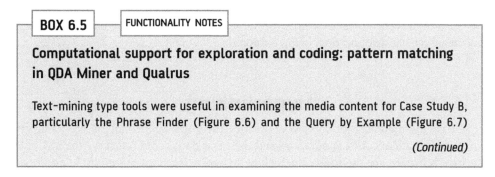

BOX 6.5 — FUNCTIONALITY NOTES

Computational support for exploration and coding: pattern matching in QDA Miner and Qualrus

Text-mining type tools were useful in examining the media content for Case Study B, particularly the Phrase Finder (Figure 6.6) and the Query by Example (Figure 6.7)

(Continued)

(Continued)

tools provided by QDA Miner. The Phrase Finder quickly lists all the phrases it can find: the user defines the minimum and maximum numbers of words that constitute the phrases, and a phrase will only be picked up in QDA Miner if it is repeated more than once (but you can define a higher minimum). This can be very useful for spotting jargon and recurring journalistic themes in media data. This analysis was more or less instantly available with the sample we experimented with (70 articles) and could be viewed in numerous statistical ways showing, for example, measures of co-occurrence. Also included are more visual cluster groupings (also illustrated in Figure 6.6). Small clusters of proximate terms were interesting to view, as much because they sometimes indicated a trend or a small example of something which took our thinking in other directions. One such surprise in the context of the Case Study B articles was the relationship the software picked out between 'good news' and 'moors railway', a small heritage railway run mainly by volunteers. This reminded us to look more closely into later group discussions concerning the role of voluntary work in a recession as well as to ask explicit questions about things respondents felt positive about in the local economy. We easily found the relevant passage, selected it and ran a Query by Example on the passage. While we allowed for the fact that local news is often positively skewed to encourage local consumers and advertisers, also often initiated by local enterprise press releases – it was the subject matter which was often useful.

The Query by Example tool in QDA Miner makes it particularly easy to select a paragraph or sentence and the software will pattern-match to find other example sentences which have something in common, throughout the dataset or within part of it. An interactive list is produced and you can then select only the sentences you want to keep (some of them might be barely relevant at all) and then code them if required (Figure 6.7; p. 151).

In the context of Case Study B this was a useful way to point to various topics which possibly needed further investigation and prompted a closer reading of the some of the articles. In the context of much larger studies of literature corpora in science or industry it is easy to see how such very quick computer-based searches (rather than researcher-led interpretive, reflective processes) enables types of analysis that would not be possible without the computer. In this moderately sized dataset such tools were a means to throw up something that might have been overlooked in the larger background data being explored.

Hyperlinking

The term *hyperlinking* is often used to describe the quick connection between objects of analysis, such as codes, annotations and their associated data. What we mainly refer to here however, are the tools which allow hyperlinking between multiple points or

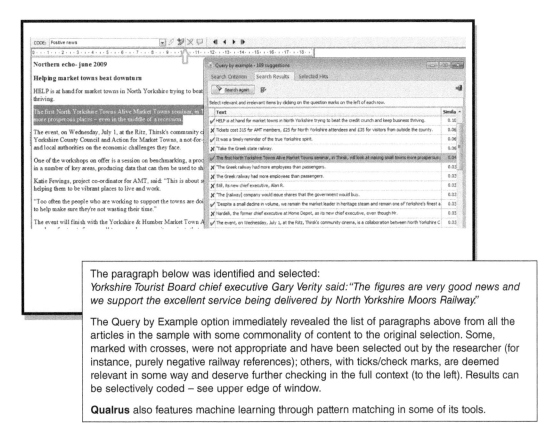

The paragraph below was identified and selected:
Yorkshire Tourist Board chief executive Gary Verity said: "The figures are very good news and we support the excellent service being delivered by North Yorkshire Moors Railway."

The Query by Example option immediately revealed the list of paragraphs above from all the articles in the sample with some commonality of content to the original selection. Some, marked with crosses, were not appropriate and have been selected out by the researcher (for instance, purely negative railway references); others, with ticks/check marks, are deemed relevant in some way and deserve further checking in the full context (to the left). Results can be selectively coded – see upper edge of window.

Qualrus also features machine learning through pattern matching in some of its tools.

Figure 6.7   Pattern recognition tool: Query by Example (QDA Miner)

segments in text or multimedia data themselves. These tools vary in effectiveness between packages, and sometimes they do not exist at all. Some offer only pairs of links, others are more flexible. We first outline some of the debate concerning software tools in respect of creating multiple links; then we discuss the practical issues, what links can do and the key differences between software programs in this respect.

The apparent dominance of coding devices in earlier CAQDAS programs caused some methodologists to question the way computerised analysis might create a homogeneity of analysis techniques (Chapter 1). Weaver and Atkinson (1995), and later Coffey et al. (1996), emphasise the need for a broader perception of what software could contribute to qualitative data analysis, particularly in ethnography. They see fragmentation of the data by a computer-led predominance of code and retrieval strategy as restrictive and a less than ideal way to handle narrative or life history accounts. As an alternative strategy they suggest hyperlinking between points in the text as a more flexible way to track varied routes through data. In actuality, it is relatively rare for those engaged in the different forms of narrative analysis to use the customised software tools to which we mainly refer. This is not necessarily due to a lack of functionality, but comes from the tendency to be deeply immersed in relatively small amounts of data. It is important however, to distinguish between needing to create a narrative in the general sense and carrying out, explicitly, a form of narrative inquiry (Chapter 1).

Practical aspects of hyperlinking

There are often moments – whatever the approach – when a need arises to 'write the story' or reflect the narrative of respondents' accounts or the situations we observe. If you are engaged in an ethnographic study and want to illustrate the story at 'data level' rather than simply summarising, it is not always possible to arrange segments of data in the precise order required. You may not want them linked or listed in vertical data order. Doing so may not track the processes or tell the story the way it logically or chronologically happened. If you also want all the other tools available, such as coding and data interrogation, currently it is ATLAS.ti and QDA Miner which provide the ability to make chains of multiple links (Figure 11.2; p. 265). MAXQDA and NVivo enable pairs of links to be made. In MAXQDA you insert pairs of links which are then indicated by underlined blue text. You can move forwards or backwards. In NVivo it is a little more complicated. 'See also' links enable different types of pairs of links (between the top levels of files or between places in the text) and become hyperlinked when a particular view is switched on.

When considering the value of hyperlinking for the needs of your analytic approach and evaluating the subtle differences between software packages in terms of their specific utility for your way of working, remember that hyperlinking tools are not always available; that they vary in ease of use where they are present; and that they can be used for different reasons. For example, you can:

- Link a trigger with a reaction (pairs of links)
- Link contradictory statements (pairs of links)
- Associate one document with places in another (pairs of links)
- Track logical reasoning (pairs or multiple links)
- Link specific parts of different documents together (pairs or multiple links)
- Link parts of an interaction or process together sequentially or based on chronology or logic and allow the user to impose order of navigation backwards and forwards (multiple links)
- Link points in data where certain types of behaviour occur, for example where strong reactions are demonstrated or very hesitant behaviour occurs (multiple links)
- Link relevant parts of multimedia sound or video in order to more quickly navigate to key areas (multiple links).

ATLAS.ti, Dedoose, Qualrus and Transana enable the creation of 'quotations', 'extracts', 'clips' or 'segments' which can be listed independently for later attention. ATLAS.ti quotations can be linked together in the required order and either navigated in their source context by clicking on indications in the margin of the data files, or illustrated in a 'network' showing graphically how the passages at quotes are linked together (Figure 11.2; p. 265). In Qualrus segments can be visualised in the Categorisation workspace, and 'stacked' as an additional way of grouping based on similarity. In Transana segments from transcripts liked to associated media can be created as clips and placed into collections without being coded. This can be useful for ordering in a linear fashion, presented as a list.

When working with multimedia data it will also be useful to consider how your chosen software allows the marking and exploration of audio/video. ATLAS.ti is the only software discussed in this book which provides effective ways of creating hyperlinked paths through data segments (of any type); see Box 6.2. An important aspect of this may be the ability to order those linkages in the appropriate way for your current purposes.

In Case Study C, Coca-Cola Commercials, with a collection of video files, it would be useful to jump from one place in one video to another place in another video, and then back to another video higher up the list. It is this hyperlinking functionality that might really enhance data-level work with sound or video files. Coding (Chapter 7) only brings together clips in a loose way, and is not fine enough a tool to define the association between them (Silver and Patashnick, 2011).

If you simply want a tool to illustrate hyperlinkages in the data, it may be that a different set of software, customised to just that feature is required. Hypermedia or hypertext editors or software packages are available (e.g. StorySpace). There may be a tension here in the context of computer assistance. It helps to be open to the potential of managing diverse entry points and navigation paths through data, but at the same time also to be able to fit the tools at your disposal as closely as possible to your specific needs. Technology is never the central reason for choosing an analytic technique, but it has changed the possibilities, so in designing research it has to be considered as one of the enabling factors for certain types of analysis.

| **BOX 6.6** | ANALYTIC NOTES |

Questions to ask yourself when exploring data

- Might the fast exploration tools provided by CAQDAS packages open up your study to larger data corpora or alternative ways of thinking about data? Or are they not appropriate to your analytic needs?
- To what extent are you interested in the way language is used in textual materials? Will consideration of key words and phrases add a useful dimension to your work?
- To what extent is your analytic strategy reliant on coding? If it is not, could you use coding tools creatively for the purposes of accessing segments of interesting data, or will you rely on other tools to navigate passages of analytic significance?

Concluding remarks: appropriate use of data-level tools

We have discussed many tools which keep us close to the data: fast exploration tools and the slower, closer work of annotation. For some types of interpretive research, technical competence with content-based searching tools can never replace the more thorough perusal of data and careful identification of meaning and significance. In their appropriate place, these tools may have multiple uses in the flexible toolkit of qualitative inquiry. Interpretive researchers often use these tools on the spur of the moment, while in careful reading and coding mode. A phrase or word in the text prompts a need to find out if it occurs anywhere else in the data, and in what context. The ability to react in this manner to a sudden thought, and to gain direct access to all relevant areas in the data, is arguably one of the spontaneous aspects of computer use which has most changed the processes of interpretive analysis. Used as part of the process of seeing and understanding all the data, it changes the speed at which we delve into the data, and therefore makes us more ready to do so!

In terms of searching the context of textual data there are many debatable aspects to using software, and as functionality increases so do the complications. We discussed this in the previous chapter, as part of the process of getting started. The pros and cons of searching full-text PDFs when not all your literature sources can be incorporated fully constitute one such complication. Text search tools generally, however, provide really efficient ways to flick through data and provide visualisations which can provide surprising insights and perspectives. Pattern searching and related types of tool are very exciting, but they do not take the burden away from you to check for actual relevance. Where the various ways of measuring and counting occurrences in qualitative data are seen as useful, the researcher needs to be doubly sure that the software is counting 'good stuff' – not rubbish. There is less to critique in slower work with the data – annotating, marking and linking can enhance recall of nuanced thinking which will impact on everything else you do. Such tools are useful to any type of researcher, or even to a non-researcher, gathering different material together in one place and managing ideas about it. Chapter 7 discusses coding tools which can also be used flexibly and appropriately by many different types of researcher.

EXERCISES: EXPLORATION AND DATA-LEVEL WORK

This chapter has concentrated on working closely with data, marking, annotating exploring, searching and linking passages. The processes may help familiarise with data and move further towards analysis, but the steps in themselves are based at data level. The purpose of working like this may be different across contexts and strategies. It may just be data familiarisation you are working towards, or you may have a specific methodological interest in the content of the data. Think about how the exercises could be relevant to both primary data and literature.

1.   Embedding notes in data or in other material

   (a)   Read through an entire data source (e.g. interview or focus-group transcript) in the software project and enrich your later recall of subtle significance by recording the insights you have, annotating the data segments that prompted the thoughts. Different annotation tools are enabled by each software. Some are simply called 'memos' and are flagged up against text passages, some are specifically called 'annotations' or 'comments' and are included wherever the relevant text is listed. Find a way to create notes which are in some way flagged in the data (but do not clutter up the data).

(b) When checking out software, decide how important this is for you. Different analytic approaches might primarily rely on such note-making devices, and not all software packages deliver this.

(c) If working with video or audio, compare the different ways of embedding notes which are synchronised or linked to particular clips. In the software packages which enable embedded annotations in text, similar tools will be available for sound/video.

2. Experiment with the integration of literature references. Import literature lists – and where enabled, annotate each reference to record their relevance to your study, contribution to the field or stance taken.

3. Experiment with the marking or compiling of useful data segments requiring later attention.

(a) Use tools explicitly for the purpose, or use workarounds by coding for 'relevance' without explicitly coding on a topic/thematic basis.

(b) If you are allowed to edit data (and only if you are involved in an individual research project, rather than a collaborative project), simply mark data by changing the colour of the font (keep this simple – do not be tempted to start colour-coding text on the basis of theme – unless it is a specific colour coding device (see Chapter 8)).

4. Make links (hyperlinks) between passages of data or between literature and analysis (where this is enabled).

(a) Link two places in the data where contradictory or confirmatory statements occur or where connected processes are documented or observed (e.g. in text or audio/video).

(b) Link something you are writing in a memo to a segment of data or to a literature reference.

5. Explore textual data for the occurrence of individual key words using word frequency tools (where possible).

(a) Carry out a word frequency search across all your textual data, or experiment with scoping such a task to just one folder or set.

(b) In some software packages results can be generated to differentiate frequencies across each separate data file.

6. Explore textual data for the occurrence of collections of key words or phrases using text search tools.

(a) Familiarise yourself with data along several lines of interest – perform lexical or text searches to explore the content of data on different bases. Use these devices to locate the 'hits' quickly at an exploration level.

(b) It may be appropriate later, or when doing certain types of searches, to code the results. See Chapter 7 on coding, and Chapter 13. Such tasks are also related to possibilities of auto-coding based on structures in the data.

7

Qualitative Coding in Software: Principles and Processes

This chapter discusses principles and processes in coding textual and multimedia data using qualitative software. We illustrate what qualitative coding is and how it works in software, discussing methodological and practical approaches and the possibilities software provides in supporting and integrating them. Code and retrieve capabilities underpin the development of CAQDAS programs (Chapter 1), but software does not dictate whether, how or why to generate or apply codes. While specific coding functionality varies, packages allow a similar degree of flexibility and a range of different ways to apply and combine coding techniques. Chapters 8 and 9 build on the discussions presented here, and Chapter 10 can usefully be read in conjunction as it discusses the ways writing tools can be used to document processes and further analytic thinking as you proceed.

What is qualitative coding?

Qualitative coding is the process by which segments of data are identified as relating to, or being an example of, a more general idea, instance, theme or category. Data segments from across the whole dataset are placed together, or 'tagged' in order to be retrieved together at a later stage. In so doing you build up a coding system to organise data and your ideas about them (Chapter 9). Coding therefore contributes to the management and ordering of data (Figure 2.1; p. 45). It enables easier searching for similarities, differences, anomalies, patterns and relationships. As such, coding is often an integral part of the analytic process, but it is not analysis in itself.

How coding works in qualitative software

When a code is applied to a data segment in a CAQDAS package, a link is created between the segment and the code. It is useful to think about CAQDAS packages as comprising two elements of a database system. One stores the data files, the other houses the codes. When the link is created, the quick retrieval of material is enabled. This is shown in Figure 7.1, illustrated in MAXQDA and NVivo. The right-hand part of the MAXQDA screen displays the Document Browser, which in this example was initially an empty document in which we made notes (or developed 'critiques') about a literature file (Chapter 5). The left-hand side shows the Code System, which lists codes (grouped hierarchically according to type) being used to manage critiques of materials included in the literature review.

The code 'un-substantiated claims' is highlighted in the Code System, as is one data segment to which it has been applied in the Document Browser. The technical process of coding links positions in the Code System to selected data segments within different *documents*. The principle is the same in all CAQDAS packages. Any number of codes can be applied to a single data segment of any size and to overlapping or embedded segments. Codes can be defined and analytic annotations/memos attached (Chapters 6 and 11). Coded data can be retrieved in different ways (Chapter 8); interrogation based on the position of codes as applied to data and combinations of coding and factual data characteristics (e.g. socio-demographics) are discussed in Chapter 13.

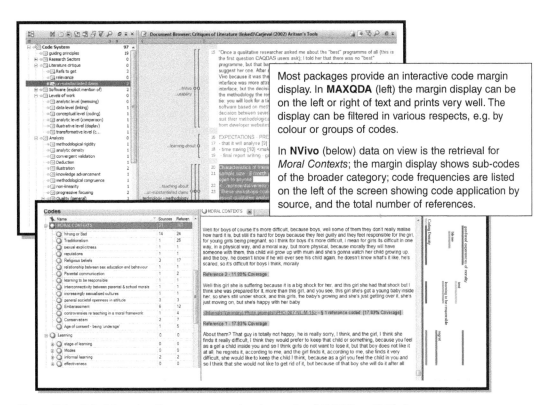

Figure 7.1 Principles of coding processes and code margins (MAXQDA and NVivo)

Approaches to coding

Coding is often seen to be central to the 'qualitative method'. Some approaches, however, resist organising and categorising data through coding (Chapters 1 and 6). CAQDAS packages are not methods of analysis but provide a range of tools which can be used to facilitate various analytic processes. Although some provide assistance in coding (see discussion below), decisions about coding *always* rest with the researcher. Tools continue to increase as software develops (Chapters 1 and 14). We encourage you to take a critical view of software and make informed decisions as to whether particular tools within a package are appropriate to the overarching methodology and the specific analytic needs.

Induction, deduction, abduction: logics of reaching explanations

In developing a strategy for coding data – whether using CAQDAS packages or not – many researchers draw upon distinctions between *inductive* and *deductive* approaches to analysis, which resonate with ways of going about coding. These terms refer to two contrasting logics of explanation. As described by Gibbs (2007: 4–5), the first works up from the data level, the second down from the theoretical:

> *Induction* is the generation and justification of a general explanation based on the accumulation of lots of particular, but similar, circumstances. … *Deductive explanation* moves in the opposite direction, in that a particular situation is explained by deduction from a general statement about the circumstances.

It is often assumed that because quantitative research primarily employs deductive processes, qualitative research must therefore be inductive, yet such distinctions are simplistic. As Gibbs (2007: 5) continues:

> Much quantitative research is deductive in approach. A hypothesis is deduced from a general law and this is tested against reality by looking for circumstances which confirm or disconfirm it. A lot of qualitative research explicitly tries to generate new theory and new explanations. In that sense the underlying logic is inductive. Rather than starting with some theories and concepts that are to be tested or examined, such research favours an approach in which they are developed in tandem with data collection in order to produce and justify new generalisations and thus create new knowledge and understanding. Some writers reject the imposition of any a priori theoretical frameworks at the outset. However, it is very hard for analysts to eliminate completely all prior frameworks. Inevitably qualitative analysis is guided and framed by pre-existing ideas and concepts. Often what researchers are doing is checking hunches; that is, they are deducing particular explanations from general theories and seeing if the circumstances they observe actually correspond.

Similarly, Sibert and Shelly (1995: 115) distinguish between conceptual and mechanical tasks involved in conducting analysis, illustrating that inductive and deductive processes are inherent in both:

> *Conceptual tasks* are those tasks by which the researcher generates the products of the analysis process. Through reading, questioning, categorizing, inferring by induction and generalizing, the researcher generates coding categories, relationships, generalisations and perhaps theories. These products are generated for the purpose of conceptualizing constructs in the data at higher levels of abstraction.
>
> *Mechanical tasks* are those tasks by which the researcher manipulates the products of the analysis process. The researcher stores, organizes and retrieves data by using coding categories. The researcher deduces (that is, makes deductive inferences about) the validity of relationships, generalizations or theories by re-examining the data. These products are manipulated for the purpose of organizing and reorganizing the data which is the basis, the grounding, of the conceptual tasks.

Many other authors also discuss the nature of qualitative (and mixed methods) analysis in terms of a combination (or dialectic) of deductive and inductive processes and reasoning (see below). Indeed, the premise of this book, and inherent to the way we view the value of customised CAQDAS packages, is that different analytic processes, ways of thinking and possibilities for cutting across datasets accordingly, are significantly enhanced through the systematic and creative use of software tools. We discuss this in relation to data retrieval and moving on from early coding tasks in Chapters 8–13. In specific terms of computer-assisted coding, we conceptualise inductive and deductive approaches as existing on a continuum. In practice, researchers may find they employ both inductive *and* deductive approaches iteratively, throughout the whole process of the research project.

However, we think it useful to distinguish explicitly between how software can support inherently inductive and inherently deductive approaches to coding before illustrating how they are combined in practice (Figures 7.2; p. 162 and 7.3; p. 171). Our experience of working with researchers from various sectors, disciplines and methodologies, and in teaching students and analysts with different levels of technical and analytic expertise, illustrates the range of approaches that are adopted. Some researchers have very clear ideas about their need to work entirely (or predominately) in one direction. As the reach of CAQDAS stretches beyond the academic social science disciplines in which they largely developed, this has become more obvious. We therefore discuss inductive and deductive approaches to coding, before moving on to illustrate how combined or 'abductive' approaches may proceed. First, we make some comments about coding terminology.

Coding terminology

There is much literature about the principles and applications of qualitative coding – both with and without the support of customised software. Reflecting

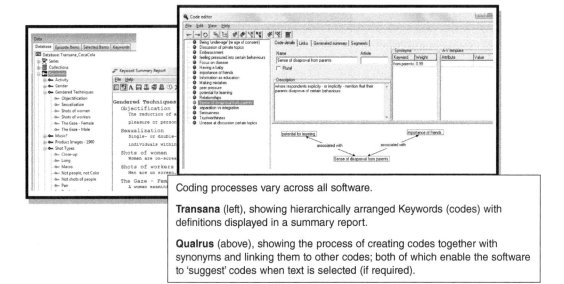

Coding processes vary across all software.

Transana (left), showing hierarchically arranged Keywords (codes) with definitions displayed in a summary report.

Qualrus (above), showing the process of creating codes together with synonyms and linking them to other codes; both of which enable the software to 'suggest' codes when text is selected (if required).

Figure 7.2 Early code creation processes (Qualrus and Transana)

different nuances in approach, authors tend to use a range of terms to refer to different types or purposes of coding, stages at which they occur within analysis and technical mechanisms for their use within software. Sometimes, the same or similar terms are used to refer to quite different processes. We list some here:

- descriptive, interpretive and pattern coding (Miles and Huberman, 1994);
- provisional, core and satellite codes (Layder, 1998);
- objectivist and heuristic codes (Seidel, 1998);
- open, axial and selective coding (Strauss and Corbin, 1997);
- literal, interpretive and reflexive indexing (Mason, 2002);
- descriptive, topic and analytical coding (Richards, 2009).

It is not within the scope of this book, however, to summarise, describe or reflect on these different conceptualisations or uses of coding. However, we do want to highlight the variety in the area, and in so doing to encourage you to become familiar with relevant literature and to develop as clear an idea as possible about how you intend to proceed before you begin in earnest with coding your own raw data within any software package.

Inductive approaches to coding

The general principle underlying inductive approaches to coding is a desire to prevent existing theoretical concepts from over-defining the analysis and obscuring the possibility of identifying and developing new concepts and theories. As Abrahamson (1983: 286) states: 'an inductive approach begins with the researchers "immersing"

Table 7.1 Coding in software: some suggestions in the context of case study A, Young People's Perceptions

Tasks from PHASE THREE: First wave coding: deductive, broad-brush coding across the dataset	
Creation of empty codes which reflect theoretical focus	• Create a basic coding scheme structure reflecting the theoretical context as identified by the literature review • Define codes precisely, including reference to where in the literature they come from • Name or otherwise mark codes to indicate they are literature-derived
Content-based auto-coding for keywords and phrases	• Identify keywords/phrases that are indicators of potential themes, auto-code on that basis across the dataset
Topic-based auto-coding for repeated structures	• Broadly auto-code primary data by section

Tasks from PHASE FOUR: Inductive recoding of broad-brush codes	
Identify broad-brush codes that require recoding	• Read through memos and coded data • Identify and prioritise codes relevant to each research question, add to memos notes about current thinking • Create short-cut groupings for codes on the basis of aspects relevant to each research question
Inductively recode broad-brush codes	• Retrieve data coded at a broad-brush codes • Inductively recode into more detailed and analytic aspects, in relation to the research questions • Name and define new codes in specific terms • Use hierarchical positioning or pre-fixing to indicate
Build on analytic and process writing	• Make notes about what you are doing as you proceed o Comment on how what you are identifying through recoding relates to the literature and research questions

themselves in the documents (that is, the various messages) in order to identify the dimensions or *themes* that seem meaningful to the producers of each message'.

BOX 7.1 ──── ANALYTIC NOTES

Considerations when coding inductively

It can be tempting to introduce data to a software project and begin coding immediately. However, exploring data is important when adopting inductive analytic approaches because these processes serve to focus subsequent coding. You may have generated an initial list of codes as part of the process of data familiarisation (Chapter 6). If not, you will at least have made notes about areas of interest and possibly also annotated some data segments. Refer to the notes already made when coding. Also keep in mind the

(Continued)

---

overall aim of the analysis by continually reflecting on the research questions which underlie your work. Inductive code development and assignation is instigated by what is 'seen' in data, but codes should not be created without purpose. The research questions provide that overarching purpose; the processes of data familiarisation help focus the detail of code development. Reflect, as you create codes, about how they might later help you to interpret data and answer the research questions. Always define codes upon their creation.

The well-known and frequently discussed 'grounded theory' (originated by Glaser and Strauss, 1967) comprises a methodological approach to qualitative research rather than simply being an analytic or coding strategy. It is not our purpose to describe or discuss grounded theory in detail (see Strauss and Corbin, 2008, for a detailed discussion). However, proponents suggest that grounded coding is an iterative process, frequently distinguishing between open, axial and selective coding procedures. In our experience many researchers work in grounded ways, without necessarily strictly adhering to the processes of grounded theory as they have been described. It is nevertheless useful to briefly discuss these procedures and indicate ways software tools can facilitate them.

- Open coding refers to the first coding phase in which small segments of data (perhaps a word, line, sentence or paragraph) are considered in detail and compared with one another. This process usually generates large numbers of codes from the data level, which encapsulate what is seen to be 'going on'. These codes may be descriptive or more conceptual in nature. They may be very precise, or more generally specified. Often terminology found in data is used as code labels, termed *in vivo* coding. Open coding fragments the data, 'opening' them up into all the possible ways in which they can be understood.
- Axial coding is a more abstract process. It refers to the second pass through the data when the codes generated by open coding are reconsidered. Code labels and the data linked to them are rethought in terms of similarity and difference. Similar codes may be grouped together, merged into higher-level categories, or subdivided into more detailed ones. Data are revisited and compared continually as the way codes represent the data is examined. Axial coding thus brings back together the fragmented data segments identified in the open coding phase by exploring the relationships identified between the codes which represent them.
- Selective coding refers to a third stage of coding when the researcher again revisits the data and the codes. Instances in the data which most pertinently illustrate themes, concepts, relationships, etc. are identified. Conclusions are validated by illustrating instances represented by and grounded in the data. Identified patterns are tested and core categories in the developing theory are illustrated. This process will lead to segments of data being chosen to quote and discuss in the final written product of the research project.

Whether following the principles of grounded theory explicitly, or using elements in informing the design of a bespoke analytic strategy, adopting an inductive approach allows for naturally occurring elements within data to be identified and interrogated, in terms of how they reflect substantive areas of interest. In Case Study C, Coca-Cola Commercials, this included the devices used to promote the product, the subtle and explicit representations of gendered relationships and how the commercials reflect their time more generally. The other case-study examples also included inductive coding processes, but their positioning within the broader analytic design was different (see Tables 2.1; p. 39, 7.1; p. 163, 7.2; p. 169 and 7.3; p. 173). For instance, in Case Study A, Young People's Perceptions, we illustrate a process of inductively recoding areas of interest initially identified through a deductive coding process (see below). Conversely, in Case Study B, The Financial Downturn, the three types of data are coded sequentially, such that the analysis builds incrementally, with inductive coding of focus-group data being sandwiched by deductive coding of open-ended survey data and deductive coding of media materials.

BOX 7.2 — FUNCTIONALITY NOTES

Software tasks supporting inductive approaches to coding

All the packages discussed here provide flexible means by which to generate codes and analyse qualitative data in an inductive way. These include the following specific tasks:

- creating codes grounded in the data (open coding) or based on language used in the data (*in vivo* coding);
- retrieving data segments based on how they have been coded;
- grouping similar codes together and viewing the data coded at them together (within or outside the software);
- defining codes, printing lists of codes, renaming codes;
- increasing and decreasing the amount of data coded;
- uncoding data;
- recoding data;
- commenting upon and writing about what is seen.

It is important to view these tasks as occurring in explicit relation to the processes of data familiarisation and exploration that will have taken place earlier (Chapter 6) and as providing the basis upon which analytic work will continue (Chapters 7–13).

Working inductively is characterised by careful and detailed inspection of data on a number of levels (Chapter 1). This 'bottom-up' approach starts at the detailed level and moves through recoding, regrouping, rethinking, towards a higher level of abstraction. The aim may often be to generate theory from the data, although this is not a pre-requisite for adopting an inductive approach.

Questions to ask yourself when coding inductively

- How do the codes you have created differ? Are some more broadly specified than others?
- To what extent does first-wave coding help you to think about the data differently from how you had been thinking after initial data familiarisation?
- How did your initial conceptualisation of the research questions affect the way you coded? Has your thinking about the research questions changed as a result of initial inductive coding?
- Have you been defining codes as you create them? How has this helped with your thinking about potential themes?

Deductive approaches to coding

Deductive approaches to coding are more explicit at the outset about the themes or categories to be considered. There may be many reasons for taking such an approach, for example, where the intention is to test an existing theory or hypothesis on newly generated data or to investigate its transferability to a different social context; or due to perceived time constraints or for other pragmatic reasons. The design of Case Study A, Young People's Perceptions, is theoretically deductive in the sense that the initial coding of primary data is explicitly directed by the prior review of the literature (Box 7.4). You may not be testing a theory or a hypothesis, but may simply know what you are looking for. This is often the approach taken in non-academic research settings, where the focus may be a more applied and practical understanding for a specific and fairly immediate objective, or a set of specifically identified outcomes. Case Study B, The Financial Downturn, for example, includes elements of this type of approach, in that the first phase of analysis constitutes content-based deductive coding of a sample of survey respondents' open-ended responses. In academic settings, as Berg notes, it is typical that a theoretical framework guides code development and application (Chapter 9): 'In a deductive approach, researchers use some categorical scheme suggested by a theoretical perspective, and the documents provide the means for assessing the hypothesis' (Berg, 2001: 6).

Miles and Huberman (1994) describe a deductive method of coding. They suggest that a variety of factors (e.g. the conceptual framework, research questions, hypotheses, problem areas) inform the generation of a provisional list of codes prior to commencing fieldwork. They illustrate how a segment of text can be read on different levels, suggesting that (re)consideration of data in the following terms leads to the identification and explanation of themes and patterns:

- *Descriptive codes* are fairly objective and self-explanatory in nature; they are used at the outset in the coding process when considering a segment of text for the first time. They allow the organisation of data according to what it is descriptively about. They are based on predefined areas of interest, whether factual, thematic or theoretical in nature (Figure 7.3; p. 171).

- *Interpretive codes* are subsequently used to add a more detailed layer of meaning to the data coded descriptively. Coded data are revisited in relation to the broad areas of interest and considered in more detail. Similar aspects may be recoded where they exemplify a meaningful concept or relationship. Existing concepts or themes may be deconstructed into more detailed aspects. Elements of a particular theme may be seen as relating to other aspects of different themes, and perhaps linked to one another.
- *Pattern codes* are used in the third stage, which moves to a more inferential and explanatory level. It involves considering how the themes, concepts, behaviours or processes identified through descriptive and interpretive coding occur within or are relevant across the dataset. This could be within an individual account. It could also be across subsets of data, for example amongst respondents with certain similar characteristics. Similarity, difference, contradiction, etc. are investigated, the aim being to identify meaningful and illustrative patterns in the data.

In many ways, therefore, deductive approaches are similar to inductive ones. They are also iterative and cyclical, involving close and repeated consideration of the data. The main difference is that the process starts with at least some predefined, higher-level areas of interest which are explicitly looked for in the data.

BOX 7.4 — CASE NOTES

Considerations when coding deductively (Case Study A, Young People's Perceptions)

Deductive coding across all forms of data concurrently serves to integrate existing theory with primary data analysis from the outset and to explicitly and directly consider empirical data alongside literature throughout the analytic process. The literature review (Chapter 5) identified the theoretical context, and these themes direct the deductive, broad-brush coding. Work in the software begins with the creation of an empty coding scheme that descriptively represents the theoretical context. Subsequently, there are two distinct ways of approaching the coding: the traditional 'human-driven' deductive approach in which the researcher looks for data that correspond to or contradict the theory; and the 'computer-driven' deductive approach in which the researcher uses the power of content searching (for key words and phrases) to identify instances of the codes. The two can be powerfully combined in order to benefit from the advantages and mitigate the disadvantages of each. We present the combined approach here. Where data are inherently structured (e.g. according to the questions asked, or other repeated sections) these may form the basis of another layer of broad-brush deductive coding. The theoretical and topic-based coding can later be combined using matrix-type co-occurrence queries (Chapter 13).

There are many different reasons for adopting a deductive approach. Here we briefly describe just two: theoretical and question-based coding.

Theoretical coding

In projects which directly use or apply existing theoretical ideas, the coding process will be inherently deductive. This might happen as described in relation to Case Study A, Young People's Perceptions, in which the literature review defines the theoretical context (Box 7.4). In this example, there are large volumes of previous research into the specific topic of school-based sex education provision, and the related broader issues of young people's introduction to issues relating to sex(uality) and relationships, their transition to adulthood more generally and the policy context and political problematisation of teenage pregnancy in Western societies. The literature review identified gaps in scientific knowledge relating to the influence of cultural, social and political factors on the historical provision and effectiveness of school-based sex education. For example, although 'social attitudes' and socio-political factors had been identified as important impacts (Jones et al., 1986; Vilar, 1994; Rademakers, 1997; Thomson, 1994), neither the nature of these influences, their historical roots nor the nature of the relationship between these 'structural' factors and policy development, provision in practice or individual behaviour had been explored in detail (Silver, 2002). Thus the theoretical context guided the formulation of the research questions, the design of the analytic strategy and the context in which new theory was developed. However, as discussed below, theoretical deductive coding constituted just one part of the process, which was followed by an inductive recoding process.

BOX 7.5 — FUNCTIONALITY NOTES

Software tasks supporting deductive approaches to coding

In all software packages, codes can be generated independently of data – perhaps even before data are collected, transcribed and incorporated within the software project.

- Codes can be generated at any point in the process, independently of data.
- A mature and complex coding schema which represents an existing theory or hypothesis may already exist and be applied to data about a different topic.
- Broadly specified codes can be revisited in order to consider, for example, patterns in the way respondents talk about an issue, or in which a theoretical idea manifests itself.
- Deductive approaches tend to start off coding in a fairly descriptive way, capturing instances relating to a set of general theoretical ideas.

Question-based coding

Where repeated structure exists in data, such as with structured interview or open-ended questions to survey data, analysis may be based around respondents' answers to particular questions. This is often the case in applied research settings. In such

Table 7.2 Coding in software: some suggestions in the context of case study B, The Financial Downturn

Tasks from PHASE THREE: Deductive analysis of open-ended survey questions	
Broad-brush coding	• Code survey responses as whole units of context according to high-frequency occurrences of keywords and phrases which indicate salient aspects in relation to research questions and 'sensitising concepts' • Define codes in specific terms • Name or otherwise mark codes to indicate they are based on textual content

Tasks from PHASE FOUR: Inductive analysis of focus-group data	
Initial inductive coding	• Pilot code two data files, experimenting with different units of coding context, to build a coding strategy that will achieve analytic aims • Refer to research questions and previously written memos to inform the process • Generate detailed 'open' codes to capture data which appears relevant • Name codes in specific terms and define them precisely • After basic code retrieval and coding scheme refinement (see chapters 8 & 9) proceed with coding remaining focus-group data

Tasks from PHASE FIVE: Deductive analysis of media content	
Deductive coding in light of previous coding phases	• Identify keywords/phrases that are indicators of themes identified in survey and focus-group data, auto-code on that basis across the media materials • Integrate media coding with primary data coding by merging codes or using short-cut code groupings • Build on existing memos to comment on what is seen in the media content and how that relates to the content of the primary data

projects it may be useful to code all the answers to each question across the dataset separately in order to view and analyse the answers in isolation. This can usually be achieved semi-automatically if data are formatted in a particular way (Chapters 4, 6 and 12). Case Study B, The Financial Downturn contains two forms of data which are inherently structured (open-ended responses to survey questions and focus-group discussions) and they were thus approached, in part, in this way. The open-ended responses to the survey were coded first in the context of theoretically derived 'sensitising concepts' according to the questions asked, and through use of content-based searching tools. The focus groups were auto-coded according to speaker sections (Chapters 4 and 12, Box 4.3). Case A, Young People's Perceptions, also contains various structural elements, but this time based upon broad topics in the interview guide, the vignette scenarios and the photos shown as prompts to elucidate attitudes. Chapter 12 discusses processes for auto-coding on the basis of such structures and Chapter 13 ways in which these can be used as the basis of revealing interrogations.

Figure 7.3 illustrates the potential of being able to recode descriptive (perhaps question-based) coding, in more detail. Another aspect of the analysis was more explorative, cutting across the question structure to consider, for example, the enablers of and barriers to creativity and innovation in the workplace. Question-based analysis is often required by commissioned research in various applied settings, for example, public consultations, service evaluations and some forms of government research. Sometimes, though, coding *only* in this way can restrict your flexibility and ability to think outside the question structure.

Combining approaches:
the practice of abductive coding
strategies using software

Discussions concerning inductive and deductive approaches to coding are necessarily simplistic and should not be viewed as dichotomously opposed or mutually exclusive. We present them separately in order to illustrate ways software tools can support a range of different approaches. As Gibbs (2002: 59) states, 'you do not have to do either one or the other or even one and then the other'. The dialectic, combination or relationship between inductive and deductive practices is sometimes referred to as 'abduction' (Blaikie, 2000; Guba and Lincoln, 1994). Some authors argue that abduction is the 'guiding principle of empirically-based theory construction' (Timmermans and Tavory, 2012). Whatever the preferred terminology, there is always an interplay between ideas and data, as emphasised by Dey (1993: 7):

> We cannot analyse the data without ideas, but our ideas must be shaped and tested by the data we are analysing. In my view this dialectic informs qualitative analysis from the outset, making debates about whether to base analysis primarily on ideas (through deduction) or on the data (through induction) rather sterile.

Similarly, Mason emphasises the sense in which 'qualitative research design and research practice are imbued with theory throughout' (2002: 179), referring to inductive/deductive approaches by characterising the *stage* at which theory comes into play – first, last, or simultaneously with data generation and analysis (2002: 180). Indeed, many authors have developed particular approaches to qualitative research and analysis which formally advocate a combination of approaches to coding. Layder's (1998) 'adaptive theory', for example, is a multi-strategy approach to the whole process of analysis in which he argues that particular aspects cannot be viewed in isolation. In coding data this approach takes account of both existing theoretical ideas and those which develop directly from the data under consideration.

Case Study A, Young People's Perceptions and Case Study B, The Financial Downturn provide examples of this type of dialectic between theory and data (Table 2.1; p. 39). The use of software facilitates the interplay and allows the process of integration to be made transparent. You do not have to code everything. In Case Study A we initially employed deductive, broad-brush coding across the dataset. This was important in establishing a relationship between theory evidenced in the literature review and the analysis of primary data. Data collected at the broad codes were subsequently recoded inductively in order to begin integrating the analysis of different types of data. Software supported topic and content based coding quickly gathers related material together. Working with literature and critical appraisals about them first ensures the analysis is driven by theory. Conducting inductive coding of previously deductively generated bodies of coding allows in-depth analytical work to be carried out without other data confusing thinking. This is important with Case Study A because there is much material contained in the literature and the primary data which does not specifically relate to the present research questions. This is illustrated using NVivo in Figure 7.1.

The code 'Moral contexts' contains a large number of references (167) from a range of data sources (21). The sub-codes hanging beneath have been created through inductive recoding. Some are quite specific with as yet relatively little data recoded at them (e.g. 'Controversies re teaching in a moral framework', 'Interconnectivity between parental and school morals' and 'Sexual explicitness').

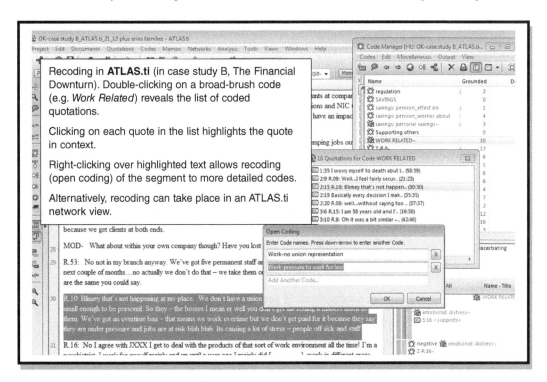

Figure 7.3 Inductively recoding descriptive or broad-brush codes in context (ATLAS.ti)

Others are more broadly specified and are already relatively prolific (e.g. 'Religious beliefs' and 'Embarrassment'). Primary data coded at 'Moral contexts' derived from the photo-prompt material were later recoded to a range of sub-codes – including 'Too young to be parents', 'Gendered experiences of morality', 'Blame' and 'Impact of religion'. Working with various visualisations within software offers the researcher flexibility to consider data in different ways. Figure 7.3 illustrates a similar recoding process in Case Study B.

The left-hand part of Figure 7.1, lists data sources coded at 'Moral contexts', showing data sources by type (e.g. literature and primary data); indicators of frequency of application (Reference column) and volume of data coded as a percentage of the whole data source (Coverage column). Such 'quantitisation' of qualitative coding contributes to the prioritisation of themes as part of analytic reflection and theoretical refinement. However this should not be construed as 'mixed methods' or 'quantitative analysis'; it is simply a means to see which 'piles' are bigger (Chapters 8 and 9). Other visualisations when recoding are also possible, including focusing on how data of different types (e.g. interviews, vignettes and photo prompts) contributed by one respondent in order to consider whether data collection tools impact on thematic content of material; and sorting coded material according to factual data characteristics, such as socio-demographic variables (Chapter 12), in order to facilitate the visualisation of comparisons on that basis (Chapter 13).

In Case Study B, the main idea framing the design of the analytic strategy was to work inductively with the primary data in order to enable a participant-grounded analysis. Given the currency of the substantive topic, however, and the intention also to include an analysis of media content, it was important to be explicit about the general theoretical backdrop which both framed our thinking about the data, and the design of the survey and the focus-group discussions. That said, at the time of designing the project and collecting the data, there was little published research into the implications of the global financial crisis to draw upon. However, the research questions informed the survey design and four of the following five questions asked are open-ended questions and therefore constitute qualitative responses.

1. How secure do you feel in your job? (scale of 1–5)
2. How have you been personally affected by the financial crisis?
3. Please indicate who you feel are most at fault for the financial crisis. (Government, banks, Eurozone – pick up to 2 choices)

    a. Please provide comments about your answer to question 3.

4. Are you planning a holiday over the next 6 months?

    b. Please provide comments about your answer to question 4.

5. Please comment on any special non-routine purchases or expenditure you have made in the last 6 months (of over £400 in value).

Perceptions around job security and potential impacts on lifestyle of losing one's job were the contextualising topics, and general literature concerning unemployment and poverty provided the theoretical context. We were explicit about the role of these theories and our own preconceptions and expectations in formulating the research problem, designing the data collection and developing the analytic strategy. Four types of code were generated through the different phases of work; a few examples are listed in Table 7.3. The survey data were collected first, with the intention to conduct a preliminary analysis of them before conducting focus groups in order to investigate key themes identified in the survey in more detail. Some survey respondents were invited to participate in the focus groups in order to compare responses to the different data types.

Table 7.3 Code development in a 'theory-informed' abductive approach (Case study B, The Financial Downturn)

Name and type	Code definition/explanation
SENSITISING CONCEPTS	
(derived from literature and included as deductive codes at the outset of the coding process)	
Stigma of unemployment	from the literature about poverty/unemployment – unemployment stigma exists and can lead to a hiring bias against the unemployed
Reduction in self-esteem	from the literature: crises of confidence in the view of self – caused by low expectations and reducing circumstances
Alienation	not quite the (Marxist) theory of, but in the context of being alienated from the area of work – not part of that world – forcibly prevented from affirming self-worth – related to *self-esteem*
CONTENT-BASED CODES	
(generated by keyword/phrase searching of open-ended survey responses/media content)	
Spending behaviour	captured by words – bought, buy, spend, purchase, afford, essential, avoid, credit. Initially captures discussion of spending in any context – but in terms of equivalence – needs to be broken down in terms of whether talk is about the need to spend the attempt to curb spending purchases made and feelings about them changes in what can be afforded perceptions of what is 'essential' spending and how that is conceptualised
Impact on income	captured by words – money, income, pay, balance, bills, pinch
Indicators of transition	captured by words – change, prospect, plans, pension, affected. This body of coding occurred during PROCESS FOUR (inductive coding of focus-group data). Allows the consideration of transition in all spheres of life – and changes that have already happened and those that are envisaged in the future
BROAD-BRUSH CODES	
(derived from the main topics thrown up by the focus-group discussions)	
Concern for younger	explicit but general concern about younger members of family re security, employment mortgages etc – for re-analysis later
Affects on social-formal	impacts on social organisations – for re-analysis later

(Continued)

Table 7.3 (Continued)

Name and type	Code definition/explanation
Affects on social-informal	all mentions of day to day impacts on social-life, meeting places – for re-analysis later
Security	any reference to personal sense of security of employment, financial, in future etc etc – for re-analysis later
Political statements	collection of any views about the 'politics' of the downturn – to be examined and re-analysed later
Economy statements	collection of any views about the 'economics' of the downturn – to be examined and re-analysed later

EMERGING CODES
(generated inductively from focus-group transcripts)

Name and type	Code definition/explanation
upsetting exit	redundancy not handled well, exacerbating negative aspects of losing job
'you're an ex'	in vivo code – no longer part of organisation
compulsion to get job	the sense that you do not have a choice about getting work, nothing else to fall back on
poor morale	any mention of how, where, when is this happening
bad timing	life-stage – bad moment to be in difficulties
back at home	having to depend on parents again
manner of restructuring	how news was broken, the mechanics of negotiation
vulnerability of weakest	any mention of the impact on the vulnerable members of society

The flexibility of combining approaches

Contrasting the suggested analytic processes for the three case-study examples illustrates that approaches are flexible, designed in relation to the specific needs of each study. Table 2.1 lists the analytic processes in summary format and Tables 7.1, 7.2 and 7.4 provide more detail for each Case Study so that you can compare the ordering of processes. Many researchers who use software combine grounded approaches to coding with more deductive processes. Even those following a prescribed method, or working within a particular paradigm, often want to be able to incorporate an element of flexibility for working in other ways. For example, where a project is commissioned and the brief specifies certain outcomes, a fairly mature coding schema may be identified at an early stage. In such projects, however, researchers usually also want to allow for the identification and analysis of 'surprising' or contradictory aspects. You might be looking for something specific now – but this does not preclude the use of your data to answer additional, perhaps unrelated questions, or to be considered from a different perspective later. CAQDAS packages support this very well (see also Chapter 9 on developing and managing coding schemes).

Coding visual data: 'indirect' and 'direct' approaches

Discussion in this chapter so far has largely concerned the coding of textual forms of data, but many research projects also utilise visual materials. CAQDAS packages vary in how they handle visual data, particularly in terms of whether they require moving images to be associated with written transcripts in order to be coded. Chapters 4 and 6 introduced this distinction in terms of whether visual data are accessed and analysed 'directly' (i.e. without the need for an associated written transcription) or 'indirectly' (i.e. where some sort of written transcript is required in order to code and analyse). In this chapter we discuss both, although it is important to note that your chosen software may not support both (Chapter 3).

Coding visual data 'indirectly' via synchronised transcripts

Written transcripts can often be generated within CAQDAS packages and associated with the corresponding media. If the process of generating written transcripts has been undertaken independently, then coding forms a secondary stage. In such an approach, transcript development will have constituted an analytic act in its own right. The resultant written representation might usefully be explored in ways similar to those discussed in Chapter 6, but also as a means of checking accuracy and to quickly locate particular areas of interest.

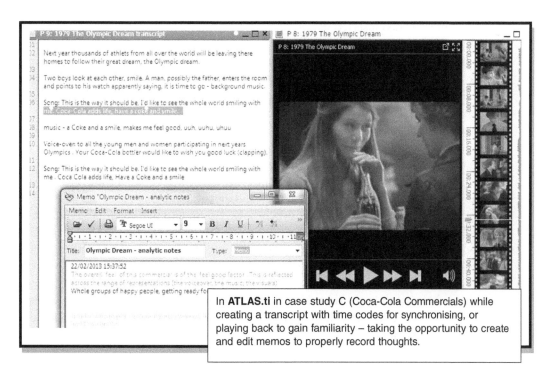

In **ATLAS.ti** in case study C (Coca-Cola Commercials) while creating a transcript with time codes for synchronising, or playing back to gain familiarity – taking the opportunity to create and edit memos to properly record thoughts.

Figure 7.4 Synchronised playback of single transcript (ATLAS.ti)

Working inductively, with limited 'external' or 'theoretical' direction concerning code development, it is useful to be as familiar as possible with data before coding commences. This might not always be possible, however, when working with extensive datasets. The transcription process itself can be important in this respect, as decisions involved during that stage will necessarily direct analytic focus. Having developed the transcripts and associated them with the corresponding video, playing them back in synchronised mode one after the other will constitute another moment of data familiarisation. In the context of Case Study C, Coca-Cola Commercials, for example, watching each commercial at the same time as reading through the corresponding transcript offers a multidimensional representation that would be lacking if only one or the other were available (Silver and Patashnick, 2011). This is illustrated in Figure 7.4 in ATLAS.ti. The written transcript (P9 on the left) and the corresponding video (P10 on the right) are opened side by side. When in *Synchro Mode* they can be played back together – the red dots visible in the transcript are the *anchors* which synchronise the two documents – the text in the transcript is highlighted in blue as the video plays. Also visible in Figure 7.4 is a memo – entitled 'Olympic Dream – Analytic Notes' – which was initially created during transcription. Having this open during synchronised playback and adding to it as additional insights are developed is fundamental in developing detailed and incremental 'audit trails' of analytic and process notes (Chapter 10). In Figure 4.3, three different textual transcripts are synchronised with one video in Transana; in Figure 6.2 the Transana illustration shows that the researcher has made use of 'snapshots' of the video inserted in two of the transcripts, which may be useful when the transcript is exported.

It can be tempting to start the process of inductive coding as soon as transcripts have been created, and in some situations this can work well. However, ensuring coding is as purposeful as possible from the outset is important when their generation is data-driven. This is especially true when working with visual data because of their multidimensional nature. Reflect upon the elements within data which seem to be relevant to the type and level of analysis you want to achieve. This may include considerations as to the content and interaction as well as the form and structure.

Working in tandem with memos (see Figure 7.4; p. 175) during the various moments at which you engage with visual data before coding processes (e.g. initial data familiarisation, transcription, synchronised playback) will ensure that inductive coding remains analytically focused and grounded. Adopting an 'indirect inductive coding' approach as described here (Table 7.4; p. 177) values the contrasting perspectives provided by textual, audio and visual representations. This type of work is all about creating codes that closely reflect your interpretations of the meaning of what is being seen in the data. Having already gone through the process of generating transcripts, it is valuable to make use of this earlier work in coding data and generating themes.

Although the bulk of the work relating to the generation of transcripts might have been conducted as an initial, earlier, stage, it should nevertheless be remembered that transcription of visual material – when the intention is to work with both

Table 7.4 Coding in software: some suggestions in the context of case study C, Coca-Cola Commercials

Tasks from PHASE TWO: Exploration and identification of analytic focus	
Familiarise with commercials	• Watch each commercial several times • Create a memo for each commercial and make notes about first impressions generally, and in relation to each research question • Informed by the capabilities of your chosen software, decide whether to work directly or indirectly
Working directly	• Rationalise and justify the decision not to generate transcripts; what might you gain or lose in adopting the direct approach? • Experiment with creating clips and annotating them (where this is possible to the exclusion of coding)
Working indirectly – transcript development	• Use software transcription tools to develop synchronised transcripts for each commercial (experimenting with developing multiple transcripts where this is possible) • Consider the importance of the placement of timestamps (time codes) in terms of subsequent qualitative retrieval and quantitisation (these implications differ depending on the software) • Be clear in your mind about the different role of annotations and transcripts in terms of your methodology and the capabilities of the software you are using

Tasks from PHASE SEVEN: Integration and analysis of publicity materials	
Focused reading, exploration and coding	• In light of the write-up of the preliminary primary data analysis (Phase Five), explore publicity materials • Use text searching tools to quickly locate passages likely indicative of the themes you previously generated • In memos write about the connections seen between the commercials and the publicity materials

representations simultaneously – is a dynamic and iterative process. Within the software, transcripts can be revisited and edited incrementally, even after coding has begun. Coding may even occur in tandem with transcript development.

Coding visual data 'directly', without an associated transcript

Several software packages enable visual data – both still and moving images – to be handled without the need for an associated or synchronised textual transcript. We call this 'direct' analysis (Silver and Patashnick, 2011). This technological possibility raises issues concerning the direction of the relationship between technology and methodology (Silver and Lewins, forthcoming). In relation to developing strategies which result in relevant, targeted, or 'good quality' analyses, an awareness of the implications of technical subtleties such as this are important. It might feel like the possibilities for direct analysis obviate the need for a transcript, or offer a 'short-cut' to analysis. Be cautious about proceeding in this way, however, unless there are good methodological reasons for working directly with visual records.

The issue is quite different depending on whether you are working with still or moving images. In the former, there may be many good reasons for working directly. With respect to the latter, however, it is rarely the case that time will actually be saved; what you save at the transcription stage, you use up at the analysis stage; as without any form of written representation, you have to work with moving images in 'real time' (Silver and Patashnick, 2011).

There are, however, instances when working directly has analytic benefits. Figure 7.5 illustrates how a moving image file might be directly coded using ATLAS.ti. In this example, clips have been created based on changes in action, with clips of varying length appearing as thick brackets in the margin view. The clips have been coded according to several action- and interaction-based codes. Different types of code appear in different colours in the margin view, enabling a visual overview in patterns sequentially (vertically) through the commercial. Individual and collections of clips coded in a particular way can be retrieved, played back, recoded, etc. at any point (Chapter 8). This particular commercial provides a good example of when the direct coding of moving images can be particularly useful as there is very little verbal dialogue. The dialogue which does occur takes place at the beginning and the end of the commercial and is very repetitive ('It's eleven-thirty' and 'Diet Coke break' at the beginning as the women gather to watch the 'performance', and a short exchange at the end where two of them reflect on what they have seen: 'oh that was great', 'see you tomorrow', 'eleven-thirty'). This is reflected by repetition in non-verbal actions – principally in the middle section, where a series of shots showing the male building-site worker removing his shirt and drinking

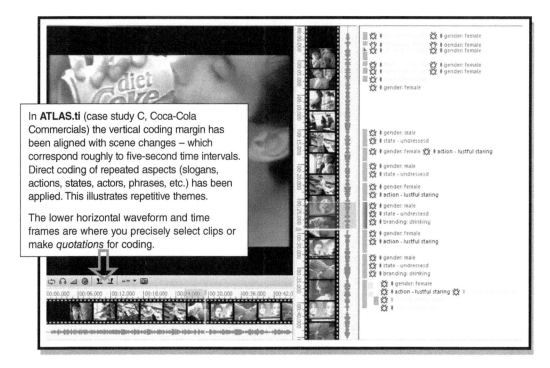

Figure 7.5 Direct coding of video (ATLAS.ti)

a can of Diet Coke are interspersed with shots of the group of female office workers looking at him through the window. Creating clips (or quotations, as ATLAS.ti calls them) for each section of action in this way (which corresponds closely to camera shots in this example) serves to indicate patterns in the speed of interactions and the length of time a certain type of action is displayed. In Figure 7.5 this is indicated visually by the relative length of the quotations as represented by margin brackets. In Chapter 8 we discuss both qualitative and quantitative retrieval options. Length of clip is an example of the latter type which can be retrieved in precise, quantifiable terms.

With respect to still images there are similar issues, but some added possibilities in Transana. 'Snapshots' can be taken from video sources and saved as stills, which can be embedded within transcripts for illustrative purposes (see Figure 6.2; p. 142). In addition, these can be visually annotated, which is a form of coding (Figure 7.6; below). Codes (called keywords in Transana) can be assigned a unique combination of coding shape (rectangle, ellipse, line, arrow), colour, line width and line style (solid, dash, dot, and dot-dash). This offers distinctive means of handling visual data and, particularly, of indicating emphasis in non-verbal interactions (see also Figure 6.3; p. 144).

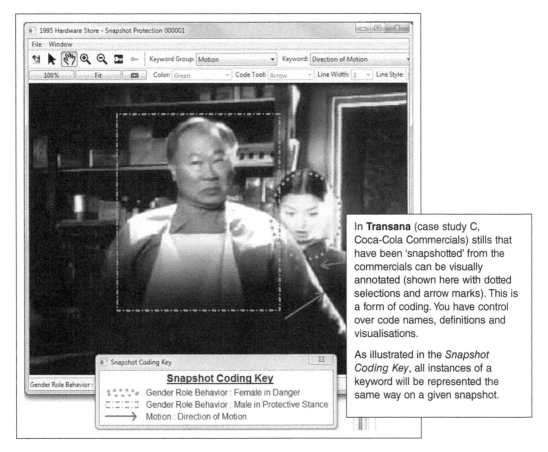

Figure 7.6 Visual annotation and coding of still images (Transana)

For certain types of visual data, then, there may be several benefits of working directly. But in developing a strategy you will also need to be aware of what might be lost or compromised by the analytic choices you make. However, the decision as to whether to work directly or indirectly is not necessarily a binary choice – it might be most appropriate, for example, to combine the two – and some packages allow visual data to be handled both indirectly and directly. Where this is the case, it is particularly important to develop a strategy for when and why each technique would be used.

BOX 7.6 | ANALYTIC NOTES

Questions to ask yourself when coding visual materials

- When coding indirectly (via the transcripts) how has your prior placement of time-stamps affected the units you chose to code? (Note that software packages differ with respect to whether timestamp placement defines 'minimum codable segment'.)
- If coding directly, how does the content of the media and what you are interested in analytically affect the size of data segment you create?

Coding in software, whatever the approach

The use of software enables the combination of approaches to coding in ways which are more dynamic than is possible when working on paper (e.g. using highlighter pens on hard-copy transcripts) or with non-bespoke software packages (e.g. word-processor or spreadsheet applications). Whatever the approach, using software encourages the cyclical and iterative nature of qualitative research. The structure and functionality of CAQDAS packages do not promote in themselves a linear progression of tasks. Coding qualitative data is part of a flexible process, and coding using software can also be cyclical and iterative in nature, regardless of the approach(es) employed.

There are two main issues to think about in approaching coding when using software:

- the basis upon which codes are generated;
- how different types of codes and coding techniques help at different times in the analysis.

Whilst no qualitative software program will, on its own, solve either issue, they can support different approaches to both.

The overriding aim of coding is to facilitate developing a detailed understanding of the phenomena which the data are seen as representing. This may involve gaining an insight into the underlying meaning respondents attribute to a social situation or particular experience, identifying patterns in attitudes, or investigating processes of social interaction. Employing a systematic coding strategy will allow you to revisit significant instances, to think about them again and to produce further insights. Be clear how the codes you use are helping you make sense of the data.

Bases for generating codes

The codes you develop may be influenced by a number of factors, including:

- theoretical context
- study aims
- research questions
- methodology and analytic approach
- amount, kinds and sources of data
- level and depth of analysis
- constraints
- research audience.

A code may represent a deeply theoretical or analytical concept; it could be completely practical or descriptive; or it could simply represent 'interesting stuff' or 'data I need to think about more' (Chapter 6). A project will usually consist of different types of codes. As analysis proceeds, the purpose and use of codes will usually change and you may collect them together in different ways. Above all, codes provide access to those parts of the data which allow you to think about the phenomena you want to examine (see Chapter 9 for more on making the most of coding schemes).

As well as having multiple functions, codes may be generated in a number of ways. For example, they may be based on:

- *ideas or concepts* – derived from existing literature in the research area and/or developed from close reading and thinking about the data.
- *themes or topics* – identified within data through close reading and thinking.
- *language or terminology* used in the data – whether words or phrases used by respondents or found in documentary evidence, or (un)conventional structures in discourse or narrative.

Labels and definitions need to be *meaningful* in the sense that they indicate the nature of data grouped at that code in some way. This may have a descriptive or more analytic purpose, which in turn may vary according to the approach to and stage of analysis.

BOX 7.7 — ANALYTIC NOTES

Limits and cautions when using software coding tools

What do you gain/lose in your approach to coding? It is important to think carefully about the analytic and practical implications of different ways of working. Among the issues that can cause problems are:

- Seeing coding as analysis in and of itself
- Generating too many codes

(Continued)

(Continued)

- Not knowing when to stop coding
- Not keeping on top of code definitions
- Misunderstanding the difference between code application counts and counts of the occurrence of an aspect contained within data (Chapter 8)
- Misunderstanding the purpose of coding schema structures (Chapter 9).

Concluding remarks: using software to support *your* approach to coding

There are many ways in which to organise qualitative data through coding. The processes and sequences you go through may be influenced by a range of factors. However codes are generated and applied, their purpose is to enable you to revisit data and to carry on thinking about them. As such, codes function as 'heuristic devices for discovery' (Seidel and Kelle, 1995: 58). Coding is not about perfectly capturing an instance or concept. Codes act as signposts to remind you to go back and think about an issue and the data linked to it again. Using software offers flexible ways to code and supports discrete and combined strategies. This flexibility, however, requires being clear about how and why different codes are generated, applied and used. There are various ways of achieving this, including consistent and meaningful code definition (Chapter 7), the use of integrated memo tools (Chapter 9) and modelling ideas and relationships (Chapter 10).

We are not advocating adherence to a particular methodology, process or strategy. Conversely, we would argue that different coding strategies are suitable in different situations rather than that there is a 'right or wrong' way of coding. It may be appropriate to follow different procedures and processes for coding different types of data within the same project as well as in different projects.

It is important to be aware of the ways your chosen software handles coding processes and to develop your own strategy of coding within your project efficiently. A balance needs to be found between your analytic needs *vis-à-vis* coding and the ways in which your chosen software will support you during the various coding phases. The following chapters have been written to help you reach such a balance.

CHAPTER EXERCISES

The following exercises are designed to help you become familiar with the coding functionality within your chosen software and to think about the suitability of different approaches to the generation and use of codes such that you can develop a technologically informed strategy for the use of coding tools in your own work. As stressed throughout the main body of this chapter, although software coding tools can open up the way we think about the descriptive, thematic and conceptual indexing of data, working with them in a methodological vacuum is likely to lead to more, rather than less, confusion.

We therefore assume that you will have considered the broader literature concerning qualitative coding before embarking in earnest on coding your own raw data. That said, early experimentation with coding tools in the ways listed in the exercises below, and contained within the software-specific instructions on the companion website, can usefully contribute to the development of an effective and transparent coding strategy. In the experimentations you undertake, we encourage you to think explicitly about the relationship between qualitative (and mixed methods) methodology and the possibilities technology affords. Whether your end result will be an undergraduate dissertation, postgraduate thesis or journal publication, reflective discussion about the nature of software-supported coding and the analysis which it supports will always be of value (see Silver and Lewins, 2014, for more in-depth discussion of these issues).

Generating codes

1. *Create a priori codes.* Any key issues or themes you know you will be interested in can be generated independently of data at any stage. They may be fairly broadly specified and/or identified from existing literature and theory.

    (a) Generate some empty groups of codes for any deductively derived themes, name them appropriately.
    (b) Create deductive codes for each case-study example.
    (c) Create sub-codes as appropriate to the case study and software you are using.

2. *Create codes grounded in the data.* Whatever their type or purpose, new codes can always be created whilst reading/looking through data, and linked immediately to the precise segment which prompted that new idea, concept or category. Generate codes for interesting aspects you identify inductively in the data which seem to be relevant to your thinking about the research questions, and name them appropriately.
3. *Create in vivo codes.* If you are particularly interested in the language used in the data, or if a term is identified which neatly encapsulates an idea or theme, you can create codes *in vivo*. Many packages allow words and phrases used in the data to be quickly and automatically turned into a code label. Be aware though that if you use this tool widely, it has methodological implications. It may seem very useful as a short-cut to code generation, but if working interpretively you should use it critically, being aware that it only has a temporary role to play in the whole process of producing more analytic ideas about the data.

Apply existing codes to data

1. *Define the amount of text to be coded.* Whether it is the word, phrase, sentence, paragraph or whole document, the researcher specifies the relevant unit of context.
2. *Apply codes as relevant.* Apply as many codes to a text segment or to overlapping segments as relevant, if this seems methodologically appropriate. Most software packages allow this sort of deductive coding (i.e. where you apply existing (probably broadly specified) codes to data segments as you identify them) in several different ways. Experiment with them all and think about which best suit your preferred way of working.

3. *View codes appearing in the margin.* Viewing codes this way is useful because it allows you to see co-occurring codes and visually identify interesting patterns and relationships as you proceed. Make notes in memos or annotations for interesting early patterns you are seeing.

Define and list codes

1. *Define the meaning, scope and intended application of codes.* It makes sense, where possible, to do this as codes are generated. Therefore, consider the function and impetus for generating the code and revisit and refine definitions. Date any changes in definition so you can track developments in thinking. Small leaps in reasoning are important, and increasing the transparency of your work in this way will add to the potential quality of your work. Experiment with defining codes using memo, comment or description tools.

    (a) Working deductively, it usually makes sense to add code definitions at the time of code creation. This is often particularly important in team projects when a high level of agreement about the meaning and intended application of codes is needed in order to achieve as much consistency as possible.

    (b) Working inductively, it is often the case that the defining of codes does not happen immediately upon their creation. This can be both because code names themselves are often more specific, but also because researchers want to 'get on' with the task of coding without being distracted or held up by generating carefully worded definitions. Where either is the case, you can go back at any point to add code definitions. Some packages provide easily visible ways of seeing which codes have definitions.

    (c) See Chapter 9 for discussion about the role of code definitions in rationalising coding schema structures, moving on from descriptive or thematic indexing of data through coding and ensuring you do not end up with an unwieldy, inefficient or too prolific coding schema.

2. *Generate code reports.* Listing codes and their definitions is useful for analytic and practical reasons. Generating a code list can help at various stages, for example when thinking about grouping codes, generating higher-level categories, or reorganising the coding schemes. Retaining these reports can provide a useful 'snapshot' of the various stages of the analytic process.

Refine coding

1. *Increase or decrease the amount of text coded.* Refining the coding in this way may be useful when considering themes or concepts in more detail and moving on beyond the first pass through the data. Experiment with both increasing and decreasing the amount of data assigned to particular codes, and notice how the changes appear in the margin view.

2. *Unlink a code from a point in the data.* It is just as easy to uncode data as to code it if you change your mind about the need for a code at a point in the data, or make an error. There will usually be several ways to uncode data, so become familiar with these. In packages where marked data segments are independent objects in their own right, notice that uncoding does not automatically unmark the segment; it can still be considered as a segment of interest (and annotated, linked, etc.).

3. *Experiment with colour coding tools.* Most packages allow codes to be assigned colour, which is usually reflected in other windows as well as in the code margin view (although you may not be able to retrieve on that basis). Consistent application of colour can add an additional dimension to coding, for example to differentiate between types of or purposes for coding, so think carefully about how colouring codes can have an analytic function in your project (this is discussed in more detail in Chapter 8).

4. *Experiment with assigning weight* to individual code assignations (where possible). Some packages allow individual coded data segments to additionally be assigned 'weight'. This might have several purposes, including to specify how strongly a particular attitude is being expressed (this is discussed in more detail in Chapter 8).

8

Basic Retrieval of Coded Data

This chapter builds on the tasks discussed in Chapters 6 and 7 to introduce some retrieval options. Whatever your purpose in coding, you will inevitably want to retrieve data based on that work at various moments. 'Code and retrieve' functionality is a basic tenet underlying the packages we discuss in this book (Chapter 1). As illustrated in Figure 2.1, retrieval is essential to the processes of analysis, whatever your methodology or analytic approach. This chapter is practical in orientation, considering some ways of and reasons for retrieving data based on how they have been coded without using the query tools, although the tasks discussed in this chapter are related to those covered in Chapter 13. Tables 8.1, 8.2 and 8.3 provide suggestions for retrieval for the case-study examples.

We illustrate tasks within software and how to generate reports to get information out of software. Despite the placing of this chapter, retrieval is not a task conducted only after a particular coding phase has been completed. Just as you continually reflect on data and how you are coding as you proceed, you will see interesting patterns, relationships, contradictions, etc. whilst retrieving coded data. As always, we encourage you to capture these thoughts as they enter your mind by writing about them (Chapters 6 and 10).

Be critical in how you think about and use retrieval tools. Consider how they may support your analytic approach and style of working. Be flexible in integrating them into other aspects of work. Above all, experiment. Retrieving coded data is about reviewing progress so far. It is about cutting across your dataset in different ways, to gather together similar data, to think about them again, to begin moving towards working on more conceptual and abstract levels. You may subsequently continue coding, as you identify gaps or inconsistencies and rethink data and the concepts that they represent. Always be alert to what is *not* apparent. Coding and retrieval inevitably reinforce what is in the data. But it is also important to think about what you are not seeing, what people are not talking about or doing, that might have been expected. Write memos about what you do and do not see. Coding is a way of managing your ideas about your data, and retrieval allows you to consider how these processes are informing your developing interpretations.

Principles of basic retrieval

There are many benefits to query tools which provide retrieval based on complex combinations. However, these should not distract from the usefulness of simpler forms. Many researchers do not make significant use of complex query tools – perhaps because their project does not require this level of interrogation, because they feel intimidated by options or user interface, or sometimes because they 'run out of time'. Chapter 13, on interrogating the dataset, addresses these issues. In this chapter we distinguish between purposes and types of retrieval to illustrate ways in which these tasks contribute to the process of 'moving on' from the indexing of data through coding, to more conceptual and abstract levels of analysis.

The main purposes of retrieval are to:

(a) remind you where you got to last time you were working with the software;
(b) generate snapshots of coding status;
(c) help identify areas of further interest;
(d) facilitate the recoding of data;
(e) compare coding.

Box 8.1 discusses purposes and considerations for types of retrieval.

BOX 8.1 ──── ANALYTIC NOTES

Purposes and considerations for types of basic retrieval

Purpose: to retrieve and reconsider coded data in various ways in order to generate a preliminary analysis and direct subsequent work such that analysis moves on to a higher level.

Considerations. Whatever your approach to coding, it is important to view the process as iterative. The use of software encourages this, as it is so easy to change your mind about how data have been coded (Chapter 9). Retrieving coded data supports these tasks, and when using software, coding and retrieval go hand in hand. Visualising and thinking about coded data in a range of ways (e.g. within context and out of context; in quantitative summary format and in traditional qualitative format; sequentially throughout one data file and comparatively across several, etc.) provides more potential for seeing the unexpected as well as for checking consistency in coding. These are the building blocks of analysis.

Retrieval options in software provide ways to review, reflect and move on with analysis. It is easy to change your mind about how data have been coded. You may be doing this as you look through one document. Retrieving coded data across (parts of) the dataset, however, can further support the cyclical and iterative processes of conducting analysis when using software. Retrieval is an iterative, incremental process, which occurs throughout analysis, rather than constituting an isolated activity or discrete stage of work. Essentially, it allows you to cut through the data according to how you have so

(Continued)

far coded, vertically and horizontally. Vertical cuts allow you to pick out sequences in coding within one data source; horizontal cuts to consider one body of coding across the whole (or parts of) the dataset (Chapter 1). Some packages allow you to do both concurrently. The design of your analytic strategy, however, will affect the type of retrieval you engage in at various moments, and the role doing so has in the work you are engaged in at that point. The ways we discuss retrieval with regard to the case studies are just examples; the utility of retrieval in software is not restricted to just these tasks or, indeed, the suggested analytic processes we discuss here. You will find additional ways in which retrieval is useful in your own work, and can pick and choose the examples we discuss to suit your practical and methodological needs.

Purposes of basic retrieval

There are many different purposes for retrieving data. We distinguish between practical and analytical purposes and illustrate how they can be useful whatever your analytic strategy.

Aiding continuity: where did I get to last time?

Perhaps the most practical reason for retrieval is to check what and how much has been coded so far. This is a useful exercise at the start of a software session when you are in 'serious coding mode'. Remember the ways in which software can act as a project management device (Chapter 2). Revisiting components of your coding scheme through retrieval will aid your continuity. Similarly, it can also be very useful to reread the last entry in your project process journal at the beginning of each software session (Chapter 10). These tasks are invaluable in getting your mind back into the project. In Case Study A, where data are diverse and complex, reminding ourselves of what we had done previously enabled us to ensure we coded consistently. Although the first wave of coding was deductive, and therefore, to an extent, relatively descriptive, it was being undertaken in direct relation to earlier work with literature. It is not always possible to work on any research project without sometimes encountering breaks of several days or even weeks between significant analytic work sessions. It is valuable to conduct a few quick retrievals of previous coding at the start of each software session as well as to reread the last few entries in key memos.

Aiding continuity: generating snapshots of coding status

Another task in aiding continuity is about recording your processes and the results of your work. This is in significant part achieved through writing (see Chapters 2, 5, 6 and 10). Recording the results of your work is also related to saving versions of your entire software project at strategic moments; in addition to a routine back-up procedure (Chapter 5). It is always useful to generate snapshots of particular aspects of work at different times. In relation to coding processes, for example, when following an analytic strategy which employs more than one phase of coding, as in all three of our case-study examples, it will always be useful to snapshot the coding status at the end of each process. This will usefully entail both qualitative and quantitative representations (see below). In longitudinal projects in which phases of data collection and/or analysis are explicitly discrete, or in projects where different types of data have different roles and statuses within the design, this will be especially important.

BOX 8.2 ——— CASE NOTES

The importance of snapshotting stages of work (Case Study C, Coca-Cola Commercials)

Generating snapshots of at the end of each data-type coding stage is important in generating an overview of resultant thinking. In the Coca-Cola project the inductive coding approach necessitated significant reorganisation of the initial coding scheme (Chapter 9). Before such work is undertaken it is particularly important to snapshot coding status. This was usefully undertaken at the end of Phase Three (initial coding: inductive indexing), before Phase Four (basic code retrieval and provisional analytic commentary) started in earnest, and then again before Phase Seven (integration of analysis of publicity materials). Being able to illustrate how thinking develops in projects in which coding schemes evolve in this way is crucial to demonstrating rigour in process. An account of coding processes will be all the more powerful when coding schemes can be represented visually through output reports or screen dumps than when they are only described.

Moving the analysis on: identifying areas for further consideration

Whatever the direction of your analytic work, there will be several stages at which you will need to identify areas for further investigation. This involves prioritising the work you have done so far, for which you will need to step back and consider coded data and how the way you have gone about coding is helping you with the analysis. All types of retrieval (whether qualitative or quantitative in flavour) will help in this task. Remember that it is unlikely to be feasible – or necessary – to code all your data to the same degree or in the same way. Whether you are starting off broadly or at a detailed level, first-stage coding is just that – the first stage. It may not have constituted the first time you have looked at data, but it will have been your first attempt at systematically gathering together segments that you consider to be instances of the aspects you are interested in. This is an indexing process. Now you need to revisit those data segments and make some decisions about what to do next.

Revisiting data to identify areas of further consideration (Case Study B, The Financial Downturn)

Case Study B is a good example of this process. The three forms of data are varied in terms of their origin, nature and breadth. The suggested analytic strategy is designed such that preliminary results arising from each form directly and intentionally inform subsequent work. We started off broadly, coding data derived from survey respondents deductively (Phase Three). This could be done relatively quickly within software through the use of content searching tools, which first served to gain familiarity with the data, and subsequently to achieve broad-brush coding (see Chapter 6). As is common in most surveys, responses to the open-ended questions were relatively short. Hence, although data are quite broad in terms of the number of individuals providing responses, they are relatively shallow in terms of the understanding of issues. The purpose of coding in Phase Three was to identify – in relation to the research questions – attitudes and opinions commonly found amongst the survey sample and to develop a preliminary analysis that could be augmented with the focus-group data and media content. Quantitative overviews (see below) as well as qualitative retrievals and writing about what appeared important to respondents in each respect were an essential part of being able to do this.

However, identifying areas for further consideration is not only about prioritising the apparently 'most important' areas. It is also about deciding what is insignificant to the focus of your analysis. Frequently we generate a great deal of data not specifically relating to the research problem we have formulated or the questions we are seeking to answer. Just because you have data does not mean it is relevant to the current analytic task. Be prepared to decide *not* to focus on particular areas, but be clear about the reasons for doing so, and justify them in your memos.

Questions to ask yourself when retrieving to help you move forwards

- How do different ways of retrieving and visualising coded data move your thinking forward?
- To what extent do the primary data reflect the issues discussed in the literature?
- What questions do you still need to consider in order to answer the research questions?

Similarly, avoid falling into the trap of thinking that codes which are prolific in terms of the volume of data coded, or the frequency of code application, necessarily indicate salience. Just because codes are 'big' does not necessarily mean they are more analytically important. Often this is the case. But not always. Do not be afraid to decide not to focus on a particular area because it is 'too common' in some sense. In qualitative work it is often the infrequently occurring comments (or, indeed, what is not said) that leads to the most interesting analysis.

Moving the analysis on: recoding

Having identified the areas you intend to consider in more detail, it is almost certain that data already coded to these areas will need recoding. In making the decisions as to which bodies of initially coded data are worthy of reconsideration, you will have retrieved data and, as part of the rationalisation process, made notes about how codes – and data at them – need to be refined. Recoding is an inherent part of all coding approaches, and not only does the use of software facilitate the process, but also the tools provided by software – when used appropriately – can help ensure the process is systematic, and therefore rigorous.

When starting out coding deductively, data are recoded to differentiate between instances of the general, to account for the nuances within a theme. The analytic process suggested for Case Study A works in this way (see also Chapter 7). Primary data (interviews, vignettes and photo-prompt discussions) are coded first

Table 8.1 Basic forms of retrieval: some suggestions in the context of case study A, Young People's Perceptions

Tasks from PHASE FOUR: Inductive recoding of broad-brush codes	

Horizontal retrieval	• Identify broad codes relating to each research question
	 • Use horizontal retrieval (i.e. retrieving individual and groups of codes across all data so far coded) to
	    o identify areas of further interest
	    o compare coding
	    o decide which data to recode

Vertical retrieval	• Use vertical retrieval to visually identify patterns in coding
	    o sequentially through a data file
	    o through a body of broadly coded data

Tasks from PHASE SIX: Code retrieval, theoretical refinement, analytic reflection	
Qualitative retrieval	• Qualitative retrieval (horizontal and vertical as described above – but now also in relation to factual data organisation (Phase Five – chapter 12)
Quantitative retrieval	• Quantitative code retrieval o consider results of all retrievals quantitatively as well
Output retrievals	• Output results of different retrievals o for purposes of snapshotting status of work and to use when writing up (Phase Nine).

(Phase Three: first-wave coding – deductive broad-brush coding across the dataset). The purpose is to gather all data broadly related to the key areas of analytic interest as identified from the literature review. This might have proceeded using a 'human-driven' deductive approach, a 'computer-driven' approach, or a combination of both. However this sort of coding occurs, codes are essentially used as 'buckets', to gather together all data broadly relevant to each area likely to be of analytic interest. Those bodies of coded data are then retrieved and recoded inductively (Phase Four). The purpose is to conduct in-depth analytical coding of general 'themes' only when all data broadly relevant have been gathered. This serves to make the inductive coding process 'easier' – because you can focus entirely on one area without being distracted by other data. Software packages that enable recoding from separate windows in which data are lifted out of context (i.e. without seeing the surrounding source context) are particularly useful in this regard (Figure 7.1; p. 159). Most packages enable this, but do so in quite different ways. Usually, in lifting coded data out of context, information provided concerning co-occurrence pertains to the exact data segment, rather than overlapping segments. Although there will be interactivity back to source data where it is possible to view overlaps, this is not always a desirable action when wanting to focus on data coded in a particular way. NVivo's equivalence between 'source browser' and 'node browser' functionality provides an effective solution because the 'node browser' contains the same code margin functionality as the 'source browser'. This means that the user has complete control over which codes to view in relation to a broad body of coded data, thus facilitating the process of recoding. A similar process is enabled within the ATLAS.ti network view (Chapter 11). The difference with other packages is that NVivo and ATLAS.ti enable you to see the coded segments together, thus facilitating comparison, whereas other packages show you each coded segment one at a time, in the window from which you recode.

Moving the analysis on: comparing coding

Comparison is inherent in all analytic work. Much comparative work relates to considering how respondents with different characteristics view, experience or talk about an issue or theme. This is achieved in software by querying coded data according to the socio-demographics attributed to speakers (Chapter 13). In large or diverse datasets, it might also be related to comparing how certain codes occur across data of different types, as discussed above in relation to Case Study B. Retrieval of coded data horizontally across the whole – or parts of – the dataset enables this sort of comparison. We also discuss this below in terms of qualitative comparisons (considering the nature of the data coded across respondents, cases or data types), and quantitative comparisons (looking at the distribution of code application in terms of frequency of application and volume of data coded). Both give indications that are used as the basis of comparison based on the indexing work done in the earlier coding processes.

But comparing coding is also much more than this. Even in small datasets, where the concern is not to make comparisons across diverse data or respondent types, the comparison of coding has an important analytic role. The basis of the comparison will then be according to how codes occur in relation to one another, rather than – or as well as – in relation to other data. We illustrate this using Case Study C below.

Types of basic retrieval

Within software there are many different tools that enable coded data to be retrieved for the purposes outlined above. Here we discuss quantitative overviews, horizontal and vertical cuts, simple filtering devices for early comparative interrogations, and generating reports within and outputs from software.

Quantitative overviews

CAQDAS packages provide a variety of means by which qualitative data, and your coding of them, can be quantitised. This is particularly useful when employing a quantitative approach to analysis, when working in mixed methods contexts or with large datasets (Chapters 1 and 13). Viewing data according to how frequently codes have been applied or how much data has been coded (often referred to as 'coverage') may to some feel like a rather crude way of retrieving data. Of course, if this sort of work contravenes your analytic approach, you should not engage in it. However, similarly to how we view word-frequency tools – as means of familiarising with and exploring textual data (Chapter 6) – generating quantitative overviews can help to appraise data in alternative ways. Numeric information need not be reported, and certainly it would not usually be relevant to do so in projects comprising relatively 'little' data.

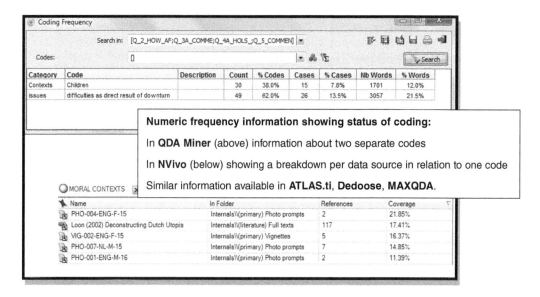

Figure 8.1 Code frequency information (QDA Miner and NVivo)

We discussed above ways in which code retrieval contributes to identifying areas for further investigation. Quantitative overviews are generally available in frequency form within the main code list view – showing, for example, the number of data segments to which a code has been applied, across the whole dataset, although in some packages (e.g. Dedoose) such information sits in a separate location and in others (e.g. QDA Miner, Transana) a search needs to be run to extract this sort of information. Packages also vary in the type of quantitative overview provided. This is illustrated in Figure 8.1 for QDA Miner and NVivo, and in Figure 8.2 for Dedoose.

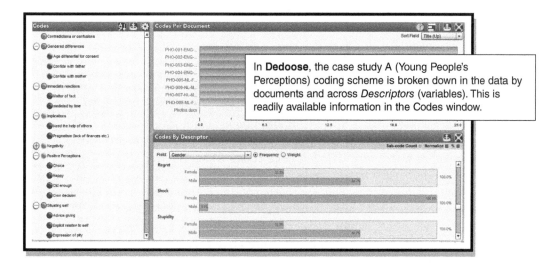

Figure 8.2 Codes by document and descriptor (variables) (Dedoose)

Dedoose and QDA Miner generally provide more different types of frequency information, including percentage as well as frequency counts for whole codes (NVivo provides that information concerning the breakdown according to data source coded, rather than for the code itself). In both these packages, the application of coding across different subsets can be interrogated in simple ways from these views. The QDA Miner Code Frequency dialogue, for example, allows for individual or combinations of variable to be searched in, and thus compared, as well as to be scoped to certain category of code. This sort of functionality is particularly useful at the stage of conducting retrieval for initial interrogative purposes.

BOX 8.6 — ANALYTIC NOTES

Questions to ask yourself when retrieving data

- Do the codes which have the highest number of applications across the dataset constitute the most 'significant' aspects? To what extent is this related to the way you have coded – especially in terms of the size of coded segments, and the way coded segments overlap?
- What is going on at codes which have relatively few data segments coded at them? Are these codes candidates for merging with others? Are they relevant to the analysis?
- Are data segments at each code equivalent in meaning? Or are they related to the same topic/theme but elucidating different or contradictory aspects? If yes, do they need 'splitting'?
- Are there some codes which are named similarly or have similar data coded at them? Could several codes be combined to create a theme or category? Do you want to bring them together but maintain the ability to view them independently? What tools does your chosen software provide to enable this?

Similar tasks can usually be enacted in other packages by filtering to short-cut groupings of data (termed sets or families) that have previously been created. However, this usually works on the basis of one set at a time, rather than in a comparative sense such as illustrated in the Codes by Descriptor view in Dedoose (Figure 8.2; p. 194). Nevertheless, CAQDAS packages provide a range of ways of quantitising qualitative data and your coding of them. This might form the basis of more complex interrogations as discussed in Chapter 13, but, throughout analytic processes, simple quantitative overviews point your attention to 'gaps and clusters' in coding, which offer pointers for further work.

Horizontal cuts

Cutting through data in different ways is inherent to the way analysis occurs and the benefits that using software provides (Chapter 1). Cutting across the whole dataset horizontally is at the heart of 'code and retrieve' functionality and as such fundamental to analytic processes involved in moving on from early indexing. For example, you might focus on an individual code or theme and retrieve all data segments linked to it, regardless of the data files in which they occur. You are thus able to start thinking about how a particular topic or theme occurs across the whole dataset, to think more analytically and start interrogating more deeply. This is useful at various stages of work, but in a project such as Case Study B, The Financial Downturn, plays a particular role in bringing coding of diverse materials together and therefore forms the basis of integrating analyses. Earlier we discussed how concern for younger generations was a theme identified in the first coding wave (Phase Three: deductive analysis of survey data). The intention to explore in more depth the contexts in which such concerns manifest themselves was one focus of coding undertaken in Phase Four (inductive analysis of focus-group data) and Phase Five (deductive analysis of media content). Phase Six (integration of coding across data types) is focused around bringing the coding of Phases Three–Five together in order to compare how topics are discussed in each form of data such as to enable the development of themes present across all. Basic code retrieval options facilitate these processes because they allow the focus on data and themes irrespective of the socio-demographic characteristics attributed to respondents. This is important because we wanted to develop general themes before exploring the impact of socio-demographics on their presence or articulation. Figure 8.3 illustrates two forms of this horizontal type of work in MAXQDA.

The two different displays shown in Figure 8.3 provided different opportunities for reflecting on data thus far coded and helped move on the thinking about this body of material. The tabular list of retrieved segments provides a general overview, revealing in summary format a sense of how prolific the code is across the different forms

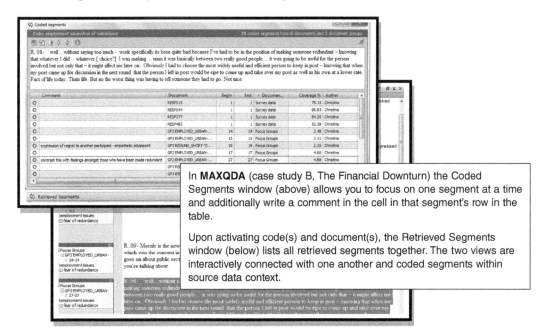

In **MAXQDA** (case study B, The Financial Downturn) the Coded Segments window (above) allows you to focus on one segment at a time and additionally write a comment in the cell in that segment's row in the table.

Upon activating code(s) and document(s), the Retrieved Segments window (below) lists all retrieved segments together. The two views are interactively connected with one another and coded segments within source data context.

Figure 8.3 Horizontal retrieval of coded segments – two interactive views (MAXQDA)

of data. Note, however, that the first four documents in the list – RESP015, RESP044, etc. – contain individual responses to open-ended survey questions, whereas the other documents visible are whole focus-group transcripts. Therefore, a simple comparative count of the number of documents in which the code 'Fear of redundancy' occurs, would be misleading, as documents do not equate to the same unit of analysis. For the same reason the coverage statistic in this example is not meaningful. However, the list of retrieved segments does provide the opportunity to view each coded segment in isolation and add analytic comments as appropriate. Data segments can also be easily outputted and recoded from this window. Detailed consideration of individual coded segments in this way is analytically very useful, but sometimes it is also important to view coded data segments more comparatively.

In the Retrieved Segments window (Figure 8.3) some pertinent information about the source of each segment is given in the flags adjacent to each segment, but this is less quantitative than the information provided in the list view. More important in retrieval terms, however, is the value of considering coded segments in relation to one another. The code 'Fear of redundancy' was created early on in the coding process, inductively, in response to the identification of this as an issue for one particular respondent. Looking at the retrieved segments, however, it is clear that the

Table 8.2 Basic forms of retrieval: some suggestions in the context of case study B, The Financial Downturn

---

Tasks from

PHASE THREE: Survey data-analysis & Media familiarisation

PHASE FOUR: Inductive analysis of focus-group data

PHASE FIVE: Deductive analysis of media content

In each of Phases Three, Four, Five, the retrieval builds up upon earlier work, such that the understanding of the topic in relation to the research questions deepens

Horizontal retrieval	• Identify broad codes relating to each research question
	• Use horizontal retrieval (i.e. retrieving individual and groups of codes across all data so far coded) to
	o identify areas of further interest
	o compare coding
	o decide which data to recode
Vertical retrieval	• Use vertical retrieval to visually identify patterns in coding
	o sequentially through a data file
	o through a body of broadly coded data
Qualitative retrieval	• Qualitative retrieval (horizontal and vertical as described above – but now also in relation to factual data organisation (Phase Five – chapter 12)
Quantitative retrieval	• Quantitative code retrieval
	o consider results of above quantitatively as well
Output retrievals	• Output results of different retrievals
	o for purposes of snapshotting status of work and to use when writing up (Phase Nine).

---

term 'fear' does not adequately capture the nature of many of the segments subsequently coded amongst other respondents' talk. The retrieval process, therefore, has highlighted that the code label requires redefining, to reflect the broader context of discussion about redundancy that is coded. Subsequently, the code needs splitting, in order to reflect the different ways in which redundancy is discussed and experienced. Cutting through data horizontally in this way allows you to ask questions like: are the segments coded here equivalent, or do they need recoding in order to handle peculiarities, contradictions, nuances? Are there some segments which are not adequate instances of the code? Do they need uncoding, reconceptualising, disregarding? How does this sort of retrieval change the way you are thinking about the code? What further questions does cutting through the data in this way raise?

Vertical cuts

Vertical cutting is all about considering one data file, case or instance in its entirety, sequentially. This can lead to further questioning of data, to ascertain, for example, whether a pattern in coding identified in one data file also occurs in other, related data. Language-oriented approaches can benefit from this type of visualisation, or projects in which the sequence of code application is of particular interest. For example, in analysing political discourse there may be a focus on how an argument is constructed. Considering the position of codes that capture particular linguistic devices according to the way sentences are structured would enable a comparison of how different politicians craft an argument. This type of coding can be combined with more content-based, descriptive or thematic types, in order subsequently to investigate whether arguments relating to particular topics are constructed differently. Consideration of the relative position of code occurrence in this way enables you to remain entirely at the data level, or to combine the indexing and data levels (Chapter 1).

Case Study C, Coca-Cola Commercials, is another example of how vertical cuts can be useful. The focus on mechanisms used to advertise the product necessitates coding on the basis of means by which associations are made between the visual content of action within the commercial, the messages conveyed by the soundtrack and voiceover, and the placement of the brand. It was clear from early familiarisation with the commercials (Chapter 6) that repetition was an important device on several levels. We therefore wanted to be able to compare how certain features occurred within and were repeated throughout individual commercials, and how these patterns compared between commercials. Vertical cuts offer a powerful visual means by which to do this, as illustrated in Figures 7.5 and 8.4,

Figure 7.5 shows a 'Diet Coke Break' commercial having been coded directly, without an associated transcript (though a synchronised transcript would also be possible), in ATLAS.ti. Clips (quotations) have been created for each scene, represented by the grey brackets visible in the margin. Codes capturing different actions, actors, speech and brand placement have been applied to the quotations. Colour has been assigned to the code labels in order to more easily be able to visualise the patterns in occurrence.

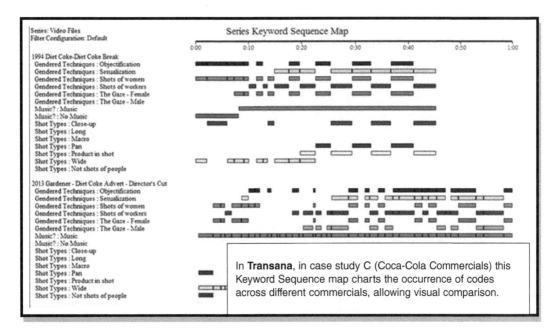

Figure 8.4 Keyword sequence map – sequential comparison of coding (Transana)

Figure 8.4 provides a different type of visualisation, comparing how two similar commercials have been coded. The two commercials being compared are directly related in that the 2013 'Gardener – Diet Coke' commercial is a remake, an updated version, of the earlier 'Diet Coke Break' commercial (1994). The same soundtrack is used, and similar characteristics are displayed – notably that a group of women are watching ('ogling') a lone male manual worker who removes his T-shirt and drinks a can of Diet Coke. In order to create the comparison illustrated in Figure 8.4, the two commercials were transcribed and coded similarly. The codes on display for the comparison unpack similar issues as discussed above, but the codes themselves are differently labelled. Using Keyword Visualizations, we can see a visual representation of the presence of coding over time, illustrating the relative occurrence and frequency of code application, in a sequential sense. There are clear differences identified through this visualisation on a number of analytically interesting levels. In addition to investigating code assignation over time, it is illuminating to consider the amount of time gendered techniques and shot types are present in each commercial. Transana's Series Keyword Bar Graph and Series Keyword Percentage Graph enable this interrogation.

Different visualisations of how data files have been coded in their entirety, in a sequential comparative sense, are just one example of how different ways of representing coded data provide different ways of reviewing work and identifying patterns and relationships. All CAQDAS packages provide tools which allow you to retrieve in ways which open up your thinking about data, thus moving you forward with your interpretation.

Table 8.3 Basic forms of retrieval: some suggestions in the context of case study C, Coca-Cola Commercials

Tasks from PHASE FOUR: Basic code retrieval and provisional analytic commentary	
Quantitative retrieval	• Broad overview via basic quantitative retrievals
	i) considering the length of clips coded as well as any transcript content coded
Qualitative retrieval	• In-context qualitative retrieval
	i) viewing coded clips one after another as basis of comparison on the visual content
	• Out-of-context retrievals
	i) compare coding sequentially (vertically) through related commercials to identify patterns and relationships
Outputting retrievals	• Outputting for reflection out-of-context
	i) unless your chosen software allows coded media content to be outputted in file format this will be based on the associated transcript content (where working indirectly)
Tasks from PHASE FIVE: Secondary analytic coding: developing themes, concepts, categories	
Review, revisit, refine	Revisit broad codes and recode them into more detailed (sub)codes
Tasks from PHASE SEVEN: Integration of analysis of publicity materials	
	Comparative retrieval, cross-referencing and concept refinement

Simple filtering devices for early comparative interrogations

In packages that enable it, filtering to short-cut groupings (sets, families) offers a quick and simple way of making initial comparisons. We introduced the analytic use of sets in Chapter 5 as they offer ways of identifying early comparative elements, thus focusing your mind on project design issues and signposting areas requiring further attention. We discuss the use of filtering for analytic purposes in more detail in Chapter 9, in the context of coding scheme refinement. Here, we simply make the point that filtering whilst in code retrieval mode offers an additional layer to your thinking and the ability to move on to the next phase of work. Horizontal cuts provide a means to consider a body of coded data in its entirety, helping in the development of generic themes. Vertical cuts provide patterns and relationships to be identified and visualised on a sequential basis, either one data file at a time or comparatively. Filtering offers the means to focus in on important subsets of data, one at a time.

Generating output

Most discussion in this chapter has been about ways of retrieving data within software. We mentioned above the value of saving copies of software projects and other reports as snapshots of progress, perhaps at significant analytic stages. When thinking about whether and how to recode, for example, consider printing out coded data and code frequency reports as well as viewing data within the software (Figure 8.1; p. 194). Such lists can be outputted in several ways, Figure 8.5 shows just three: a list of codes with frequency information, taken from an early version of Case Study B in ATLAS.ti, and a similar output format (with text segments) from Case Study A, from NVivo and also from HyperRESEARCH.

Quantitative information about qualitative data, however, should always be viewed in context. Qualitative samples are often not random or representative, and this needs to be accounted for when manipulating frequency information in a statistics package. Treated appropriately, however, summaries can add another dimension to qualitative work. When writing up a final report, therefore, consider whether some forms of frequency information will be useful to present. If you have a large dataset and are conducting a mixed methods project, then outputted frequency information can be further manipulated in a statistical package, if appropriate.

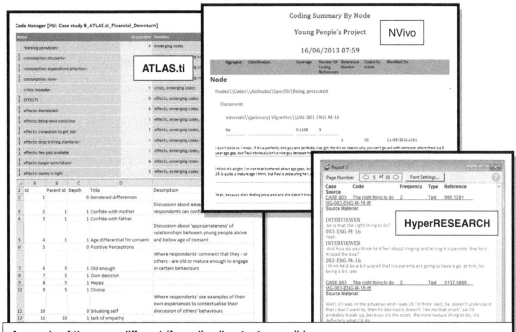

A sample of the many different (formalised) outputs possible.

1. **ATLAS.ti** (left), showing an HTML output of the Codes Manager: a list of all codes, frequency of application, how they grouped in short-cut groups (*Code families*) and the definitions etc.
2. **NVivo** (middle), showing *Code Summary by Node* report: a selected Node (code), all coded passages, statistics and source information.
3. **HyperRESEARCH** (right), showing a report on all codes and their segments, with a page for each code (could alternatively be sorted vertically by cases, with a page for each case).

Note: Less formal outputs can often be generated by exporting an individual code or selection of codes.

Figure 8.5 Various reports: getting retrieval information out of the software (ATLAS.ti, NVivo and HyperRESEARCH)

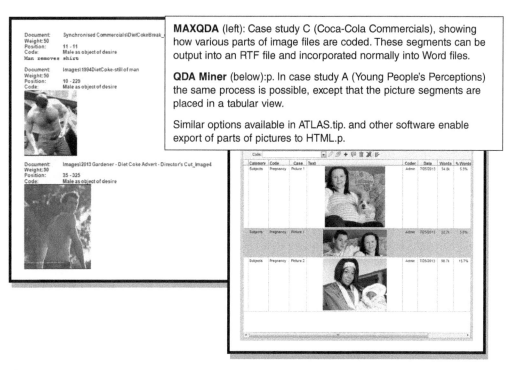

Figure 8.6 Output of coded segments of still images (MAXQDA and QDA Miner)

More qualitative forms of output are also possible. Usually it is easy to simply copy coded data segments from any retrieval window within your chosen software and paste into a word-processing application. Beware when doing this, though, that often this does not take with it the additional 'metadata' about the source of those coded segments, such as the data file from which they derive, the code name and other related content.

It can therefore often be more useful to use the bespoke output or report functions in order to get more meaningful outputs. Figure 8.6 shows coded parts of pictures which have been output into RTF format.

Concluding remarks: reflexivity and rigour

Coding processes are not straightforward, uncomplicated or easy from a theoretical or analytical point of view. Retrieval of coded data is central to all CAQDAS packages and to the way most researchers working with unwieldy amounts of qualitative data will expect to work. Studying and annotating coded output, recoding, and combining codes are all aspects of retrieval following on in turn from coding tasks. Focused retrieval is a major aspect of the systematic management of data, enabling concentrated and iterative work on significant data.

Coding is a cumulative rather than a one-stage process, and the meaning and application of codes will change over time, as will the development of the coding scheme (Chapter 9). Using software will not automatically resolve any of these issues. Neither will software ensure reflexivity or rigour in itself. Some tools, however, when used systematically, can help illustrate the processes you have gone through. However, you remain accountable. Reviewing all data so far assigned a code, for example, can help you decide whether the code label adequately captures the concept, theme or category. Does the code label need refining? Should all data currently coded there remain there? Are there subtle or key differences in the way respondents talk about the same issue? Does the code need deconstructing into more precise concepts, or perhaps combining into broader ones? We introduced these issues in Chapter 7. In this chapter we have encouraged you to think more deeply about them. You may eventually use more complex ways of interrogating data using query tools, and it will be useful early on – in order to be aware of what they might further achieve for your analysis – to have in mind a broader picture of what is possible (Chapter 13).

CHAPTER EXERCISES

CAQDAS packages provide many ways to retrieve data based on earlier tasks. We now present generic retrieval tasks they support, focusing on what can be achieved within the software and how to get information out of the software. These exercises can be carried out using sample data for any of the case-study examples using the step-by-step instructions for specific software packages on the companion website.

Retrieve all data coded so far

Software packages vary in the ways they provide retrieval. One aspect to consider, in comparing packages, is how 'close' you remain to the original source data when in retrieval mode.

1. Within the software. You can retrieve coded data based on any individual code, or based on different groups of codes. Whatever stage you are at, retrieval will help you to think about one issue exclusively, in isolation from other aspects. You will also be able to see these coded segments in their original source context and to continue coding where necessary.
2. Generating output reports. As well as reviewing coding within the software, it is always possible to pull this information out of the software by printing or saving to view in other applications, such as MS Word.

View all codes appearing in one document

It can be useful to view how one document has been coded in its entirety. This can usually be achieved in a number of ways. (For retrieval based on groups of documents see Chapter 12.)

1. Inside software:
    (a) The margin view. You can usually see within the software how a document has been coded in its entirety. Most packages also allow you to filter the margin view to different groups of codes.

(b) Code listings per document. Generate a simple list of codes appearing in a document, to gain an overview, without necessarily viewing the data.

2. Generating output:

(a) Print a document with margin view. This can be useful for many different reasons. Software packages vary, however, in terms of the presentation and 'readability' of such output.

(b) Report on all codes for one document. Output how one document has been coded according to 'all codes' or selections of them.

Recode data

You are likely to change your mind about how data are coded as you proceed. Similarly, as you retrieve coded data you may see them in a new light and identify additional aspects of significance. As well as altering the amount of data linked to a particular code and reorganising your coding scheme, you will probably want to recode. If taking an inductive approach, this may involve thinking about how more detailed codes are related, whereas a more deductive approach may necessitate the deconstruction of broader concepts into more precise ones (see Chapter 7).

1. Recode while in retrieval mode. Software provides flexible means by which to recode data, whether into related categories or subcategories, or into codes which are completely unrelated.
2. Recode while considering how a document has been coded in its entirety. You will also find it useful at times to view how one document has been coded in its entirety, either within the software or by printing a document with its margin view showing codes.

Overview current coding status

Qualitative software provides up-to-date frequency information concerning the status of your coding, showing, for example, how many times across your whole dataset a code has been applied to discrete segments of data.

1. View coded references building up as you code. Seeing code frequencies increase while you code serves to reassure you at the same time as providing you with a useful and immediate guide as to which themes, categories and concepts are occurring more than others across the dataset. Some lists can be organised by frequency.
2. Generate output. Various types of output report can be generated which reflect frequency information relating to the application of coding. In some cases this type of tabular summary information is also fully integrated with your project.

9
Working with Coding Schemes

This chapter is about coding schemes and how they develop, what they mean to different researchers and how they can be variously represented and refined inside software. Coding scheme structures and what you make of them can have a great effect on how you work. They function rather differently across software packages. We discuss typical distinctions because of the importance of coding scheme structures in managing your ideas about data. At the same time we are pragmatic about how the coding scheme is represented. It is merely how the software lists your codes, after all. What is more important is that you can manipulate the coding scheme for your purposes, group codes differently if you need to and rationalise connections between codes as part of the development of your explanation or theory. This chapter was difficult to place. Some researchers might need to think early on about a coding scheme because it represents the theoretical backdrop to their study or the general ideas that inform the project. Others might be waiting to create codes in a grounded or inductive way (Chapter 7). Whichever combination of ways you use to develop codes, this chapter aims to assist in the 'moving on' phases of analysis. It is well documented that the end of a first-pass coding process can produce a 'block': where to go next, what to do with it all? Being clear about your objectives and the analytic tasks required to achieve them is what determines the steps you need to take and the sequencing of the use of tools. Practically, however, we often find that the way forward involves moving beyond the face-value structures of the coding scheme. Consequently, we see other ways of grouping codes as critical to thoughtful progress and some software programs excel in this respect. In some packages you can reorganise codes without affecting the main listing; having them appear in new collections for different purposes. Although tools to enable this vary in name and effectiveness, we illustrate that, whatever constraints you perceive in a coding scheme, there are simple strategies which will help you move on in theoretical, analytical and practical directions. These practical activities are always driven by the specific needs of an individual project and therefore the way you work with coding schemes will differ from project to project.

We have two main objectives with this chapter. We want to encourage a confidence in coding scheme tools as early as possible so that you can avoid the constraints of over-caution which can stop you playing with ideas and using tools creatively. We also want to convey in a constructive sense that, although it may seem natural for your coding scheme to begin or end as a reflection of the way your theory is modelled, or how you perceive the framework of your final analysis or write-up, it probably will not be either of these things. In fact if you see your coding scheme as a reflection of the latter the chances are you are not so much facilitating analysis as simply filing. The danger is that you may close down your ideas, not leaving room for subtle discoveries through later interrogations. We focus on the Case Studies in overviews of process in Tables 9.2, 9.3 and 9.4. Almost every process we talk about in the detail of this chapter was applied to the Case Studies to help us fix a problem or to help us move on.

Breaking down data, building them back together

Qualitative data analysis often involves initially breaking data down – sometimes called 'drilling down' or 'fragmenting' – into the many different significant parts, especially when coding inductively (Chapter 7). The later processes of analysis often necessitate bringing those fragments back together into other collections for different purposes. This may help you to see data in different ways and arrive at multiple levels of understanding about the nature of connectivity between themes, emotions, actions, outcomes, etc. Such processes often do not necessarily have to change the way your main coding scheme is structured – it will depend on the software you are using. Some of these strategies may also provide ways to recover from perceived coding scheme dilemmas but, at the same time, preserve what you have done already. Everything achieved so far will have value. Deductive processes tend to work the other way; the drilling down

Table 9.1 Coding scheme tasks

Coding scheme tasks	Comment
Coding can begin in a broad-brush way	Deductive approaches which are informed or driven by theoretical frameworks often start in this way
Broad-brush codes can be recoded to create new areas of a coding scheme. Broad codes are thus split into sub-codes that represent nuances of the more general theme	Re-analysing for more depth
Codes can begin as detailed codes and be collected into higher concepts or broad-brush categories	Grounded, bottom up, inductive method emerging from the data

Label/relabel and redefine codes	Define and describe, stay on top of development of thinking Keep past definitions – see evolution of ideas
Move codes around (if hierarchical scheme)	Change your mind about whether a code belongs where it is
Add prefixes to impose structure on codes list (or to clearly label sub-codes)	Keep codes you want to see together close to each other Sub-code prefixes are helpful to remind of the hierarchical association when seeing subcodes out of context
Copy virtual versions/short-cuts of codes into any number of temporary (or permanent) sets/collections/families,	Alternate analytic function to main coding schema Good for reminders, thinking, easy retrieval/export – a good way to manage ideas and potential focus
Merge codes to create higher concepts or categories	Analytic task in which you can by mistake lose the original detailed codes: make sure you want this
Colour codes	Visualise/retrieve on the basis of colour to indicate a particular status or relevance of code or origination
Change the 'sort' order of the codes listing, or tabular views	Useful for seeing most frequently used?

or recoding processes happen as a secondary stage on earlier broadly coded themes. Table 9.1 summarises some aspects of coding scheme structures as we discuss them.

Structures of coding schemes in software

Chapter 7 covered some methodologically specific aspects of coding and more pragmatic combination methods. However codes are generated, and whatever methodological approach underpins this process, what we mean by the 'coding scheme' in terms of software is the manifestation of the way codes are listed and organised within the software in its main codes window (see Figures 9.1; p. 208 and 9.2; p. 209 for examples from different packages). Three of the packages we discuss in this book offer additional, more flexible and complex ways to manipulate codes. These are ATLAS.ti, MAXQDA and NVivo. The other packages offer a simpler set of coding scheme choices in terms of the ability to manipulate and regroup. This does not mean you cannot make these coding scheme structures work for you; but being aware about how your chosen software functions in this regard is important before you start working in earnest as it may affect how you proceed. All packages have their own individual characteristics in terms of code-based visualisations and outputs, and simple coding scheme functionality is frequently sufficient.

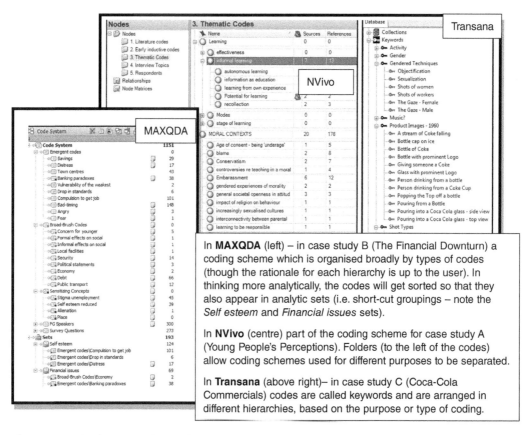

In **MAXQDA** (left) – in case study B (The Financial Downturn) a coding scheme which is organised broadly by types of codes (though the rationale for each hierarchy is up to the user). In thinking more analytically, the codes will get sorted so that they also appear in analytic sets (i.e. short-cut groupings – note the *Self esteem* and *Financial issues* sets).

In **NVivo** (centre) part of the coding scheme for case study A (Young People's Perceptions). Folders (to the left of the codes) allow coding schemes used for different purposes to be separated.

In **Transana** (above right)– in case study C (Coca-Cola Commercials) codes are called keywords and are arranged in different hierarchies, based on the purpose or type of coding.

Figure 9.1 Differing hierarchical coding schemes in three Case Studies (MAXQDA, NVivo and Transana)

Functioning and implications of hierarchy

Researchers often discuss the benefits and limits of hierarchical and non-hierarchical coding schemes. We often spend significant amounts of time in training workshops debating the relative benefits of different systems and supporting researchers design efficient and effective systems. Practical distinctions between coding schemes in respect of hierarchy and how this is manifested in terms of functionality are not predictable (see below). Many packages, including MAXQDA, NVivo, QDA Miner, Transana and Dedoose, appear to encourage an inherently hierarchical organisation of the coding scheme. Within them, however, you can be as non-hierarchical as you like. Equally, a less hierarchical-appearing system in software may in fact offer alternative ways of grouping and linking codes. It is up to you to choose how the structures at your disposal best fit your purpose.

The behaviour of hierarchical coding schemes

Not all packages that list codes apparently hierarchically provide *functional* hierarchies. Some have simpler structures. It is often assumed that higher-level codes in hierarchical schemes automatically contain all the data coded by all of their sub-codes. This happens in some packages, not at all in others, and in some it can be arranged but does not happen by default. This means that, initially at least, a hierarchy may not serve any functional purpose except as a way to tidy up, or, more importantly, to visually group codes which are similar in some way. Transana and QDA Miner, for instance, do not enable data to be coded at the 'top level'; therefore those top-level codes are simply organisational devices or 'coat-hangers'. Data coded at sub-codes can nevertheless be retrieved 'globally' from the top level in QDA Miner, and in Transana this can be done through the search tool (Chapter 13). Figure 9.2 shows two versions of the apparently hierarchical coding scheme for Case Study B in Dedoose compared with the 'flat' non-hierarchical listing of codes in ATLAS.ti where prefixes have been used to impose order.

In other packages there are useful ways of making hierarchies behave functionally. In NVivo, for instance, you can make different hierarchies and even different levels within individual hierarchies function in different ways, by 'aggregating' codes in successive stages to the next level. This means you need to be clear about which areas of the coding scheme are functioning in which way, why, and to what effect. MAXQDA does something similar; upon data retrieval, you can choose whether to 'activate' or switch on top or intermediate-level codes along with all successive sub-levels – although individual sub-codes can also be activated separately. Unusually, MAXQDA has an optional way of treating a whole hierarchy as one code when interrogating. This means, for instance, that you can look for the co-occurrence of a whole hierarchy of codes with any other codes. This can be switched on and off as required.

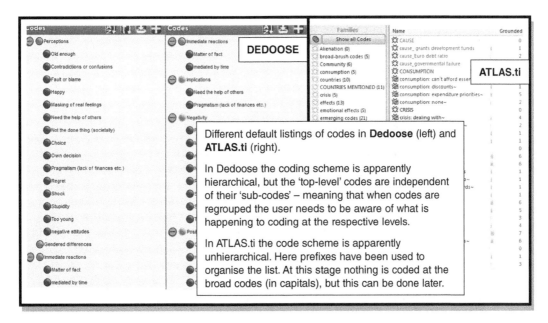

Figure 9.2 'Apparently hierarchical' and 'apparently non-hierarchical' coding schemes (Dedoose and ATLAS.ti)

Non-hierarchical systems

Most packages allow you to generate a simple list of codes, all sitting at the same level (as shown in ATLAS.ti in Figure 9.2). This is often the way researchers working inductively initially proceed: first generating many detailed, unorganised codes, later using various devices to merge, order and group them. Only Transana and QDA Miner require you to create a 'top level' under which to create codes (termed Keywords Groups and Root Categories, respectively). Even in these two packages (neither of which allows coding at the top group/category level) it is possible to minimise hierarchy, simply by creating a group/category called 'initial codes' or 'inductive codes' or 'unorganised codes'. That will do exactly the same job (Figure 9.3; p. 212).

In ATLAS.ti there is a lack of priority given to hierarchy in the codes list because the developers wanted to provide the ability to express relationships between codes, concepts and themes in a range of different ways and often these cannot be represented by the way they appear in a list. Subtle connections can be created and visualised when exploring codes in 'networks'; allowing the researcher to graphically map and connect related objects (Chapter 11). As illustrated in Figure 9.2, when alphabetically listed there is the potential to cosmetically group codes via prefixing code labels (possible in any software). In a cosmetic hierarchy the visibility of all the codes (rather than being hidden under clickable upper levels) can be just as effective as the more apparently hierarchical structures in other software. See also other ways of grouping codes in 'sets' as discussed below (Figure 9.4; p. 219).

What type of coding scheme will suit the way you work?

The characteristics of your project have an inevitable effect on how important coding structures are in the way you manage your ideas about data. For some analytic

Table 9.2 Working with coding schemes: some suggestions in the context of case study A, Young People's Perceptions

---

Tasks from PHASE FOUR: Inductive recoding of broad-brush codes

Identify broad-brush codes that require recoding	• Inductively recode broad-brush codes • Use hierarchical positioning or prefixing to indicate

Refine coding scheme	• Merge sub-codes with top level codes if this has not happened by default
	• Create short-cut code groupings Sets/Families (if available) to highlight further analytic directions in terms of how new detailed codes can be combined in other parallel ways if new perspectives need to be developed.
	   ○ E.g. in evaluating Effectiveness – does culture have a determinant role and does this also have a relevance in all the other key themes.
	   ○ Do the new detailed sub-codes encompass the variety in the data?

Build on analytic and process writing	• Make notes about what you are doing as you proceed • Comment on how what you are identifying through recoding relates to the literature and research questions

---

approaches coding tools may not be used in the customary sense in which researchers tend to think about coding (Chapter 1). Being able to index places in data for purposes other than thematic or conceptual interpretation might be useful, but the subtleties of coding scheme structures may be less important than other features we refer to throughout this book, which might determine the choice of package.

Some researchers are hierarchically wired, and if coding mechanisms are important, the hierarchical structure is attractive. Researchers working in teams often begin with simple hierarchical structures, having identified key areas of interest, but may also construct the coding scheme to allow space for emergent codes to be incorporated.

Some researchers are bothered by hierarchy because it seems to force decisions about where things belong. For some the focus is entirely on the nature of the relationships that can be built between codes. They see hierarchies in terms of code listings as a distracting irrelevance. In fact, as illustrated above, hierarchical coding schemes do not have to be very hierarchical, however, when multiple levels are in use it can be difficult to know what is going on and at what level. With a flat coding scheme nothing is hidden away. This benefit is clearly seen in the illustration in Figure 9.2 of the Case Study B coding scheme in ATLAS.ti.

Creating coding schemes

If you are uncertain about the way your codes should be listed, relax about the need to get the coding scheme right to start with – you can usually move codes around, relabel them and redefine them. If you are following a coding process someone else has written about you may already have a number of codes in no particular order or structure. As discussed, packages vary in terms of how easy and flexible processes can be. If you discover that the process seems awkward or inflexible, then you may need to take a little more care early on, in thinking about how you will usefully build the coding scheme.

Some packages offer other ways to get a coding scheme in place. You might be able to import a whole coding scheme (or parts of one) from a different project, using a special export/import function or simply by saving a list of codes in a word-processing application and importing it in a particular way. You might (e.g. as in ATLAS.ti and Qualrus) be able to create a coding scheme in a map or network. You might just save a copy of an existing software project, delete all the data from it and leave yourself with a coding scheme which you can then to adapt to a new set of data. This is a good workaround to get a project started, particularly if you are working in a team, or if you are an individual researcher using a previous project as a framework. Often a lot of work has gone into that framework and it can be very useful to know that none of it need be lost. In a team this means you are all working from exactly the starting point – using the same labelling protocols and code descriptions. As an individual you can now start to change it and adapt it to the current project; as a team member you will negotiate that process.

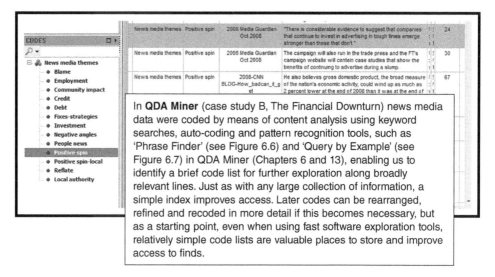

In **QDA Miner** (case study B, The Financial Downturn) news media data were coded by means of content analysis using keyword searches, auto-coding and pattern recognition tools, such as 'Phrase Finder' (see Figure 6.6) and 'Query by Example' (see Figure 6.7) in QDA Miner (Chapters 6 and 13), enabling us to identify a brief code list for further exploration along broadly relevant lines. Just as with any large collection of information, a simple index improves access. Later codes can be rearranged, refined and recoded in more detail if this becomes necessary, but as a starting point, even when using fast software exploration tools, relatively simple code lists are valuable places to store and improve access to finds.

Figure 9.3   Simple indexing of news media (QDA Miner)

Project-related factors influencing the development of coding schemes

Although understanding the architecture of the software is important, there are many other factors which influence the development and use of codes and coding schemes, not least analytic approach, research questions, methodology, style of working and research context (Chapter 7). It is imperative to give thought to this early on; do not just launch into coding without a clear sense of purpose. Factors which may contribute to the way the coding scheme develops include the following:

- A coding scheme does not have to be about carefully conceived 'codes' in the sense of a qualitative method. If a mechanism is simply required for indexing topics and where they occur in background material or information, the index can be as brief and straightforward as in Figure 9.3. Such an index might be useful for any approach.
- Researchers using grounded theory (Chapter 1), or pragmatic derivatives thereof, may generate most of the coding frame from the 'bottom up' as 'things' are identified inductively in the data, later combining codes to create higher concepts, themes or categories (Chapter 7). Usually the early part of this process is not hierarchical. To decide too early how to organise codes is often seen to undermine the 'open coding' process. Later the codes will be rationalised, possibly by using hierarchies or 'sets'. See discussions below on how aspects of this process were supported in Case Study B by structures in individual software.
- Many researchers, particularly in applied contexts, will use an *a priori* coding frame, embodying a clear set of objectives which help to govern and inform thinking from the outset (i.e. a deductive approach); see Chapter 7 on deductive coding and the discussion below about Case Study A.
- Others look to expand on existing theories, and the coding scheme can reflect this in part – acknowledging the role of existing research – to use some of the concepts to sensitise the way data is viewed, but will also be open to issues and themes directly arising from the text.

- We mention horizontal coding in Box 9.4, which can be a reason to focus on a smaller coding scheme initially – with the idea that more in-depth reanalyses of those coded segments will occur later.
- Pragmatic reasons for organising codes in a certain way might include groups of codes which serve different purposes or reflect different stages of work. In Case Study B this way of working is reflected in MAXQDA using top-level codes called Broad-brush Codes, Emergent Codes and 'Sensitizing Concepts (Figure 9.1). For Case Study A, Figure 9.1 also illustrates the use of folders in NVivo to separate different types of codes (literature codes, early inductive codes, thematic codes, etc.) as well as using the actual hierarchical structure of codes themselves.

Table 9.3 Working with coding schemes: some suggestions in the context of case study B, The Financial Downturn

Tasks from PHASE THREE: Deductive analysis of open-ended survey questions	
Broad-brush coding	• Question-based auto-coding of survey questions for later interrogation of broad brush across questions ○ List codes in a structured way in coding scheme to distinguish from later inductive codes
Tasks from PHASE FOUR: Inductive analysis of focus-group data	
Rationalise and refine	• Evaluate similarity of inductive codes to survey broad-brush codes • Identify very similar inductive codes which are really the same as each other (and data is similar) and merge them into one code • Identify concepts or more analytic themes that inductive codes might be contributing to ○ Create Sets with view to adding collections of codes to them for following up later (or No sets? Create explicit Report areas inside or outside the software with view to adding collections of exported codes and data to them for following up later) • Consider sensitising concepts ○ Create Sets/Reports on those bases gather codes that contribute to concepts – also make one new code out of all codes in each of these Sets (for experimentation while interrogating)– (or No sets? Copy and merge codes together that contribute but don't lose detailed codes) • Rationalise in places by creating a new broad-brush code out of gathered codes (e.g. all codes in a set?) • Carefully label and describe each time to be clear about origins of codes while rationalising in these ways • Write commentary at each stage about why and what plans are later
Tasks from PHASE FIVE: Deductive analysis of media content	
Deductive coding in light of previous coding phases	• Integrate media coding with primary data coding by merging codes or using Sets to gather them together – (no Sets – put them or export them to Report areas)

Escaping the confines of coding scheme structures

However you start off and make use of coding scheme structures in the early stages, it might be useful later, especially when you have many codes or have coded inductively in a grounded way, to escape the structures of the main code listing. In order to think about themes, categories and higher concepts it can be productive to combine codes in different ways and express connections between them. In one way or another this might be possible, though some software packages will provide a more explicit set of tools for these purposes. In a very real sense, then, think early on how it might be possible to step back later from structures in the coding scheme (see Table 9.1; p. 206, Box 9.6; p. 222 and Chapter 11). The thing to remember is that in most software you can change your mind about where codes sit, and you can do so over and over again. Given that flexibility, there are some factors that influence the ways coding schemes are developed and also guiding principles which would be useful to take forward. We therefore discuss ways and purposes for separating areas of the coding scheme; the relationship between the coding scheme and the theoretical framework; and the use of short-cut groupings to better express and collate theories.

Separating areas of the coding scheme for pragmatic or theoretical reasons

You can always achieve separation of codes by prefixing. Always a good idea, for example, is to keep codes that have been created via auto-coding or text search exercises separate. As discussed in Chapter 5, codes generated in this way are particularly useful as means of familiarising with and exploring the content of textual data, but they also have their limitations. If you have worked in this way, keep them separate while you decide whether they are worth keeping, what needs rethinking, refining, building upon and what needs to be thrown away! When discussing cleaning up large coding schemes (below) we mention using a 'z' prefix for codes which are little used in order to keep them in the system but put them out of sight at the bottom of a code list or particular hierarchy. In packages which require the use of codes for certain types of socio-demographic, structural or other types of non-thematic or non-conceptual based coding, prefixing is also very useful in managing these different types of codes. We discuss this in Chapter 12 concerning the organisation of data.

NVivo's folder structure provides a useful way of incorporating all codes in the project as a whole but totally separating those which do quite different tasks (codes are held at 'nodes' in NVivo); the folders thereby separate parts of a coding scheme. For instance, you may have quite different collections of data with rather different requirements in terms of handling and coding; or, you may not be sure to start with how much you want to integrate all codes together. Folders give you the option to keep them separate for now. Figure 9.1 illustrates folders in NVivo that separate codes generated directly from the literature in advance of coding the primary data: *Early inductive codes* created during primary data familiarisation; *Interview topics* represent the structures inherent in the primary data. The *Thematic codes* folder constitutes the main coding scheme, the development of which was driven by the literature review; at a later stage, some of the inductive codes were transferred to the *Thematic* folder. This worked well for the needs of Case Study A but might not be appropriate in other projects.

Figure 9.1 also shows a simple hierarchical coding scheme for Case Study B in MAXQDA. Here, folders are not available to isolate parts of a coding scheme. The same thing, however, is achieved by means of creating top-level codes for 'Emergent codes', 'Broad-brush codes' and 'Sensitizing concepts'. In this example, code sets, visible at the bottom of the code system, act as the means to bring together selected codes from across the broad groupings. For example, the 'Financial issues' set contains short-cuts to codes from both the 'Emergent' and 'Broad-brush' lists. At this early stage both the main listings and the sets are relatively descriptive, but as work continues and more in-depth analytic thinking occurs, the sets become more specific and theoretical in terms of the combinations of codes they contain.

The relationship between the coding scheme and the theoretical framework

Not all researchers will have theoretical frameworks at the outset. Working in a grounded, inductive way (Chapter 7), your analysis may be working towards a theory or an explanation (Figure 9.7; p. 226). As you build up ideas you move away from the groundedness in the data and become more conceptual and abstract; as we discussed above, you begin to find connections and categories which take you further analytically. You might also be acknowledging the influences on your thinking which come from previous literature. This is the case in the way we approached both Case Studies A and B (Chapter 2). In the former, the coding scheme was explicitly and intentionally *driven* by the literature review, in the latter particular sensitising concepts are kept in mind but, alongside those, an inductive approach was taken to the development of other codes (Figure 10.1; p. 236). It would be difficult to express all the connections in a theory (Box 9.1), but in ATLAS.ti and Qualrus particularly different ways to create a coding scheme are offered since you have the choice to create links and relationships between codes from the outset (Figures 7.2; p. 162 and 10.1; p. 236). This suits a theoretical or deductive approach well, or indeed the later stages of an inductive process where you have done enough work to be able to express connections. Relationship nodes in NVivo might offer something similar (Figure 11.5; p. 274).

Economy when developing codes

Copying codes all over the coding scheme can seem an intuitive thing to do – but the software now sees those copied codes as quite distinct objects, and if more coding is done subsequently, care would have to be taken to either code in all those places or just in the one correct place. There is no hard-and-fast rule here, but having several similar codes in different places is more taxing and subject to human error. Take the example of the 'Poor morale' code in Case Study B. If you copied it so that it became three separate codes each under, for example, hierarchies of codes about *Family*, *Community* and *Fiscal*, so that from then on you coded 'Poor morale' separately for each circumstance, you would have the coding sorted into various contexts but you would lose an easy opportunity to have all the material on '*poor morale*' together. If it remained just one code it could be interrogated across gender or publication or region, or be subject to quick co-occurrence checks in the data to see what other codes seem to be impacting (e.g. the sensitising concepts 'Stigma', 'Self esteem', 'Place', 'Alienation'). The query tools provided by software (Chapter 13) allow for the investigation of co-occurrence and proximity between codes as they have been applied to data. So it is possible to leave more room for discovery and exploration with the larger code.

The danger with trying to create the perfect coding scheme is that you waste time because, actually, it can neither perfectly replicate the theory or relationships or the explanation you are edging towards. Nor will it be malleable into a perfect bullet-point representation of your thesis (which can sometimes be tempting). Trying to do either of these things in the way coding schemes are structured in the main listing tends to close down the ability to discover patterns and relationships using query tools.

Rules of thumb when working with hierarchies in software

- *Try to keep the coding scheme as flat as possible.* If you have several levels, be sure you can justify why, to what effect, and that you know what is going on in terms of what is coded where, at each level. This is especially important when working with software that allows flexible aggregation of top-level codes to work differently in different hierarchies.
- *Try to avoid having copies of codes* (see Box 9.1). If you feel a code belongs in more than one place, this is likely an indication that it should be a top-level code in its own right. Only have more than one version of a code if you can clearly justify the analytic benefit of this.

- *Try to think about the physical manifestation of your coding scheme like an index –* simply listing in simple ways the areas of analytic interest you have. Try to avoid the temptation of representing the connections you are seeing between codes by their physical placement in the codes list. There are other ways to keep track of these connections – i.e. sets (below) and maps (Chapter 11), or just on paper.
- *Consider carefully before having different coding schemes for different data.* If you do want to separate parts of the coding scheme (e.g. through the use of folders or prefixing) it is useful to do this on the basis of the *function* of codes (e.g. separate codes derived from auto-coding or question/topic-based codes), the *stage* at which coding occurs (e.g. codes derived from literature, early inductive codes, later thematic codes), or *contributions of different coders*, or for *completely different types of data* which require different ways of thinking. Sometimes any of these separations can be temporary – have in mind that you may eventually bring these different areas or elements of them together somehow. Remember that if you do separate codes based on type of primary data or factual characteristics, doing that will mean it is much more difficult later to make comparisons irrespective of data type or respondent. Evaluate how different types of data need to be coded differently or similarly with these things in mind.
- *If your software provides short-cut groupings (sets or families) use those to play* with alternative ways of gathering codes and starting to think about the connections between them (see below). Build on this work through your use of maps (Chapter 11).

When your approach rests on a theoretical framework (or combination of different theories) gleaned from literature, it might be easier and certainly tempting to reflect elements of the framework in the coding scheme. However, the discovery element needs to be optimised and parts of a coding scheme can represent parts of the theory without needing to replicate it. The small to grand range theories and concepts that might be informing your theoretical framework are themselves the result of detailed work. They are likely to be based on different populations and samples, located at different times or places, and perhaps the result of quantitative rather than qualitative research. Though you are not wishing to reinvent the wheel, your own work is always exploratory; whether the outcome has the effect of confirming, enriching or challenging some of the *a priori* concepts.

BOX 9.3 — ANALYTIC NOTES

Questions to ask yourself when working with a theoretical backdrop

- Do the principles and concepts of a theory *represented as codes* allow enough room for manoeuvre?
- Are some of the analytic concepts you are developing likely to be fed by codes which 'feed' more than one concept?
- Are you ready to define how a concept is broken down into other elements?

To that end, the coding scheme is an adjustable instrument for accessing data which confirm, enrich or challenge a theory. Via meaningful labelling of codes you can contribute fresh ideas to join with the extant ideas in the theoretical melting pot. The theoretical framework is always in the background, providing a perspective or lens through which data are viewed in the light of which the account is created. Box 9.4 focuses on one of the ways in which the deductive coding of the data can be achieved followed by recoding or 'coding-on' of those segments to a more detailed understanding of the theme.

BOX 9.4 — CASE NOTES

Horizontal coding then coding on to add sub-codes (Case Study A, Young People's Perceptions)

In Case Study A one approach to the coding of Gendered Discussions is that this particular coding could be achieved horizontally across all the data; codes which are broadbrush or broad theoretical concepts can all be done in this manner. Keeping the focus just on one subtle area of talk at a time and coding across all of the data saves the stress of recurring decision making about which of many codes fits when working vertically. Having done that, do the same with any other appropriate broad themes in turn, and you can then look at each individual theme and recode by building sub-codes (or appropriately prefixed codes) which relate to the detailed distinctions and deeper analysis of what is going on at the broad theme. After coding-on in a few files, the Gendered Discussions coding area began to look like this:

    Gendered discussions

    Lack of accessible info for boys

    Differing opinions about legal age

    Confiding in mother

    Confiding in father

    Trusting a woman (rather than man)

We come back to the idea expressed in Chapter 7 of viewing codes as 'heuristic devices for discovery' that enable you to revisit data and to carry on thinking about them (Seidel and Kelle, 1995: 58). Therefore the coding scheme, and the position of the codes within it, is simply an organised expression of ideas – an artifice which enables us at least to tidy up, to separate data in different ways, and at most to combine, interrogate and compare, to test relationships, to get back to the data.

Better ways to express and collate theory – mapping and short-cut groupings

Whereas we advocate simple uses of coding schemes to represent your general ideas about important themes evident in data, we suggest two strong candidates for the collecting and connecting of codes which are related by theory, account or process. The first encourages a stepping back from data by mapping; the second is by grouping codes – or data segments – in multiple alternative ways.

There are various other tools outside CAQDAS packages to perfect the expression of theory if you need to do this graphically (it is important to keep in mind that your chosen software does not do everything you may want to do). It can test relationships based on the coding and organisation you apply (Chapter 13), but it may not on its own carefully map out a whole theory. Having said that, mapping tools, where they are provided, can facilitate the visual expression of theories (Figure 10.1; p. 236 and Chapter 11). However, it is still completely down to you, the researcher, to make the connections, to define the relationships and to arrange the layout to maximise clarity. Essentially maps fall into two categories, those that are basically 'scribbles', having no impact on the background functionality of codes and the retrieval of data segments (MAXQDA and NVivo), and those that have deeper implications and

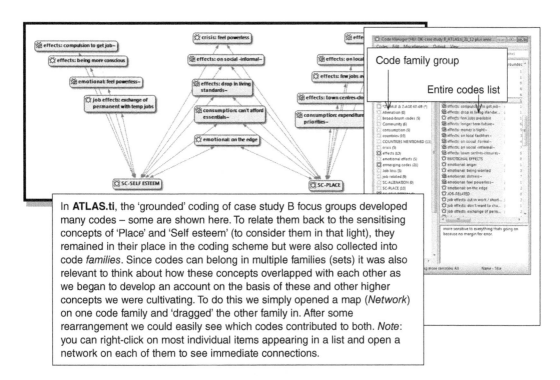

In **ATLAS.ti**, the 'grounded' coding of case study B focus groups developed many codes – some are shown here. To relate them back to the sensitising concepts of 'Place' and 'Self esteem' (to consider them in that light), they remained in their place in the coding scheme but were also collected into code *families*. Since codes can belong in multiple families (sets) it was also relevant to think about how these concepts overlapped with each other as we began to develop an account on the basis of these and other higher concepts we were cultivating. To do this we simply opened a map (*Network*) on one code family and 'dragged' the other family in. After some rearrangement we could easily see which codes contributed to both. *Note*: you can right-click on most individual items appearing in a list and open a network on each of them to see immediate connections.

FIGURE 9.4 Families (sets) of codes for grouping 'sensitising concepts' or 'analytic directions' (ATLAS.ti)

functionality once connections are drawn (e.g. ATLAS.ti and Qualrus). We discuss mapping, modelling and networking much more in Chapter 11.

The second and more functional option, in terms of moving on with thinking and retrieving data segments outside of the main coding scheme, are short-cut groupings for codes, generally known as 'sets' (Figure 10.7; p. 247; 'families' in ATLAS.ti, Figure 9.4; p. 219). These allow 'virtual' versions of codes to be gathered from around the coding scheme – contributing to analytic directions; hunches, hypotheses and larger theories; or, more pragmatically, phases of work. Sets are important tools enabling you and your codes to escape the rather more solid structures (or lack thereof) of the main listing of your software coding scheme. We discussed sets in Chapter 5 as alternate listing mechanisms to folders with respect to source data files (Figure 5.2; p. 116). We also refer to them in Chapter 10 in discussing ways to organise writing up (Figure 10.7). Sometimes sets are visible with other main lists of, for example, codes and documents, sometimes they are somewhat hidden. Sets are places to gather things together and think about them differently. They provide short-cuts to the originals, and this is good because an idea embodied at one code can contribute to several sets and so contribute to several aspects of how you might move on with analysis. This was of great relevance to what we wanted to do in Case Study B and is illustrated in Figure 9.4 and Box 9.5. In any project using inductive coding processes you will probably end up with many more codes after the first-pass coding phase than with a deductive 'top-down' (theoretically informed or not) approach. Opportunities to let those inductive codes contribute to more than one higher concept or theme or, as in grounded theory, axial or selective coding stages (Chapter 7) are invaluable, and sets representing those more abstract combinations are just one way to do that.

The three software packages that allow codes to be grouped in sets are ATLAS.ti, MAXQDA and NVivo (and each enables sets to be illustrated graphically in a network, map or model – see Chapter 11). This is illustrated in Figure 9.4, using Case Study B in ATLAS.ti as an example. Visualising sets, and the families within which you have placed them, graphically offers additional flexibility to think about how they might be further connected. If you wanted to make a statement about the relationship between the codes themselves in these software programs, then you could view the collection in a map or model and then connect them and label the relationship (Chapter 11). Short-cut groupings of codes work in similar ways to codes themselves – retrieving data, incorporating in queries, outputting, etc. As such, short-cut groupings simply allow for another layer of thinking to cut across the basic structures of the indexing that occurs when coding, and these can be represented parallel to the main coding scheme. This way of working is much more flexible than creating ever more complicated coding scheme structures.

In a different way, but with similar outcomes, QDA Miner's Report Manager provides a place within the software project to gather outputted retrievals, results and tables along certain lines, similar to how you might work with sets in other packages (see more on this in Chapter 3 and Figure 5.4; p. 121). Again, the coding scheme does not change, but you choose to create a storage space in which to collect certain aspects of a particular report topic for later attention and writing up.

BOX 9.5 — CASE NOTES

Use of sets to think about codes differently (Case Study B, The Financial Downturn)

In Case Study B some of the coding was informed by theory, embodied in codes representing 'Sensitising Concepts'. Many more codes were developed in a 'bottom-up' emergent way. Sets come into their own when beginning to rationalise and rethink which codes belong together for different reasons. There were two central requirements of sets for this: one was to relate the 'emergent' codes to the sensitising concepts that we wanted to acknowledge in past literature; the other was to develop any other ideas about what we felt was going on. Code Families (another term for sets) were used in ATLAS.ti to group codes in a hierarchical organisational way but also to group them according to their possible relevance to the sensitising concepts, new identifiable themes, and other more pragmatic collections (see illustrations in Figures 9.1; p. 208, 9.2; p. 209 and 9.4; p. 219). There was a need to collect things in different ways and to allow any one code (or document) to belong in several different sets. A similar process was followed in MAXQDA and would also be possible in NVivo.

Coding scheme maintenance – routine actions

Here and there in this book we have talked about code definitions. It is most important that you and others (whether it be a colleague, supervisor, other team members in a collaborative project) see and understand your coding scheme in the way you need it to be seen and understood. There is nearly always a place for a description, definition or memo about each code – especially when there is any ambiguity. Whether you are a contributor or the main user of your software project, you must be very transparent. Part of being effectively transparent is to see ambiguity where there seems to be none. If a code could possibly be misunderstood or interpreted very slightly differently, then it likely will. Defining a code could be about its meaning in terms of the type of nuance you are looking for, it could also be about the amount of surrounding context you expect to include. Retaining some idea behind the development or adjustments to a code is important too, so if you change the definitions, keep the older definitions, make those part of the account you are developing about this particular concept or theme, part of the account of your project.

We have talked explicitly and by implication about larger coding schemes which may often be intuitively and thoughtfully created and may present no problem at all to researchers if they are manageable. But often they are not. We have also mentioned that manipulating the coding scheme usually helps to move on analytically. The strategies for dealing with either of these can be similar. Sometimes coding schemes are large because they have very many detailed or descriptive codes. This can happen when attempting to work entirely inductively, the tendency being that you initially use codes to describe what is being said or seen, rather than interpreting data and creating more analytic codes. It can also happen when researchers are concerned to make sure every slightly different occurrence of a concept is coded separately in all its different contexts (Box 9.1). We have talked about the advantages and disadvantages here. The main challenge comes when the coding scheme becomes unwieldy with too many levels and far too many recurring concepts. The realisation that data and ideas about them are overly fragmented, difficult to find and to think about again is a sign! It can then become difficult to move on, to 'analyse' at a more abstract level. So what to do next, how to pull everything together to form a coherent explanation? We generally suggest that when you have more than three levels of hierarchy you can usefully ask yourself why. Is it helping? If so, then how? Just be sure it *is* actually helping you. There may be several ways to approach the problem.

This is an opportunity to come out of the software and use markers to annotate a printed codes list. Sometimes it is easier to rationalise the whole of a coding scheme on paper, to spot empty levels, to indicate codes you want to merge. We list some other general strategies for fixing a coding scheme – and they can be just as relevant to an overlarge coding scheme as to one which is just at that stage where you need to rethink and possibly rationalise. Back in the software you can do any of these things if they seem relevant (Box 9.6). We performed all these actions at one time or another and in one way or another while manipulating the codes in each of the Case Studies.

BOX 9.6 | FUNCTIONALITY NOTES

Tasks helping to refine the coding scheme and move on analytically

- Merge codes which really do represent the same thing.
- Move little-used codes aside into a special hierarchy or group called 'marginal codes' *or* 'redundant codes'.
- If the codes list is not hierarchically structured, check your little-used codes for exceptional contributions which throw up a completely new perspective – if they are not crucial to the main focus of your analysis, prefix with, say, 'zz-' to ensure they drop down to the bottom of the codes list, to stop them cluttering up the important codes.

- *Experiment with the combining or grouping functions* and read and review the coded output retrieved from the new combination. You might see something new (Table 9.3).
- *Use the grouping mechanism of sets* to merge all the codes in a set into one (but leave the detailed codes in place if you are uncertain). In some software this is enabled but in others, not. Different ways of putting such data together and a subsequent read-through can throw up new insights and can offer new ways to interrogate and compare using this larger catchment of data.
- *Without the sets function?* There are several possibilities. (i) With a large coding scheme, for instance, we sometimes work in combination with several paper printouts of the coding scheme – and indicate the relevance of codes to areas of thinking, i.e. those analytical or pragmatic reasons for grouping things. Exporting a codes list into Excel can be useful – we create columns for the groups and copy codes into each relevant group column. (ii) Create special folders outside the software based on those analytical or pragmatic reasons for collecting different exported coded files and group them that way. Specifically, QDA Miner has a tool for doing all those things inside the software – the Report Manager (see above and Chapters 5 and 12).
- *Use search/query tools to make new combination codes* or to save queries and searches which you will want to perform again and again to bring your regrouped combinations up to date (Chapter 13).
- *Draw a map to visualise your current thinking* about how codes are grouped and related to one another (Chapter 11).
- *Write a memo* about what you are thinking and how reorganising the coding scheme is helping (Chapter 10).

All codes, all data

The general nature of coding schemes and their interactive nature should have an impact on the way you view the potential of even a simple index system. Whatever shape your coding scheme is in, the principle benefit of coding schemes in software programs is the ability to navigate around the whole coding scheme in an orderly manner and see any or all of the relevant data segments.

Table 9.4 Working with coding schemes: some suggestions in the context of case study C, Coca-Cola Commercials

Tasks taken from PHASE FIVE: Refine, recode, reflect

Refinement of the coding schema	<ul><li>Output list of codes with definitions</li><li>Recode data where you have identified a need</li><li>Merge codes where data coded at two or more appear to concern the same phenomena</li><li>Move codes into new groupings</li></ul>

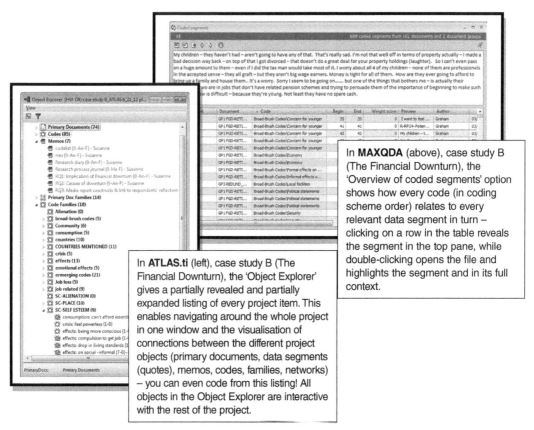

In **MAXQDA** (above), case study B (The Financial Downturn), the 'Overview of coded segments' option shows how every code (in coding scheme order) relates to every relevant data segment in turn – clicking on a row in the table reveals the segment in the top pane, while double-clicking opens the file and highlights the segment and in its full context.

In **ATLAS.ti** (left), case study B (The Financial Downturn), the 'Object Explorer' gives a partially revealed and partially expanded listing of every project item. This enables navigating around the whole project in one window and the visualisation of connections between the different project objects (primary documents, data segments (quotes), memos, codes, families, networks) – you can even code from this listing! All objects in the Object Explorer are interactive with the rest of the project.

Figure 9.5   Overview of the whole coding scheme and/or the whole project (ATLAS.ti and MAXQDA)

This is illustrated in Figure 9.5 in MAXQDA, which creates a seamless environment to keep the structure of the coding scheme interactive and parallel with retrieval. For example, asking for an overview of coded segments breaks down the entire coding scheme by respective segments at each constituent code in a long list; a single click on each line reveals the data. That means all your coded data are viewable from this one window. In ATLAS.ti, the HU (project) Explorer literally gives you clickable interactive access to every project item in one pane; your entire project including coding scheme, code families (sets) and their constituent codes, the connections between them and the coded data are all accessible here (Figure 9.5).

For some smaller projects the 'all data' view will be enough. For many projects, however, once you start needing to know where specific catchments of data or types of people feature at those codes, other organisational structures in the software and variables/attributes used to classify data come into play. Now the coding scheme and its structures are no longer enough on their own (Chapters 12 and 13).

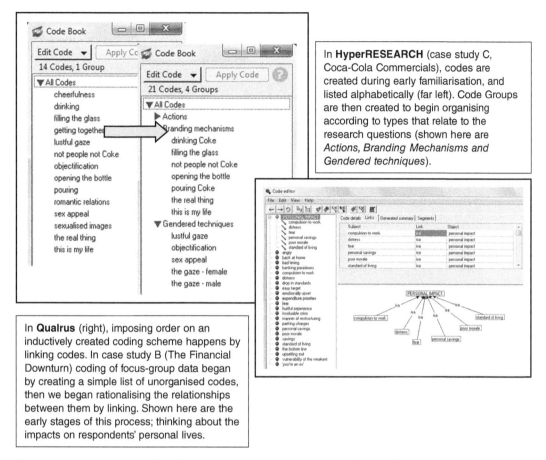

In **HyperRESEARCH** (case study C, Coca-Cola Commercials), codes are created during early familiarisation, and listed alphabetically (far left). Code Groups are then created to begin organising according to types that relate to the research questions (shown here are *Actions, Branding Mechanisms and Gendered techniques*).

In **Qualrus** (right), imposing order on an inductively created coding scheme happens by linking codes. In case study B (The Financial Downturn) coding of focus-group data began by creating a simple list of unorganised codes, then we began rationalising the relationships between them by linking. Shown here are the early stages of this process; thinking about the impacts on respondents' personal lives.

Figure 9.6   Early rationalisation of inductively generated codes using grouping and linking devices (HyperRESEARCH and Qualrus)

Concluding remarks: manipulating coding schemes for your needs

It is useful to gain early perceptions of how the coding scheme in your chosen software can be manipulated. There is no one right way to begin. CAQDAS packages can facilitate the management of ideas represented in a coding scheme to facilitate different methodological and analytical approaches and practical needs. This is the case whether working in a hierarchical or non-hierarchical software system. Without suggesting that 'anything goes', the coding scheme can always be manipulated to a certain extent. Such a process is an important step not only in order to 'tidy up' but also to help you to move on to a next level of analysis. What is important is that you can independently justify the way you are working, and that this fits in with your project design and methodology. Fitting in with what the software can do will be a secondary (but inevitable) factor, and optimising

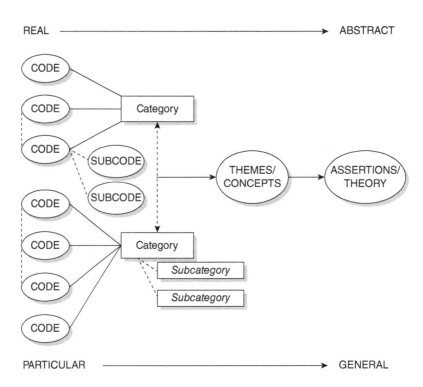

REAL ⟶ ABSTRACT

PARTICULAR ⟶ GENERAL

Figure 9.7 A streamlined codes-to-theory model for qualitative inquiry (Saldaña 2013: 13)

its benefit to your work in the ways described above (and more) will nearly always be to do with subsequent manipulation of the coding scheme. Remember to escape the software occasionally; printing out codes lists can be a constructive first step to sit back and rationalise away from the computer. Later, in combination with organisational tools (Chapter 12) and visualisation and interrogation devices (Chapter 13), the ability to test and compare what is going on in the data is now feasible at several different levels. Chapters 10 and 11, about managing interpretation and mapping, will remind you that managing 'messy' qualitative work has to include keeping a careful log of why and when things are done, and this process might benefit from other dimensions such as being able to step back and then to create or see connections.

EXERCISES: MANAGING AND MANIPULATING CODING SCHEMA STRUCTURES

The following tasks are designed to help you understand the logic of the coding scheme in your chosen software, to visualise codes and their potential connections in different ways and alter the structure of the scheme as required. It is common, as you proceed through different coding phases, to feel the inclination to reorganise codes to more accurately reflect the development of your thinking. Your coding scheme is not likely to be a neat encapsulation of theoretical ideas (whether preconceived or emerging from the data); however, it is unusual not to reorganise the coding scheme at some point. Software provides several useful tools to facilitate this. Experimenting with these tasks will help you in moving on from basic indexing to a more conceptual and analytic level of work.

Refine coding scheme structures within software

1. *Output code lists.* Any output report generated from software is a snapshot of that moment in time. Reports are fully editable, and you can save them as files (see Chapter 10). Always print a codes list report before and after making major changes to the coding scheme. There will always be an easy way to do this from the export functions associated with the project or main menus. This is important in keeping track of the processes you are going through and the analytic decisions you are making in refining coding scheme structures.
2. *Rename codes.* Renaming codes can indicate more precisely the phenomena they represent. This will probably be necessary whether you started off generating codes deductively or inductively. This work will happen in tandem with the processes of basic code retrieval as discussed in Chapter 8.

    (a) Where deductively created codes derive directly from literature be careful about renaming them if you need to explicitly and systematically compare your data with existing theories.
    (b) When working inductively, renaming codes to more precisely represent the data segments is an essential process. You will need to ensure data segments are equivalent as part of this process, and where necessary split codes by recoding (see Chapter 8).
    (c) In packages which are 'flat' in terms of the main listing, experiment with prefixing codes to order them or to manufacture hierarchy.

3. *Refine code definitions.* When renaming codes it is important to keep track of why you are doing so – appending existing definitions rather than overwriting them is important in terms of keeping an audit trail of your processes (see Chapter 10).
4. *Merge codes.* You might merge codes either because the difference between them is not as meaningful as you first thought, or because a broader theme is more appropriate.

    (a) Experiment with merging codes which have similar data segments coded to them.
    (b) Remember that if you want to bring coded data segments together without losing the difference between individual codes, you might move codes into hierarchical listings (see next point) or use alternative groupings (see below) as an alternative.

5. *Group codes into hierarchical listings.* For example, if you started coding in an inductive way you might later want to collect similar codes together – perhaps into a hierarchy where this is supported, or a looser collection of codes (see below).
6. *Move codes.* For example, if you began with a more deductive coding schemes, you might want to reorganise the structure in light of growing interpretations or reconceptualisations. Be aware of how your chosen software works in terms of the hierarchical relationship between the different levels (i.e. top-level codes and sub-codes).
7. *Delete codes.* You may want to delete codes because they have become redundant. Doing so, however, will remove all the references the codes have to data across your whole dataset,

and it will not usually be possible to retrieve that coding at a later stage. Consider, therefore, isolating redundant codes from the main coding schemes by grouping them into alternative groupings, rather than deleting them (see below), unless of course you are sure they really are no longer relevant.

Use alternative code grouping tools

1. *Create short-cut groupings.* Sets, families or collections are not always provided. Where they exist, they offer additional ways to group codes which can be useful for a range of purposes.

    (a) Create a short-cut grouping called 'codes I'm not sure about yet' and add to it codes which you know need to be refined or worked on more carefully.

    (b) Experiment with creating short-cut groupings that represent the broad research questions and other theoretical ideas, analytic conceptualisations or hypotheses. These groupings can form the basis for gathering evidence for your interpretations and later outputted (see Chapter 10).

10

Managing Processes and Interpretations by Writing

In many senses this is the most important chapter in this book. Whatever your topic, methodology, research design, analytic strategy and requirements for an eventual outcome, interpretation is the essence of what you are doing, and writing is fundamental to how you achieve and represent it. You may well use various quantitative and qualitative visual representations to interrogate your data and illustrate your interpretations, but they will only ever augment what you actually write in an account, report, article or thesis. We have touched on various forms of writing in other chapters. For example, Chapter 4 discusses transcription, Chapter 5 the development of critical appraisals of literature and other supplementary materials, Chapter 6 the universal utility of annotation tools, Chapters 7 and 9 the importance of code definitions, Chapters 8 and 9 the need to write about what you see when retrieving, rethinking and reorganising coded data. Different types of writing occur throughout and are essential components in your analysis. Writing, therefore, is not a discrete activity, but forms an essential part of all types, levels and stages of analytic work. This is illustrated by the centrality of reflection in our model of analytic activities (Figure 2.1; p. 45).

In this chapter we bring together previous discussions about writing when using CAQDAS packages. In so doing we discuss forms, purposes and spaces for writing, encouraging you to use the tools at your disposal to develop a systematic, structured and evidenced final write-up. We discuss writing about general themes or aspects of your study in centralised locations, linked to the data that prompted and contributed to the formulation of those ideas. Part of making progress in the analytic process is a movement away from data-level annotations (Chapter 6) to more abstract analytic and theoretical memos. In addition, you will need to keep an audit trail of the research process to track the development of the more practical aspects of the project and the analysis.

This chapter builds on the issues discussed previously to consider strategies for effectively utilising the range of writing tools available in CAQDAS packages. We illustrate how the use of software not only allows for different types of writing, but also through the use of linking tools (see also Chapter 11) enables writing to be integrated with and outputted along with data and other materials. We first consider the importance of writing when conducting research. We then outline types of writing and spaces for doing so within software, illustrating ways in which you can manage your writing. As always, consider your own project needs and personal style in deciding which tools and strategies are most appropriate. Table 10.1 provides an overview of types of, spaces for and levels of writing within software.

The importance of writing in analysis

The process of becoming aware of what is interesting and significant about the information and data you are collecting begins during the first moments of conceiving the research project and continues throughout (Chapters 2 and 5). One of the key tasks we face as researchers is to ensure we note these thoughts, insights, questions and theories when they occur in order that they are useful when we return to them later. Doing so encourages a more consistent approach as it helps to ensure we follow up all potential avenues of inquiry, prompting us to revisit and rethink earlier ideas and build on them where appropriate. Whilst this is a necessary task in facilitating the analytic process and ensuring rigour in qualitative research, it is also a messy one. As human beings our minds are able to continually have thoughts about different things, frequently simultaneously. It can often be very difficult to record them all, or to feel we can take the necessary 'time out' from the particular task we are currently performing to note them down. When working manually these issues are compounded because it is also difficult to subsequently search written logs in order to retrieve those thoughts reliably.

Using a CAQDAS package can significantly help with the process of spontaneously noting observations and thoughts, linking them to the data that prompted them, managing them in systematic and useful ways, retrieving them in order to use at a later stage of analysis, and outputting them in order to make use of them in final written products.

Thinking carefully about how to handle writing within your chosen software package is as important as organising and managing the data and the coding scheme. As discussed in Chapter 2, it is when these aspects of work come together in a systematic and structured way that your use of software to manage your project as a whole can really start to be effective.

Writing as a continuous analytic process

In describing the process of conducting research it is common for the various aspects involved to be presented as discrete stages which happen sequentially and in isolation from one another. It is not unusual, for example, to hear researchers refer to their progress in a given research project in terms of whether they are engaged in 'data collection', 'analysis' or 'writing up'. Similarly, methodological texts often refer to such stages and discuss them separately. On one level, treating these aspects independently is both logical and necessary; it is common to distil a complex and multifaceted process into more easily manageable, digestible and understandable summaries. However, viewing the nature and process of conducting qualitative research as sequential in this context is misleading, as one of its main characteristics (whatever the approach) is its emergent, iterative, reflexive and cyclical nature (Chapter 2). This is the case during design and data collection as well as analysis (Chapters 7–9). Writing tools in software reflect and facilitate these processes (Figure 2.1; p. 45).

Whilst some analytic tasks do occur sequentially, others are ongoing. For example, in Chapters 7–9 we discussed the sense in which various forms of coding and retrieval may occur sequentially or in tandem and be revisited for various purposes. At some point, however, coding comes to an end. Interpretation through various forms of writing is, however, the one set of analytic tasks that starts at the beginning of the research process and continues throughout. This is illustrated in relation to our three case-study examples, as listed in Tables 10.2, 10.3 and 10.4.

Writing about what is going on in data, and the patterns, relationships and anomalies you identify, will help in the process of analytic prioritisation as you inevitably have to formalise those ideas through the act of writing.

Forms, purposes and spaces for writing

There are many different forms of and purposes for writing that can be undertaken and organised within software. The extent to which you engage in these and the function they play will depend on the nature of your research project. Table 10.1 lists types of, spaces for and levels of writing.

Appraisals

Chapter 5 discusses ways in which you can use CAQDAS packages to conduct systematic literature reviews. One of the main benefits of doing so is that later it becomes possible to integrate your critical appraisals of relevant literature and other contextual materials into the analysis by comparing them directly to other forms of data (Figure 5.7; p. 129). Some packages provide specific functions for linking your appraisals (stored within the software) to the media which they are about (stored outside of the software). Even where this is not the case, you will be able to approximate the functionality. The point is that these critical appraisals can constitute data in their own right. You will usually have the choice whether to store them in document-based format like most other primary data sources are. If you do so, you can treat (i.e. annotate, code, search, etc.) them in exactly the same way. Alternatively, you might prefer to view these appraisals as notes about data rather than data in their own right. You would then store them separately from 'data', using your chosen software package's specific memo functions, thus treating them in more customary ways (see process and analytical/theoretical memos, below).

Table 10.1 Types of, spaces for and levels of writing in software

Types of writing	Spaces for writing in software	Level of work
Appraisals (of literature or other relevant contextual materials)	Documents (data files) if you want to code summaries/appraisals Memos if you do not intend to code this type of writing	Data level
Field notes (of observed (inter) actions)	Documents (data files) if you want to code your memos Memos if you do not intend to code this type of writing	Data level
Transcriptions (of recorded interviews, focus-group discussions, meetings, etc.)	Documents (data files)	Data level
Annotations (specific to and anchored at data segments)	Special spaces linked directly to the data segments which they are about. Sometimes provided in a central list. Often a completely separate function from memos, sometimes memos used for the purpose of annotation	Data level
Definitions (describing the purpose and meaning of codes and how they are applied to data segments)	Special spaces linked directly to codes. Usually there is a code properties dialog where definitions can be viewed and edited	Indexing level
Process memos (relating to research progress in general and the tasks being undertaken within software)	Stand-alone document type memos – potentially linked to other memos and project objects later on	Conceptual level
Analytic memos (relating to research questions, theories, code/concept development, etc.)	Stand-alone document type memos – potentially linked to other memos and project objects later on	Conceptual / abstract level
Summaries (of coded data, or in the form of a preliminary analysis)	Special function in some software, in others memos or documents can be used for the purpose	Conceptual / abstract level
Writing up	Initially starts off in memos – later to be outputted for finalisation within word processing application	Abstract level

Field notes

When conducting ethnographic or observational research, field notes are likely to be a primary source of data. Depending on the nature of the study and the technology available to you in the field, you may be able to write directly onto a computer – for example, if using a mobile app version of a software package (Chapter 3). Even if you are not conducting an ethnographic study, keeping notes about thoughts and observations made whilst in 'the field' will be useful. If your field notes constitute data in themselves, think carefully about how you can best structure them for your chosen software (see below and Chapters 2 and 11). Alternatively, notes about the field situation may be kept as memos, rather than being treated as data in the way formal field notes usually are. It is up to you, informed by your research design and analytic needs, to decide how to store field notes and integrate them with the rest of your work. None of the case-study examples we refer to in this book are ethnographic in the customary sense. However, for Case Study B, The Financial Downturn, it might have been worthwhile making notes about each focus-group discussion immediately after it took place, in order to note down the contextual information about the group dynamics, the general nature of the discussion and issues raised that seemed worthy of in-depth consideration, or follow-up in subsequent groups. This sort of note-taking can be treated in similar ways as ethnographers might treat field notes.

Transcriptions

In Chapter 4 we discussed different approaches to generating and working with transcriptions using Case Study C, Coca-Cola Commercials, as an example. We differentiate between working indirectly with audiovisual data via written transcripts and working directly, without an associated written representation in the form of a transcript. For many forms of qualitative research transcripts constitute the main form of data, and therefore how they are generated is significant. In the context of the use of CAQDAS packages for data management and analysis, the key consideration rests with whether to enable a synchronisation between the raw audiovisual data and the written transcription or to work with the transcripts only.

Annotations

Chapter 6 focuses on data-level exploration in which the processes of marking and annotating are key. Although often undertaken at these early stages of work, as an essential means through which you become familiar with data, and start identifying areas for analytic focus, these writing spaces can also be used at other moments. For example, when retrieving coded data in order to refine ideas and generate themes, it can be useful to annotate segments which are particularly powerful examples of a concept or category, and indeed, those that are not. This is discussed in Chapter 8 in terms of checking coded data for equivalence. In addition, when you are deciding which segments of data to quote in a final report, conference presentation or other publication, it can be useful to annotate those that you will use, including notes about why certain data are more 'quotable' than others. These examples are not the only additional uses for annotation tools, but they both speak to the need to be reflective about how you use data to evidence an argument. It is important always to caution against using 'juicy quotes' to the exclusion of others which may contradict the general view. This might be a criticism of qualitative analysis generally, and the write-ups of some research projects specifically. The use of a CAQDAS package will not in and of itself reduce the likelihood of you overquoting a particular respondent or case, but the creative and systematic use of

Table 10.2 Managing processes and interpretations: some suggestions in the context of case study A, Young People's Perceptions

Tasks from PHASE ONE: Data preparation and project set-up	
Data preparation	• Transcribe and format primary data o Consider nature and form of transcriptions (see chapter 4)

Project set-up	• Create locations for storing different types of writing
	   o research question memos
	      o make notes about what you expect to find
	• respondent memos
	• analytic memos
	• process memos

Tasks from PHASE TWO: Review of the literature and identification of theoretical focus	

Familiarise with the articles	• Annotate literature in relation to research questions
	   o be systematic in use of annotations
	   o consider how what you write in annotations differs from what you will write in memos

Generate and organise critical appraisals of literature	• Generate a critical appraisal of each literature file o use colour and other formatting devices to structure your writing systematically
Tasks from PHASE THREE: First wave coding – deductive, broad-brush coding across the dataset	

Read through and content-based data familiarisation	• Define codes precisely upon creation
	   o in reference to the theoretical focus as identified in literature
	   o in reference to how you intend to apply them to data segments

Analytic writing	• Make notes about what you are seeing
	   o what strikes you as interesting as you familiarise with data
	   o use annotations and/or analytic memos systematically

Process writing	• Write in process memos about
	   o how you are coding (i.e. in terms of the use of auto-coding tools and more manual methods)
	   o how the coding process is helping think about and bring together different forms of data

Tasks from PHASE FOUR: Inductive recoding of broad-brush codes	
Identify broad codes relating to each research question	• Refer to previous memos in tandem with reviewing coded data to generate ideas for recoding
Inductively recode broad codes	• Name and define new codes precisely
Build on analytic and process writing	• Make analytic notes concerning the relevance new codes to theoretical focus and literature • Append process notes
Tasks from PHASE FIVE: Factual data organisation	
Group respondents' contributions according to socio-demographics	• Make analytic notes about how the awareness of respondents' socio-demographic characteristics adds to your interpretation o are you surprised about any of their characteristics?

Tasks from PHASE SIX: Code retrieval, theoretical refinement, analytic reflection	
Qualitative and quantitative code retrieval	• Make analytic notes about how different retrieval options contribute to the identification of patterns
Analytic writing	• Review all previous memos and write a summary of preliminary findings
Refinement of coding scheme	• Make process notes about how you intend to refine the coding scheme, if at all

Tasks from PHASE SEVEN: Interrogate data to establish findings	
Compare coding across the dataset	• Save and define all queries you run • Summarise results of queries in terms of how they contribute to your ability to answer research questions

Tasks from PHASE EIGHT: Theoretical reconsideration in light of primary data analysis	
Integration of analytic results with literature	• Review early memos and maps concerning theoretical focus; compare with the results of data interrogations and preliminary analysis/ summaries • Write about how the analysis relates to previous literature
Develop theoretical models	• Write memos about any maps you generate, explaining clearly what they represent and how they contribute to the interpretation

Tasks from PHASE NINE: Building the interpretation and writing up	
Write-up research design and analytic process	• Create a draft structure of the final write-up
Write authoritative and evidenced accounts	• Read-through all previous forms of writing, marking the sections which will contribute to each section/chapter
Report and output for illustration	• Output combinations of memos together with relevant data as they relate to the section you are writing about

certain tools can help you to establish more rigour in your processes, and importantly, to trace the processes you went through and decisions you made (see also below, concerning process memos).

Definitions

Chapter 7 discusses the development of codes and Chapter 9 coding schemes and their refinement as analysis proceeds. Keeping on top of code definitions is important in these processes. We usually find it useful to write definitions upon code creation, however they are generated, and indeed, to note in definitions (or in the way codes are labelled) information about how they were generated. For example, codes which originate from the fast, high-level work performed using content searching tools (Chapter 6) should be labelled such that you remember they may not contain all relevant material concerning that topic, theme or category. Those that derive from the literature in more theory-driven approaches should be labelled such that you remember the ideas behind them were *a priori*. Labelling codes according to how they were derived as well as noting their function and role in definitions will contribute to the tracking of analytic process. The point about code definitions is that they are more than just descriptions of what code labels 'mean'. This of course is an important function; however, as discussed below in relation to analytic memos, your writing about the use of codes, how they contribute to your analysis, is fundamentally important. Being clear in code definitions, therefore, about how you intend to apply codes, their scope and contribution to your thinking, and how that changes over time, will always be valuable. Later, these definitions may morph into more fully-blown analytic memos.

Analytic memos

Analytic memos are larger, more general writing spaces than annotations and definitions, but you may use them within software in tandem. Analytic memos are used to record the development of your interpretation, and therefore are likely to build on the notes written in annotations and the descriptions and commentary written in definitions. Discussion in the literature about the writing of analytic memos is often framed in relation to inductive, theory-building approaches. For example, writing analytic memos is a key aspect of grounded theory, seen as the place to theorise and comment about codes (concepts) and the coding process. For example, they are used heavily during the phase of axial coding (Chapter 7). Writing in relation to NVivo, but equally relevant to other CAQDAS packages, Gibbs (2002) notes that software provides the

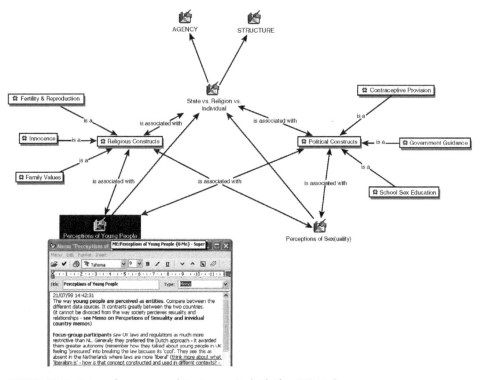

FIGURE 10.1   Integrating memos with other work via linking (ATLAS.ti)

ability to treat and work with memos as originally endorsed by Glaser (1978), that is, as entirely separate from primary data. In so doing you can sort and search memos, using them to develop categories inductively (see also Chapter 7). Gibbs goes on to illustrate, however, that software provides an added flexibility in working with memos: the ability to link them to other objects (including codes and data segments) is a way of directly integrating your writing with the other elements of the project (see below). Similar processes are possible in most (but not all) CAQDAS packages.

BOX 10.1 ——— FUNCTIONALITY NOTES —————————————————

Rationalising the use of writing spaces

The fact that there are many different writing spaces within most CAQDAS packages means that you need to reflect critically on their uses and benefits for each project you undertake in software. Together with the different forms and purposes of writing, which may change as an analysis proceeds, the adage 'less is more' holds true for your use of tools. Do not be tempted to use all of the options available unless there is a real purpose in doing so. There might well be, but just be sure there is, because often economy is the best policy. Reflecting on your need for different writing spaces will relate to how you intend to bring together the different strands of your writing later on, at the stage of preparing a written report or publication of some sort. Having your outcomes in mind in these terms as soon as possible will mean not only that the direction and purpose of the analysis are more focused, but that the note-taking you engage in throughout the process also has some concrete end in mind. It is one thing to say (which we do) that it is important to get all your ideas out of your head and into the software (linked to the data that prompted them), but to do so in a haphazard way, with little sense of purpose, will not help you in the long term. As always, therefore, planning is important (Chapter 5).

Layder (1998) refers to theoretical memos in a similar manner. Although discussing ways to analyse data with theory in mind, the following excerpt provides a useful illustration of the role of memos in qualitative analysis more generally and the practical processes involved in using them:

> From ... extended memos I developed discussions of many important concepts and ideas ... I did this by constructing a running discussion or commentary on the data contained in the interview transcripts and this involved two main elements. First, it required a continual reshuffling or rethinking of what the data meant (how, what and why questions) in order to produce new angles, ideas and explanations. Secondly, it involved a sustained teasing out (elaboration, extension, modification) of the concepts and ideas that were already playing a significant role in the analysis and interpretation of the data. (1998: 60–61)

You may have different memos relating to specific themes, concepts and ideas. In them you can flesh out your ideas and build upon them to develop a cohesive and coherent interpretation. Charmaz (2000) sees analytic memos as a pivotal intermediate step between coding and writing up the final report. This way of working is reflected in the suggested analytic processes for our three case-study examples (Tables 10.2; p. 234, 10.3; p. 243 and 10.4; p. 250).

Chapter 9 discusses the ways coding schemes can be manipulated to reflect the development of your analytic thinking. Memo-writing is closely related to such work. Whether your analysis is directed by or leading towards theory, or, indeed, free from theory, writing memos will be an element of your process. As you progress, keep track of puzzling observations and lines of thought requiring further inquiry. For the key analytic or theoretical aspects you may create spaces for this type of writing as part of your project set-up (Chapter 5). You may choose to do so in a general research process journal (see below), particularly if you want to keep hold of the sequence of their occurrence. You may use annotations for data segments that strike you as interesting, but you are as yet unsure how, and you just want to quickly make notes and embed them at points in the text. However you start off, at some point you will want to gather writing about general themes or topics together. You might do that simply by moving writing around (using cut/paste), or use grouping/linking tools to bring notes together (see below).

It usually makes sense to use methods consistently rather than switching between them sporadically, but noting observations and questions will act as reflective ponderings, to return to later once you have pursued a line of inquiry and built on an idea, or noticed something else of salience.

Process memos

Writing about what you are doing, how it is going, and recording significant changes in direction are important parts of documenting the processes you go through. Some of this will happen as you write analytic memos, but a central research diary – what we like to call a 'project process journal' – can also perform several functions in your

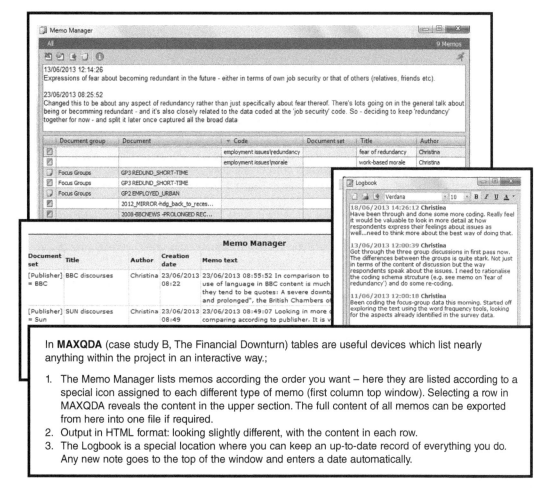

In **MAXQDA** (case study B, The Financial Downturn) tables are useful devices which list nearly anything within the project in an interactive way.;

1. The Memo Manager lists memos according the order you want – here they are listed according to a special icon assigned to each different type of memo (first column top window). Selecting a row in MAXQDA reveals the content in the upper section. The full content of all memos can be exported from here into one file if required.
2. Output in HTML format: looking slightly different, with the content in each row.
3. The Logbook is a special location where you can keep an up-to-date record of everything you do. Any new note goes to the top of the window and enters a date automatically.

FIGURE 10.2 Logbook, Memo Manager and HTML output (MAXQDA)

project. It is usually the main place where we record the various phases and day-to-day processes, together with our thoughts about them. Researchers can add to transparency and rigour by systematically recording such information. This is invaluable if you need to justify your methodological approach, and will act as a history or 'audit trail' of your project if you keep it up to date!

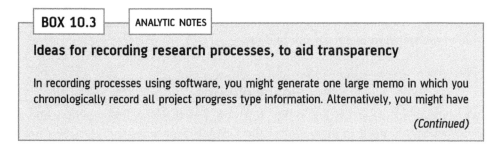

BOX 10.3   ANALYTIC NOTES

Ideas for recording research processes, to aid transparency

In recording processes using software, you might generate one large memo in which you chronologically record all project progress type information. Alternatively, you might have

(Continued)

several memos about different aspects of project progress and processes. In either case, consider the following:

- cross-referencing with literature;
- including research proposal to assess progress;
- tracking the various phases of the project (significant changes in direction, refinements in coding scheme, etc.);
- recording the practical aspects of using the software (e.g. what was useful, how and why);
- visualising your progress in a map (Chapter 11).

Being systematic about how you write process memos, and ensuring you have an adequate account of all the work you do, will be important when you come to write up your account of methodology and analytic strategy. Therefore, also reflect on how your chosen software is impacting upon the way you are working.

Summaries

Writing critical appraisals of literature and other relevant contextual materials is a form of summarising (Chapter 5). In addition, summarising your work at various stages is an important exercise in building an interpretation. This is relevant to both process and analytic memo-writing, and will draw on writing you have done in other spaces within the software as well. Some CAQDAS packages (e.g. MAXQDA and NVivo) provide special spaces for writing summaries that can be generated from and linked to previous coding work (Figure 10.3; p. 241).

Working in this way can have multiple functions. It might be that you are employing an analytic strategy that explicitly seeks to reduce data to the level of summaries, such as framework analysis (Chapter 1). Indeed, NVivo's Framework Matrices incorporate functionality which was originally developed by researchers at NatCen who also developed the framework method. The aim might be to abstract quite quickly from the original source material and thus it is possible to work directly with framework matrices (i.e. stepping over the coding process entirely). Although you would need to create codes in order to add them into the matrix through the dialogue box, they need not have any data coded at them for you to work with the frameworks. The logic in the MAXQDA Summary Grid function is slightly different in that summaries are linked to coded data. Even where your chosen software does not include a special function for writing summaries, you will be able to use standard memo spaces to do so.

Final write-ups

We always encourage writing within software, but there will inevitably come a point when you need to move out of the CAQDAS package and prepare a final

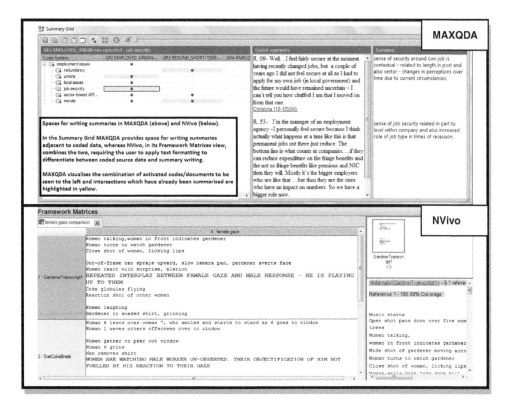

FIGURE 10.3   Framework Matrices (NVivo) and Summary Grids (MAXQDA)

report, publication, presentation or other representation of your analysis. It can be important to plan for this as there will be no dynamic relationship between what you write outside the software and the versions originally started within the software. Reports outputted from software will always only be snapshots of the status of work at the time they are generated; subsequent changes within the software project will not be reflected in previously generated output reports. Alternatively to generating reports, you might just copy and paste the relevant parts of writing from any software space into a word-processing application. Some software packages have centralised systems for managing all or some of the forms of writing that you have done within the whole software project. These tools provide particularly easy and useful ways of outputting large bodies of writing around a theme or topic into one file that can be further manipulated and polished in a word-processing application for publication.

Considerations when writing in software

Software allows not only systematic management and retrieval of different forms of writing, but also crucially the integration of writing with the rest of the project. First, the flexibility of software makes it very easy to record thoughts and ideas and

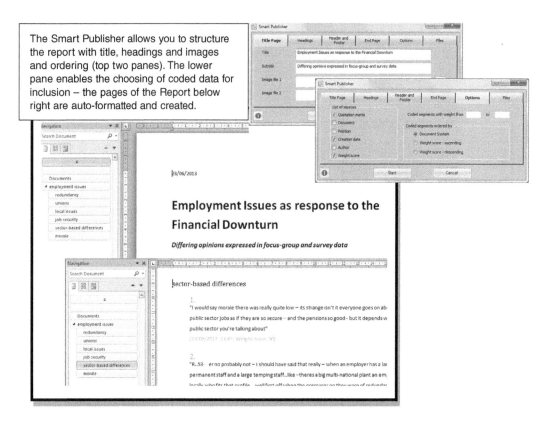

The Smart Publisher allows you to structure the report with title, headings and images and ordering (top two panes). The lower pane enables the choosing of coded data for inclusion – the pages of the Report below right are auto-formatted and created.

Figure 10.4 The Smart Publisher for building professional reports (MAXQDA)

link them to the data source which prompted them. Second, software allows the content of memos to be searched and retrieved with ease. These are the key reasons why it is useful to write within your software project, rather than elsewhere; the ability to integrate writing with other aspects of work offers more potential for making systematic use of your writing than is conceivably possible when writing is disconnected from data.

Nevertheless, as with all software tools, this does not happen automatically simply because you happen to be working within a software package. Packages have different places in which to write and ways in which to manage that process. We argue that effective use of software writing tools, together with efficient management of the resultant material, can enhance the process of analysis and result in increased rigour, transparency and quality (Silver and Lewins 2014). In order to develop an effective strategy you need to become aware of the subtleties of how the writing tools available in your chosen software work. It is unlikely that you will need to use all of the writing spaces and tools provided by your chosen software. Keep in mind the ways you like to write, and critically evaluate the available tools in light of this as well as the methodological and practical needs of your project.

Table 10.3 Managing processes and interpretations: some suggestions in the context of case study B, The Financial Downturn

---

Tasks from PHASE ONE: Data preparation and project set-up

Data preparation	• Transcribe and format primary data
Project set-up	• Create locations for storing different types of writing

	o research question memos;
	        o make notes about what you expect to find
	    o respondent/group memos
	    o analytic memos
	    o process memos

Tasks from PHASE TWO: Factual data organisation

Group data according to socio-demographics	• Write analytic notes about what you expect to find in the data relating to the different groups

	o e.g. retired professionals,
	    o employed urban,
	    o redundant short-time etc.

Tasks from PHASES THREE, FOUR, & FIVE: Analysis of survey, focus-group and media data

Read through and content-based familiarisation	• Make notes about words and phrases that seem to be indicative of themes, requiring further investigation as a result of the data familiarisation process • Reflect on data and processes arising from initial interrogations
Coding and retrieval	• Name and define codes as they are created, identifying those resulting from auto-coding processes, related to sensitising concepts and generated inductively • Whilst coding and retrieving, make notes about how individual coded segments compare to one another, how they contribute to your thinking about the research questions, and how they relate to code labels and definitions
Analytic writing	• Summarise key results that require validating with other data
Process writing	• Make notes about the role of content-searching and auto-coding in the process, and how this process differs from more inductive work

---

Tasks from PHASE SIX: Integration of earlier stages

Quantitative and qualitative retrieval	• Retrieve data across data types and make notes about how the different forms relate, reinforce or contradict one another • Review all previous notes and coded data
	o Make notes about the structure of the coding scheme and ways in which it might usefully be refined. Which bodies of coded data need revisiting, combining, splitting, etc.
Analytic writing	• Summarise results of interrogations conducted across the dataset, and within subsets of it • Write about the dynamic between sensitising concepts and primary data

---

Tasks from PHASE EIGHT: Building the interpretation and writing up

Write-up research design and analytic process	• Create a draft structure of the final write-up
Write authoritative and evidenced accounts	• Read through all previous forms of writing, marking the sections which will contribute to each section/chapter
Report and output for illustration	• Output combinations of memos together with relevant data as they relate to the section you are writing about

---

Managing your writing

Because of the flexibility software provides in terms of writing, it is important to think carefully about how to manage and organise your writing. Some packages provide more complex memo organisation facilities than others. Whichever software package you are using, however, organising your memo system is as important as organising the data (Chapters 5 and 12) and the coding scheme (Chapters 7–9). Here we discuss managing your writing in three ways: creating, naming and dating memos; grouping memos; and structuring writing.

BOX 10.4 — CASE NOTES

Organising writing from the early stages of analytic work (Case Study C, Coca-Cola Commercials)

In Case Study C we first created memo groups for the two broad research questions, each of which have their own memo where general commentary is kept as thoughts develop (Figures 10.5 and 10.6). Other more specific memos are also contained within particular groupings – for example, first impressions of the Diet Coke Break and Gardener commercials which are particularly important in the interpretation of differences in gendered representations over time. In this example, we also broadly distinguish between process and analytic memos at the memo group level to enable a quick way to access and output these two types of writing later on. As more detailed work progressed we began also memo groups for key aspects of comparison – for example, the two commercials about the Olympic Games (1979 and 2012) and the Diet Coke Break (1994) and its remake, the Gardener (2013).

Creating, naming and dating

It can be tempting when using software to create a new memo every time you have a new idea. This tendency might indeed be encouraged when using software because you can so easily create as many as you like. Doing so is less problematic in some software packages than others, but it is usually advisable to begin bringing together your writing about similar aspects early on. Study the devices provided which help you to retrieve memos, and think ahead about this issue.

Your approach may necessitate the creation of many very specific memos, for example if you are interested in discourse or narrative. That is fine as long as you know where they are and what their purpose is. Consider carefully what a memo's function is before you create it. Avoid creating large numbers of memos unless you have specific analytic requirements for doing so; proliferating writing in many different places can fragment your thinking. That said, you can both split broad memos (using cut and paste) and pull many detailed notes together (using grouping tools). Figure 10.5 shows notes in Transana in the database structure and in the centralised Notes Browser.

As with most other packages, writing can be linked to various points within the project (database) in Transana. Notes are used for both memo-writing and annotating. They are visualised as sticky note type icons in the database system and can be accessed from there as well as the Notes Browser window. Whatever database item they are linked to (Series, Episode, Transcript, Collection, Clip or Snapshot), the Notes Browser lists the name of the item as well as the author. Naming notes precisely and succinctly makes the management and outputting of writing easier (see also below) and finding relevant content easier – although there is a search function. This is particularly important in packages such as Transana that do not have additional means of gathering writing – such as short-cut grouping functionality (discussed below).

Naming your memos precisely and using consistent protocols for similar types of memo will help considerably in organising your writing in a way which facilitates rather than hinders your analysis. If developing an accurate audit trail is important to you, always remember to date each entry you make in any memo (Chapter 2). This can also be seen in Figure 10.2, where the Logbook function in MAXQDA is being used as the central research process journal. Note that entries are listed such that the most recent is at the top. MAXQDA does this automatically, which means you do not have to scroll down to the bottom of a long memo in order to add a new entry. In other packages you will have to manage the sequencing of notes within memos yourself.

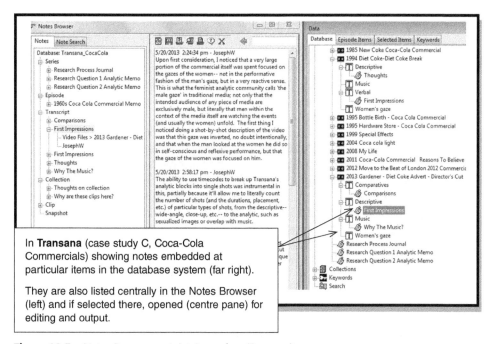

In **Transana** (case study C, Coca-Cola Commercials) showing notes embedded at particular items in the database system (far right).

They are also listed centrally in the Notes Browser (left) and if selected there, opened (centre pane) for editing and output.

Figure 10.5 Notes Browser and database view (Transana)

Grouping memos

Organising your writing by grouping memos can be very helpful. Some software packages provide specific tools for grouping memos. Even where this is not the case, you can usually artificially group memos together by prefixing their titles. Groups may be based on research questions, emerging findings, theoretical ideas or perspectives, thesis chapters or report sections, etc.

Figure 10.6 shows the Memo Manager system in ATLAS.ti with different families of memos for Case Study C, at an early stage of work (Box 10.3).

Packages which allow you to create short-cut groupings of different types of item (e.g. to bring together data files, codes, memos and maps in one place) offer additional means to gather evidence from across the dataset relating to a particular research question, case, setting or concept. This is illustrated in NVivo in Figure 10.7. Similar functionality is provided by QDA Miner through its Report Manager tool (Figure 5.4; p. 121). Where you cannot put items of different types into one short-cut grouping (e.g. as in MAXQDA and ATLAS.ti), it might be that you can approximate the functionality through the use of linking tools (see below).

BOX 10.5 — CASE NOTES

The various purposes of short-cut groupings in context (Case Study A, Young People's Perceptions)

Short-cut groupings such as sets are useful devices for focusing thinking as they can act as 'hypotheses', 'hunches' or areas you need to investigate further (see also Chapters 7 and 9). In Figure 10.7 you can see listed on the left several different types of set. As well as sets for the research questions for Case Study A, there are sets which reflect ideas to be followed up ('HYP – Dutch more positive re content + process' and 'HYP – Transition more gradual amongst Dutch'). These are prefixed by 'HYP' (meaning 'hypothesis') so that they are listed together in this view. Other types of set visible in Figure 10.7 are ideas to follow up from having read the literature (prefixed by 'LIT') and the more practical set 'codes I'm not sure about yet' which serves to remind us to review the coding at particular nodes later on. The set 'WRITE – Thesis Chapter 4' is highlighted and the project items which are contained within it are listed on the right. This sort of practical set helps to gather materials that will be drawn upon to develop a particular part of the final write-up – in this example, Chapter 4 of the thesis. The lower part of Figure 10.7 shows the partial contents of two of the memos in this set, where notes have previously been made concerning the idea of young people as entities, as evidenced societally through health policies and laws/regulations; and initial ideas about the use of Giddens's (1984) theory of structuration. These two memos are kept separate as they contain commentary that needs to remain independent; but NVivo's 'see also' links are used to relate commentary across the memos (see below for more on this and other linking functionality).

Although we encourage the grouping of memos as a means of managing writing, some of your memos may be about a general aspect of your project and

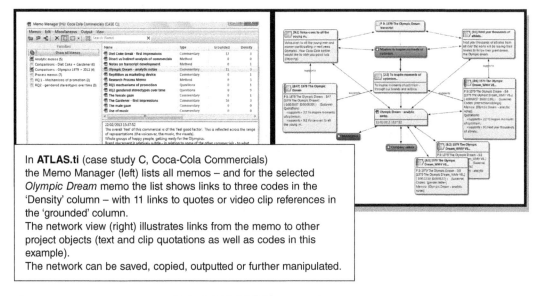

In **ATLAS.ti** (case study C, Coca-Cola Commercials) the Memo Manager (left) lists all memos – and for the selected *Olympic Dream* memo the list shows links to three codes in the 'Density' column – with 11 links to quotes or video clip references in the 'grounded' column.
The network view (right) illustrates links from the memo to other project objects (text and clip quotations as well as codes in this example).
The network can be saved, copied, outputted or further manipulated.

Figure 10.6 Memo Manager – linking and networking (ATLAS.ti)

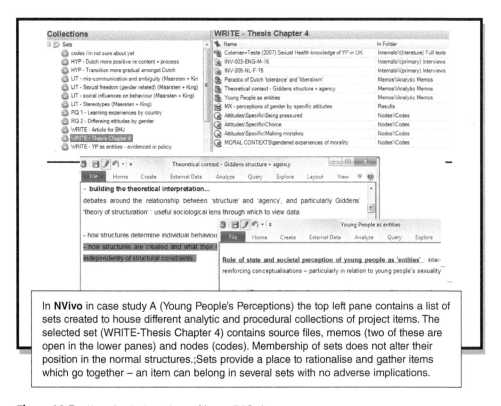

In **NVivo** in case study A (Young People's Perceptions) the top left pane contains a list of sets created to house different analytic and procedural collections of project items. The selected set (WRITE-Thesis Chapter 4) contains source files, memos (two of these are open in the lower panes) and nodes (codes). Membership of sets does not alter their position in the normal structures.;Sets provide a place to rationalise and gather items which go together – an item can belong in several sets with no adverse implications.

Figure 10.7 Use of sets to gather evidence (NVivo)

therefore usefully remain centralised and free from other aspects of your work. Logging the research process is a case in point (as discussed above in relation to MAXQDA). You may have one research log where you record all aspects of the research process, or you may prefer to keep different aspects of the process in separate logs (e.g. by creating one log to record the research process and another to act as a reflective diary). You do not have to put all your memos into groups; but grouping elements of your writing will serve to keep you focused on the eventual outcome in terms of the needs of your written account, and help you access and output relevant writing when you need to.

Structuring writing

However you use memos and other writing spaces, there will inevitably be overlap in their content and the purpose of the writing within them. The way you handle this is something to consider carefully. You may decide to impose structure on your writing from the outset, or when reviewing previous thoughts. Alternatively, you may decide that to structure your writing would disrupt the free flow of thoughts and ideas too much. The key thing is to think about these issues and decide on a general approach at the outset (whilst maintaining, as always, the possibility of changing it).

If you are conducting a commissioned study, you may have predefined parameters for what is expected and therefore a mature reporting framework explicit from the outset. Undertaking a more explorative study, however, is inherently less formalised, and an idea of what the final written product will look like will therefore evolve more iteratively. In both cases, however, stepping away from data and thinking more abstractly about how you will eventually pull your work together in a written format can be a welcome 'break' and also serve to refocus the mind and see the study in a different light. Stepping away from the data can often provide renewed direction and motivation. This can be achieved through the grouping of memos (and other material) as discussed above, but the structuring of your actual writing in terms of the content of memos, for example, is another element.

There may be many different ways that you could usefully structure your writing, and not necessarily one best way. Tools for structuring memos are generally very basic – headings, fonts, colour, etc. – but can have great effect when used consistently. This is discussed in more detail with respect to the generation of critical appraisals of literature in Chapter 5 but is relevant to all types of writing.

Integrating your writing with the rest of your work

The ability to integrate your writing with the rest of your work may be one of the main advantages of using software. Grouping (as discussed above) is an aspect of linking – but this functions in a relatively 'loose' way. Putting memos (and other items) into short-cut groupings (sets or families) essentially only illustrates that they are in general terms related – for example, all these materials will be used to write 'Chapter 4' of the thesis (see Figure 10.7; p. 247). You are not making any statements about the nature of the association between items simply by putting them into a short-cut grouping.

At a practical level, linking objects to one another can simply serve to move around the different aspects of work in your software project more quickly. Importantly, when you are fleshing out an idea in a memo, linking relevant codes, documents and data will allow you to pull together those connected aspects later on. Writing analytic memos at relevant moments in tandem with the other analytic tasks stimulates progress. The links you make to other aspects of your work will only serve to improve the continuity of your thinking and cross-referencing. This is closely related to the ways you may work when mapping and coding, and linking tools are discussed further in Chapter 11.

Linking writing

Linking whole memos to whole data files and other source materials can be useful for writing contextual information concerning those documents. This is distinguished from linking *parts* of data files (whether coded or not) to one another (Chapters 6 and 11). For example, in working with one-to-one interview data you may wish to compile descriptive information or build typologies concerning individual respondents at corresponding memos. This approach was taken in Case Study A. Respondent memos were used to generate summaries of each respondent, acting as a means to bring together their contributions to the project through the three different forms of data (interviews, vignettes and photo prompts) which themselves remained as separate source data files. A similar approach can be very useful in life history work when much contextual information is relevant. Another purpose of linking memos to documents may arise with focus-group data when you wish to link field notes about a particular discussion to the transcript.

Similar functionality is sometimes available for linking whole memos to whole codes. This can help when thinking and writing at an abstract level about the relationships and connections within the data. Often this can serve the very practical function of reminding you about previous trains of thought, particularly when visualising connections in a map or network (Figure 10.1; p. 236 and Chapter 11). ATLAS.ti is distinctive in its ability to link memos to data segments (quotations); see Figure 10.6. These can be visualised and opened in several different ways, in the margin view next to the data, in networks and in the Memo Manager.

Visualising memos

Having linked memos to other project content, you will want to visualise those connections. The options for doing so vary quite significantly (see also Chapter 11),

Table 10.4 Managing processes and interpretations: some suggestions in the context of case study C, Coca-Cola Commercials

Tasks from PHASE ONE: Data preparation and project set-up	

Data preparation
Project
set-up
	• Transcribe and format primary data
	• Create locations for storing different types of writing
	    ○ research question memos
	        ○ make notes about what you expect to find
	    ○ commercial memos
	    ○ analytic memos
	    ○ process memos

Tasks from PHASE TWO: Exploration and identification of analytic focus	
Familiarise with the **commercials/make** **analytic notes**	• Create a memo for each commercial and make notes about what is seen as you watch each commercial through in its entirety • Add commentary to each research question memo as seems relevant, noting which commercial has prompted each thought
Transcription/early **annotation**	• If intending to work indirectly, develop one (or more) transcript per commercial Make notes about analytic decisions you are making in deciding how and what to transcribe • During play-back of synchronised transcripts create clips and annotate them, indicating why they are meaningful in the context of the research questions
Tasks from PHASE THREE: First wave coding: inductive indexing	
Initial coding **(indirect and direct** **processes)** **Process notes**	• Output all notes. Read them and generate a list of ideas to refer to as you code. • As you generate clips and codes, name and define them precisely. ○ Make notes relating to the possible implications of different sized clips • If experimenting with both direct and indirect coding, make notes about the differences in working in each way, and their relative advantages and disadvantages
Tasks from PHASE FOUR: Basic code retrieval – early analytic commentary	
Qualitative and **quantitative** **retrievals**	• Make notes about the how different retrievals of coded clips (with and without associated transcripts) offer different ways of interpreting data
Tasks from PHASE FIVE: Secondary analytic coding: developing themes, concepts, categories	

Review, revisit,
refine
	• In light of reviewing memos and annotations, refine the coding schema
	    ○ write about what you are doing and to what effect
	    ○ in terms of moving from descriptive indexing to more conceptual coding work
	• Write up a preliminary analysis, focusing on how the themes/concepts/categories you are developing relate to the research questions
	• Reference and link to data segments that evidence your argument
	• Write detailed notes about how you are moving up towards an interpretation/theory.
	    ○ How are you using software tools, how are they helping you think about data?

Write-up **preliminary** **analysis**	• Review all previous memos and write up a summary of preliminary findings

Tasks from PHASE SEVEN: Integration of analysis of publicity materials	
Focused reading, exploration and coding	• Make notes about how your reading and analysis of publicity materials relates to your preliminary write-up, considering in particular how an awareness of the company values impacts on your thinking about the data

Tasks from PHASE EIGHT: Interrogate data to establish findings	
Compare coding across the dataset	• Save and define all queries you run • Summarise results of queries in terms of how they contribute to your ability to answer research questions

Tasks from PHASE NINE: Building the interpretation and writing up	
Write-up research design and analytic process	• Create a draft structure of the final write-up
Write authoritative and evidenced accounts	• Read-through all previous forms of writing, marking the sections which will contribute to each section/chapter
Report and output for illustration	• Output combinations of memos together with relevant data as they relate to the section you are writing about

depending on the memo linking functionality itself, but also the existence and functioning of mapping tools. In many senses, it seems pointless to create links if these cannot be visualised satisfactorily. Therefore, be sure to investigate the options for visualising memos and their links to other objects before actually embarking on linking them.

Coding your own writing

Where memos have the same status as data files within the software, they can immediately be treated equivalently (i.e. be searched, coded, etc). Even where this is not the case, you will always be able to approximate the functionality (i.e. by turning a memo into a data source). Most packages store data files as rich text and allow them to be edited within the software, so you can continue writing in them once they have been converted. Treating your own writing as 'data' in this way is related to the discussion of generating critical appraisals of literature and other supplementary materials, above and in Chapter 5.

Searching the content of your notes

It will be frustrating if you know you have previously written about an issue, but you can no longer find where. Searching the content to find a key word or phrase you know you have used in your own writing can be invaluable in such circumstances. This may also get you out of trouble if your memo system becomes unwieldy or overly fragmented. Sometimes this searching functionality is included with the main software query tools (see Chapter 13), but often there is an option within the centralised memo system or a find tool similar to that found in MS Word.

BOX 10.6 — ANALYTIC NOTES

Considerations when writing up the results of visual analysis

Writing dissertations, reports or articles and presenting findings at academic conferences are among the most common research outputs. Systematic use of writing tools from the outset of software use will enable you to be transparent about the processes you employed, and be convincing in the presentation of your argument. Presenting the results of visual analysis poses particular challenges, and traditional linear and text-based expectations can be restrictive. This is especially the case when analysis focuses on the interactional dimensions of visual material as well as, or to the exclusion of, their content. When planning for publication, explore the possibilities of presenting visual material dynamically. There are some online journals, for example, that allow video clips and still images to be embedded in documents, which can be much more illustratively powerful than describing (inter)action in textual narratives. It is also imperative when working with some forms of visual data to consider the ethical issues pertaining to the dissemination of results. When research participants have generated visual material themselves, this will need to have been considered as part of gaining informed consent. When working with publicly available data you will need to ensure you have sufficient rights to reproduce material for scientific purposes.

Outputting writing

Being able to get your written thoughts and ideas out of the software in flexible ways and in a format that you can easily convert, to form part of a final report, will probably be very important to you. This will especially be the case if you have taken the time to formulate your ideas clearly within a memo and want to use some of the content directly. Efficient output has much to do with efficient organisation of memos in the software. Take a careful note early on to see the ways this is enabled in each package. In Figure 10.8 some of the output options available in Dedoose are shown which are similar to those in other packages. It is usually possible to vary several aspects for any output; for example, whether linked content is provided at all, in summary or full context, and whether description or other associated meta-information is included.

Some packages provide more choices for the format in which output will be saved, but even where this is not the case, you will usually easily be able to convert. Common formats include rich text, comma-separated and HTML.

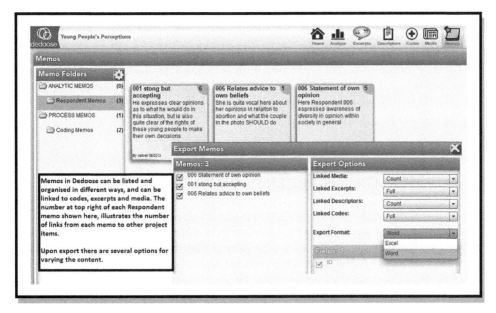

Figure 10.8 Output options for memos (Dedoose)

Outputting memos, just like outputting coded data, can be constructive at various moments throughout the analytic process. There is often no substitute for printing information off and reflecting upon it away from the computer. This is just as true for your own writing as for bodies of coded data.

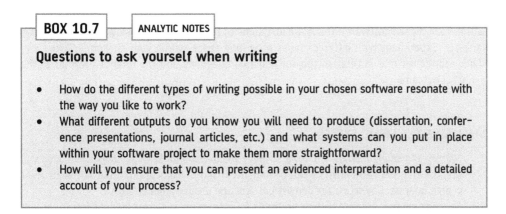

BOX 10.7 — **ANALYTIC NOTES**

Questions to ask yourself when writing

- How do the different types of writing possible in your chosen software resonate with the way you like to work?
- What different outputs do you know you will need to produce (dissertation, conference presentations, journal articles, etc.) and what systems can you put in place within your software project to make them more straightforward?
- How will you ensure that you can present an evidenced interpretation and a detailed account of your process?

Concluding remarks: integrating writing

There are many differences in how memo systems work in CAQDAS packages. That said, each enables you to integrate your thoughts with the rest of your work and retrieve writing in various ways. If you are already using a software package you will be able to make effective use of memo tools to help you manage your interpretations about the data. If you are choosing between packages, the attractions of each system may rest as much on the way you work, and the way your mind works, as on the methodological needs of your project. Either way, the ability to integrate different forms of writing with the data that prompted the ideas represented within them, to search, organise and build on writing, within CAQDAS packages constitutes the main advantage of using these tools rather than continuing with paper-based note-taking.

EXERCISES: MANAGING PROCESSES AND INTERPRETATIONS

This chapter discussed the different forms, purposes and spaces for writing within CAQDAS packages. You need not use all of them, but you will need to be aware of how they work in your chosen software in order to devise a strategy for using them to support your analytic needs efficiently. It is therefore advisable to experiment early on with the different options – it will be to your advantage later to be structured from the beginning. The exercises listed here relate back to some of those in Chapter 4, in which we encouraged you to think about the key aspects of the project you will need to keep notes about. You may, therefore, already have created and used different writing spaces. Usually, making use of a few of the writing spaces systematically rather than all of them sporadically will be more effective.

CREATE SPACES IN WHICH TO WRITE

Think about the different forms of writing that will be useful for your project. Will you distinguish between process and analytic writing? Will you use annotation tools as well as memos? Do you intend to write summaries, and if so, where will be the best place to do so within your chosen software? These are just some of the questions to ask yourself as soon as possible. Experiment with different types of writing space within your chosen software and think about their role in relation to your research questions and the intended format of the eventual outcome.

MANAGING THE MEMO SYSTEM

1. *Naming and dating memos*. Whatever strategy you develop for keeping notes about what you see, the way you name memos will be important. Simple naming protocols will be of great benefit later on. Devise a clear naming protocol and use it systematically.
2. *Grouping memos*. Efficient naming protocols for memos serve a grouping function as you will often be able to list them according to their name. Some packages enable the additional grouping of memos by type (e.g. 'method', 'theory', 'commentary'). Where this is possible you can usually create your own types. Some packages also enable you to group memos with other items – such as data files and codes – using short-cut groupings (see Chapter 9). Where enabled, this is particularly useful for gathering 'evidence' for a particular hypothesis or in relation to research questions, and when deciding what the final dissertation or report structure will look like (see also point 2 in the next section).

3. *Structuring memos.* Consider how best to structure your own writing. Experiment with the use of formatting functionality – such as bold, italics, underlining and colour as well as the use of paragraph styles and other options (where supported). Devise and note down a systematic way of using these functions and ensure you do so consistently across all memos. Such visual marking of your own writing will help you later on when you want to transfer notes from within the software out into a formal report, paper or dissertation.

LINK YOUR WRITING WITH THE DATA THAT PROMPT THE IDEAS WITHIN THEM

Where your chosen software enables the linking of writing spaces (principally memos) to other aspects of your work, consider whether and how this might be useful.

1. *Linking memos to documents.* This might be useful when you need to write in detail about a particular respondent, setting, event or subset of data. Some packages offer more flexibility with how to link writing spaces to whole documents – so if this type of work is likely to be a core activity for you, experiment with the options. Usually this is essentially a means of quickly accessing your writing space from a list of data files – or vice versa.
2. *Linking memos to codes.* Not all packages allow this, and those that do, enable it in quite different ways. Therefore if you think it will be useful to link whole bodies of writing to whole bodies of coded data, it is important to experiment with how to do this, and to what effect – that is, how can linked memos and codes be retrieved and outputted?

INTEGRATE YOUR WRITING WITH THE ANALYSIS

Remember that writing is an analytic act and therefore your own notes and memos are important in terms of how your interpretation is developing. Linking writing spaces to data is one aspect of this, searching and coding your own writing might be another.

1. *Coding your own writing.* Where memos are data files in their own right, you can treat your own writing similarly to how you may have worked with other forms of qualitative data. Coding your own writing might be one way to integrate your comments with the data that prompted those ideas.
2. *Search the content of memos.* Sometimes you will not be able to find a passage you have written because you cannot remember which writing space you used. Having a simple and systematic memo system will reduce the likelihood of this being an issue, but most packages also enable you to search your own writing for words and phrases. Experiment with searching for content within your own writing – but be aware that not all packages allow you to search for words and phrases across all writing spaces, so this might be problematic. You need to be able to rely on this sort of searching, so test this by searching for a word or phrase which only occurs in a particular form of writing, and check that your chosen software retrieves what you expect.

OUTPUT YOUR WRITING

Although we encourage you to use the writing tools offered by your chosen software, at some point you need to write an article, report or dissertation and therefore outputting your writing from the CAQDAS package to a word-processing (or other) application is a key process.

1. *Output by copy and paste.* The easiest way to get any text (whether your own writing or text from within data files) is usually simply copy and paste. Formatting might not always transfer over, however – depending on which application you are pasting into – so experiment with this and explore alternative ways of getting your writing out of your chosen package.
2. *Experiment with different formats for output reports.* It is usually possible to generate reports on aspects of your work – including your own writing – in many different ways (see also Chapter 13). Sometimes you want the actual content of what you have written, sometimes a simple overview in list format is sufficient. Try out all the options available. Often there is a central tool within the software from which reports can be generated, but several packages also incorporate quick ways of generating output from other dialogue windows or views.

11

Mapping Ideas and Linking Concepts

This chapter is somewhat different from most of the other task-based chapters because we view the purposes of mapping ideas and linking concepts in a wide variety of ways. Some researchers make significant and continued use of mapping tools, others hardly at all. But this does not mean that those who do will be doing 'better' analysis, using software more efficiently or in some way to a 'fuller' potential. In addition, the packages we focus on do not all have mapping tools, and those that do, function quite differently. It is therefore very difficult to take a broad view about the role of mapping in analysis generally, or the functionality of CAQDAS mapping tools specifically. We therefore offer practical principles of and ideas for using maps, as well as discussing general and exceptional tools, in the hope that these become starting points for your own creative use of them.

This chapter aptly follows the chapter on managing processes and interpretations, since the relationship between writing, managing interpretation and mapping can be strong (Figure 2.1; p. 45). This is illustrated in the way mapping can be used to step back and view the processes of grouping and connecting (Figures 10.1–10.6; pp. 236–247 and 11.1; p. 258). We concentrate here on tools which allow a diagram of connections to be made. Where such maps are available, whatever the connections being made (whether between codes, memos, documents or data segments or a mixture of those things), it is up to you, the researcher, to make the decision about what goes in a map, what is connected and how it is arranged.

We really just want to open doors here to all sorts of ideas based on the general and special functions within CAQDAS mapping tools. We paint a picture about the practical possibilities of maps and touch on their potential to illustrate, or in some way expand on, theory. This is just one use of maps; there are many more. The processes of analysis might include the development of many small theories, stories and connections, and each of our illustrations is an expression of such developments in the case-study examples. If we had to sum up mapping possibilities in one phrase, we would suggest they are for 'stepping back'. Within that one phrase many possibilities present themselves. To give a sense of those possibilities we include general lists of routine tasks and also exceptional and software-specific

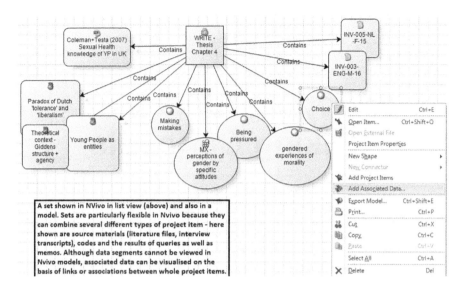

A set shown in NVivo in list view (above) and also in a model. Sets are particularly flexible in Nvivo because they can combine several different types of project item - here shown are source materials (literature files, interview transcripts), codes and the results of queries as well as memos. Although data segments cannot be viewed in Nvivo models, associated data can be visualised on the basis of links or associations between whole project items.

FIGURE 11.1 Model showing members of a set with mixed items – codes, memos, documents (NVivo)

functions, suggestions for different uses of maps and ways to integrate them with other aspects of your work. We refer generically to the visual spaces created to manipulate ideas as 'maps', but the tools we mainly focus on here operate on differing principles. They are well supported in ATLAS.ti as *networks*, in MAXQDA as *maps* and in NVivo as *models*. HyperRESEARCH and Qualrus also have some map-like functionality but they function rather differently. Therefore we primarily refer to them in the section about special functions since they each have their own rather different emphasis related to the unique behaviour of each respective package. At the time of writing, Transana and QDA Miner do not include mapping tools of the kind we discuss in this chapter.

Mapping traditions and other software

Before focusing on how CAQDAS programs enable the integration of source data with mapping processes, we touch briefly on the traditions of mapping and the bespoke tools which have developed around those traditions, as they provide some useful context. We draw attention to three approaches in the traditions which led to the development of mapping software in its own right: mind mapping as conceived by Buzan (1995), who also authored the software packages iMindMap and ThinkBuzan; concept mapping (Novak, 1993; Novak and Gowin, 1984); and cognitive mapping (Eden, 1988; Eden and Ackermann, 1998). Mind mapping generally focuses on a 'main idea' and the aspects which radiate from it. Concept and cognitive mapping tend to produce more complex maps concerning multiple interconnections and more main focal points. The links between objects in these maps might be said to express more causal or directional connections. Cognitive mapping involves drawing 'mental maps' which model a theoretical approach, such as the mapping conventions created (Ackermann et al., 1992) on the model of personal construct theory (Eden, 1988). Mapping software packages have sometimes been created to emulate particular theoretical models. Decision Explorer, for example, a tool widely used in academic and strategic management fields, was created with personal construct theory in mind, though its application and analytic functions are adaptable to other mapping traditions and modelling purposes. Other mapping tools such as CMap have grown out of learning initiatives in higher education. Many others have been created to support strategic management decision making. If you are using a CAQDAS package which does not have an in-house mapping tool such as we focus on in this chapter, there are many options to experiment with in these alternative solutions (see Chapter 3 and the companion website). Thus you can represent the ideas resulting from your analysis graphically even if your chosen CAQDAS package does not include bespoke functions.

Other types of 'mapping'

There are also other tools in CAQDAS packages which might be said to 'map'. We mention these briefly but do not cover them in depth here since they tend to operate at the level of interrogation and either are based on content (Chapter 6) or provide visualisations and 'quasi' quantifications of what you have already done in the software (Chapter 13). *Maps* and *mapping* are terms which are of course relevant to many methodologies, situations and sciences. The production of diagrams, charts and the use of tools which 'map' quantitative visualisations of content often have different beginnings. For instance, text-based manager or text-mining programs, using a constructionist, language-based approach to analysis, can find the occurrence of words (and codes) mapped in a number of different representations. In QDA Miner, *dendrograms* and *cluster maps* chart proximity and correspondence relationships between words and codes; interactive *heatmaps* map the position and concentrations of words within files according to variables. NVivo too offers a degree of content analysis 'mapping' in the visualisation of content with cluster charts. Dedoose automatically maps the quantification of codes across documents, and these visualisations are ever present in some windows, giving the software its mixed methods emphasis. The unusual MAXQDA Document Portrait and Document Comparison Chart offer several different ways to map codes by means of interactive blocks of colour within a file or compared across files. Some of these are discussed in Chapter 13.

Purposes of mapping in CAQDAS packages

There are many different starting points, reasons and implications for mapping in CAQDAS packages. Some of these are summarised in Box 11.2 in the context of specific functionality. Whatever the reason for creating them, maps provide another

Table 11.1 Mapping ideas and linking concepts: some suggestions in the context of case study A, Young People's Perceptions

---

Tasks from PHASE FOUR: Inductive recoding of broad-brush codes

(Refer to previous memos in tandem with reviewing coded data to generate ideas for recoding – chapters 8 & 9)

Visualise coding scheme in a map	• As part of the process of code refinement, move codes around to help you think about...

      o the prioritisation of codes
      o potential connections between codes
      o codes that need recoding
      o how coding relates to research questions
      o how coding relates to background theory

Tasks from PHASE FIVE: Review of literature & identification of theoretical focus

Create theoretical models arising from literature appraisal	• In terms of 'grand theory' (e.g. Giddens' Theory of Structuration) • In terms of previous findings that relate to the research questions • In terms of what you expect to find in primary data

---

Tasks from PHASE SIX: Code retrieval, theoretical refinement, analytic reflection

Review and explore previous work visually	• Generate maps representing current thinking in relation to various aspects

      o the research questions
      o an expression of different aspects of interpretation

           o E.g. the differences in experiences according to the country in which the respondents live
           o E.g. the differences in socio-sexual attitudes according to gender

      o how you intend to structure the final write-up

Tasks from PHASE SEVEN: Interrogate data to establish findings

Map-based interrogation	• Use mapping tools as basis of interrogating patterns in coding

      o how young people in the two countries evaluate the different modes of learning
      o how young men and women differ in attitudes and experiences
      o how primary data relates to literature and theory

Tasks from PHASE EIGHT: Theoretical reconsideration in light of primary data analysis

(Review early memos and maps concerning theoretical focus; compare with the results of data interrogations and preliminary analysis/summaries)
(Write about how the analysis relates to previous literature)

Summarise interpretation in maps	• Model your aspects of your interpretation

      o in relation to each research question
      o in relation to the key ways in which your study contributes to the field

---

dimension in which to express what is going on in data. To provide an overarching context for the use of maps in qualitative analysis, we comment first on their utility as a means to **express theoretical connections**. However, not all projects are theoretically framed, and as the chapter progresses we provide other ideas for more practical reasons for using CAQDAS mapping tools.

Mapping to express theoretical connections

For some projects theory is an important dimension and may be a contributing factor to the early conceptualisation of a whole project, or the development of the coding scheme (Chapter 9). Alternatively, theory development may be the object of the research, as is typical in many inductive approaches (Chapter 1). Theoretical explanations are all about models, generally in terms of grand theory, and specifically in terms of particular authors' writings. Some projects are informed or driven from the outset by theoretical models, for others the approach to analysis is developed after prior examination of the literature, as in Case Study A. For others, theory or explanations are developed during the process of research.

In Chapter 7 we refer to various ideas concerning the role of theory and coding processes as part of the development of theory. Maps might help express the connections between aspects of theory. Layder (1998) suggests that models act as 'templates' against which data are evaluated to see whether they fit into the 'conceptual scheme' of the model. Models therefore can contribute to the whole research process, imposing order upon it. However, they are also open to constant reformulation in light of empirical findings. Layder is not referring explicitly here to a graphic visualised model of theory, however, such representation is just one aspect of a whole set of practical uses that this set of tools can offer in terms of how these visualisations can support the development of ideas and connections between things (Chapters 7 and 9).

BOX 11.1 — CASE NOTES

Mapping grand theories and data-specific interpretations (Case Study A, Young People's Perceptions)

Case Study A is an example of a 'theoretically driven' project. This can be seen to operate on a number of levels. As discussed in Chapter 5, the review of the literature framed the project in terms of contributing to the theoretical focus, the questions asked of the respondents in the interviews and the use of hypothetical vignette scenarios and photo prompts to elicit underlying attitudes. Mapping had a prominent role in the software project from the outset, and maps were used in various ways. For example, Giddens's (1984) theory of structuration constituted important theoretical contextualisation, and it was useful to have the model within the analysis software to refer to at various moments. The visual representation made it possible to 'mess around' with how elements of Giddens's theories were contributing to understanding. The purpose was not to apply the theory to this dataset or to allow it to determine our view of the data, but it provided a useful theoretical lens through which to think about the issues. Indeed, this was just one element of the theoretical context of the project derived from the literature review. Towards the latter stages of the project, writing in analytical memos (Chapter 10) was integrated with the model in order to start rationalising the final write-up and the extent to which to draw upon the theory in constructing the interpretation (Figure 10.1; p. 236).

(Continued)

(Continued)

Although in many projects 'grand theory' impacts upon coding processes and the structures of coding schemes, in this instance a looser approach was adopted, informing but not restricting the approach to coding. The integration between the visual and what the young people were actually saying when they talked about their experiences of learning within the interview data, in expressing their attitudes to young parents elucidated from the photo prompts, for example, made it possible to not take codes and the data linked to them at face value. In terms of the levels at which analysis happens (Chapter 1), it was the interplay with the data level (what the respondents actually said), the indexing level (where we catalogued the similarities in the meaning of their statements), the conceptual level (where we started thinking about the development of themes and the connections between them) and the abstract level (represented in this example by theory) that could be illustrated and explored through maps.

Drawing connections and defining relationships between codes is part of this process and, as suggested by Gibbs (2002), can be facilitated by a diagrammatic mapping process. He describes how, in going beyond what is illustrated in a hierarchical coding scheme, 'a richer and more complex set of linkages can be represented' (Gibbs, 2002: 207). His suggestion is to vary the appearance of links and symbols available in software to illustrate explicit connections to express different types of connections.

General mapping functionality in CAQDAS packages

It is the tools of ATLAS.ti, MAXQDA and NVivo which we generalise about when listing the main functions and suggested starting points for making maps (Box 11.2). We then discuss specific functions in each of these packages separately, since some of them offer additional choices in the way data can be handled. Some of the exceptional tools also add to the versatility of mapping devices and the flexibility with which you manipulate them; some are methodologically significant in terms of how they make different ways of working with and managing data possible.

BOX 11.2 — FUNCTIONALITY NOTES

General mapping functions common to ATLAS.ti, MAXQDA and NVivo

You can perform the following tasks in the graphic diagram or map (network or model):

- View codes, memos, documents
  - o Just visualising objects in a map provides a different way to collect and group them together, and options for differentiating collections (based on the name you give the map) (Figure 11.1)

- Make links between any of those objects

  - The way you are thinking can be summarised by the links you make between things. Different 'levels' of work can be supported, depending on what type of project item the link is connecting.
  - An awareness of what the right timing for making links between codes is important.

- Define links between objects in most situations

  - Add a label to a connection to make the relationship explicit.
  - Illustrate theories or small connections by building a series of explicitly labelled links between objects.

- Make a schematic summary

  - A schematic overview, to capture key elements or features of a respondent, case or process.
  - Use as an illustration to support an explanation.

- Integration with relevant data

  - Ask to see (possibly in another window) data or objects directly related or linked to the object (e.g. coded data, memo and document content).

- Interrogation via a map

  - Generally much interrogation at a high abstract level happens when you add things related to objects already in a map – these functions are distinct in each software package (see Figures 11.5 and 11.6; p. 274).

- Create new abstract objects

  - Add new 'symbols' to represent a process or timetable, a hunch or a new abstract idea. Link those to other objects or project items if required.
  - Create a map of a process or a timetable for project work.
  - Add a caption for the map by naming new objects.

- Change the format

  - Change the look of the fonts, icons, backgrounds, etc. to make a representation suitable for a presentation medium.
  - Insert a graphic to flesh out what a symbol represents.

- Export/copy a map to other applications or print it out

  - Choose to copy or export areas or the whole map to any application which can take file insertions or use print screen /copy /paste options to insert clipboard material into e.g. a presentation or MS Word file.

- Use the map for high-level interrogation

  - Ask to include a project item (e.g. a code, a memo or a document) – then action a right-click menu option to include associated or linked items to view what work has been done that impacts on or is related to the object.

Software-specific functions and specialities

The differences in how CAQDAS packages work with respect to their mapping tools are important to understand since they affect what you are able to do and the impact of creating maps. If you are choosing between packages then mapping functionality may be a key consideration, especially if this sort of visualisation is important to your methodological approach, or just if you are a visual thinker.

We discuss six key aspects to consider concerning mapping functionality, which differ between packages: the extent to which the links made in maps are 'remembered'; the extent to which you can work completely 'in' the text (i.e. at data level) within maps; whether layers can be created within maps and the utility of doing so; whether code co-occurrences can be visualised within maps; whether it is possible to create new codes or memos within a map; and the existence and operation of 'intelligent' links and 'functional' relationships created and visualised in maps.

Remembered vs. scribbled links

In ATLAS.ti the principle is different than in MAXQDA and NVivo. In the latter two packages the physical lines or arrows linking objects in a map only endure beyond that map if they reflect work done elsewhere. So for instance, the lines connecting top-level codes and sub-codes in either package would be remembered, because their connection is based on their 'hierarchical' position within the coding scheme (Chapter 9). However, any new connections you make in a map (e.g. connecting one code with another because you feel they are related) are only relevant to the map in which you create them. This means that the same two codes can be

Table 11.2 Mapping ideas and linking concepts: some suggestions in the context of case study B, The Financial Downturn

---

Tasks from PHASES THREE, FOUR & FIVE: Analysis of survey, focus-group and media data

(Reflect on data and processes arising from initial interrogations & summarise key results that require validating with other data)

Create maps to represent your developing interpretations	• In terms of the answers to each open-ended survey question
	• With respect to each focus-group discussion
	• In terms of how the international and local media represents the issues
	• How work thus far relates to research questions
	• How work thus far relates to 'sensitising concepts'

Tasks from PHASE SIX: Integration of earlier stages

Review and explore; previous work visually	• Review all previous work and generate a map that represents your current thinking in relation to various aspects
	○ the research questions
	○ an expression of different aspects of interpretation
	○ how you intend to structure the final write-up

---

connected differently in separate maps. In both MAXQDA and NVivo the map (or model as it is called in NVivo) is saved unless you choose to delete it, so the link endures in that map, but only in that map. This essentially means that models and maps in these two packages can be regarded as scribbles. They are important for the purpose they are serving at that moment, but have no knock-on effects or implications outside that particular map – in terms of the functioning of other software tools. In MAXQDA, however, you can ask the mapping tool to create models automatically for you, based on earlier work. This can happen on several bases: a one-case model, a one-code model, a code theory model, a code co-occurrence model and a code sub-code segments model. These models, however, are essentially starting points for your further work rather than means of interrogating patters according to coding or linking tasks.

This independence is often very useful. For example, in Case Study B we mapped out a picture of each focus-group discussion after the first-pass coding had been completed. That we could save 'snapshots' of these maps to refer back to later

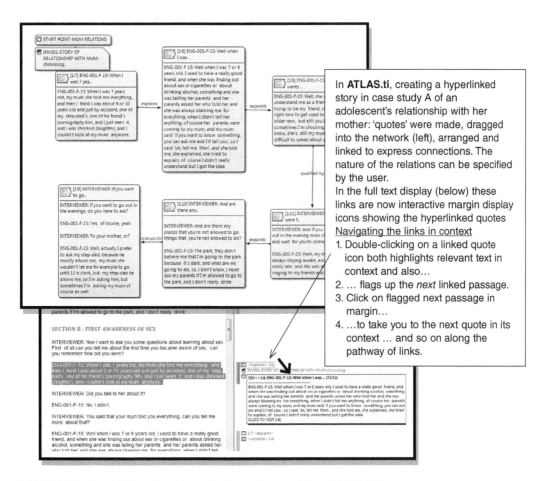

FIGURE 11.2 Hyperlinking to track a set of narrative associations (ATLAS.ti)

on meant that we could not only compare how each group discussed and rationalised the issues but also easily track how our thinking had changed as the analysis proceeded and our codes changed.

This is very different from how the ATLAS.ti networking tool works. Here, the links you create (whether between codes, quotations, memos, documents, families) all endure beyond the life of the particular network view in which you first made them. Therefore, when you express a connection between two codes (part of which is defining the relationship between them) you are in effect making a statement which will endure. In that sense, then, the links you create between objects are generalisable in some sense. The timing of making connections (called relationships in ATLAS.ti) is therefore important. When, for instance, coding to emergent or grounded codes, you may identify a relationship you want to express between two or more codes, in working in one particular data file. In connecting them, you must either be prepared to disconnect them if you later find them to be contradicted or not occurring in other data; or delay making connections until you see a pattern emerging *across* the dataset. It is possible to create a 'spin-off' of a particular network, but this remains dynamic in that changes made outside of it are reflected within it. Therefore you need to export a graphic of a network to preserve your thinking at particular stages.

Working at the data level within maps (ATLAS.ti and MAXQDA)

The central architecture of ATLAS.ti rests on the independence of quotations (data segments) as objects in their own right (Chapter 3). Data segments can be created as quotations and treated in isolation from other objects and software tools (as well as being integrated with them). This means that quotations can be manipulated on their own in a network (Figure 11.2; p. 265). This functionality lifts the software into a different category since the ability to work at data level is of use to those less reliant or wholly unreliant on coding. Quotations can also be illustrated in networks by importing the 'neighbours' of a code (i.e. coded passages). If an exact quotation happens to be linked to two codes it will tell you by means of a dotted line linking both codes to the quotation within the network view. As a result of the architecture, the manipulation of quotations in a network is exceptionally smooth, efficient and flexible.

BOX 11.3 | ANALYTIC NOTES

Suggestions for working at the data level within ATLAS.ti networks

1. Linking data segments

    •   You can link quotations to create a functional hyperlinked trail of quotes to track a process or story. This allows you to work entirely at the data level, to the exclusion of coding.

- You can use the network simply as a graphic display, to represent the set of associations you have made.
- You can also see the hyperlinks indicated in the source context – displayed and clickable in the margins of each data file.

2. Coding from within a map

- You could achieve broad-brush coding in a network. Drag quotations into a network space; drag codes into the network or create new codes within it; create links between quotes and codes – this codes them.
- Recode broader codes into more detail from within a network. Drag a code into the space and ask for its 'neighbors' – this brings in the linked quotations. Make piles of quotes based on dichotomous aspects you wish to apply (e.g. negative–positive) or particular sub-aspects or nuances of the general theme – then link them to new codes.

MAXQDA also allows data segments to be visualised and linked within a map (Figure 11.3; p. 268). There are a number of subtle differences in comparison with ATLAS.ti, however. Firstly, in order to get individual data segments into a MAXMap they need to have been coded first. Although you might simply create data segments using a 'proxy' code (called, perhaps 'interesting segments' (Chapter 6)) in order to be able to manipulate them within a map, there is an extra step involved, and thus coding functionality is more fundamental to the way you work. In ATLAS.ti it is possible to simply select data from a document and drag it into a network; you need not have first made it into a quotation, the act of dragging it into the network will do that for you. Secondly, the links created at the data level within a MAXMap need not be defined upon their creation, whereas they must be within ATLAS.ti. You can label the links in MAXQDA but this is essentially a cosmetic exercise for the purposes of illustration, with no functionality beyond that particular map. Therefore, the links created within MAXMaps do not exist as entities in their own right; whereas in ATLAS.ti, they do; centrally listed in a Hyperlink Manager, where all quotation-based links can be viewed together, commented upon, etc. There are benefits to both systems, so think about your needs.

Creating, hiding and revealing layers in maps (MAXQDA and NVivo)

Layers can be created within maps to hide or reveal objects in MAXQDA and NVivo. They can be used for various reasons; for example, to form higher categories or concepts, to indicate stages or types of coding or other analytic and process-related information. A layering effect is created when filtering tools change what is visible within the map or model, effectively providing the ability to temporarily remove areas or groups of items. This enables you to simplify a more complex map, when you need to focus in on one particular aspect. You might not want to permanently remove other, related aspects, but keeping a large number of complex connections on view can sometimes be confusing when you want to think about only one aspect at a time. As well as contributing to your conceptual and analytic thinking, layers can help remind you of aspects of your process. They may, for instance, be used to represent the development of different types of coding in an inductive approach. This can be useful when remembering the stages at which certain codes were developed and is important for tracking the development of an interpretation. In Case Study B, for instance, in which the focus-group data were coded inductively, it was useful to create a map for each focus group (Figure 11.3) in which we visually represented the general group view about the various core topics discussed. Putting the detailed ('open') codes into a separate layer from those developed at later stages of work and sorting the display according to these category-based layers enabled us to visualise the process of coding concurrently with mapping out the essence of each group discussion, and comparing on that basis. Doing this in MAXQDA, which includes the ability to incorporate coded data segments as illustrations of a code within the map (see above), contributed to the ability to evidence the move from more detailed codes to broader themes and concepts. Layers can also be effective when using a software project 'live' in a conference presentation, when you want to slowly build up an argument, illustrating and discussing certain aspects one at a time.

Layers are usually discrete to the map in which they are created, and remain specific to the ideas embodied within that map, and the connections you make there. This is useful when, for example, you are making separate maps to represent

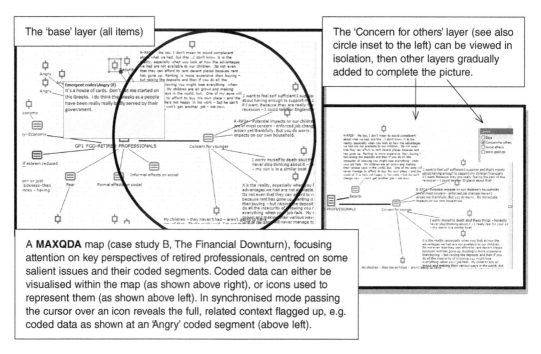

The 'base' layer (all items)

The 'Concern for others' layer (see also circle inset to the left) can be viewed in isolation, then other layers gradually added to complete the picture.

A **MAXQDA** map (case study B, The Financial Downturn), focusing attention on key perspectives of retired professionals, centred on some salient issues and their coded segments. Coded data can either be visualised within the map (as shown above right), or icons used to represent them (as shown above left). In synchronised mode passing the cursor over an icon reveals the full, related context flagged up, e.g. coded data as shown at an 'Angry' coded segment (above left).

Figure 11.3 A map divided into layers on the basis of thematic aspects (MAXQDA)

the views or experiences of an individual respondent, group, case or setting (as discussed above). Alternatively, some types of layer can be made available for use in other maps, thereby potentially being used to represent a more general set of ideas, a core theme, theory or stage of work. But this only works in certain respects. In NVivo, this can happen on the basis of colours previously associated with codes (Figure 11.4), or you could create a model based on all respondents who fall into particular socio-demographic groups and layer on those bases (if the right organisational things have been done in prior steps). However they precisely function, you might use layers to overlay the way you have been thinking about data through the process of coding (Chapter 7), the organisation of ideas through their physical positing in the coding scheme and the use of short-cut groupings to tentatively explore hunches, hypotheses, theories, etc. (Chapter 9). Working in this way reinforces the idea that maps can be used as high-level, abstract interrogation devices.

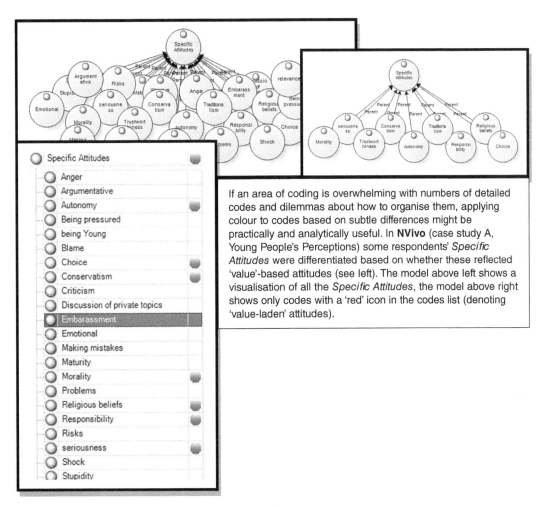

If an area of coding is overwhelming with numbers of detailed codes and dilemmas about how to organise them, applying colour to codes based on subtle differences might be practically and analytically useful. In **NVivo** (case study A, Young People's Perceptions) some respondents' *Specific Attitudes* were differentiated based on whether these reflected 'value'-based attitudes (see left). The model above left shows a visualisation of all the *Specific Attitudes*, the model above right shows only codes with a 'red' icon in the codes list (denoting 'value-laden' attitudes).

Figure 11.4   Filtering codes in a model, by colour (NVivo)

Table 11.3 Mapping ideas and linking concepts: some suggestions in the context of case study C, Coca-Cola Commercials

---

Tasks from PHASE TWO: Exploration and identification of analytic focus

---

(Create a memo for each commercial and make notes about what is seen as you watch each commercial through in its entirety)

Map your expectations	• Create maps that visualise your intended analytic focus and process
	o E.g. aspects of gender you want to consider
	o E.g. your initial ideas about changes in commercials over time
	o E.g. the analytic phases you intend to go through
	• Create a map for commercials that strike you as containing powerful analytic content
	o Based on the research questions

Tasks from PHASE FOUR: Basic code retrieval – early analytic commentary

---

(Make notes about the how qualitative and quantitative retrievals of coded clips (with and without associated transcripts) offer different ways of interpreting data)

Visualise coding scheme in a map	• As part of the process of code refinement, move codes around to help you think about...
	o the prioritisation of codes
	o potential connections between codes
	o codes that might be combined to generate themes
	o codes that need recoding
	o how coding relates to research questions

Tasks from PHASE FIVE: Secondary analytic coding: developing themes, concepts, categories

---

Review and explore previous work visually	• Generate maps representing current thinking in relation to various aspects
	o the research questions
	o an expression of different aspects of interpretation
	o how you intend to structure the final write-up

Tasks from PHASE EIGHT: Interrogate data to establish findings

---

(see also chapter 13 and Table 13.3)

Map-based interrogation	• Review all previous work and generate a map that represents your current thinking in relation to various aspects
	o the research questions
	o patterns in coding in the commercials aired during different decades
	o patterns in coding relating to how gender is represented in the commercials over time
	o how you intend to structure the final write-up

Visualising co-occurring codes in maps (ATLAS.ti and MAXQDA)

Interrogating co-occurrence in terms of how you have previously coded data is often a core way to identify patterns in coding across the entire dataset, or within particular subsets of it. This is discussed in more detail in Chapter 13 with respect to querying.

However, ATLAS.ti and MAXQDA additionally enable co-occurring codes to be retrieved and visualised within their respective network and mapping tools. This allows you to focus on one code within a map, and pull in any code which somehow physically overlaps with it across the rest of the dataset, providing a very quick way to identify all the codes which potentially relate to the original code. Often we do this as an initial step, just to get an overview; we then flick to a particular query function which enables us to interrogate the exact nature of the co-occurrence (its frequency, location within data, etc.) in more depth. It is particularly useful to focus on a broad code, which is likely to have large segments of data coded at it, perhaps across the range of materials present in the study, and get a sense of what else is related generically. In some ways, this offers a similar type of visualisation to that possible when seeing data coded at a broad code, and visualising co-occurring codes in the margin view (Figure 7.1; p. 159). The difference is that when doing so in a map, you are working at a more abstract level, focusing on the codes themselves, rather than on the data segments that are coded to them. You can get at the data segments from the map or network view, but the benefit is that you are thinking at a higher level, useful when generating themes. The point, as always, is that you can flick between the levels of work, checking the nature of the broad connection visualised in the map, with the detail of the data actually constituting the co-occurrence (Figure 11.7; p. 275). It is important, however, to be aware that the effectiveness of asking for co-occurring codes in a map or network will depend on how you have previously been coding. You need to have been consciously applying more than one code to the same or overlapping segments within data for it to be effective, as there the tool is looking for actual co-occurrence, not proximity.

| BOX 11.4 | ANALYTIC NOTES |

Bases for retrieving co-occurring codes in maps and networks

- If you are applying codes-based contexts to broad areas of text, e.g. *Family discussion* (or *Work-related talk, Employment matters*, etc.), and if you are also coding to more detailed codes at the same time to possibly smaller chunks of data, e.g. *Embarrassment, Maturity, Traditional beliefs*, then you will be able to right-click on *Family discussion* (having dragged it into a map or a network) and import co-occurring codes – this will tell you something in terms of patterns in existing coding that you can investigate further.
- You can right-click on a code which has been applied to all of one speaker's contributions to, say, a focus group (Chapter 12) and see at a glance which conceptual or thematic codes are relevant to the speaker. This might be the starting point for reviewing individuals and what motivated them to talk in particular ways.

Creating codes (and other project items) in a map (ATLAS.ti and MAXQDA)

ATLAS.ti and MAXQDA allow the creation of certain project objects from within a network or map. This means that all sorts of work can start from within the graphic 'space' rather than within the main structures of the software, adding flexibility to the way you can work. With respect to the creation of codes in this way, since this is where you can also express connections between them, when starting off with a theoretical framework – or simply with a set of looser assumptions or expectations that you want to bear in mind from the outset – you can accommodate them right from the start.

- Suggestions: If you are trying to capture the structure and connections of a theoretical model, create the whole coding scheme in the network or map (whilst also remaining clear about the varied ways the eventual list of codes can work for you in the Code Manager in ATLAS.ti and the codes list in MAXQDA (Chapters 7 and 9)).
- In an ATLAS.ti network you can additionally create memos, write in them and add and create new codes or drag existing codes into the network to link to the memo (i.e. codes which will contribute to your thinking in that memo). A further advantage of this option is that all those added codes can be converted to a code family (set), offering ongoing retrieval and inter- rogation via that family later. Memos can be linked to quotes in a network and then the memo icon will appear (and can be opened) in the margin area of the relevant document. Memos will also 'remember' the link they have to codes or to quotations, so a memo can later be dragged into a network and you can remind yourself of the links it has to anything by right clicking to import its 'neighbours'.
- In MAXQDA, although memos have to be created outside the map view, they can be subse- quently dragged into any map and then linked as described above.

BOX 11.5 — CASE NOTES

Using maps to step back and take stock (Case Study B, The Financial Downturn)

In Case Study B we used maps in many different ways, depending on particular possibilities in individual packages. In each instance their use enabled us to step back and take stock at a number of levels.

Co-occurrence and scatter-type visualisations were useful to gain a general overview across and within data types and according to types of respondent.

The creation of clickable routes through data on the basis of individual respondents' contributions (to the survey and focus-group discussions) allowed us to more easily under- stand particular respondents' stories, to identify tensions in their responses and to create connected pathways around data files – particularly in ATLAS.ti (Box 11.3, Figure 11.2).

Figure 11.3, for instance, shows how we used layers in MAXQDA to focus on a key theme in the retired focus group: 'Concern for others' (or 'Concern for younger').

In the ATLAS.ti network tool (and similarly in MAXQDA) we focused in on one speaker- based code at a time to see what thematic codes co-occurred. We built up in turn an idea of the connections and exceptions in terms of what they did or did not talk about.

In NVivo and MAQDA, because we could effectively use each model or map as a scrib- bling pad, we used them to create summarised accounts of different aspects of work and for each respondent and each group discussion.

'Intelligent' links and functional relationships in maps

ATLAS.ti 5, NVivo, HyperRESEARCH and Qualrus allow later 'suggestive' or special retrieval functionality based on certain relationships created between codes which go beyond a purely visual expression. There are wide differences here between packages since they rest upon central features of software architecture. Here we provide an overview of some of these types of 'intelligent' links, to give you a flavour of how the tools of individual packages might support your work. If you are choosing between packages and mapping tools are likely to be important to the way you will need to work, we strongly suggest you look into these tools in more detail by visiting the respective developer websites, as we simply cannot do full justice in this book to all the subtle differentiations between them in functionality terms or the implications of their use with respect to different analytic strategies.

- In ATLAS.ti, select from a list of predefined relationships when linking codes – or create your own new relationship. You can choose whether the 'transitive' property is added to a directional link, and this will enable special retrieval options for connected codes in the Query tool. A specific, different set of relationships exists for hyperlinking quotes together.
- In HyperRESEARCH, as well as creating simple maps which act as visual reminders of connections between codes, you can either simply highlight elements of the map or tell the software that you want to make a case selection based on the presence/absence of codes that you have highlighted in the map. You could use this as part of an incremental process of switching on cases which satisfy various criteria in order to get coded output. Remembering that the structure of HyperRESEARCH is based on the case card (Chapter 3), moving from the visual arrangement of thoughts to retrievals based on the resultant selection of cases might help to validate or disconfirm the links that you are illustrating in a map.
- In NVivo you can use a *Relationship node* to register a connection between two conceptual or thematic codes to create a more complex code: for example, 'Making mistakes' *contributes to* 'Informal learning'. The relationship between the two codes is another code in itself. It can then be assigned to where evidence is found in the data to support the relationship. Visualising relationship nodes in a model illustrates that relationship nodes constitute several elements (Figure 11.5; p. 274). A different use of the same tool can express and visualise relationships between people as in social network analysis; see the inset in Figure 11.5 where we illustrate how people are connected. In some projects a visual reminder of such a relationship might be relevant when considering whether they reflect each other's views, etc.
- In Qualrus a map is manifested as the visualisation of each code and its links to other codes (there is no ability to control the creation of maps as a standalone dimension). However, if you set up the coding scheme and you make links between pairs of codes – and if transitive or predictive properties are assigned to the link – this can impact on subsequent coding processes. When coding the 'suggestive' or *Q-coding* function the program will suggest other codes based on links existing with other codes (you do not have to accept the suggestions). In order to make appropriate use of this function we would tend to suggest that the coding scheme be created early, might be extensively based on looked-for content, or might be theoretical, taking a constructionist or a more linguistic approach to analysis (Figure 11.6; p. 274).

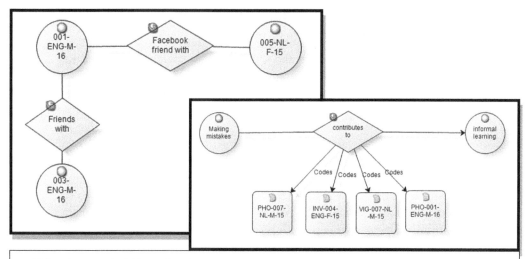

In **NVivo**, (case study A, Young People's Perceptions) two different uses of relationship nodes illustrated in a model. Above left: respondent nodes representing interviewees linked by a relationship type to indicate different aspects of their social network. Above right: two thematic nodes (joined by the relationship type, 'contributes to') and then applied to a number of documents where the evidence for the relationship exists. The way it is illustrated in the model means you can ask to see the documents where the relationship node has been applied or the documents where the individual constituent nodes have been applied.

Figure 11.5 Relationship nodes illustrated in a model (NVivo)

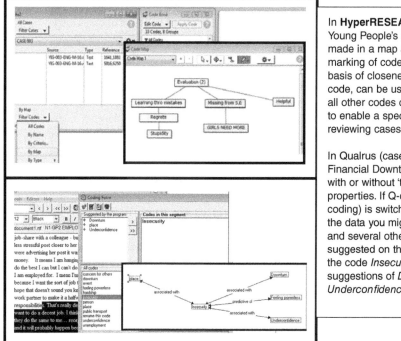

In **HyperRESEARCH** (case study A, Young People's Perceptions) the links made in a map and the subsequent marking of codes, possibly on the basis of closeness to a selected code, can be used as a filter to switch all other codes off in the case cards to enable a specific focus, while reviewing cases or reporting.

In Qualrus (case study B, The Financial Downturn) links are created with or without 'transitive' or predictive properties. If Q-coding (suggestive coding) is switched on, when coding the data you might select one code, and several other codes might be suggested on the basis of those links: the code *Insecurity* has prompted suggestions of *Downturn*, place and *Underconfidence*.

FIGURE 11.6 'Intelligent' links impacting on coding and selections elsewhere (HyperRESEARCH and Qualrus)

Questions to ask yourself when creating maps

- Will maps help *me* in the way *I* like to work? If yes, how?
- Is this the right time to make a map?
- Will a map help me present my ideas to other people?
- Can I validate the connections I have expressed in a map in the data?

Concluding remarks: extensive possibilities for mapping

The possibilities and creative uses of graphic mapping tools far exceed the suggestions we can make here. We have highlighted some of the uses and differences between tools because they can be important to the way work happens. Each tool has useful subtleties and some limitations, but you will usually be able to make CAQDAS mapping tools suit your needs. The multifaceted dimensions of qualitative data analysis are enriched significantly if you can become familiar with the flexibility within the mapping functions of your chosen software. The integration and interactivity of these tools with source data and with the other items within the software project will help to validate the connections which you as the researcher are making. If the software you are using does not have a mapping element, we have mentioned just a few standalone software packages that may help, some of which are low-cost or free. In the next chapter we focus on the factual

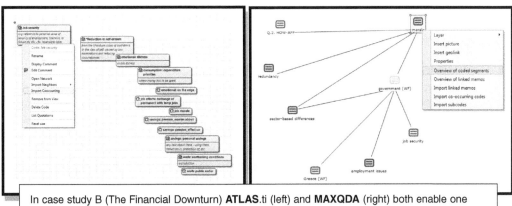

In case study B (The Financial Downturn) **ATLAS**.ti (left) and **MAXQDA** (right) both enable one code to be selected in an otherwise empty map and, on right-clicking, to select *co-occurring* codes. This imports into the map any codes which overlap in the data with the originating code.
In MAXQDA it is possible to then build in more co-occurrences on imported codes because the software sees what is already there and strikes uplinks to show commonality.

Figure 11.7   Map-based interrogation for co-occurrence (ATLAS.ti and MAXQDA)

organisation of data – some elements of which we have illustrated at times in the mapping tools. Organisation, interpretation and visualisation are all different dimensions of qualitative inquiry which can be interwoven throughout your work.

EXERCISES: MAPPING IDEAS AND LINKING CONCEPTS

This chapter has discussed many different reasons for mapping ideas and linking concepts and starting points for doing so. The ways in which you use these tools (where they are enabled) will depend on your analytic strategy (in particular, the direction you are working in) and your own preferred ways of working (i.e. whether you like expressing ideas visually). The chapter exercises listed here provide just some suggestions. You do not have to make use of all – or any – of these options, although we do suggest using mapping tools early in your work with software in order to think about how they could be useful.

Understand how mapping works

CAQDAS packages vary significantly in terms of how mapping tools are enabled and function. Not all include this functionality at all. Therefore, if this type of functionality will be important to your work, it is important to experiment early on so you can make the best use of the mapping tools available in your chosen software.

Creating early maps

Experimenting with mapping tools during the stages of designing your project and devising a strategy for using software serves multiple functions, not least becoming familiar with the mapping tools themselves. Always give a map a meaningful name and datestamp it (see Chapter 2 for advice on consistent naming protocols). Define its use in the map description.

1. *Mapping your research design.* Create a model of your project plan and timeline, by creating new abstract objects and linking them in a logical way. Experiment with layout and formatting options to familiarise yourself with the mapping tool.
2. *Mapping the literature.* If using a CAQDAS package to manage literature and generate critical appraisals (see Chapter 5), create maps which present a visual overview of key ideas contained within them. You might create a map for each of the key articles, or one map which summarises several related articles.
3. *Mapping the theoretical landscape.* When working deductively, using an *a priori* theoretical model, or generating hypotheses, create objects within your chosen software (codes, memos and links) which represent abstract features of the theory, and visualise them in a map.

Maps as part of your interpretive processes

Stepping back from the intense work of exploring, organising, interrogating to reflect on progress thus far is an important task in deciding how to move forward with analysis. Visualising data and connections using CAQDAS mapping tools helps with working on this more conceptual and abstract level, whilst maintaining the ability to drill back down to the source data for checking purposes. Do not spend hours beautifying these early maps. They will change as your ideas develop, structures change and connections become established, and therefore they are largely, if not exclusively, for your eyes only.

1. *Mapping key comparative elements*. Depending on your research design, this might be for each respondent, case, setting, etc. as relevant. For example, having examined and coded a document, create a map that illustrates the prominent features of the particular respondent or case. When you have coded across the dataset to a particularly important theme, create a map to illustrate what you have seen.
2. *Visualising a coding scheme*. Changing your mind about the physical positioning of codes in the main listing is a common activity (see Chapter 9). It can be a useful exercise to visualise the current coding scheme in a map before embarking on making extensive alterations to it. This may serve both as a record of the initial scheme and as a means of thinking about how best to alter it. Creating abstract 'objects' or 'shapes' within the map can act as a means of thinking about how to split broad codes into more detailed aspects and/or generate broader categories out of a collection of more detailed codes.
3. *Mapping changes thinking*. Whether working inductively, deductively or abductively, your thinking develops throughout the process. Tracking those changes visually provides a record and helps refine your thinking.

    a. *Working deductively*. Experiment with creating new theoretical maps which account for the peculiarities found in your set of data and then compare with the initial theoretical framework.
    b. *Working inductively*. Experiment with bringing codes and data files into a map to conjecture how things are starting to fit together. Create new abstract objects within the map that help your thinking. Create maps that represent early versions of your theoretical ideas.
    c. *Working abductively*. Experiment with all of the above.

Exporting maps

Experiment with exporting maps to other software applications. They can usually be exported in several different image formats and pasted into word-processing applications. Print off different maps to view and consider away from the computer. Remember that even if you can edit them outside of the CAQDAS package, those changes will not be reflected back inside the package.

12

Organising Data by Known Characteristics

This chapter focuses on the importance of data organisation, considering typical and exceptional organising features, discussing processes using the three case-study examples. As outlined previously (Chapters 1 and 2), CAQDAS packages are powerful project management tools. Chapter 5 covers getting a software project started and putting various basic organisational structures in place, perhaps as a means of reflecting initial research design. Chapters 10 and 11 discuss managing interpretations using creative ways to organise and connect ideas. This chapter could have been placed anywhere in between since the work in it can largely be prepared and put in place at any stage prior to the processes of interrogation that rely on it. In most qualitative projects it will help to organise data according to known characteristics. This enables you to narrow your focus onto subsets (or combinations) of data, thereby facilitating comparison and deeper levels at which to identify patterns and test relationships. When conducting large-scale projects these aspects are very important. Even projects comprising relatively small numbers may benefit from the potential of factual organisation to allow the cutting of data in different ways. Doing so might throw up patterns and exceptions, confirm or disconfirm hunches. When used in combination with other tools, such as conceptual coding, effective data organisation supports wide-ranging interrogations according to careful permutations of data. All such possibilities help to support and reflect research design (Chapter 2) and varied and rigorous interrogation (Chapter 13).

Organisational tools vary enormously in structure and potential. In addition, it can be difficult to orientate to the way a CAQDAS package provides such support. We therefore include the basic practical principles of organising whole or parts of data files. There are also reminders about more basic organising devices which all contribute to the idea that the visual identification of important features through good naming protocols and useful groupings can help you feel in control – through systematic data and project management. Tables 12.1, 12.3 and 12.4 list organisational processes in the context of our case-study examples. Table 12.2 provides an overview of main organising functions in CAQDAS packages. Each varies in emphasis, and we do not discuss every function in each package.

The importance of good organisation in reflecting project design

In most studies, there is an inherent element of comparison and inquiry based on differences between the origins and characteristics of data. The larger the dataset, the more important it is to organise data efficiently, and the more reliance you will probably place on known characteristics when interrogating the dataset (Chapter 13). If you are undertaking a small-scale study and have collected and transcribed all the primary data yourself, you will know and recall more readily the characteristics which are important about individual respondents and settings. A small or particularly homogenous dataset may mean less emphasis needs to be placed on organisation, as in Case Study C. For methodological approaches where in-depth submersion in a few cases is required, there will be less need to interrogate data in multiple combinations. Conversely, when working with medium to large-scale datasets, taking the trouble to organise data using 'attributes' or 'variables' within the CAQDAS project can open up many different routes of inquiry. This might be in the light of detailed facts and figures you already know about the data – and perhaps sampled for – or it might concern features about data that you discover through the process of analysis. Sometimes an implicit dimension of research design involves the need to focus on one respondent's story or one case at a time. Thus the ability to separate out or gather together all the elements related to that unit of analysis is an aspect of organisation that needs to be incorporated (Box 12.1).

Research design therefore has a dominant impact on how you will organise data. Even in projects using snowballing sampling strategies, at a fairly early stage you will identify 'factual' features about respondents and data which you intend to compare, ask questions about or isolate in order to explore in more depth. This process will continue to evolve as the project progresses, as we discuss below.

The earliest basics of organisation – and the limits

At a fundamental overarching level, if your project comprises data collected from multiple sources it will be useful, as a minimum, to organise the data according to type or origin: interview, focus group, journal article, official guidance, email exchange, meeting minutes, online discussion, etc. Where possible, this can happen within the software project by storing materials in folders on this basis, or at the very least by carefully naming files so they can be identified in a list (Chapter 5). Ideally storage locations reflect data collection strategies in complex projects. In projects utilising only one type of data, folders might instead reflect major aspects of the sampling process. In a longitudinal project, for instance, you might have folders representing the phase or year of data collection. What is important, though, is also to categorise this feature using attributes or variables in order to effect queries which look across and differentiate on that basis. Folders do not enable the differentiation of results in queries, only

Table 12.1 Organising data by known characteristics: some suggestions in the context of case study A, Young People's Perceptions

Tasks from PHASE FIVE: Factual data organisation	
Group data according to type	→ (if not already done during project set-up – phase one, chapter 5) group data according to type using folders (where enabled) • Literature • Interviews • Vignettes • Photo-prompts
Group respondents' contributions according to socio-demographics	→ If relevant to software create 'respondent' codes and assign to each interview and respective vignette etc. → Organise respondents' data in more complex ways according to socio-demographics by assigning variables • Country of residence • Age group • Gender etc ○ Add a 'Name' variable, so that the three contributions by each respondent can be unified in queries or interrogated together rather than separately → Where possible create sets based on complex combinations of data for continued scoping of searches and interrogations • E.g. Female Dutch respondents • E.g. Male 15 yr old respondents etc.

Tasks from PHASE SEVEN: Interrogate data to establish findings	

Add variables or short-cut groupings to handle analytic fact as they become apparent	→ Assign further evolving organisational groupings, with a view to later interrogation
	
	• E.g. broad evaluation of sex education
	  ○ Generally positive
	  ○ Generally negative
	• E.g. Strictness of parents
	  ○ Strict
	  ○ Laissez faire

initial 'scoping' or 'filtering' to set the parameters of the query (Chapter 13). Short-cut groupings to source data files (usually termed sets) are also important tools for basic organisation and for the basis of all sorts of more complex filtering operations. They are also important analytic markers and collection points for codes and documents (Chapters 5 and 10). As long as they are not seen as the only way to organise a dataset, their functionality is very useful. The ability to scope some operations to a folder or set adds an extra dimension to interrogating data; combined with other organisational steps or structures, is invaluable. With the exception of ATLAS.ti which incorporates dynamic 'super' sets (super-families), however, sets and folders cannot be combined in one easy step within queries, whereas attributes/variables usually can.

Not all the CAQDAS packages we discuss utilise folders anyway. Some rely entirely on variables as the means of organising factual features (e.g. QDA Miner and Dedoose). Others (e.g. Transana) require the use of codes (keywords) for the purpose. Most studies incorporate an inherent element of comparison within their design. The ability to differentiate conceptual coding across and within variable/attribute values (Chapter 13) usually supports this comparative dimension in more flexible and potentially complex ways. To complicate matters, not all the software packages we have focused on in this book have these additional tools. If the assignation of variables and attributes is not possible in a software package, then factual organisation happens by coding (see Table 12.2)

Table 12.2 Devices for organising factual features of data and respondents

Consistent file naming	Ensures that lists of files are seen in the order you want and grouped the way you want (does not work in all software).
	Identify key features of files by good naming. Always abbreviate prefixes. Do not waste space on full words like 'Interview'.
Folders	Organising at the whole document level. Can be changed.
	Actual files are in folders. Keep them simple. Useful to base on type of data.
Sets	Alternative to folders – but *shortcuts* to files sitting in folders.
	Ways to organise differently from folders.
Respondent or case-based codes	Required to organise parts of data files; e.g. speaker sections within focus-groups, or other repeated structures in data.
	Might be achieved step-by-step or by auto-coding. (May lead to categorisation of codes to socio-demographics via variables.)
Socio-demographic codes	Used in tandem with respondent/case-based codes when there is a need to use coding devices to organise e.g. socio-demographic values (male/female etc.). They are assigned directly to relevant parts of documents. This is often the way to assign factual characteristics where no bespoke attribute/variable function exists.
Auto-coding	Used to gather data on respondent or socio-demographic bases. Usually reliant on good, software-specific formatting of data (chapter 4 and companion web pages). (Can also be used on the basis of content.)
Variables/Attributes/Descriptors for organising whole documents by e.g. gender, age group, role, region	Ways to organise whole files and later combine to create complex sub-sets. Can be achieved step-by-step via spread-sheet import. Differentiate on this basis in queries; e.g. qualitative cross tabulations of codes by attributes (chapter 13).
Variables/Attributes/Descriptors (for codes) (not always available)	Ways to organise parts of files which have been coded in certain ways but with similar functions to document level attributes/variables. Sometimes the work can be semi-automated through the importation of spreadsheet.

Timing: when to put more complex organisational structures in place

It is debatable whether the structures reflecting all these aspects of project design should be the starting point of work in the software project. In Chapter 5 we suggested the utility of starting off with some simple organisational structures, such as folder-type storage locations, and good file naming protocols. It is always advisable to be organised at the basic level; this will help you gain familiarity with your chosen software generally, as well as contribute to your feeling your way towards its efficient use. Where it is clear what needs to be done, and how to do it, further steps can be taken regarding the assignment of variables to data. For Case Study A we deliberately delayed this organisational work because of a need, in the first instance, to keep clearly focused on concepts irrespective, for example, of 'who' and 'where' data derived from. Conversely, in Case Study B, the introduction of variables coincided with the incorporation of the survey responses through a specific survey-import function (see below, Table 2.1; p. 39 and Figure 4.4; p. 102). The way you proceed is always determined by the complex needs of the individual project.

In addition to the needs of your analytic strategy, a key issue in terms of the timing of factual organisation is knowing how to do it efficiently within your chosen software. If that seems opaque (and it can!), the process is better left to one side until you feel more familiar with the software. Get on with other things, rather than wasting time worrying about it! Gaining an awareness of the potential of this sort of additional organisation for later inquiry is the important thing. All the potential ways of classifying data may not be immediately obvious anyway. In addition, the decision about when 'organisation' is put in place may depend on the kind of organisation it is. You can apply basic socio-demographic variables at any stage; but other ways of classifying data might not be identified until later in the analysis.

Other factors influencing timing relate to whether you need to organise at the document level only or *within* data files as well (as with speaker sections within focus-group data). A more complete understanding of the mechanics of how everything fits together in the software is necessary when organising parts of data files, and usually nothing is lost if left until later in the process.

Secondary data and supplementary or background material may also contain known characteristics or metadata which can be handled at this level. Chapter 5 discusses some processes of handling literature and background material. Some software packages can import directly from bibliographic software; creating spaces to write appraisals, and bringing with them the metadata to organise those spaces; sometimes also bringing with them full-text PDFs (Figure 5.6; p. 128). The timing of this type of work will depend on the timing of the literature review within the project timetable. Whether this work is integrated with the handling of primary data may depend on a number of issues, not least your confidence with software.

Organising individual speakers contributing to different forms of data (Case Study B, The Financial Downturn)

As discussed in Chapter 4, for Case Study B we wanted to be able to create a narrative for each focus-group respondent. In addition, we wanted to marry up the data contributed by respondents who had taken part in both the survey and a focus group. To do this we created a speaker-based code to represent each focus-group respondent and, where relevant, added open-ended survey responses to them, that is, for those who had contributed to both forms.

For one respondent, bringing together his 'written' response to a question in the survey with his 'spoken' contributions in the focus-group provided additional substance and context.

Well.... as for me – the financial mess cost me the final 3 years of my working life. I worked for an European inter-governmental organisation. It got income from airlines and other stakeholders ... that was reducing significantly. I mean commercial aviation was just contracting in the wake of the downturn – fewer passengers. The scope of its work had to be cut. My contract came to an end in July last year. (From Focus-group 1. Talking about his financial situation)

Have got deep feelings of suspicion about Europe. Completely controlled by undemo-cratically appointed commissioners who spend their lives trying to make a name for themselves and this is the result. I worked in Europe and saw the utter waste and profligacy first hand. There was a saying about one large project – '2 years into the project and 2 years behind schedule' that was typical and you know why – it was a total waste of everyone's time. Some DG making a name for herself and in the ground – no will to do it just everyone going through the motions – getting paid public money to waste time. (From Question 3.A in the survey (Further comments about blame for the financial crisis))

Different steps could be taken to bring all these elements together. In a step-by-step way the process might, for example, be to create one 'case' code and assign it to all the various segments of data (you might already have one code with all his speaker contributions in it). See also Box 12.3.

Illustrating the potential at the interrogation stage

We illustrate some examples of how variables become useful for interrogation in Chapter 13. They might be used to create subsets on which to focus attention, without the use of complex queries (Figure 13.4; p. 318). Dedoose charts are there waiting to be viewed, providing you are in the right window. You can make them a little more complex and export them for different effects (Figure 13.5; p. 319). Figure 13.7 illustrates a cross-tabulation matrix result using several different bases for comparison. These query results bring attributes and conceptual codes together

Table 12.3 Organising data by known characteristics: some suggestions in the context of case study B, The Financial Downturn

Tasks from PHASE TWO: Factual data organisation	
Group data according to type	→ (if not already done during project set-up – phase one, chapter 5) group data according to type using folders (where enabled) • Survey responses • Focus-groups • Media content
Group respondents' contributions according to socio-demographics	Survey data → Earlier import of survey (phase one, chapter 5) creates variables to organise qualitative fields (open-ended questions) automatically (and places all mini-documents based on respondents in a folder/set) • E.g. Region • E.g. Gender • E.g. Age group Focus group data → Either manually within the software or via the importation of a spreadsheet, associate factual information with the corresponding qualitative records (this can be done using 'socio-demographic' codes if using a software that does not have a separate 'variable' function) • Use some of the same variables used in the survey to categorise respondents, and additional ones as relevant → Code or auto-code respondents' speaker sections either to speaker-based codes (*to get all of each respondent's data together at one code) or code relevant speaker sections to basic socio-demographic type codes → *Combine relevant qualitative records from survey with matching speaker-based respondent codes for respondents who also took part in both focus groups and survey, to complete process of compiling and checking individual 'respondent narratives' in case useful.

Tasks from PHASE SEVEN: Interrogate data to establish findings	
Add variables or short-cut groupings to handle analytic facts as they become apparent	→ Assign further evolving organisational groupings, with a view to later interrogation • E.g. according to strength of concern about implications on their children • E.g. according to where respondents attribute the primary fault for the downturn

in initial tables. Some such visualisations seem to stress quantitative results, but in fact are just entry points to the qualitative data sitting behind the various cells.

What does a data file consist of?

When one respondent or case contributes to the research process in different ways (e.g. several interviews over time) there can be uncertainty about whether transcripts should be combined or kept separate. The issue is compounded when data

Documents	Name	Time Phase	Gender	Role
IV-GITA-P1	GITA	1	Female	Staff Nurse
IV-GITA-P2	GITA	2	Female	Staff Nurse
IV-GITA-P3	GITA	3	Female	Ward Matron
IV-PEDRO-P1	PEDRO	1	Male	Health Care Assistant
IV-PENDRO-P2	PEDRO	2	Male	Staff Nurse

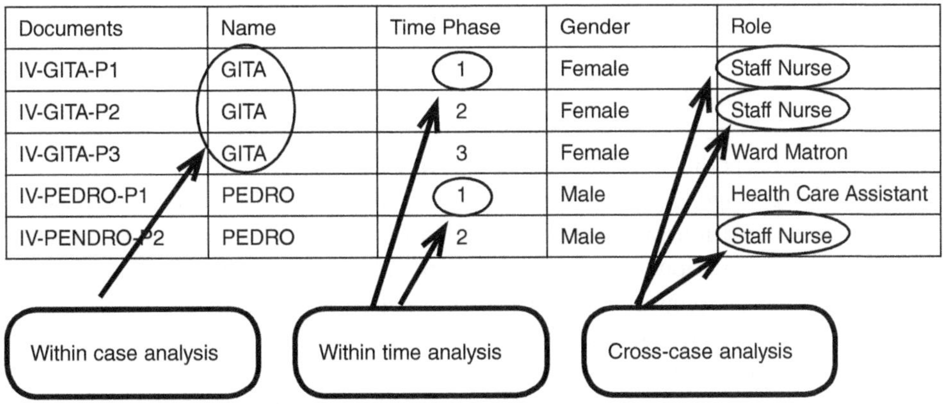

Within case analysis   Within time analysis   Cross-case analysis

Keeping the three interview transcripts for each respondent separate enables each contribution to be considered in isolation and characteristics about respondents at each data collection point to be recorded. This enables, for example, the time phase of each interview to be logged, and changes in individuals' characteristics to be handled (e.g. that Gita becomes a ward matron after the phase 2 interview). The name variable enables all data from each respondent to be considered together, regardless of time phase or any other variables (within case analysis).

Codes are assigned to interview data as normal, irrespective of any of these characteristics, but can later be broken down by any individual set of variable values (e.g. longitudinally, or by role) or complex subsets can be created (female staff nurses in phase 2).

Figure 12.1 Assigning variables to enable different types of analysis in a longitudinal project

files are small. Although there is no hard-and-fast answer, generally software packages offer easier organisation on the basis of the whole 'file'. In an illustration of a hypothetical longitudinal project (Figure 12.1), keeping Gita's three files separate means they can be 'organised' individually, which would be important if needing to compare over time.

If, conversely, one interview is completed on two separate occasions, and you are not really interested in change, it is more likely you will combine the transcripts into one file. If, in addition, there are parts of other files which are about Frank, it becomes more complicated and you may have to think about coding his contributions from all forms of data at a respondent-based code to bring them together (see below). Case Study A, although not longitudinal, comprises three forms of data contributed by each respondent (Chapter 2). We kept each separate as it was useful to be able to consider each type of data separately. Therefore, coding was used to bring all contributions of each respondent together, such that they could be viewed as a whole. The lack of a longitudinal element makes this process simpler, but there are always ways of organising complex research designs within CAQDAS packages; it is just a case of understanding how the particular organisational tools function, and working out the intermediate tasks that need to occur to get the organisation done.

Circumstances, conditions, contexts, cases

Often socio-demographic information such as age, gender, marital or employment status are important. These may be aspects of the project design and key elements in the sampling processes of medium to large qualitative studies. In Case Studies A and B such aspects dictated data collection. In Case Study A key features included country of origin, age group and gender. In Case Study B respondents lived in either rural or urban locations, were employed or otherwise. The news media data were sorted by local or national, year of publication, etc. Your own project may be part of a larger study, be longitudinal, or have a more quantitative element as well. If you have quantitative data from a survey, you may wish to incorporate them with qualitative material – for example, if interview or focus-group respondents have also filled in a survey (as in Case Study B). Software usually enables the integration of tabular quantitative data for such purposes. There are variations in the principles of preparing such data (see Chapter 4 and the companion website).

BOX 12.2 — FUNCTIONALITY NOTES

Differentiating between organisational features and 'conceptual' codes

We sometimes encounter confusion among researchers about when it is appropriate to use variables as opposed to codes. It is useful to differentiate between them by stating that organising data using variables or the equivalent allows you to capture 'known characteristics' or 'factual' information in the data. These aspects generally will not change, although there are situations when they will – particularly if you are conducting a longitudinal study, for example. Coding, conversely, is used to bring together segments of data which are similar in some way, as deemed by the researcher (Chapter 7). As such, in relation to primary data, codes will generally be applied to parts of data files, where respondents are talking about a particular topic or where the researcher identifies data as representing a theme or concept. It can be particularly confusing when a known fact or variable is the same as a concept you are interested in for more analytic purposes. To take a simple example, if conducting a study about perceptions of gender in newspaper articles about 'teenage pregnancy', you may need the organisational feature 'gender' to differentiate between whether the journalist is male or female, but you will also need conceptual codes to identify where perceptions of gender generally are being discussed, and the differences in the way judgements are made about boys and girls specifically. This will allow you to investigate, for example, both how the gender of journalists affects the way articles are written, and the way men and women are discussed in the articles or in different publications.

The evolution of data organisation

There may be other types of 'facts' that come out during the research process. When collecting data, sometimes almost without thinking, you begin the process of classifying by various features showing up in interviews or field notes. As more and more data are gathered together and analysed, you might begin to identify new and interesting ways in which you are beginning to catalogue respondents in your mind. Normal coding processes deal with the things respondents say (Chapter 6). At other times you are instead concerned with general characteristics, behaviours or opinions that seem to typify respondents. You may then need to consider their presence or absence on the level of individuals or cases, and the differences between them (Box 12.3). Variables can handle these sorts of 'interpretive facts'.

BOX 12.3 — CASE NOTES

Evolving factual organisation: splitting variables to handle additional nuances (Case Study B, The Financial Downturn)

In Case Study B, much factual organisation at attributes happened relatively early in Phase Two (see Table 12.2; p. 281). As analysis proceeded, thinking about how people viewed their personal financial circumstances was obviously important. This was not included in the socio-demographic data routinely elicited from them, though we did include employment status in the survey (with values: employed, self-employed, unemployed, retired). However, inevitably something of their financial circumstances came out in each discussion. We debated the necessity of more detailed classification about Financial circumstances.

> In normal circumstances I would have expected to have been kept on for another 3 years, to take me up to 65. Those 3 years would have made all the difference to – I don't know just feeling comfortable – able to do things I have to be careful about now. (Rural, retired professional respondent)

This information was interesting just from the point of view of it helping us to understand 'who' he was, but a new category, Forced Early Retirement, suddenly became a factor that might be relevant for further inquiry or as an 'attribute' to assign generally to those who fell into the same category. So 'retired' was not necessarily a simple category of employment. Possibilities included Retirement as a natural course of action at the expected age; early retirement, perhaps accompanied by a golden handshake; forced early retirement, meaning a loss of income; partly retired; all of those having different effects on perceptions of security and well-being.

Importing a spreadsheet containing descriptive information can 'organise' qualitative materials (see below). The column headers become attributes/variables and the values in the cells categorise the qualitative data correspondingly. There is nothing to stop the values being changed or added to, once imported into the software (Box 12.3; above, Figure 12.2; p. 288). You decide whether there is enough information about data with which to carry out such new attributions.

'Document families' in ATLAS.ti (case study A);

Create and populate basic document families (e.g. English, Dutch, Male, Female). Use the Super-family tool to set up more complex dynamic groupings (e.g.;'Years=15 & English'). Super-families are automatically updated as basic families are populated.

Information can be imported in a spreadsheet. Filter to families for basic retrieval (Chapter 8) and more complex query scoping (Chapter 13).

'Source' or 'Node Classifications' and Attributes in NVivo (case study A)

Decide which classification type is required. Use node classifications for handling parts of documents or longitudinal-type data. Create and code nodes for respondents first (if using node classifications). Create classifications for the entity you are organising, and link the Nodes or Sources to the relevant Classification. Then create and assign Attributes and values.

With care, this information can be imported in a spreadsheet. Attributes can be employed in queries to make comparisons (Chapter 13).

Document or Code Variables in MAXQDA (case study B)

Assign variables to documents or codes as relevant. This is done automatically upon import of survey data from a spreadsheet (as above), or can be done by hand.;

This information can be imported in a spreadsheet. Activate based on individual or combinations of variable values (Chapter 8), access instant comparisons of coding across variables via matrix tables, or use in queries to make more complex interrogations (Chapter 13).

FIGURE 12.2 Factual organisation at the document level (ATLAS.ti, NVivo and MAXQDA)

Imperfect categories

There are always dilemmas. You can probably never tweak values until they are perfect in every respect. For instance, one of the partly retired speakers in the focus-group sample (Case Study B) had been forced into that status by cutbacks in the NHS – so he falls into the 'partly retired' *and* 'forced early retirement' categories (Box 12.2). A judgement has to be made based on a realistic assessment of what is interesting in the context and purpose of your research questions. There are occasions when you just need an entirely new attribute which takes care of a subtly different set of possible circumstances. But it is also important to remember that whatever software tools you make use of, the output you generate and the inferences made are ultimately moderated by you. Part of that entails adjusting a write-up based on what you are actually seeing in the data and keeping in mind that prior

Table 12.4 Organising data by known characteristics: some suggestions in the context of case study C, Coca Cola Commercials

---

Tasks from PHASE SIX: Factual data organisation

Group data according to type	→ (if not already done during project set-up – phase one, chapter 5) group data according to type using folders (where enabled)
	• Commercials
	• Publicity materials
Record meta-data about commercials	→ Either manually within the software or via the importation of a spreadsheet, associate factual information with the corresponding qualitative records (this can be done using 'meta-data' codes if using a software that does not have a separate 'variable' function)
	• Data characteristics
	o e.g. length of commercial, date of airing, visual properties etc.
	• Actor characteristics
	o gender, ethnicity, apparent age, attire etc.
	• Interaction characteristics
	o between actors within the commercial and directly with the viewer
Integrate analytic facts derived from earlier work	→ Consider the extent to which any analytic characteristics you have identified thus far may usefully be attributed to data as factual characteristics
	• E.g. in working with the commercials you may have noticed that some employ very direct advertising tools (e.g. 'Coke vs Pepsi', 'The Olympic Dream') whereas others are much more subtle (e.g. 'Sing Along with Me', 'Diet Coke Break'). Such 'analytic facts' can be handled at the 'attribute/variable' level.
	→ You might use some aspects for which you have codes as 'factual' characteristics as well
	• E.g. consider how capturing instances of different gendered stereotypes through coding ('sexualisation of women through attire'; 'traditional domestic tasks') contrasts with recording the fact that some commercials include such stereotypical content, whereas others do not.

---

decisions about structures in terms of software set-up (Chapters 2 and 5) may have been pragmatic and not perfect for every circumstance.

Case studies

The term 'case' can have various meanings. In NVivo 'case' is used to denote various smaller units of analysis such as the 'respondent' as well as to describe functional aspects of the software. This can be confusing, however, since to some researchers the term is about a central architectural feature of their research. There might be many respondents, but they contribute to cases (which represent organisations or settings). In the context of case-based research the level at which the term is used

Table 12.5 The way software usually handles the formalised 'case' element of organisation in case-based research (HyperRESEARCH excepted)

Sources	Gender	Age	Case
Interview1-C3	Fem	20–29	Case 3
Interview2-C2	Fem	30–39	Case 2
Interview1-C2	Male	30–39	Case 2
Fieldnotes8-C3	n-a	n-a	Case 3

in software can be confusing. The predominant focus for case-based research is to study within and around an individual case and possibly, depending on project design, to compare across cases. The foci of large international collaborative projects, for instance, are often case-based since within the context of the whole project, the region or country becomes the case. Within each case there will be conditions, contexts and socio-demographic information about data which if effectively attributed will enable dimensions of inquiry within the case, but also if needed (and if applied consistently) will enable dimensions of inquiry across cases. The purpose then would be to ask questions such as: are the same conditions producing similar results within the case as they produce across cases? What are the differences – and why?

It is important to understand that software does not really differentiate between the organisation of data at the case level and the organisation of data within those cases. Consequently, a table representing organisation via *variables* in a case-based project (i.e. constituting several cases) might look something like Table 12.5 (where the file naming protocol for sources relates in part to case). As discussed below and illustrated in Chapter 13, any combination of these aspects of organisation can be interrogated.

Whatever the structure of your project, interrogations can be handled across the different cases, or across socio-demographic aspects, such as gender (irrespective of case) or across a combination of case and other variables/attributes (e.g. all the case 1 data for ages 20–29 and females).

When variables are not enabled, as for instance in Transana and HyperRESEARCH, there will be ways to organise data via the assignment of codes that represent socio-demographic or other factual dimensions.

Organising whole documents in software

You may have a project where each individual data file represents one respondent, instance or case. Examples of such data include one-to-one interview transcripts, journal articles, and focus-group discussions (where you are interested in the group as a whole, not the individual opinion). In this situation the organisation of data is straightforward because it is usually possible to apply the relevant known characteristics to the whole data file. Doing so varies in terms of detailed processes and the complexity with which it happens in particular software packages. We only point out the key features here in order to provide starting points for using the different packages (see **companion websites** for more detail for specific packages). There is no escaping the fact that with some software packages the process is more straightforward than with others, and straightforward tools are easier to describe than more complex ones. More complex tools make it difficult to see your way through the decision paths and processes and it can be more difficult to troubleshoot when things go wrong.

- **ATLAS.ti** uses document families (that function like sets), such that a *Female* document family contains all the female documents – this can be done step-by-step or a table can be imported. Dynamic super-families can easily be created out of combinations of basic families – *Females aged 20–29 years*. Queries can be easily scoped on the basis of families and super-families.
- **Dedoose** uses descriptors that are assigned to documents (media), enabling instant charts and breakdowns of coding on the basis of descriptor information. Organisation can be carried out as a step-by-step process or via the import of a table.
- **HyperRESEARCH** uses case cards (see below), relevant to organisation at document level especially when just one document comprises a 'case'. More complex organisation is possible by assigning a socio-demographic style code (e.g. *Female*) to the case.
- **MAXQDA** uses document variables and values, applied in a step-by-step way or through the importation of a table. An easy to manipulate cross-tabs tool allows comparison of conceptual codes across variables (as well as other queries). Variables can also be applied to codes, where for example they are used to code speaker sections in a focus group.
- **NVivo** uses source or node classifications with attributes under each. Several decisions have to be made and elements have to be linked accordingly. Choose between source or node classifications and link sources or nodes accordingly to the relevant classification, then create attributes under the classification – step-by-step or import a table. Varied matrix and coding queries are enabled.
- **QDA Miner** uses variables and cases. The structure is rather different since in the mixed methods emphasis of the software, variables are the main placeholders for any data that it handles. The process can be automated as you import data (this will also happen if you create a new project on the basis of a selection of files or a spreadsheet).
- **Qualrus** uses attributes assigned to codes; to organise whole data files, the socio-demographic codes are assigned to all segments in whole file.
- **Transana** uses keywords (codes) and the creation of collections assigned to video/transcripts as a way to organise both hard facts and conceptual categories.

BOX 12.4	CASE NOTES

Using variable-type functionality for recording 'analytic facts' (Case Study A, Young People's Perceptions)

Case Study A contained a number of socio-demographic facts which were known about from the outset (e.g. the nationality, age and gender of respondents). However, factual organisation took place at a relatively late stage of work (Phase Five) because we wanted to think about respondents' views and experiences together first, before considering how their

(Continued)

(Continued)

socio-demographic characteristics might help explain their views. However, a similar evolution and adjustment of ideas about categories for classifying respondents influenced decisions about ongoing organisation at the variable-type level, as discussed in relation to Case Study B. But the incorporation of additional variable-type information related to analytic facts rather than socio-demographic ones. For example, it became apparent that respondents evaluated the various forms of information concerning sexuality and relationships rather differently. Their evaluation could be ranked and considered a 'fact' and treated at the same level in the software as the 'facts' pertaining to their nationality, age and gender. It then became possible to interrogate whether the way they evaluated different forms of learning was related to the country they lived in – or other aspects – or needed to be explained in different terms. Queries using the variable might subsequently reveal whether those satisfied with school-based sex education behaved in different ways, or experienced relationships differently, or had more detailed knowledge about contraception, etc. Such analytic facts were identified and classified by the researcher, as part of the analysis, and only applied once the closer familiarisation with data through processes of coding and annotation had taken place. Often researchers see the organisation of facts as a one-stage process; but as this example illustrates, you have the flexibility to add new variables as and when you identify new analytically interesting aspects which relate to a whole respondent, case or other unit of analysis. You can therefore incrementally build up a more analytically useful and project-specific set of variable-type information as the project proceeds.

In discussing organisation at document level we indicated that a case can consist of more than one document (this is very likely) and that the case assignation of a file usually happens via the same process as socio-demographic variables (Table 12.5; p. 290). With HyperRESEARCH, however, the case card (like a cardex system) is the basis of work (see Figure 12.3; p. 293). This package is completely unique in the way it handles its case-based structure. While most of the other packages we mention can feature the case dimension, the default unit of analysis in them all tends to be the document (except QDA Miner whose structure is case-based in a different way). Not so with HyperRESEARCH. A 'study' (project) is created only by the creation of any number of *case cards* – which gradually accrue coding entries in documents relevant to the case. The software does not care how many documents feature within one case; indeed, an individual document can be linked to more than one case. Equally, an individual case card might just have one linked document. The point is that the case, not the document, is the main basis upon which navigation and interrogation happen (see additional information in Chapter 13 regarding its theory tester, and the software summaries in Chapter 3).

Organising at document level – step-by-step advice

Each process is slightly different, and document-based organisation can be achieved with varied degrees of simplicity. Working out how to create and apply variables can

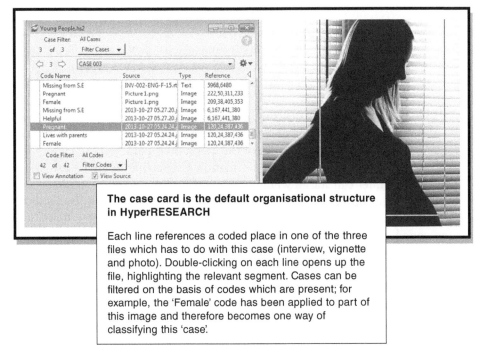

The case card is the default organisational structure in HyperRESEARCH

Each line references a coded place in one of the three files which has to do with this case (interview, vignette and photo). Double-clicking on each line opens up the file, highlighting the relevant segment. Cases can be filtered on the basis of codes which are present; for example, the 'Female' code has been applied to part of this image and therefore becomes one way of classifying this 'case'.

FIGURE 12.3   The case card (HyperRESEARCH)

be a little opaque, depending on the architecture of the software; dialogue boxes are not famous for telling you what to do next. Remember the companion website and the help menu. When there is a Variable menu – this is a good start! Generally you feel in control when doing it in a 'hand-done' (i.e. step-by-step) way. You will be able to create as many variables as you need, whenever you need to. Keep labels short. Only you need to understand them.

If using codes to assign socio-demographic attributes to documents, the process is as easy as other forms of coding. The principle will be that instead of using queries which look for variables (together with concept codes) you will look for socio-demographic or factual codes – where they co-occur with conceptual codes. Alternatively, you might want the co-occurrence of the 'female' code and the '20–29 yrs' code – to produce and save a new subset of coded documents or cases at a new code 'female 20–29'. Software varies in the way such codes have to be assigned. This may also have to do with the type of query you are framing.

Organising at document level – by importing a spreadsheet (or survey)

Some software packages can enable organisation at document (or code) level via the import of a spreadsheet. This could organise documents already in the software project or import qualitative data which are included in the spreadsheet along with corresponding quantitative information. When formatted properly they are in effect pre-coded, enabling auto-processing as part of the import process. They usually need particular syntax to indicate particular kinds of information at the column header (e.g. a dollar sign '$' or a cross-hatch symbol '#'). This is illustrated in Figure 4.4 where the survey file in spreadsheet format (for Case Study B) is ready for import into MAXQDA. ATLAS.ti, MAXQDA (and QDA Miner with a slightly different outcome) can import a survey in this way, and as a result of the pre-coded format at column headers the import process creates respondent-based mini-documents out of the qualitative 'comment' fields and the rest of the descriptive or quantitative information assigns the variable information to them. QDA Miner can start a whole project off with a similar spreadsheet, and processes data appropriately. NVivo requires that you process a similar table by making choices in several dialogue boxes about the purpose of each column – is it to be coded, or is it for classification purposes? Here though, the qualitative data stays in the table, so in a sense the respondents in the survey are not turned into 'documents' in their own right, but stay with the rest of the information. There are advantages and disadvantages with each system.

Starting a table off in the right format?

Most programs enable a separate spreadsheet to be imported with just the descriptive or socio-demographic data in order to organise qualitative files which have already been incorporated. A good way to start this spreadsheet off is to export a 'proxy' spreadsheet out of the software (possibly with one 'dummy' variable created) which has the correct data file names contained within it. Opening that file in Excel would give you the minimum columns and content expected by the software in the subsequent table you are about to prepare. Importantly, too, if the data files had already been imported into the software project, they would also feature in this table. So adding the rest of the quantitative or descriptive data into the cells of the spreadsheet (with suitable column headers as variable names), you can then be sure that each row of data will match up to exactly the right documents, because they are already listed correctly, in the exported spreadsheet, exactly as they appear in the software project. This general starting point information is applicable to several packages which use variables (or something similar); but watch out for slightly different procedures in each.

Organising within the document (parts of documents)

If you have focus-group data or any other files divided into recurring and exactly matching sections (in terms of the header information) it may be the parts within the file that need to be organised (e.g. the speaker sections in focus-group data). Conversely, if the file needs to be treated as a homogeneous whole and organised on that basis, the process will be similar to that described above. There are generally three things you may have to decide in organising parts of files (though there might be more than one way of achieving each of them):

1. Do you want to create a code where you can gather together all of one speaker's contributions in order to isolate, interrogate, filter to or just to view his/her 'narrative'?
2. Do you just want to categorise the respondents or sections of the file by general factual categories such as gender/female, or age/16?
3. Will you want to do (1) as above *and also* organise the speaker codes with, for example, socio-demographic categories?

The answers rest on the need to treat the individual contributions, cases or speakers as separate entities to compare across or within things you know about them; or to interrogate just one of them. If you do not want or need to do that, each file should be treated as one homogeneous unit. There is one other factor to do with practical feasibility. For instance, focus groups are notoriously difficult to transcribe to include the identification of each speaker reliably (because it is not always clear from the audio who is speaking). For now we assume you have managed to achieve this; in that light we summarise software options for organising parts of documents, and then provide a little more information on the actual process.

- **ATLAS.ti** uses Codes and Code families (similar to sets). You can either use codes to apply socio-demographics direct to speaker sections or make respondent-based or section-based codes, and then sort them into Code Families. One respondent-based code can belong in as

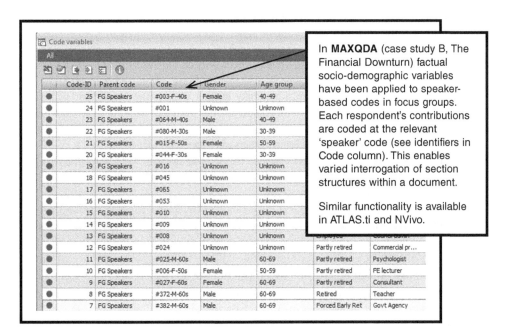

Figure 12.4   Organising at the level of parts of documents (MAXQDA)

many families as required. Dynamic super-families can easily be created out of combinations of the basic families (e.g. 'Females aged 20–29 years'). It is easy to switch between families in any query result. The **auto-coding** device based on text searching for elements can be used to search within speaker identifier or section titles for the relevant flags.

- **Dedoose** uses codes that are **assigned** to parts documents (media) after segmenting. This can be based on socio-demographic information or, for example, speaker identifiers, but the process of applying codes is step-by-step. Instant charts and breakdowns of coding within documents or across them are available.
- **HyperRESEARCH** uses codes assigned to parts of cases and files. Certain types of selection by criteria will find co-occurrence of codes (e.g. concept codes with socio-demographic codes or speaker-based codes). The case-based focus of the software frames results by case not by document, though a 'case' (i.e. the case card) can represent any aspect of analysis, so all coded references to many data files could be gathered in a case, based for example on a time phase or geographic location. Thus because coding references can sit in many different types of case there may be many different ways to approach the organisation of parts of documents.
- **MAXQDA** uses codes that are applied to parts of documents to create section-based or speaker-based codes. Variables (similar to Document variables) are then applied to the speaker-based codes. This allows 'activation' of multiple combinations and making of sets of codes via those combinations. A table can be created step-by-step or imported (Figure 12.4). Easy cross-tabs tool and instant matrix views allow comparison and retrieval of conceptual codes across respondent or speaker-based codes. Lexical search can auto-code based on elements in speaker identifiers to code, for example, speaker sections.
- **NVivo** – uses *Nodes* (codes) applied to parts of data, then linked to node classifications with attributes under each. This can be achieved manually or via the importation of a table (this is a complex process and needs care). The auto-code device for qualitative text can code multiple matching heading levels based on matching style and text at headers or speaker identifiers. Various matrix and coding queries are enabled. When importing surveys ('data-sets') the software keeps the comment style open-ended questions in the spreadsheet. Further auto-coding of the survey may be required.
- **QDA Miner** uses codes assigned to parts of documents on the basis of socio-demographics. Much variable frequency information is available on those codes, and Boolean (AND, OR, NOT) queries can be combined with proximity queries to find how specific parts of documents (e.g. multiple respondents with one document) feature at thematic codes. QDA Miner naturally associates every qualitative comment field in a survey with its associated quantitative or descriptive data, so that interrogation can happen on that basis.
- **Qualrus** uses codes with attributes assigned on the basis of facts, socio-demographics, etc. There are multiple ways of querying codes combined with attribute values to produce thematic coding filtered to precise subsets.
- **Transana** uses keywords (codes) and the creation of collections to categorise segments in different ways. Thus codes are used to organise both hard facts and conceptual categories.

For the rest of this section we generalise since the specifics of software are so different. To start with we discuss codes as simple devices that do one of the things suggested in points (1) or (2) at the very beginning of this section. Then, more appropriate to point (3), we add on more functionality (available in some software only) where variable and attributes can themselves be associated with codes similarly to the way they are associated with documents.

Coding in step-by-step ways

You can create codes in a step-by-step way for all the eventualities covered in points (1)–(3) above. Codes have to be created for respondents' speaker-based data (e.g. 'R.481' or 'Robert'; or codes for 'female', 'male'). Then these codes need to be applied to all the bits of data that fall into each category. They should not just be sitting somewhere in those segments; the codes should be applied to the whole of each relevant segment. Thereafter the co-occurrence of any of those codes and the more conceptual codes which will give you bases for interrogation and comparison is enabled.

However, when such places in the data are repeated *and* identified clearly *and* consistently transcribed *and* you have given some thought about their relevance for your data type, then it may be that auto-coding tools may enable the quick organisation of those sections of data at socio-demographic codes.

BOX 12.5 — ANALYTIC NOTES

Questions to ask yourself when considering the factual organisation of your project

- Are you clear – analytically and technically – about the difference between coding conceptually and the use of hard factual characteristics when using attributes/variables?
- Are there circumstances in your data which might necessitate the combining of codes with, for example, socio-demographics?
- How has recording the known facts altered the way you are thinking about the dataset?
- If you are importing factual data about your respondents from elsewhere, are you sure you will make use of all those categories in the software project?
- Are new, softer characteristics about the data evolving? Are they characteristics that could categorise the whole respondent or file? Or are they simply codes that need applying to a few instances in the data?
- What questions do you now want to ask about how certain codes, themes or categories occur according to the more factual data?

Auto-coding

Chapter 4 discussed 'basic' and minimal (but useful) guidelines for transcription, in order to benefit later from auto-coding tools, providing some guidance to structures and units of text recognised by software. Nearly always these will include paragraphs – so a clearly defined paragraph (ended by pressing the Enter key and separated from the paragraph above by pressing the Enter key, forming a 'hard return') so passages that look like this can be auto-coded (via text/lexical search tools) in ATLAS.ti, MAXQDA, NVivo and QDA Miner:

N1–015: Well obviously they had to deal with the loss of funding – but I think management take the easiest way out to fix the numbers. I was a soft touch – already part-time – but I'd been there for 15 years – and they forget how much extra you do – so when you leave they suddenly wonder how they will cope and start hiring in all sorts to fill the gaps. It really did make me feel ill at the time. Just worthless too.

MOD: Can you explain a bit what do you mean hiring in all sorts?

In reference to points (1), (2) and (3), in turn:

(a) You can perform an auto-coding operation or text search for 'N1–015' anywhere in this particular file (or across all files) and save the paragraphs which enclose the 'hits' and then code them all at code called 'N1–015'.

(b) If N1–015 was instead N1-F..015 (the -F.. indicating female) you could similarly search for '-F..' and then save all the female data at a code called 'Female'.

(c) It will nearly always be possible (instead of (b)), to create and apply a code for the speaker and then copy that code (which will copy the coded segments) into any number of other socio-demographic type codes.

With respect to option (b), you are unlikely to be able to include all the facts or socio-demographics about a respondent at his/her identifier, but it can be useful to consider the inclusion of really important features about the data here. In particular, regarding auto-coding abilities, it is worth bearing in mind that NVivo takes those possibilities a step further by recognising the use of consistent heading levels with matching text to enable in one step the auto-coding of all heading level 2 headers, for example, together and concurrent with (any) matching text across all the data. So here the potential is for multiple codes to be created in one step (e.g. one for each speaker in a focus group, or all topic sections across all files); see Box 4.4; p. 92. This means much more care has to be taken at transcription and formatting stages (see Chapter 4) so that the right format and styles can easily be inserted – possibly via Find and Replace in MS Word.

Whatever software or tool you are using, it is important not to force essentially unstructured or semi-structured data into a structured form just because you are aware of auto-coding tools!

The implications of coding cases, respondents and parts of files in terms of their further organisation

We saw above that codes can simply be applied on the basis of socio-demographic information. This is always a possible workaround even where other organisational tools such as attributes and variables are present, but especially where they are not available. When you have created and assigned, for instance, speaker-based or respondent-based codes in your data, in all software you can organise them in groups or sets of codes based on defining characteristics. In some packages you can combine the groups in complex ways. ATLAS.ti makes this easy with the dynamic Super-family tool.

Finally, MAXQDA and NVivo allow an extra possibility where these structural codes you have created and assigned to sections or speakers, etc. can be associated with special code-based attributes or variables, thus enabling (similar to ATLAS.ti) quicker, ongoing and complex ways to combine subsets of coded data.

Concluding remarks: potentials and cautions

There is no limit on the number of factual features you can incorporate to organise data and respondents within a software project. How many attributes, variables or codes you create for this purpose will depend on your research design and the functionality to support their creation and use in your chosen package. Incorporating these features within your project provides the potential to make comparisons on many different levels and to interrogate patterns and relationships through the use of query tools in complex ways. Chapter 13 focuses on ways of interrogating the dataset.

However, a cautionary note should be voiced here. When it comes to organising data, there are many different starting points. Sometimes step-by-step ways are easier to control. Some of the processes which aim to combine and marry up work from different software applications with entities already in the qualitative software project (e.g. importing spreadsheets) work really well and are relatively simple to understand. However, using a mixture of different routes and using many different starting points for organisation can cause a bit of a muddle, and it can be difficult to spot when things have gone wrong. Later on, it can become difficult for less experienced users to diagnose where the problems lie. Researchers tend not to work in tidy, set procedural ways, simply because qualitative research design is emergent and things never happen to plan. Sometimes small steps need to be taken and then tested to see whether they work. In learning new software versions ourselves so that we can teach them effectively, we do precisely that. We test everything. Will the steps produce the expected outcome if we experiment with a small query? Have we understood what needed to happen? In a real project the danger is that the wrong inferences might be made from queries which produce results out of patchy or erroneous organisation of data. So it is a question not just of 'garbage in, garbage out', but of forced errors because of misunderstandings. Often mistakes are not discovered until query tools produce nothing at all in the way of expected results. We talk generally about what are the good potentials of these organisational tools, but there are so many varied starting points that we have to gloss over some of the complications and stumbling blocks of software which are in themselves more complex in this respect. We make small experimental queries, to understand when things are going right. We take the trouble to do a query on something we know the answer to. We do a little organisation at attributes or variables or document families.

Then we do some coding. We practise the relevant query in the software (e.g. which of the women (or the men) talk about 'job security'?). If we know we should be getting a result and we get nothing back, something has gone wrong. It has either gone wrong with the coding of job security or with the way we organised data. We go back to basics and investigate each part of that equation. This should put us in a position to understand for sure which bit went wrong. This is the way to gain confidence with a more complex software program.

In deciding on which features to include as attributes or variables, therefore, think about the kinds of questions you want to ask, the ideas you want to test and the parts of your dataset you want to isolate. This is all connected with research design and analytic strategy. An awareness of how you can add or change things later is useful as the analysis evolves to prompt new questions. Chapter 13 takes this further in talking about complex, but also very simple, ways in which interrogation can happen. The more complex dimensions of interrogation depend on organisational structures, but these can be relatively simple structures. Evaluate your project and the complications of your dataset and your objectives and put them in the context of the software you will use.

EXERCISES: ORGANISING DATA BY KNOWN CHARACTERISTICS

The focus of this chapter has been on the organisation of data files and respondents' contributions according to factual characteristics. We made a number of distinctions in order to help you decide the best approach for doing this type of work within the context of your own research design. There are usually many ways of proceeding and it is unlikely that you will need all – or even several – of them. Each software package that we comment on provides a different set of functionality for doing so. Some provide simple ways of recording factual features, which although usually adequate for many designs are limited when datasets become particularly large or designs more complex. Other packages provide many more and varied options for handling factual features, thus enabling very complex designs to be managed. However, sometimes understanding the most efficient way of going about factual data organisation using these packages can be difficult and cumbersome.

To reflect the range of possibilities available across software packages and for different research designs would result in an extensive and cumbersome list of exercises. We have therefore kept these chapter exercises relatively generic, presenting options for you to consider in the context of your own research design. Refer to the companion website for detailed instructions on how to achieve factual data organisation using your chosen software. You can experiment with any of the case-study example materials.

Organising data in whole files – simple research designs

1. *Where individual data files constitute units of analysis.* This includes transcripts of recorded interviews with individual respondents (where you have one document per respondent); literature articles saved as PDF files; focus-group discussions in which you are interested in the group rather than the individual view.

(a) Use attributes, variables or families according to the functionality of your chosen software.

    (i) Create the attributes/variables and their values within the software and experiment with applying them to data files using the tabular or list-based functions available.

    (ii) Experiment with importing the information in tabular format from a spreadsheet or statistical application. This will usually create all the attribute/variables and apply the values to the data files automatically.

(b) Where these tools are not available you can achieve the same through coding. Create codes for each characteristic you need to record (e.g. for socio-demographics you will need a code for 'male' and 'female' separately). These can then be applied to the whole of each data file (thus creating one large coded segment).

2. *Where multiple data files combine to constitute a unit of analysis.* Case-study designs and those in which the same respondents have contributed to more than one form of data (e.g. answered a set of survey questions and taken part in a focus-group discussion, or in ethnographic studies where respondents' actions have been observed, and they have been interviewed) are examples of more complex studies which require more careful factual organisation. In designs such as this, there are multiple discrete units of observation that contribute to the same unit of analysis (i.e. multiple forms of data corresponding to the same case). Assuming data have been collected at the same time point – or that differences in data collection time are irrelevant – multiple forms of data need to be combined via coding in order to associate with factual characteristics, only once.

    (i) Software packages which include the ability to assign attribute/variables to coded data or enable the use of short-cut groupings (families or sets) to group codes will usually be more flexible for organising these sorts of designs.

    (ii) You will need to code all the contributions provided by each respondent at an individual code (e.g. 'Resp001:Frank') and then apply the corresponding socio-demographic values or codes to those bodies of respondent-oriented data.

3. *Where changes over time need to be tracked.* Longitudinal designs require data contributed by each respective respondent to be isolated such that within- as well as across-case analysis can be conducted. Attributes or variables applied to whole data files work well for this where data are interview transcripts (or similar). Where encounters with respondents are handled within larger data files (e.g. field note observations, survey data, focus-group discussions), contributions first need to be coded to respondent codes which also account for the time at which data was collected (e.g. 'Resp001:FrankA', 'Resp001:FrankB', 'Resp001:FrankC', ...). Applying socio-demographic characteristics to those coded data can thus account for the fact that the respondent Frank moved house or became divorced, say, between phases A and B or B and C.

Organising parts of data files

1. Where you have data files that contain several speakers or other important structures which you need to differentiate between in terms of factual characteristics, use codes for this purpose.

(a) This might include focus-group discussions where you are interested in the individual (as well as the group) view, and you know the socio-demographic characteristics of the speakers, or (semi-)structured interview data or group discussions/meetings where topics are discussed in broad terms, or field note data where observations about particular events, settings or actors are made repeatedly within a data file.

   (i) Where you have formatted data files according to the required software-specific conventions.

13

Interrogating the Dataset

This chapter builds on tasks covered previously to discuss functions allowing you to interrogate, search or query a database. Chapter 2 outlined the broad potential of queries. Chapter 6 covered the exploration of data. Chapters 7–9 focused on coding and where it can lead. Early organisation of data and more advanced organisation in the light of their further potential for interrogation are covered in Chapters 5 and 12, respectively. The processes of interrogation as discussed in this chapter can bring all these elements of work together. In our model of analytic activities (Figure 2.1; p. 45), interrogation is closely linked to the processes of reflecting on interpretations and results, and is oriented around identifying patterns, relationships and anomalies, comparing cases and subsets, and testing theories and quality more generally. Despite the placing of this chapter, interrogation can be undertaken throughout the iterative analytic process; it need not be left until, for example, coding has been completed. We list ideas and reasons for querying, illustrating how it can help you delve around the project for interesting relationships, patterns of occurrence and exceptions. We raise some cautions and debates about these tools and discuss ways in which they provide methods of interrogation additional to those practically possible when working manually. It is important to have a rounded understanding of the potential of query tools. Appreciating how different phases and elements of work can come together in your chosen software is an important part of familiarisation with and optimisation of software use.

The role of interrogation in moving on

Interrogation broadly concerns many kinds of delving into data and the analytic and organisational work already achieved. Querying is a key means by which work moves from simple code-and-retrieve to more in-depth analysis. We use the term 'query' since it is often the generic label used within software packages for the functional area where all manner of queries are built. In fact, interrogation happens very often without building 'queries' *per se*. In some packages the term is not used because interrogation is enabled via short-cut icons or specific menu options. We tend to use the term 'query' when we are making a conscious effort, however that is enabled, to explore connections in data and to discover and test relationships. We distinguish 'querying' as discussed in this chapter from 'searching' as discussed in earlier chapters. Searching relates to using software tools to pick out key words, phrases and patterns used in texts.

BOX 13.1 — ANALYTIC NOTES

The value of querying in contributing to 'quality'

Most query tools focus on where items specified exist in data, but it is important to be aware that absence can be just as analytically significant as presence. Therefore view results in context and be reflexive about how searches are contributing to your understanding. Queries and searches will not in themselves produce good-quality analysis.

It is not possible to describe all the interrogation options; there are simply too many across the packages we are concerned with here. Instead, we discuss commonly used queries and some of the more sophisticated interrogatory functions, the aim being to provide an overview to help you begin using tools with confidence. Remember, you cannot damage your software project by searching or querying. The only dangers lie in being confused or uncertain about how to build a query or where the coding on which they rely is unsound, patchy or inconsistent. The consequence may be dubious results, thereby leading to mistaken thinking. Preparing the groundwork and interpreting the results lie with you.

The incremental, iterative and repeatable nature of querying

Sometimes, having coded for some time, it may be hard to know where to go next. Your research questions generally and your analytic needs more specifically guide your direction with software, but query tools can be used to gain confidence in handling data. There may often be more than one way to achieve a similar result, and early experiments will help you see what might be possible later. When the answer to a question is already known, a confirmatory result will provide confidence in the way the query was built. Querying supports iterative analytic processes, enabling you to check out hunches as you progress. Queries can also facilitate incremental analysis, in that further queries can be performed on the results of earlier ones, by either building a previous search term into a new query or using coded results of previous queries as the basis of subsequent ones (Box 13.4). The variety of ways to combine work provides vast potential in interrogating the dataset.

Table 13.1 Interrogating the dataset: some suggestions in the context of case study A, Young People's Perceptions

---

Reminders of research questions:

- To what extent do young people living in England and the Netherlands have similar experiences of learning about sex and relationships?
- How do the socio-sexual attitudes of young women and young men differ? Can these differences be related to aspects of their family background?
- To what extent do the attitudes of this sample of young people reflect other research findings?

Tasks from PHASE SEVEN: Interrogate data to establish findings

Interrogate connections and illustrate structures using visual tools	• Explore broad connections between codes visually (where possible) to highlight patterns and relationships that warrant further in-depth interrogation using query tools (this can be achieved both according to data type and across the whole dataset)
	
	  o e.g. (where possible) to gain a broad overview of co-occurrence between subject codes ('contraception', 'pregnancy' etc.) with attitudinal codes ('too young', 'embarrassment', 'stigma' etc.)
	  o e.g. to make broad comparisons of codes used in different forms of data (interviews, vignettes, photo prompts and literature)

Compare coding across the whole (or subsets of) the dataset	• Compare coding concerning learning styles (informal/formal) and modes (school/media/friends) by nationality
	
	  o Frequency of application of coding (quantitative matrix of learning styles/modes codes by nationality)
	  o Review data behind each cell in matrix
	
	    o how do they speak about learning styles
	    o to what can you attribute differences in the nature and content of discussion?

Identify patterns in coding within data files (or subsets)	• Explore the ways respondents express attitudes in response to the vignette scenarios
	
	  o In what contexts do they express negative and positive attitudes (coding query of negative attitudinal codes ('fault or blame', 'not the done thing') and broad socio-sexual context codes ('teenage pregnancy', 'age of consent')
	  o Are there any patterns in the application of codes within interview transcripts that help further understanding (code proximity or code sequence queries/visualisations)
	
	    o E.g. do broad gendered discussions about young men and young women occur in different relation to moral context or negative attitudinal codes?

Combining different dimensions of data

As discussed throughout this book, analytic work happens on all kinds of levels (Chapter 1). Organisational categories, interpretive coding and the examination and searching of physical content all play a part. Querying allows different elements to be combined; often within an individual query or via incremental stages. For example, Figure 13.1 illustrates the distribution of (selected) keywords across the Case Study A dataset presented in different visualisations. In the Case Study B data we performed such word distribution interrogations within data already coded in a certain way (by 'positive spin'). Thus interpretive work at different levels goes on during coding processes. Alternatively, for coding which might be structural (e.g. representing speakers; Chapters 4 and 12) content analysis can be combined with or filtered to these elements, and tested across socio-demographic variables. Other ways of combining different dimensions of data through querying are illustrated in Figures 13.5 and 13.7.

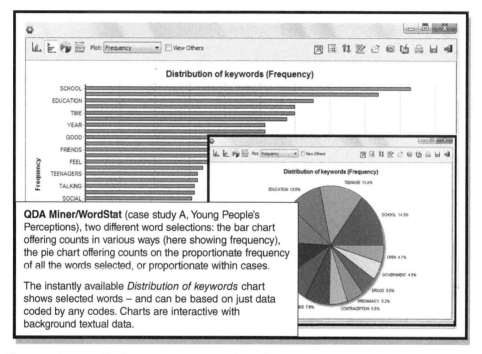

Figure 13.1   Quantification of keywords (QDA Miner with WordStat)

Test theories and expectations (hunches)

When working in explicit relation to existing theories or when testing hypotheses, there are certain questions you need to ask of your data. These will have informed the way you have gone about coding. Query tools will enable the revisiting of this work to interrogate more deeply. Being aware of your preconceptions and expectations is important whatever the design of your project (Box 13.3). When working within a theoretical framework they are more explicit than might otherwise be the case, but as you go through the processes of analysis, your ideas, hunches, theories and expectations are modified as you consider more data and think more and more in-depth about how they are contributing to your ability to answer the research questions. Even where you are not explicitly testing theories or hypotheses, you will have some expectations about what you are likely to find in the data, and via the use of queries you can validate them.

Creating signposts for and from queries

There are various ways to build 'signposts' into your work to remind you of your hunches. Memos, codes, sets and maps can all be used to record pathways to be followed and investigations deserving further attention (Chapter 5). Similarly, queries can be saved as pointers to future 'tests'. Most CAQDAS packages can save search expressions which can act as dynamic questions, repeatable on later accumulations of (coded) data (Figure 13.2; p. 308). They can be built at a relatively early stage, when running them would return few results. Where sets are available their early creation can act as a pointer to future queries, and then become the location where a short-cut to the results are saved. They can sometimes even comprise short-cuts to the data files on which a particular series of queries should be focused.

BOX 13.2 — CASE NOTES

Being aware of the need for comparison queries (Case Study A, Young People's Perceptions)

The analytic approach to Case Study A was framed by the initial literature review and is thus 'theory-driven' (Chapter 2). In the context of school-based education specifically, it was to be expected, considering previous literature, that those living in the Netherlands might be more satisfied with the information provided in school-based sex education classes than their counterparts living in England and Wales. In addition, because Dutch society is frequently upheld as particularly 'liberal' in relation to sexuality and relationships, it might have been expected that the young people interviewed living in the Netherlands would also exhibit more 'liberal' socio-sexual attitudes. The research questions (Chapter 2) were designed to investigate these issues. A key aspect was to consider how primary data reflect previous findings and contribute to understanding the apparent paradox between a lack of standardisation in Dutch school-based sex education provision and the historically low teenage pregnancy rate. Queries that enabled comparisons to be drawn were key here. Proceeding in such a way with the required organisational structures and coding processes to enable these specific predefined questions was therefore in our minds from the outset of setting up the project, and inherent in the design of the phases of work (Table 2.1).

BOX 13.3 — CASE NOTES

Being aware of your expectations and the need to test hunches (Case Study C, Coca-Cola Commercials)

Even in essentially inductive projects that seek not to be overly determined by existing theory, it is important to be aware of preconceptions and expectations, and reflexive about their role on your work.

(Continued)

Case Study C, for example, includes a focus on how gendered stereotypes are evidenced in the commercials and the way in which these reflect the times in which they were first aired. We had a number of expectations that needed to be tested. Coding of the data, whether adopting a direct or indirect approach (Chapter 7), needed to happen in such a way that these issues could be unpicked. Therefore, the exploration and identification of analytic focus (Phase Two, Table 2.1) focused on identifying instances of gendered actions and representations (e.g. contrasting the behaviours of men and women and their attire; Chapter 6). Where written transcriptions were generated, these were also constructed in such a way as to be able to access relevant material, dimensions which would be brought together in comparisons to answer research questions: the years in which commercials were first aired were recorded within the software as facts; and the inductive indexing phase generated codes in the light of research questions (Chapter 7).

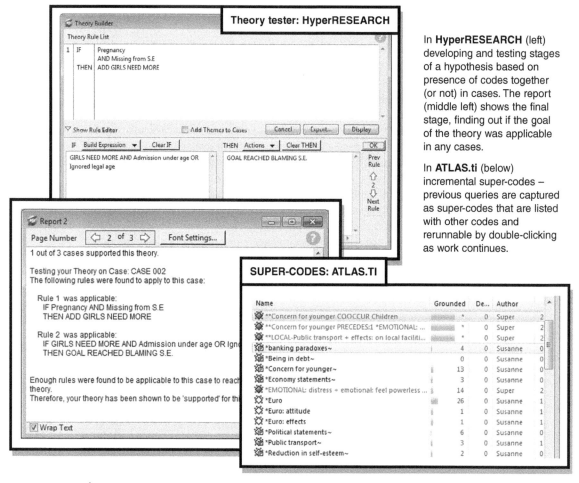

In **HyperRESEARCH** (left) developing and testing stages of a hypothesis based on presence of codes together (or not) in cases. The report (middle left) shows the final stage, finding out if the goal of the theory was applicable in any cases.

In **ATLAS.ti** (below) incremental super-codes – previous queries are captured as super-codes that are listed with other codes and rerunnable by double-clicking as work continues.

Figure 13.2 Incremental and multiple stage queries (HyperRESEARCH and ATLAS.ti)

Identify patterns and relationships

The identification of patterns in how data have been coded contributes to establishing relationships. Indeed, testing theories and expectations is all about the identification

Table 13.2 Interrogating the dataset: some suggestions in the context of case study B, The Financial Downturn

---

Reminders of research questions:

- In what contexts are the implications of the financial downturn expressed by the focus-group respondents? Do their experiences reflect the wider sample in the survey in terms of the major impacts on lives?
- What are respondents' understandings of the causes of the downturn and how are these expressed?
- How are the issues constructed in media reporting and to what extent are respondents' understandings reflected by them?

Tasks from PHASE SEVEN: Interrogate data to establish findings

Interrogate connections and illustrate structures using visual tools	• Explore broad connections between codes visually (where possible) to highlight patterns and relationships that warrant further in-depth interrogation using query tools (this can be achieved both according to data type and across the whole dataset) ○ e.g. to get a broad overview of main causes of the financial downturn amongst respondents ○ e.g. to make broad comparisons about how different types of media represent the issues ○ e.g. to begin exploring the extent to which survey responses are reflected by the more in-depth focus-group discussions

Compare coding across the whole (or subsets of) the dataset	• Patterns of responses to each open-ended survey question
	○ Matrix of open-ended question codes by thematic codes
	  ○ E.g. compare responses to questions about the major effects of the downturn and comments about where the fault lies according to thematic codes around 'Emotional effects' (e.g. distress, anger, uncertainty etc.)
	• Patterns in application of coding
	○ Coding queries looking for the contexts in which respondents express major concerns
	  ○ E.g. the 'concern for younger' code in relation to 'job security', 'expenditure priorities' etc.
	• Comparison of responses according to socio-demographic characteristics of respondents
	○ Matrix of key responses (across primary data types) by key socio-demographics
	  ○ E.g. codes relating to the effects of the financial downturn according to employment status, location, gender etc. of respondents

Identify patterns in coding within data files (or subsets)	• Consider the interactions between respondents and the moderator as the discussion proceeds – within each discussion separately ○ To what extent does the moderator have to keep respondents on track with respect to the general topic? ○ Do certain respondents dominate the discussion? How does this seem to affect the direction and nature of the content covered?

---

of patterns. We discuss these aspects separately because researchers who consider their projects to be about 'building' rather than 'testing' theory often conceptualise the identification of patterns and relationships in more flexible ways. In fact, as illustrated by the case-study examples, deductive and inductive ways of working occur in almost all projects, often in tandem (Chapter 7). The use of software generally, and especially when interrogating, reinforces this interaction.

- Theory 'building' necessitates theme generation in a general or global sense. This requires the reconsideration of codes to assess their potential to be treated as themes. Within software, 'horizontal' retrieval of an individual broad-brush code (when working deductively) or of several more detailed codes that appear to be related (when working inductively) is an initial task (Chapter 8). Data segments are compared for equivalence and uncoded where they are deemed not precise enough to constitute examples of the theme. Initial coding is a process of indexing data (Chapter 7). Theme development is the process of analysing the codes. Working inductively when large numbers of codes may be generated in the initial coding pass, this is likely to involve deciding which to merge or group to form a theme (Chapters 8 and 9). Search and query tools can help with this work considerably, as can mapping tools (Chapter 11 and Box 13.4), the use of other visualisations (see below) and the continual writing about what you are doing and what you are seeing in the data (Chapter 10).

BOX 13.4 — CASE NOTES

Incremental or multi-part queries to discover patterns (Case Study B, The Financial Downturn)

Queries can find where two codes occur together. In Case Study B this was especially relevant for question-based and thematic codes. For instance, in data coded to 'Question 2' (How have you been personally affected by the financial crisis?) we queried to find out where respondents also mentioned 'Concerns for younger'. We ran a query and saved the finds at a new code called 'Q2-Concerns for younger'. This was the first stage in establishing the generalities of concerns and implications of the downturn on younger generations. We then wanted to find out where these references occurred in specific relation to respondents' own family members, rather than the younger generation in general. In order to consider this possible pattern in more detail, two further, more complex coding queries were run (there are various ways to do this, depending on the software being used).

Method 1: using the result of the first query, the new code, 'Q2-Concerns for younger'. A similar query was run, asking for the co-occurrence of this new code with the code 'Children' (all the data coded across the whole survey to mentions of children or offspring in any context).

Method 2. The initial query was refined in order to retrieve co-occurrence of three codes: 'Question 2', 'Concerns for younger' and 'Children'. This allowed counting the number of times concerns for the younger generation are mentioned in specific relation to respondents' own children, and to view and interpret how such comments are framed.

Results of these queries established more clearly that some respondents have concerns related to specific issues (e.g. the house-purchasing power of their children, or their job security), whereas others expressed concerns in more general terms (see also Figure 13.2; p. 308).

In order to double-check the relevance of this in relation to discussion of younger people in general, a further search was conducted to find all data segments coded at 'Concerns for younger' but *not* at 'children'. This served the purpose of comparing how respondents express concerns for the younger generation in general, with the way they express concerns about their own family members in particular. In addition, it made it easier to identify any errors in coding, and examples of respondents whose statements differ significantly from the majority of discussion relating to the topic.

In addition, it was useful to consider *how* respondents were discussing these issues, in terms of the language used, as well as *what* they were actually saying. In this Case Study, in which an additional focus is to identify how issues are constructed in media reporting and the extent to which respondents' understandings are reflected by them, for example, the searching for key words and phrases across the primary data and the media content would contribute. Here a mixture of deductive and inductive searches were conducted to look for expected topical words, whereas QDA Miner's Phrase Finder and Query by Example tools were used as a type of 'blind shot' mechanism to gain a sense of what software would simply throw up in terms of anything found to be recurring in both types of data.

Compare subsets, cases and interpretations

At the heart of all analysis is comparison. It happens on many levels and at many moments, when routinely retrieving coded data (Chapter 8) and looking at the differences between respondents. Some research designs are explicitly comparative; for example, comparative research, cross-national research or qualitative comparative analysis. Equally, some analytic approaches explicitly employ comparative strategies; for example, the constant comparative method in grounded theory. Even where your design is not conceived in these ways, or where you are conducting a case-based or ethnographic study in which the focus is on a particular setting, event or organisation, there will be certain aspects you need to compare in order to be able to answer your research questions.

Compare on the basis of codes by subsets or metadata

Researchers often think about comparison in terms of querying data to consider how themes occur and are experienced across the dataset in relation to the factual characteristics of the data. Where primary data have been collected this frequently concerns the socio-demographic characteristics of the respondents who were sampled for. Comparisons can also be made on all other kinds of other factual bases, however, including document-based metadata (such as date of publication, author and publisher when working with literature or newspaper files), or contextual information concerning settings (such as organisation type, size, location in case-based projects) (see also Chapter 12). CAQDAS packages all enable this sort of comparison, assuming, of course, that you have set up the factual characteristics and coded the data adequately and consistently.

Compare on the basis of codes occurring with or close to other codes

More complex comparisons can occur when combining different aspects or types of coding. When interested in attitudes, for example, you might need to understand what type of talk prompted an expression, as in Case Study A (Box 13.5). Being aware of the potential for querying on the basis of the location of codes in relation to one another can be important when you embark on first-pass coding. Similarly, discovering how codes are sequenced throughout an individual transcript (vertical retrieval) can be enlightening, especially when considering interactions or behaviour in particular settings (Figure 13.3).

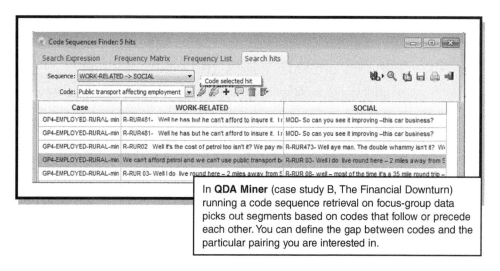

In **QDA Miner** (case study B, The Financial Downturn) running a code sequence retrieval on focus-group data picks out segments based on codes that follow or precede each other. You can define the gap between codes and the particular pairing you are interested in.

FIGURE 13.3   Querying data for code sequences (QDA Miner)

Queries not only need concern patterns in the use of topic or conceptual codes, but also can be based on the nature of talk, the stage in an interview, the non-verbal indications (if these are contained within transcripts) the hesitations, the long silences, the heated moments. In Case Study C, for instance, there was an interest in the dynamics of the juxtaposition of camera shots of individuals and groups. Reviewing all clips coded as *close-up* shots followed by *panning-out group shots* might indicate a repeatedly used device meriting further attention. What sort of person appears in close-up shots – how are they dressed? How does the soundtrack alter during the sequenced panning-out shots?

Table 13.3 Interrogating the dataset: some suggestions in the context of case study C, Coca-Cola Commercials

---

Reminders of research questions:

- How do the advertisements reflect the gendered stereotypes of their time?
- What are the cinematic and advertising mechanisms used to promote Coca-Cola as a brand, and how have these changed over time?
- To what extent do the content of the commercials reflect the company's stated mission, vision and values and its history?

Tasks from PHASE SEVEN: Interrogate data to establish findings

---

Interrogate connections and illustrate structures using visual tools	• Explore broad connections between codes visually (where possible) to highlight patterns and relationships that warrant further in-depth interrogation using query tools (this can be achieved both according to data type and across the whole dataset)
	
	   o e.g. to get a broad overview of the mechanisms used to advertise over time
	   o e.g. to make broad comparisons of the gendered role behaviour over time
	
	• Use visual tools to interrogate connections between data segments and codes that were created in PHASE FIVE. Create more connections as you identify additional relationships
	
	   o e.g. differences in the types of activities engaged in amongst male and female actors using visual co-occurrences
	
	• Use visual tools to illustrate structures in data
	
	   o e.g. the use of repetition within commercials using code margin views and compare how they change over time.

Compare coding across the whole (or subsets of) the dataset	• Compare codes relating to gender stereotypes of men and women across the adverts
	
	   o e.g. are women objectified differently over time
	   o e.g. how does male and female attire change and what can we infer from this?
	
	• Compare the stated company values and mission from the publicity materials with coding for similar aspects and your notes about these themes in earlier memos
	
	   o e.g. does the way you had initially thought about feelings evoked by the commercials tie up with the brand's stated vision etc?

Identify patterns in coding within data files (or subsets)	• Explore use of advertising devices (e.g. visual and aural repetition) throughout individual commercials (code proximity or code sequence queries/visualisations)
	
	   o e.g. in the 'Diet Coke Break' (1994) commercial how do observed actions (e.g. 'the female gaze', 'the male gaze') occur in relation to different states of undress and the use of the soundtrack?
	
	     o how do these compare with the 'Gardener' (2013) commercial?

Quality control

Quality: queries improving interpretive processes

Consideration of what is not in the data, and the identification of anomalies, are crucial to testing theories and hunches, uncovering patterns and relationships, and comparing subsets, cases and interpretations. Search and query tools cannot find what is not present, but it is important for you, the analyst, to 'read between the lines', to consider what underlies data in terms of what is not obvious or immediately apparent, as well as what is. This is the essence of what moves you on from description to interpretation. Search and query tools will help you identify anomalies, data which contradict the way most respondents talk about an issue or experience an event. Retrieval of coded data (especially broad-brush or theoretical codes) will not by itself produce meaningful analysis unless the passages are reread carefully and interpreted further. Counting the segments coded might be of use for getting an overview of salience for a respondent or if the dataset is very large, but otherwise would not give you many insights. Sensitive rereading might pick up important nuances. Often, though, it is in the iterative aspects of querying that subtleties are uncovered. That might be during serendipitous discovery via content searches (Chapter 6) or queries which look for interesting co-occurrences or sequencing (Boxes 13.4 and 13.5).

BOX 13.5 — CASE NOTES

The quality of interpretive work (Case Study A, Young People's Perceptions)

Though the young people interviewed for Case Study A have fairly consistent but pragmatic views about the age at which sex actually happens, despite the legal age of consent, none of them explicitly draws attention to the mental or emotional maturity that might be needed. We therefore initially paid little attention to this aspect in the context of sex education. However, the following comment about the loss of face which boys can suffer because of a lack of maturity in handling the aftermath of such an event prompted us to look again at talk about maturity generally;

> ENG-001-M-15: Because of maturity, not physically, because you know, you can have sex when you're 12, probably could, and it is possible, it's more about mental maturity, and I mean, I just don't think they're ready to do that, understanding emotional connection of sex, not just the physical, and I mean I've got a few friends and a classic example is, they're in year 9, 13, and a couple of them have had sex, and it's all giggling and laughing about it, and the boys actually have the piss taken out of them about it, the girl actually told his best friend that he ...

The passage had been coded fairly broadly during horizontal coding (Chapter 7) at three separate codes, 'Sex', 'About young women' and 'Embarrassment', but the passage was spotted

---

when a query was done on the basis of 'Sex' co-occurring with 'Embarrassment'. There was a perspective here that may have been missed otherwise. We then discovered that though there were no explicit mentions in the same way among other respondents, there were references acknowledging or implying similar discomfort. Further investigation concerning these more subtle social effects was required so as to understand whether or how they were covered in either of the national education contexts. We were always going to reanalyse the broadly coded themes, but doing the query brought the passage to our attention. The initial assignment of multiple broad codes to this passage had left the door open to this discovery.

Quality: flag up problems and check work

Queries can be instructive in all sorts of ways, including showing up omissions and inconsistencies. As you become more familiar with data, performing queries sometimes produces surprising and revealing results. At other times there might be a sense of discomfort because results are not as you expected in light of your knowledge about the data and the analysis achieved so far. If the queries involve codes, results should be prompts for thought and action. Is it just that a 'pet theory' or preconception is not confirmed by the query? Is there a glaring omission in your coding processes? Did you think a lot while you were reading but code in a patchy way? Attempting to solve such conundrums can only lead to improved understanding. First, it may be necessary to go back to the query and its basic components – are the constituent codes or variables as you expect, are they assigned to the data correctly? If things look as you would expect – did you build the query in a logical and accurate way? The nature of coding queries of any sort is that they rely on the quality of earlier work. Queries are helpful because they make you look at data again, often allowing you to see data differently; they can also help to refine codes or make you question how you coded in the first place (Box 13.5). It is therefore most important that your trust in the way you are working is reinforced by early experimentation with queries, giving you confidence in the use and potential of query tools and simultaneously helping reassure you that you are thinking about and processing the data rigorously.

Certain types of query can be mechanisms for showing up the absence or incorrect application of organisational structures where facts and figures about data are assigned (Chapter 12). Small tests looking for codes across different subsets of data, performed when you know what you should get back from the query, will reinforce your confidence. Subsequently, queries can be built to discover things you do not yet know, enabling you to make inferences and to rely on the quality of the results that underlie them.

Software tools for interrogating the database

There are many different tools designed to interrogate the dataset in CAQDAS packages. It is not possible to discuss all the options available in all the packages we are concerned with here, and even summarising them in a logical way is difficult because of the variety in functionality and terminology. We distinguish between broad types of interrogation: searching for content and/or structure; filtering and simple forms of retrieval; coding queries; qualitative cross-tabulations; and map-based interrogations. Content searching, filtering and map-based interrogations are discussed in earlier chapters, but we remind you about them here because they relate to the other, more complex ways of interrogating data and, in practice, are often carried out in tandem.

Searching content and/or structure

Chapter 6 covers data-level work more fully, discussing the spontaneous exploration of text using 'find', 'word frequency', 'text searching' and 'pattern recognition' tools. We distinguish between exploring data in this way as a form of data familiarisation, and coding as a result of such searches, because, although the latter may legitimately follow the former, this does not need to be the case. There are more automated pattern recognition tools such as the Phrase Finder and the Query by Example functions in QDA Miner (Figures 6.6; p. 151 and 6.7; p. 153).

Chapter 12 covers auto-coding process in the context of needing to quickly code repeated structures in data. The way textual data are formatted is a key factor in enabling these tools (Chapter 4). In the range of tools offered for this type of work, there are customary text search tools, deceptively simple tools like the Section Retrieval tool in QDA Miner and more complex tools like the auto-coding tool in NVivo. Some examples are provided in Figures 4.1 and 4.2.

BOX 13.6 — ANALYTIC NOTES

Combining auto-coding of structures in data with conceptual coding

In terms of interrogation, combining structural coding with more thematic or conceptual coding will offer means of picking out patterns in coding according to those more formal structures. We took advantage of this in slightly different ways in Case Studies A and B; auto-coding of textual data for structure within and/or across data files allows those codes to be combined with other types of codes.

In Case Study A, there were five broad topic areas which we auto-coded. It was then useful to perform a co-occurrence matrix query of codes capturing different attitudes via those five topic areas. This significantly contributed to identifying and visualising patterns and therefore establishing relationships.

In the focus groups in Case Study B, all the speaker sections were auto-coded to respective speaker codes, enabling subsequent querying for a particular thematic code within one speaker's contribution or across all the codes for all the speakers. This allowed us to review coding but to see it all quickly 'cut' and compared by speaker.

Such exercises put us back in touch with earlier coding processes in the context of the key dimensions of data collection and project design.

> Most packages that provide incremental text-searching or multi-part queries can bring two or three different dimensions of work together; for example, searching for particular words in data already coded in a particular way. In Case Study B, for example, searching for the use of the word 'government' or 'politics' in answers to data coded by 'Question 2' or in the data coded by 'Social effect'; or searches for words, the results coded, then cross-tabulated across all the values of a variable (see discussion on visualisations and matrices below).

Simple forms of retrieval

There are simple ways of retrieving coded data which take advantage of filtering devices to focus attention on particular parts of a dataset (Chapter 8). We remind you of these here since they are relevant to the routine day-to-day work in a software project, and particularly to reviewing work in a focused, selective way. We also provide some cues concerning the utility of combining views and remaining aware of co-occurring items in margin displays. In such simple ways much can be achieved.

Filtering

Filtering tools are simple ways to begin thinking about organisational structures (Chapter 5) and early retrievals (Chapter 8). In terms of more complex interrogations, their beauty lies in their safety. When conducting qualitative data analysis you need the ability to have an idea, think about it, test it, go down a 'blind alley' with it, without it 'mattering'. The creation of short-cut grouping and subsequent filtering on this basis, does exactly that. Sets can be used at several levels, allowing you to focus on aspects of the project in isolation, without necessarily making any lasting changes to the organisational framework of your software project. They can be used in straightforward ways, for example to retrieve data coded at one issue or theme or according to subsets of data. They can run in parallel.

MAXQDA and ATLAS.ti enable the whole of your current work space to be filtered to sets, thereby focusing attention on a subset of data sources and/or a group of codes. For example, in MAXQDA, by activating combinations of variables in a certain way we take advantage of this in Case Study B where 'mini' respondent data files are created semi-automatically and simultaneously categorised by the quantitative information upon importation of the survey spreadsheet (Figure 4.4; p. 102). It is easy, then, to activate or 'switch on' all the 40–49-year-olds who are also self-employed and also married; they can automatically be grouped into a 'set', which can then be activated for use in all sorts of ways from then on (Figure 13.4; p. 318). A very similar tool in ATLAS.ti is also illustrated in Figure 13.4. Combining the short-cut groupings ('families') into 'super-families' makes them 'dynamic'. This means that if any other new data, organised in the base families, also happen to satisfy the particular combination of variable values that is consolidated in the 'super-family', they automatically become members of that more complex grouping.

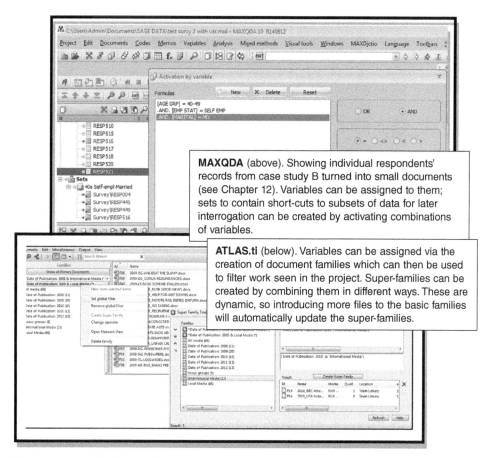

Figure 13.4 Activating and filtering to short-cut groupings (MAXQDA and ATLAS.ti)

Optimising coded retrieval with margin views

Most CAQDAS packages provide good margin displays, though they differ slightly in the way they are enabled and greatly in the further options available within or from them (Chapter 8). When reconnected to the full context of a file, always remain aware of the codes illustrated in the margin area. There are also often good ways to narrow the focus of a margin display; for instance, via filtering (as discussed above). Colour assigned to codes can often be used as a means of filtering a margin view. NVivo, for example, has an array of different viewing options, including one where you can consciously select the codes you wish to view, irrespective of the sets or other groupings to which they belong. Further, coding stripe options are available for viewing against retrieval of coded data (Figure 7.1; p. 159). Thus, while focusing on the data associated with one code you can see other selected codes against this selection. This is a simple option, but it might move you on analytically in terms of how you might be thinking about this catchment of coded data and the impact of other issues on it.

Readily available information about codes (without building complex queries)

There is much information, often only a couple of clicks away, enabling interrogation based on culminations of what you have done so far. Some of these are discussed in Chapter 8. We focus here on those that include an emphasis on mixed methods in origin and design principles of the software; principally QDA Miner and Dedoose, but also MAXQDA.

Easy access visualisations – mixed methods emphasis To some extent, mixed methods tools are all about visualisation. Most packages provide readily available basic frequency information about coding (Chapter 8). Some packages – notably Dedoose, MAXQDA and QDA Miner– provide very simple ways to get started with more complex interrogations. In some cases they readily display codes and data as they co-occur or are sequenced with other codes or variables (see below). They all differ in emphasis but are worth exploring because they can increase your familiarity with the relationship that codes have with each other. This is illustrated in Figure 13.5 in relation to Dedoose, whose 'Analyze' function and Chart Selector provide a wide variety of different visualisations.

The instant, quantitatively oriented information about codes (and content) available in QDA Miner is useful for the large datasets it was designed to handle. Two key tools offering unusual and more qualitative aspects of support (alongside the quantitative) are *code co-occurences* and *coding sequences*.

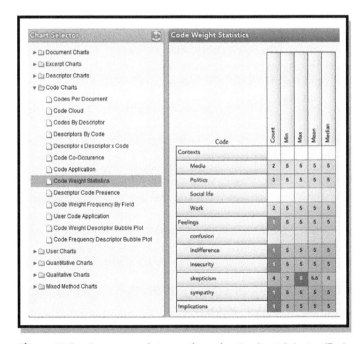

A large variety of starting points for charts are available in **Dedoose**.

The code chart on view shows an early representation of measures of 'weight' applied to data segments associated with certain codes. Weight can be used for various purposes; here denoting the strength of certain feelings (e.g. scepticism) expressed within individual coded segments.

Similar functionality is available in MAXQDA.

Figure 13.5 Easy access interrogation using the Chart Selector (Dedoose)

Code co-occurrences explore relationships among codes and similarity among cases on the basis of proximity and co-occurrence. Tables are easily created and various other visualisations are available, such as cluster analysis, multidimensional scaling, and proximity plots.

Coding sequences can be used to identify recurring sequences of codes. This is an impressive feature which is exploratory in that it produces sequencing pairs; you do not have to proactively decide for yourself what combinations to look for. It can produce frequency lists of all sequences involving two selected sets of codes as well as the percentage of time one code follows or is followed by another one (Figure 13.3; p. 308).

BOX 13.7 — ANALYTIC NOTES

The importance of framing the questions properly

Lyn Richards, co-founder of NUD*IST, and then NVivo, and the author of many methods textbooks, provides much real-world advice to researchers engaged in qualitative projects making sense out of coding queries:

> Both coding searches and text searches are of course mechanical processes. Like all mechanical techniques, they do not directly support interpretative processes, and they will never substitute for those. You need constantly to ask whether the search you can send the software to do is addressing the question your analysis raised, what the results will mean and how you can use those results so that your question is addressed. ...
>
> At first (and may be later) you will be helped by writing out the questions and searches and noting when one fits the other and when it doesn't. Never lose the habit of first framing the ordinary language question, then asking how adequately (given your categories, your coding and the search tools) you can ask it by a coding search. That habit allows you to picture clearly what the search is doing and what it can contribute. (Richards, 2009: 157, 161).

Coding queries

Coding queries are all about interrogating the way you have previously coded. They vary in complexity. Some provide summary-type overviews contributing to descriptive analysis. Others are more focused on qualitative representations. In all software packages they can be used as a means of generating more coding, testing hunches, checking consistency in previous coding, and establishing 'results' that contribute to your interpretation.

The typical bases of coding queries

Typically coding queries employ Boolean (e.g. AND, OR, NOT) and proximity (e.g. NEAR, FOLLOWED BY, PRECEDED BY) operators to enable you to search for the relative positions of codes as they have been applied to data. Results rely on the coding work you have already performed. There are many different reasons for these types of query, including:

- combining codes to represent broader categories (OR operator);
- finding where codes occur together in the data (AND or WITHIN operators);
- finding where codes overlap or occur near to each other in the data (CO-OCCUR or OVERLAPS operator);
- finding where certain codes occur in a particular sequence (FOLLOWED BY or PRECEDED BY operators);
- finding data not coded by a particular code (NOT operator).

There is usually an element of difficulty in building such queries. The dialogue boxes and the architecture behind them vary. We can only repeat that no damage can come to your software project through building and running a query. Just practise them in small ways to ask questions you know the answers to. Figure 13.6 shows three common types of coding query, using illustrations from MAXQDA.

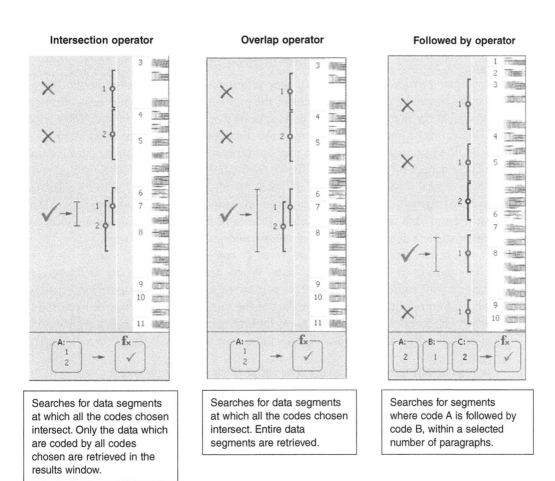

Intersection operator

Overlap operator

Followed by operator

Searches for data segments at which all the codes chosen intersect. Only the data which are coded by all codes chosen are retrieved in the results window.

Searches for data segments at which all the codes chosen intersect. Entire data segments are retrieved.

Searches for segments where code A is followed by code B, within a selected number of paragraphs.

Figure 13.6 Examples of query operators and bases of data segment retrieval (MAXQDA)

Incremental work to combine queries; special devices

Most packages enable more complex queries to be built in incremental ways. You can also the save the way the query is built for rerunning. While the results of the initial query might answer one question, if you code the results they can be fed into another query. In HyperRESEARCH everything you do is based on the incremental selection available via 'case cards'. What is visible there will be based on a series of simple selections to produce ever more focused retrieval. The closest thing to a 'query tool' is the theory tester used to create sequenced, structured questions to test (in multiple stages) the presence or absence of various conditions within cases according to previous coding (Figure 13.2; p. 308). Also illustrated in Figure 13.2 is the ATLAS.ti Super-code tool discussed earlier, which allows old queries (and their results) to be built into new, updated queries. Once a query is performed that you think might be useful again, turn the query into a super-code and it becomes a special clickable code, listed in the coding scheme with a special icon where it will always rerun the query on up-to-date data whenever you double-click on it in the codes list.

Qualitative cross-tabulations

Software provides summary frequency information concerning the application of coding across the dataset. This includes the prevalence of individual code applications as well as the number of times a code appears in a particular document. These more basic forms of frequency information are discussed in Chapter 8. In addition, most CAQDAS packages enable you to pick out various types of association across (subsets of) the dataset by generating qualitative cross-tabulations. Some of these are achieved in piecemeal ways using coding queries. Some of them are achieved using particular types of matrix query. Although the latter are easier to achieve in some packages than others and each tabulates information differently, they all allow you to overview different aspects of your project in certain numeric, or quantitative, ways.

Cross-tabulations are powerful ways to combine qualitative coding with the more descriptive organisation of data. Where these tables are interactively connected with source data, they allow you to see summary (frequency) information and the corresponding qualitative data at the same time. Tables can be exported to other applications or printed. Reasons for interrogating data through the creation of qualitative cross-tabulations might include:

- listing data files in which a code occurs at all (simple presence/absence);
- finding out how many times a code has been applied within data file (an indicator of frequency);
- finding out how much data has been coded at a particular code within a data file (an indicator of volume);
- viewing the number of times certain subsets of data or respondents have been coded in certain respects (fact-based comparison);
- constructing a 'global' matrix that provides an overview of the application of codes in relation to other codes (co-occurrence of coding).

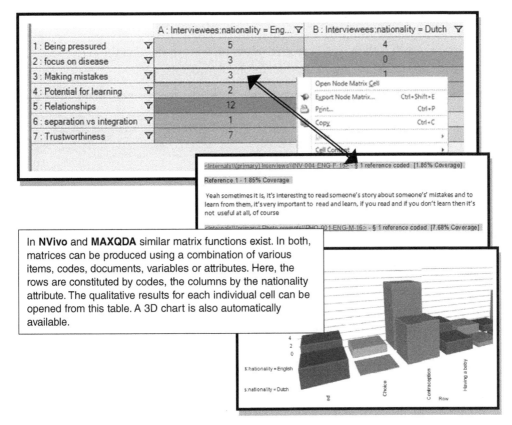

Figure 13.7 Coding matrix query, tables, charts and qualitative data (NVivo)

Visualising results

There are many different ways that CAQDAS packages can present the results of your interrogations. Interrogation in this context does not only mean via proactively created queries. Recall that interrogations also occur just by looking at readily available background information. We differentiate these since making 'queries' involves a building process. Readily available information does not. Here we distinguish between tables and matrices, and charts and graphs, highlighting and reflecting on some of the variety in how different software packages enable you to visualise the results of queries and, where relevant, how these fit in with the addition of mixed methods dimensions in qualitative research.

Tables and matrices

Tables and matrices may have connections with improved mixed methods support within qualitative software, but tables can also be simply summarised views of aspects of qualitative work, and as such they help to tidy up a proliferation of ideas.

Matrices are rather more complex, in that they provide, initially at least, a tabular sense of the relationship between multiple different aspects of work. Like tables, when they work well they are interactively connected to the text they are about and therefore comprise an important dimension of work.

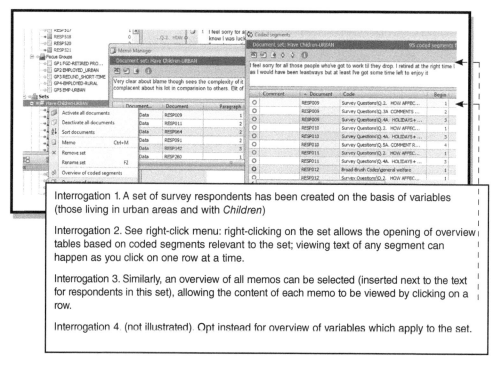

Interrogation 1. A set of survey respondents has been created on the basis of variables (those living in urban areas and with *Children*)

Interrogation 2. See right-click menu: right-clicking on the set allows the opening of overview tables based on coded segments relevant to the set; viewing text of any segment can happen as you click on one row at a time.

Interrogation 3. Similarly, an overview of all memos can be selected (inserted next to the text for respondents in this set), allowing the content of each memo to be viewed by clicking on a row.

Interrogation 4. (not illustrated). Opt instead for overview of variables which apply to the set.

FIGURE 13.8 Interactive tables for multiple aspects of interrogation (MAXQDA)

Tables

Interactive tables are nearly always means to see what you have achieved so far; they are a strong element of particular packages, and are at their best when they are just there waiting for you to access through the correct menu option. MAXQDA excels at presenting alternative such views. Lists of all coded segments or overviews of code frequencies can all be based on the filters you wish to apply. Tables about coded data for one document, a set of documents, activated codes, activated documents, all memos, memos linked to particular codes, summary grids –the are many variations in the way that tables that can be viewed in MAXQDA, yet at no point do the tables detract from the qualitative dimension since these tables are ways to access and interrogate work you have done before (Figure 13.8; above). QDA Miner also puts practically every qualitative search or query result into an interactive table where further coding can be applied on a row-by-row basis (Figure 13.3; p. 312). The level of interactivity to other dimensions is important in terms of interrogation. In ATLAS. ti for instance, the Codes Manager list provides normal frequency information, but also reminds you that some codes have been linked a number of times to other codes. Right-clicking at that point can open up a network so that you can check what type of links you have made and what items the code is linked to. In NVivo some summary information concerning the application of codes across the dataset is provided in the main codes list.

Matrices

Matrices are a way of displaying the results of queries or a current status, where multiple qualitative cross-tabulations are being performed at the same time. In fact similar outcomes can happen without matrices – but they are a resource to go back to again and again to pull out qualitative data 'behind' a particular cell. They can be developed out of combinations of codes by variables, codes by codes, or codes by documents/cases, and in terms of varied and more qualitative uses are particularly well supported in MAXQDA and NVivo.

BOX 13.8 — CASE NOTES

Exploring difference (Case Study A, Young People's Perceptions)

In Case Study A we could produce a relatively simple matrix with just one code, for example 'Making mistakes', across respondents' categorised by country variables (England and Wales and the Netherlands) to produce a summarised result in an interactive one-row, two-column table. This allowed us to focus on 'difference'. We created resources from which to compare across nationality for each code as we began to bring together an account of the way 'learning' appeared to have worked well in some situations and not so well in others and how 'Making mistakes' either contributed to that process or by contrast occurred, in spite of sex education. Expanding it in Figure 13.7, we complicated the query by including key elements from other codes to explore the relationship by nationality in other aspects where we felt influences on young people might have affected the efficacy of sex education. In both MAXQDA and NVivo, double-clicking on a cell will open the qualitative data for that cell, as illustrated for 'Making mistakes' and 'English'. We had to be sure that in doing such a query we could rely on the coding and organisational work done earlier. It was important to make sure that the variables assigned to data (Chapter 12) were correct, so that all aspects of the results could be relied on.

There are sometimes more outcomes to choose from in terms of the numeric content displayed in matrices. In NVivo, for example, the count can be varied from number of coded passages, to percentages (by row or column), to number of words, respondents or cases coded. These various measurements can be revealing. Differences in analytic approach benefit from different ways of counting. The qualitative data sitting behind each cell remains the same however they are counted. In MAXQDA matrix information is just 'there' waiting to be viewed, but the simpler execution comes with fewer optional outcomes in numeric display terms. The software programs with more mixed methods emphasis, Dedoose and QDA Miner, provide matrix-type displays which, in places, have less interactivity with underlying qualitative data, but have many more quantitative-based analytic options. Matrices and tables, wherever available, can be exported to other applications such as Excel.

Charts and graphs

Charts take various forms. Sometimes they are fairly standard quantitative visual presentations which both reinforce and reflect the idea that mixed methods dimensions are increasingly incorporated in qualitative research design. Sometimes, though, they have little to do with mixed methods and are much more about seeing the profile and proportionality of qualitative coding within a document or across several. They are nearly always about interrogation.

Charts are often available via 'wizards' offering a range of different starting points (Figures 13.5; p. 319 and 13.7; p. 323). They might additionally be enabled (as in QDA Miner) following queries or 'analyses' which have generated qualitative data. Almost everything you do in terms of queries or analyses can ultimately be viewed in different chart formats in QDA Miner or Dedoose (Figures 13.1; p. 306 and 13.5; p. 319). Data represented in them are then reduced to quantitative or quasi-quantitative presentations. Charts can summarise the breakdown of coding or content; they are too numerous to describe in detail, but it is worth mentioning that those providing charting on the basis of content usually also enable a combination of content analysis filtered to codes. In NVivo these are basic cluster analysis tools; in QDA Miner they encompass a wide range of alternative calculations about content to produce many different types of chart and breakdowns (Figure 13.1; p. 306). We use the term 'quasi-quantitative' since if your project is qualitative and data have not been sampled as would be the case in a quantitative project, the charts represent coding only; they cannot be used in a confirmatory, statistical sense. The chart may be good for stepping back and producing an overview of spikes and gaps (meriting further attention within the data) but they cannot necessarily produce numbers or data that can be used conclusively as evidence to prove an argument. They can be used to support an argument and can no doubt add polish to a presentation or article, but they need to be interpreted in the right context. At the other end of the scale, if they have been produced from, for example, a very large representative dataset and the physical content is being counted and charted, this is more likely to be conclusively useful if the research design and philosophy support that approach.

MAXQDA and Transana produce a different style of chart providing coloured profiles and comparisons of coding occurrence in one or several data files. The ability to colour codes logically can be used to create interactive portraits and profiles (Figures 13.9; p. 327 and 8.5; p. 201) which we used to chart the relative position codes based on different dimensions of video analysis in Case Study C. They allow an overview of selected codes but the mapping of them in coloured blocks to illustrate

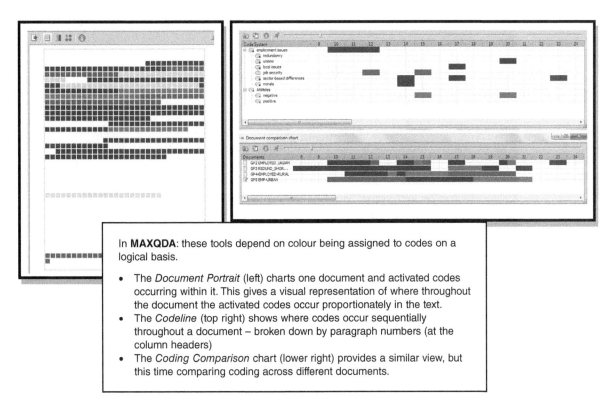

In **MAXQDA**: these tools depend on colour being assigned to codes on a logical basis.

- The *Document Portrait* (left) charts one document and activated codes occurring within it. This gives a visual representation of where throughout the document the activated codes occur proportionately in the text.
- The *Codeline* (top right) shows where codes occur sequentially throughout a document – broken down by paragraph numbers (at the column headers)
- The *Coding Comparison* chart (lower right) provides a similar view, but this time comparing coding across different documents.

FIGURE 13.9 Portraits and comparative profiles (MAXQDA)

where they occur provides an extra dimension in which to review the work done on data. Such profiles might also be useful for comparing the processes and broad interactions in a set of meetings or group interviews.

Concluding remarks: interrogation functionality in CAQDAS packages

The processes discussed in Chapter 8 in relation to retrieval options contribute to determining what might be of importance thematically, and much can be done to optimise retrieval in relatively simple ways. Query tools allow you to delve deeper to more consistently identify patterns. Queries – and interrogation in general – are where many elements of work and structures are brought together. As such, the tasks of retrieving, querying and refining codes and their position in relation to one another within the software often occur concurrently. Purely qualitative work can be enhanced where relevant by combining with descriptive or quantitative variables, and further than that, an increased emphasis on mixed methods is reflected in this relatively wide selection of software tools. These dimensions in most of the packages will continue to be enhanced.

While there are many similarities in the types of interrogation that can be facilitated by CAQDAS packages, there are also many differences. Some of these are quite subtle, while others are more significant in terms of both the sophistication of options and the ease with which results can be generated. It is not within the scope of this book to describe and discuss all the variations, but we have focused in this chapter on the types we consider important to your understanding of the way packages function and to highlight tools which are particularly useful or distinctive. Experiment with them in small ways, then in more complex ways to improve confidence in them. We have not included a separate chapter on reporting and outputting, but have mentioned at various points throughout the book how various forms of output can be generated. Much searching will be tentative and exploratory, but as you progress there will be a need to formalise your interpretations for a final report. Refer to Chapter 10 for a discussion of writing, and think reflexively about how retrieval of earlier writing can usefully be integrated with output of the evidence supporting your interpretation.

CHAPTER EXERCISES

This chapter has covered some of the many ways of interrogating data in order to establish findings. We have discussed how interrogating the dataset enables you to identify, compare and test data and results. This chapter concentrates on the query tools which retrieve data based on earlier organisational and analytical work, rather than on searching for content or structures inherent within data (these are discussed in Chapters 6, 7 and 12). CAQDAS packages vary significantly in the range of interrogation tools they provide, the types of question they can be used to answer, the way results are visualised and how easy it is to start using them.

Some packages provide simple ways of interrogating, which are often adequate for the needs of many projects. Other packages provide many more and varied types of query, options for specifying them and alternative visualisations in the way results can be presented. Some are explicitly rooted in particular analytic traditions. These can often be useful whatever your approach, although their use must be carefully thought through as some types of interrogation are not appropriate for all types and amounts of data. It is not possible to discuss the full range of interrogation options provided by each package in this chapter or to list each here as exercises; there are simply too many options. The developer website and user manual for your chosen software are the best places to get this detailed information. Here we provide an overview of the types of interrogation that are useful to be aware of and experiment with in designing your strategy for using your chosen software. The chapter exercises are relatively generic, presenting options for you to consider in the context of your own research design. Refer to the **companion website** for detailed instructions for using your chosen software. You can experiment with any of the case-study example materials.

Code searching for patterns, relationships and anomalies

Searching for the relative positions of codes as you have previously applied them to data can be done in several ways, often leading you to recode data (see Chapter 8) and refine coding schemes (see Chapter 9) as the results add another layer to your thinking.

Standard code searching options (available in most packages)

1. *Code frequencies* (see also Chapter 8). Experiment with the different ways of listing codes and the frequency with which they have been applied across the dataset in your chosen software.

    (a) The options for displaying this information vary quite a lot (particularly in terms of the amount and type of quantitative and statistical information provided).

    (b) Nevertheless, reviewing coded data in summary frequency format provides the sort of overview that illustrates basic 'gaps and clusters' in coding that will usefully constitute the basis for more in-depth queries for patterns and relationships.

2. *Boolean queries.* Experiment with operators such as AND, OR, NOT to retrieve data based on combinations of presence in data.

3. *Proximity queries.* Where these are available, experiment with operators such as NEAR, FOLLOWED BY, PRECEDED BY (or similar terms) which retrieve data based on codes having been applied near to one another within data files – but not necessarily overlapping. Usually it is possible to specify how near to one another codes need to be applied in order to satisfy the query and thus be retrieved (options include within the same paragraph or other recognisable unit of context).

Some additional code searching options (available only in some packages)

4. *Retrieving data segments based on weight assignation.* If using MAXQDA or Dedoose, both of which allow individual coded data segments to be attributed weight (indicating how important a data segment is, or the strength of the attitude expressed at that point, as an indicator of the code or theme), experiment with retrieving on this basis.

    (a) Weight needs to have been applied consistently and meaningfully, but this type of working is particularly useful when doing attitudinal-type analysis.

    (b) Experiment with the qualitative and quantitative presentation of retrievals and consider how they contribute to your thinking about the strength of attitude expressed.

5. *Semantic queries.* ATLAS.ti enables the retrieval of data segments based on the links (relationships) between codes that have previously been applied. This is relevant for those types of links that are hierarchical ('transitive') rather than more loosely associative. The operators SUB, UP and DOWN enable data segments to be retrieved based on the nature of the relationship assigned between the codes to which they are linked.

6. *Code sequence queries.* If using QDA Miner, experiment with retrieving data segments based on the sequences in which codes have been applied. This takes proximity querying to another level as the user does not need to specify the codes of interest; the software will analyse the dataset and generate pairs of codes which frequently occur in a particular sequence. You can specify the minimum and maximum distance within which codes need to occur to be retrieved and there are several ways to vary the display and output of results.

7. *Code similarity.* If using QDA Miner, experiment with the options during the early stage of coding as this tool is designed to identify as yet uncoded textual data containing similarities with existing coded data segments. It is useful for checking omissions and thus improving consistency in coding.

8. *Searching for content or language use within bodies of coded data.*

(a) If using NVivo, experiment with compound queries, which (among other things) allow for a text search query to be carried out on data already coded in a particular way.

(b) QDA Miner has similar functionality in its text retrieval functions, which can be investigated in more sophisticated ways using the WordStat add-on module.

(c) QDA Miner includes the Query by Example tool which compares a selection of text (perhaps a sentence or paragraph) you have identified as interesting or indicative of some concept, with other text, and retrieves similar passages. You then accept or reject the finds and search again, thereby incrementally 'teaching' the software to retrieve text based on meaningful patterns.

Making comparisons and investigating co-occurrence

Most CAQDAS packages enable matrices to be constructed which make comparisons according to the rows and columns they are made up of. This is often used as a means of making comparisons across subsets of data, within cases and to investigate co-occurrences in coding. Some packages require matrix queries to be constructed using the query tool, others provide the functionality in more readily accessible formats.

1. *Comparing across subsets of data.*

    (a) Experiment with building tables (matrices) that allow you to see how certain codes occur according to the socio-demographic characteristics of individual respondents.

    (b) Experiment with building matrices to investigate how individual data files have been coded in certain, similar respects.

2. *Making comparisons within cases.* Experiment with using query tools to pick out and compare how all the data pertaining to a particular case has been coded in a particular respect.

3. *Picking out co-occurrence with matrices.* Experiment with building matrices in which codes are present on both axes (e.g. as rows and columns). This will show patterns of co-occurrence according to how codes have been applied to data segments across the whole dataset (or parts of it – see the scoping exercises below).

Scoping queries

Often queries will be run across the whole dataset, where patterns need to be established 'globally' in order, for example, **to develop generalisable themes.**

1. *Scoping based on factual characteristics.* Any query can be scoped or filtered based on the presence of an individual factual characteristic, or a combination of them. This is in addition to making simple comparisons on that basis. For example, additional dimensions can be added in this way to two-way matrices such as those described above.

2. *Scoping to short-cut groupings.* In software that allows the short-cut grouping of items as discussed in Chapter 9, these can be used as the basis of scoping queries as well as (or in combination with) other organisational devices (such as factual characteristics and more basic folders in which data are stored; see Chapter 5).

Incremental querying

1. *Using the results of queries in further queries.* The results of queries can usually be saved. Where this can be done as another level of coded data, those results can themselves be included in subsequent queries. This serves two key purposes:

    (a) Queries can be used as a means of generating bodies of coded data, thus contributing to the iterative process of organising your ideas about data through coding (see also Chapters 7–9).
    (b) Running further queries on the results of previous queries allows you to delve increasingly deeper into data and ask more complex questions (e.g. of the respondents who have x in common, how many also talk in y way?).

2. *Write about what you see.* As always, write in the writing spaces you are using within your chosen software (see Chapter 10) as you view and consider the results of any interrogation. Remember that the software is only presenting the results to you – it remains always your job to interpret them. Therefore, get into the good habit early on of always writing about why you are running certain queries (what prompted you to ask this particular question?) and what you are seeing in the results (is this what you expected to see? what does it tell you? what are you going to do next?).

Creating signposts from queries

Interrogating data using query tools is not only about establishing results towards the latter part of a study. When involved in processes such as data exploration and coding, for example, you will see some interesting patterns or think about certain questions that will need to be followed up later. Indeed, based on your research questions, there will be certain questions framing the way you are working with data right from the outset. Building and saving queries in order to rerun at a later stage is one way in which you can create 'signposts' that act as reminders of areas to focus on later.

Interrogating in maps (only available in some packages)

Not all CAQDAS packages provide mapping tools, and those that exist vary significantly (see Chapter 11). Some integrate mapping tools with the principles of interrogation more fully than others. If working with one of these tools, experiment with how exploring connections visually adds to your thinking and offers alternative ways of presenting results.

1. *Viewing coding presence.* Visualise a particular data file within a map and ask to see all the codes that appear within it.
2. *Retrieving and working with coded data segments.* Visualise a particular code within a map and ask to see all the data segments that are linked to it. This is a basic retrieval activity, and packages that enable this also enable those data segments to be sorted, grouped and recoded from within the map (see Chapter 8) and those data segments to be linked to other data segments (see Chapters 6 and 11).
3. *Visualising co-occurrence in coding.* Visualise a broad (or particularly important) code within a map and ask to see co-occurring codes. This lists all the other codes that are linked to data segments which co-occur with those coded at the first code, across the whole dataset.

Selected additional interrogations and visualisations

There are many additional ways of interrogating data and visualising the results. We cannot discuss or list all of them here, but some are unique within a particular software package, or provide particularly novel ways of representing the results of interrogations. Many of these tools are found in the packages which are explicitly informed by quantitative (i.e. content analysis or text mining) or mixed methods approaches to the analysis of qualitative data. At the time of writing, of the packages we discuss in detail in this book, these are principally QDA Miner (with or without WordStat and SimStat), Dedoose and MAXQDA. Refer to the developer websites and the companion website for more information.

Outputting results of interrogations

The result of any query can usually be outputted in a number of ways (see also Chapters 6–12 which discuss output in the context of specific analytic processes and software tasks).

1. *Outputting qualitative results.*

    (a) Any selection of data from anywhere in the software project can be copied and pasted into other applications. This is quick and easy, but often does not take with it the associated meta-information (such as the name and other attributes about the data file from which it derives).
    (b) Using specific export, output or reporting functionality usually provides many more options for specifying exactly what to include in the output. This might include, for example, any annotations or other content linked to retrieved data segments, associated summary information and definitions.

2. *Outputting quantitative results.* Usually any list or table generated by a software package can be outputted, viewed and further manipulated in a spreadsheet or statistical application.
3. *Creating snapshots as graphics.*

    (a) Maps and other visualisations can usually be saved as graphics files (JPEG, PNG, TIF, etc.), which can then be used in presentations and reports.
    (b) You can also use the 'print screen' key on your keyboard to create a quick snapshot of an aspect of your work at any stage.

4. *Outputting to HTML* is particularly useful for sharing data and analysis with colleagues or supervisors who are not conversant with your chosen software.

14

Convergence, Closeness, Choice

Throughout this book we have pointed to differences among CAQDAS packages, highlighted considerations in planning for software use and offered some ideas about working with the packages. Issues raised by the case-study examples are common to many situations. We refer to them at strategic moments to illustrate some of the successes and predicaments encountered in day-to-day work. They demonstrate how researchers in different contexts manipulate software to suit their needs, selectively and critically using tools to develop analytic strategies. In this chapter we bring together strands which have permeated throughout to re-emphasise a number of aspects: the need to plan for the use of software; the sense in which a software package can be a container for your work; how software can bring you closer to data on a number of levels; how techniques of data analysis are changing; and how important it is to work with software in a focused and effective way.

Planning for the use of software

Working as an individual and working in a team raise different issues in terms of using software. Team projects are more complicated and rely heavily on the organisational aspects of CAQDAS packages as well as the dynamics of the team. They also require more planning. There is information about teamwork on the companion website and detailed support for designing collaborative projects and working in teams using different software packages on the CAQDAS Networking Project website.[1]

Researchers working individually have more choices and can allow the ways they work with software tools to evolve more organically. However, they may feel isolated and in need of local support which is not always available. Interviews collected

---

[1]http://www.surrey.ac.uk/sociology/research/researchcentres/caqdas/

as part of the 'Online support for QDA and CAQDAS' project[2] and 'Qualitative Innovations in CAQDAS'[3] strongly confirm gaps in local support. Though the CAQDAS Networking Project is often called upon to help, researchers want to be self-reliant and often do not like to 'keep asking for help'.

The rationale of this book, and the philosophy behind the CAQDAS Networking Project, is to supplement gaps in support which were the natural consequence of new technologies emerging during a period when qualitative projects, and qualitative elements in broader research studies, were increasing in number. The project itself has contributed to a significant growth in the numbers of expert users, but it remains challenging to convert this into institutional support on a local basis.

Whatever the characteristics of your project the use of software to facilitate your management of it require careful planning. Qualitative research design is emergent and the range of tools provided by these packages offer flexibility to customise to the specific needs of different designs.

Convergence of tasks and tools:
software as a container for your work

In writing this book we encountered a number of challenges. Our aim was twofold: first, to demystify the field of qualitative software by illustrating the range of packages and tools currently on the market; and second, to illustrate ways in which using software can reflect and enhance the cyclical and iterative process of doing analysis. What we found, as we wrote the chapters, was that separating tasks creates artificial differentiations. What we actually do when handling qualitative data in software is to shuffle between panes, multitasking with different tools. In a typical five-minute period we might slip from carefully reading, marking and coding data to using fast exploration tools in order to find similar occurrences of a particular word or phrase, to reviewing what has been coded so far, to annotating and linking what we see. We jot down insights, references to other work and reminders for follow-up action. It is rare that reasoning processes happen in a linear and orderly way, and CAQDAS packages certainly free us from having to be linear. The analytic activities of integrating, exploring, organising, interrogating and reflecting upon data (Figure 2.1; p. 45),and their convergence within the software container represent the key benefits of using customised CAQDAS packages. This does not happen by chance, however, and it can be difficult to work out how to combine tools effectively to achieve analytic aims. We have cross-referenced frequently between tasks to enable and encourage the meshing of different aspects of work.

---

[2]Funded by the UK Economic and Social Research Council: see http://onlineqda.hud.ac/

[3]Funded by the National Centre for Research Methods: see http://www.surrey.ac.uk/sociology/research/researchcentres/caqdas/quic/index.htm

Closeness to data: inside software and outside it

We alluded to scepticism concerning CAQDAS use in supporting qualitative data analysis (Chapter 1). We understand such concerns, but it is also important to challenge the idea that CAQDAS packages 'take the researcher away from the data'. This was raised when these packages first became commercially available and, despite subsequent developments, such concerns persist in some quarters. Fielding and Lee (1998), in their study of CAQDAS users, found some researchers felt closer to their data when working more 'manually'. The feeling is that using a computer will put an artificial barrier between the researcher and the data. Reluctance to change from carefully developed routines and systems is understandable. However, software programs have improved beyond the expectations of early users. In terms of data themselves, the increased range of formats directly handled by and the improvements in types and presentations of output make conceptual work easier. Key advances in memoing and mapping tools, basic retrieval options and searching/ querying possibilities provide researchers with options that might never have been considered before. In methodological terms, researchers place different emphases on certain tools. A narrative analysis of a relatively small amount of data might only make use of annotation and memoing tools. An interpretive approach on a larger dataset might make heavy use of coding devices. A discourse analysis might place heavy emphasis on contextual content searching and pattern matching. The relative role of theory varies how codes are created and the directions of travel in the software. One way or another, software keeps us within touching distance, throughout the analysis, of the fundamentals of information and data.

A CAQDAS package can bring the researcher closer to the data in a variety of ways. This can be true when you are *inside* the software. For example, hyperlinking and annotation tools provide ways of staying close to data without abstracting from them (Chapters 6 and 10). Software can obviate the need to use highlighter pens and piles of paper whilst coding. However, the variety of output options available allows you to be very close to different combinations of data *outside* the software and *away* from the computer. Paper can still have its place in qualitative data analysis, but the computer can help to provide you with the right bits of paper! Tactile contact with printouts is a dimension of work that enables you to see, think about and annotate data in different ways. Often the most insightful thoughts occur at unexpected times, away from the computer, and away from the data.

Changing techniques of data analysis

Ways to work with qualitative data have substantially changed with the improved access to data that software provides. The potential of CAQDAS packages to impact on the way qualitative analysis happens has been debated for many years. It is clear that many of the tools we discuss in this book allow interrogation to a level which is not possible without using a customised CAQDAS package. Indeed, it is through the use of these tools that the potential for changing the techniques of analysis, and the purposes to which they can be put, is greatest.

Analytic tasks can be integrated and methodological boundaries stretched by using tools in flexible and innovative ways. Conversely, if you are adhering to an established set of analytic procedures, then a more limited use of tools can also support specific analytic tasks effectively. From the beginning issues concerning the relationship between technology and methodology that the use of these tools raises have been pertinent. As technology continues to develop at an unprecedented pace, and the pressures of competing for market share among the businesses which typically develop the tools increase, these issues remain important. Alongside these are continuing developments in methodology which cannot be played out to the exclusion of technology. There are no easy or universal solutions to these issues, notwithstanding the fact that technology is here to stay and that to resist its role entirely is becoming an increasingly untenable position. That said, technology should always be embraced in the context of the methodological and practical needs of a given project. In Silver and Lewins (forthcoming) we discuss this in broad terms by considering the state of technological support for qualitative research generally, including discussion of technological assistance in three realms of qualitative work: data collection, preparation and/or transcription; bibliographic management and systematic literature reviews; and data management and analysis. In that publication, we discuss limitations and constraints relating to the use of CAQDAS packages in terms of: an underestimation of the time involved; an overreliance on software (in terms of its being seen as a short-cut to analysis, or conversely, that using software results in one becoming a 'slave to the computer'); the increasing complexity and proliferation of tools; and the potential for confused analytic strategy. Here we do so in specific relation to automation, quantitisation and mixing methods and in terms of tools for visual analysis.

Automation, quantitisation and mixing methods

Some tools have more potential to change the face of how qualitative data analysis is conducted than others. These include auto-coding processes that search for and code verbatim content (Chapters 6 and 13). John Seidel, himself one of the early pioneers of software development (The Ethnograph), was concerned that computer technology would lead to a sacrifice of 'resolution' in favour of 'scope'. His essays and thoughtful software manual recount how hours of in-depth examination of small sections of data revealed phenomena in midwifery care which would have been missed by faster methods of exploration and identification. He saw the value of analysis coming from careful immersion in relatively small qualitative datasets, and was concerned that this would be lost in the face of software developments which allow shallower exploration on larger and larger datasets (Seidel, 1991). These concerns were reflected in the absence of text searching tools in his own software. Conversely, Richards and Richards (1994), who were actively responsible for including such tools in early versions of NUD*IST, felt that text search functions were 'a necessary tool for gaining direct access to records rather than accessing them only through codes expressing the researcher's interpretation'. Weaver and Atkinson (1995) say something similar in describing the uses of text search tools 'as a useful means of checking the validity of analyses shaped by other strategies such as the coded segments strategy in interpretive research, or in the triangulation of methods'. Fisher (1997) stresses the slightly different efficiency dimension, suggesting that searching can counteract human failings by revealing possible 'aberrant cases', thereby ensuring that 'analysis is as comprehensive as possible'. These contrasting views are useful because they emphasise the value of two dimensions of work in qualitative data, while alerting us to the potential shortcomings of both.

Our own view is that the mechanistic text search tools with auto-coding options available in CAQDAS packages can increase reflexivity and help to plough through a mass of data. To reverse the metaphor, however, when you are working in an interpretive way, the results only skim the surface of the data. It goes without saying that your data might refer richly to topics without ever using the keywords you search for. If such tools are overused in an interpretive approach to the exclusion of other more careful work in the data, it is possible that the nature and purposes of some types of qualitative data analysis are being undervalued or misunderstood.

The development of CAQDAS packages since the turn of the twenty-first century has seen a much greater proliferation of ways of summarising qualitative data and their analysis quantitatively. This is seen across the spectrum of interrogation possibilities, from the types of simple frequency information based on code application that can be provided (Chapter 8), to the integration of functionality inspired by text-mining techniques with the qualitative analysis of texts (Chapter 6), and an increasing number of tools available specifically designed with mixed methods analyses in mind (Chapter 1 and 13). However, it will not always be appropriate to work in these ways, and therefore such tools need to be applied with caution. That said, specific tools designed for mixed methods analysis also have the potential to play an important role in the continued growth of the methodological field. There is much literature discussing mixed methods in terms of research design, but far less discussing the contributions to mixed analytic techniques provided by CAQDAS packages; as such the technology is leading the methodological literature at this time. The next years will bring continued changes, not least in this area.

Visual and social media analysis

A key developmental area since the publication of the first edition of this book is support for visual and social media analysis. More packages now incorporate the ability to handle still and moving images, and there is a move towards direct incorporation of internet-harvested material, including social media content. With respect to the former, there remains significant variability in the field – in terms of both what individual CAQDAS packages provide and other software applications. The multidimensionality of visual data raises a whole host of additional considerations when planning a project and undertaking data analysis. We have discussed some of these throughout the book. Elsewhere we have commented on the need for finer tools for visual analysis, suggesting that the tools developed for the analysis of text are often too blunt for the purposes of visual content (Silver and Patashnick, 2011). Even since then there have been some exciting developments, the most significant of which is Transana's ability to visually annotate still images and retrieve them like codes. No doubt there will be other developments in this area over coming years.

Social media analysis is a particularly fast developing field. The ability of some CAQDAS packages to incorporate social media content has a number of implications, but there are also a host of other applications and web-based tools for conducting social media analysis almost instantaneously. It remains to be seen how the field of CAQDAS adapts to the growing interest among academic and applied researchers in incorporating these types of materials into their research projects, and the extent to which other developments impact on this.

Focused effective use of software

We often see researchers using software in very innovative and sophisticated ways. However, we also frequently see projects in which relatively few tools are used, but to great effect. Researchers sometimes worry that they are not using software to its 'full potential', and that this somehow means their analysis is falling short of what is expected. We made the point in Chapter 1 that the use of software can conventionalise data and assumptions about how they should be analysed. We challenge the idea that there is *one* ideal way of using any CAQDAS package. Such ideas undervalue the usefulness of the software and the ability of the user to make discerning choices. Our central message is that *you* should determine what is useful. There will be ways to do things differently, and tools which you have yet to use. Almost every time we use and teach a package we see an alternative way of using a tool, or learn something new. Experimentation is what makes it fun.

References

Abrahamson, M. (1983) *Social Research Methods*. Englewood Cliffs, NJ: Prentice Hall.

Ackermann, F., Eden, C. and Cropper, S. (1992) Getting started with cognitive mapping. In *Proceedings of the 7th Young Operational Research Conference* (pp. 65–82). University of Warwick.

Angen, M. J. (2000) Evaluating interpretive inquiry: Reviewing the validity debate and opening the dialogue. *Qualitative Health Research*, 10(3), 378–395.

Atkinson, J. M. and Heritage, J. (1984) *Structures of Social Action: Studies in Conversation Analysis*. Cambridge: Cambridge University Press.

Atkinson, P. (1997) Narrative turn or blind alley? *Qualitative Health Research*, 7(3), 325–344.

Attride-Stirling, J. (2001) Thematic networks: an analytic tool for qualitative research. *Qualitative Research*, 1(3), 385–405.

Bazeley, P. (2006) The contribution of computer software to integrating qualitative and quantitative data and analyses. *Research in the Schools*, 13(1), 64–74.

Bazeley, P. (2009) Editorial: Integrating data analyses in mixed methods research. *Journal of Mixed Methods Research*, 3(3), 203–207.

Bazeley, P. (2011) Integrative analysis strategies for mixed data sources. *American Behavioral Scientist*, 56(6), 814–828.

Bazeley, P. (2013) *Qualitative Data Analysis: Practical Strategies*. London: Sage.

Berg, B. (2001) *Qualitative Research Methods for the Social Sciences*. London: Allyn & Bacon.

Bergman, M. M. (2008) *Advances in Mixed Methods Research: Theories and Applications*. Los Angeles and London: Sage.

Bernard, H. R. and Ryan, G. W. (2010) *Analyzing Qualitative Data: Systematic Approaches*. Los Angeles: Sage.

Blaikie, N. W. H. (2000) *Designing Social Research: The Logic of Anticipation*. Cambridge: Polity Press.

Boolsen, M. W. (2006) *Kvalitative analyser* [*Qualitative Analysis*]. Copenhagen: Hans Reitzels Forlag.

Boyatzis, R. E. (1998) *Transforming Qualitative Information: Thematic Analysis and Code Development*. Thousand Oaks, CA: Sage.

Brannen, J. (2005) Mixed methods research: A discussion paper. ESRC National Centre for Research Methods.

Braun, V. and Clarke, V. (2006) Using thematic analysis in psychology. *Qualitative Research in Psychology*, 3(2), 77–101.

Braun, V., and Clarke, V. (2013) *Successful Qualitative Research: A Practical Guide for Beginners*. Thousand Oaks, CA: Sage.

Bryant, A. and Charmaz, K. (2007) *The SAGE Handbook of Grounded Theory*. Los Angeles and London: Sage.

Bryman, A. (2001) *Social Research Methods*. Oxford: Oxford University Press.

Bryman, A. (2008) *Social Research Methods*. Oxford; New York: Oxford University Press.

Bryman, A. and Burgess, R. G. (1994) *Analyzing Qualitative Data*. London and New York: Routledge.

Buzan, T. (1995) *The Mind Map Book* (2nd edn). London: BBC Books.

Charmaz, K. (2000) Grounded theory: objectivist and constructionist methods. In N. K. Denzin and S. Lincoln (eds), *Handbook of Qualitative Research* (2nd edn). Thousand Oaks, CA: Sage.

Charmaz, K. (2006) *Constructing Grounded Theory: A Practical Guide through Qualitative Analysis*. London and Thousand Oaks, CA: Sage.

Coffey, A., Holbrook, B. and Atkinson, P. (1996) Coffey, Holbrook, and Atkinson: Qualitative data analysis: Technologies and representations. *Sociological Research Online*, 1(1). Retrieved from http://www.socresonline.org.uk/1/1/4.html

Creswell, J. W. (1998) *Qualitative Inquiry and Research Design: Choosing among Five Traditions*. Thousand Oaks, CA: Sage.

Creswell, J. W. (2003) *Research Design: Qualitative, Quantitative, and Mixed Method Approaches* (2nd edn). Thousand Oaks, CA: Sage.

Creswell, J. W., Klassen, A., Plano Clark, V. and Smith, K. for the Office of Behavioral and Social Sciences Research (2011) *Best Practices for Mixed Methods Research in the Health Sciences*. National Institutes of Health. Retrieved from http://obssr.od.nih.gov/mixed_methods_research

Daiute, C. and Lightfoot, C. (2004) *Narrative Analysis: Studying the Development of Individuals in Society*. Thousand Oaks, CA: Sage.

Denzin, N. K. and Lincoln, Y. S. (eds) (2002) *The Qualitative Inquiry Reader*. Thousand Oaks, CA: Sage.

Dey, I. (1993) *Qualitative Data Analysis: A User-Friendly Guide for Social Scientists*. London: Routledge.

Di Gregorio, S. and Davidson, J. (2008) *Qualitative Research Design for Software Users*. Maidenhead: Open University Press.

Dick, P. (2004) Discourse analysis. In C. Cassell and G. Symon (eds), *Essential Guide to Qualitative Methods in Organizational Research*. London: Sage.

Eden, C. (1988) Cognitive mapping. *European Journal of Operational Research*, 36(1), 1–13.

Eden, C. and Ackermann, F. (1998) *Strategy Making: The Journey of Strategic Management*. London: Sage.

Fenton, C. and Langley, A. (2011) Strategy as practice and the narrative turn. *Organization Studies*, 32(9), 1171–1196.

Fereday, J. and Muir-Cochrane, E. (2006) Demonstrating rigor using thematic analysis: A hybrid approach of inductive and deductive coding and theme development. *International Journal of Qualitative Methods*, 5, 1–11.

Fielding, N. (2012) Triangulation and mixed methods designs: Data integration with new research technologies. *Journal of Mixed Methods Research*, 6(2), 124–136.

Fielding, N. and Lee, R. M. (1998) *Computer Analysis and Qualitative Research*. London: Sage.

Fisher, M. (1997) *Qualitative Computing: Using Software for Qualitative Data Analysis*. Aldershot: Ashgate.

Fruber, C. (2010) Framework analysis: a method for analysing qualitative data. *African Journal of Midwifery and Women's Health*, 4(2), 97–100.

Gee, J. P. and Handford, M. (eds) (2012) *The Routledge Handbook of Discourse Analysis*. London and New York: Routledge.

Gibbs, G. (2002) *Qualitative Data Analysis: Explorations with NVivo*. Buckingham: Open University Press.

Gibbs, G. (2007) *Analysing Qualitative Data*. Thousand Oaks, CA: Sage.

Giddens, A. (1984) *The Constitution of Society: Outline of the Theory of Structuration*. Cambridge: Polity Press.

Glaser, B. G. (1978) *Theoretical Sensitivity: Advances in the Methodology of Grounded Theory*. Mill Valley, CA: Sociology Press.

Glaser, B. G. and Strauss, A. (1967) *The Discovery of Grounded Theory*. Chicago: Aldine.

Glynos, J., Howarth, D., Norval, A. and Speed, E. (2009) *Discourse Analysis: Varieties and Methods*. ESRC National Centre for Research Methods. Retrieved from http://eprints.ncrm.ac.uk/796/1/discourse_analysis_NCRM_014.pdf

Goodwin, L. D. and Goodwin, W. L. (1984) Are validity and reliability 'relevant' in qualitative evaluation research? *Evaluation and the Health Professions*, 7(4), 413–426.

Greene, J. C. (2007) *Mixed Methods in Social Inquiry*. San Francisco: Jossey-Bass.

Guba, E. G., & Lincoln, Y. S. (1981) *Effective Evaluation* (1st edn). San Francisco: Jossey-Bass Publishers.

Guba, E. G. and Lincoln, Y. S. (1994) Competing paradigms in qualitative research. In N. K. Denzin and Y. S. Lincoln (eds), *Handbook of Qualitative Research*. Thousand Oaks, CA: Sage.

Hammersley, M. (2002) Discourse analysis: A bibliographical guide. *English*, 57(12).

Hart, C. (1998) *Doing a Literature Review: Releasing the Social Science Research Imagination*. London: Sage.

Heath, C., Hindmarsh, J. and Luff, P. (2010) *Video in Qualitative Research: Analysing Social Interaction in Everyday Life*. Los Angeles: Sage.

Hesse-Biber, S. (2010) Emerging methodologies and methods practices in the field of mixed methods research. *Qualitative Inquiry*, 16(6), 415–418.

Hindmarsh, J. (2008) Distributed video analysis in social research. In N. G. Fielding, R. M. Lee and G. Blank (eds), *The SAGE Handbook of Online Research Methods* (pp. 343–361). London: Sage.

Holsti, O. R. (1969) *Content Analysis for the Social Sciences and Humanities*. Reading, MA: Addison-Wesley.

Hutchby, I. and Wooffitt, R. (1998) *Conversation Analysis: An Introduction*. Cambridge: Polity.

Ivankova, N. and Kawamura, Y. (2010) Emerging trends in the utilization of integrated designs in the social, behavioral, and health sciences. In A. Tashakkori and C. Teddlie (eds), *SAGE Handbook of Mixed Methods in Social and Behavioral Research* (2nd edn, pp. 581–611). Thousand Oaks CA: Sage.

Johnson, R. B., Onwuegbuzie, A. J. and Turner, L. A. (2007) Toward a definition of mixed methods research. *Journal of Mixed Methods Research*, 1(2), 112–133.

Jones, E. F., Forrest, J. D., Goldman, N. et al. (1986) *Teenage Pregnancy in Industrialized Countries*. New Haven, CT: Yale University Press.

Jordan, B., and Henderson, A. (1995) Interaction analysis: Foundations and practice. *Journal of the Learning Sciences*, 4(1), 39–103.

Kelle, U. (2006) Combining qualitative and quantitative methods in research practice: purposes and advantages. *Qualitative Research in Psychology*, 3(4), 293–311.

Konecki, K. T. (2011) Visual grounded theory: A methodological outline and examples from empirical work. *Revija za sociologiju*, 41(2): 131–160. doi:10.5613/rzs.41.2.1

Kuckartz, U. (2012) Realizing Mixed Methods Approaches with MAXQDA. Unpublished. Marburg: Philipps University, Department of Education.

Layder, D. (1998) *Sociological Practice: Linking Theory and Social Research*. London: Sage.

Lee, R. M. and Fielding, N. (1996) Qualitative data analysis: Representations of a technology: A comment on Coffey, Holbrook and Atkinson. *Sociological Research Online*, 1(4). Retrieved from http://www.socresonline.org.uk/1/4/lf.html#1.1

Lewins, A. and Silver, C. (2007) *Using Software in Qualitative Research: A Step-by-Step Guide* (1st edn). London: Sage.

Lieblich, A., Tuval-Mashiach, R. and Zilber, T. (1998) *Narrative Research: Reading, Analysis and Interpretation*. Thousand Oaks, CA: Sage.

Lincoln, Y.S. & Guba, E.G. (1985) *Naturalistic Inquiry*. Newbury Park, CA: Sage.

Mason, J. (2002) *Qualitative Researching* (2nd edn). London and Thousand Oaks, CA: Sage.

Mertens, D. M. (2009) *Research and Evaluation in Education and Psychology: Integrating Diversity with Quantitative, Qualitative, and Mixed Methods*. Los Angeles: Sage.

Mertens, D. M. and Hesse-Biber, S. (2012) Triangulation and mixed methods research: Provocative positions. *Journal of Mixed Methods Research*, 6(2), 75–79.

Mertens, D. M. and Hesse-Biber, S. N. (2013) Mixed methods and credibility of evidence in evaluation. *New Directions for Evaluation*, 138, 5–13.

Miles, M. B. and Huberman, A. (1994) *Qualitative Data Analysis: An Expanded Sourcebook*. London: Sage.

Morgan, D. L. (2007) Paradigms lost and pragmatism regained: Methodological implications of combining qualitative and quantitative methods. *Journal of Mixed Methods Research*, 1(1), 48–76.

Morse, J. M., Stern, P. N., Corbin, J. M., Charmaz, K. C., Bowers, B. and Clarke, A. E. (2009) *Developing Grounded Theory: The Second Generation*. Walnut Creek, CA: Left Coast Press.

Novak, J. D. (1993) How do we learn to learn? Taking students through the process. *Science Teacher*, 60(3).

Novak, J. D. and Gowin, D. B. (1984) *Learning How to Learn*. Cambridge: Cambridge University Press.

Paulus, T., Lester, J. and Dempster, P. (2013) *Digital Tools for Qualitative Research.* Thousand Oaks, CA: Sage.

Pink, S. (2007) *Doing Visual Ethnography: Images, Media, and Representation in Research* (2nd edn). London and Thousand Oaks, CA: Sage.

Rademakers, J. (1997) Meeting the contraceptive needs of the modern woman. Presented at the Symposium at the XV FIGO World Congress of Gynaecology and Obstetrics.

Reissman, C. K. (2005) Narrative analysis. *Narrative, Memory and Everyday Life* (University of Huddersfield), 1–7.

Richards, L. (2009) *Handling Qualitative Data: A Practical Guide* (2nd edn). London: Sage.

Richards, L. and Richards, T. (1994) Using computers in qualitative research. In N. Denzin and Y. Lincoln (eds), *Handbook of Qualitative Research* (pp. 445–462). London: Sage.

Ritchie, J. and Lewis, J. (2003) *Qualitative Research Practice: A Guide for Social Science Students and Researchers.* London and Thousand Oaks, CA: Sage.

Ritchie, J., Spencer, L. and O'Connor, W. (2003) Carrying out qualitative analysis. In J. Ritchie and J. Lewis (eds.), *Qualitative Research Practice: A Guide for Social Science Students and Researchers.* London; Thousand Oaks, CA: Sage.

Saldaña, J. (2013) *The Coding Manual for Qualitative Researchers* (2nd edn). Los Angeles: Sage.

Schnettler, B. and Raab, J. (2008) Interpretative visual analysis. Developments, state of the art and pending problems. *Forum Qualitative Sozialforschung / Forum: Qualitative Social Research*, 9(3 Art 31). Retrieved from http://nbn-resolving.de/urn:nbn:de:0114-fqs0803314.

Seale, C. (1999) *The Quality of Qualitative Research.* London and Thousand Oaks, CA: Sage.

Seale, C. (2000) Using computers to analyse qualitative data. In D. Silverman (ed.), *Doing Qualitative Research: A Practical Handbook.* Los Angeles: Sage.

Seidel, J. (1991) Methods and madness in the application of computer technology to qualitative data analysis. In N. Fielding and R. M. Lee (eds), *Using Computers in Qualitative Research.* London: Sage.

Seidel, J. (1998) Qualitative data analysis. In J. Seidel, *The Ethnograph v5.0: A User's Guide* (Appendix E). Salt Lake City, UT: Qualis Research Associates.

Seidel, J. and Kelle, U. (1995) Different functions of coding in the analysis of textual data. In U. Kelle (ed.), *Computer-Aided Qualitative Data Analysis: Theory, Methods and Practice* (pp. 52–61). London: Sage.

Shaw, I. (1999) *Qualitative Evaluation.* London and Thousand Oaks, CA: Sage.

Sibert, E. and Shelly, A. (1995) Using logic programming for hypothesis generation and refinement. In U. Kelle (ed.), *Computer-Aided Qualitative Data Analysis: Theory, Methods and Practice* (pp. 113–128). London: Sage.

Silver, C. (2002) The development of school-based sex education in the Netherlands and England and Wales: culture, politics and practice. PhD thesis, University of Surrey, Guildford.

Silver, C. and Fielding, N. G. (2008) Using computer packages in qualitative research. In C. Willig and W. Stainton Rogers (eds), *The SAGE Handbook of Qualitative Research in Psychology*. Los Angeles: Sage.

Silver, C. and Lewins, A. (2010) Computer assisted qualitative data analysis. In P. Peterson, E. Baker and B. McGaw (eds), *International Encyclopedia of Education* (3rd edn, Vol. 6, pp. 326–334). Oxford: Elsevier.

Silver, C. and Lewins, A. (2013) Computer assisted analysis of qualitative research: Trends, potentials and cautions. In P. Leavy (ed.), *The Oxford Handbook of Qualitative Research Methods*. Oxford: Oxford University Press.

Silver, C., and Lewins, A. (2014) *Computer-Assisted Analysis of Qualitative Data*. Oxford: Oxford University Press.

Silver, C. and Patashnick, J. (2011) Finding fidelity: Advancing audiovisual analysis using software. *Forum Qualitative Sozialforschung / Forum: Qualitative Social Research*, 12(1). Retrieved from http://www.qualitative-research.net/index.php/fqs/article/view/1629

Silver, C. and Rivers, C. (2014) Learning from the learners: The role of technology acceptance and adoption theories in understanding researchers' early experiences with CAQDAS packages. In Friese, S. and Ringmayr, T. (eds.), *ATLAS.ti User Conference 2013: Fostering Dialog on Qualitative Methods*. Berlin: University Press, Technical University Berlin.

Silverman, D. (2000) *Doing Qualitative Research: A Practical Handbook*. Los Angeles: Sage.

Silverman, D. (2001) *Interpreting Qualitative Data: Methods for Analysing Talk, Text and Interaction*. London: Sage.

Silverman, D. (2010) *Doing Qualitative Research: A Practical Handbook*. Los Angeles: Sage.

Silverman, D. (2011) *Interpreting Qualitative Data: A Guide to the Principles of Qualitative Research*. London: Sage.

Smith, J. K. (1984) The problem of criteria for judging interpretive inquiry. *Educational Evaluation and Policy Analysis*, 6(4), 379–391.

Smith, J. K. (1990) Goodness criteria: Alternative research paradigms and the problem of criteria. In E. G. Guba (ed.), *The Paradigm Dialog* (pp. 167–187). London: Sage.

Sparkes, A. C. (2001) Myth 94: Qualitative health researchers will agree about validity. *Qualitative Health Research*, 11(4), 538–552.

Spencer, L., Ritchie, J., Lewis, J. and Dillon, L. (2003) *Quality in qualitative evaluation*. London: TSO.

Strauss, A. and Corbin, J. (1990) *Basics of Qualitative Research: Grounded Theory Procedures and Techniques*. Newbury Park, CA: Sage.

Strauss, A. and Corbin, J. (1997) *Grounded Theory in Practice*. Thousand Oaks, CA: Sage.

Strauss, A. and Corbin, J. (2008) *Basics of Qualitative Research: Techniques and Procedures for Developing Grounded Theory* (3rd edn). Los Angeles: Sage.

Tashakkori, A. and Teddlie, C. (eds) (2003) *Handbook of Mixed Methods in Social and Behavioral Research*. Thousand Oaks, CA: Sage.

Tashakkori, A. and Teddlie, C. (eds) (2010) *SAGE Handbook of Mixed Methods in Social and Behavioral Research* (2nd edn). Los Angeles: Sage.

Teddlie, C. and Tashakkori, A. (2012) Common 'core' characteristics of mixed methods research: A review of critical issues and call for greater convergence. *American Behavioral Scientist*, 56(6), 774–788.

ten Have, P. (1999) *Doing Conversation Analysis* (2nd edn). Los Angeles: Sage.

Tesch, R. (1990) *Qualitative Research: Analysis Types and Software Tools.* New York: Falmer Press.

Thomson, R. (1994) Prevention, promotion and adolescent sexuality: The politics of school sex education in England and Wales. *Sexual and Marital Therapy, Sex Education* (Special Issue), 19(2), 115–125.

Timmermans, S. and Tavory, I. (2012) Theory construction in qualitative research: From grounded theory to abductive analysis. *Sociological Theory*, 30(3), 167–186.

Vilar, D. (1994) School sex education: still a priority in Europe. *Planned Parenthood in Europe*, 23(3).

Weaver, A. and Atkinson, P. (1995) *Microcomputing and Qualitative Data Analysis.* Aldershot: Avebury.

Weitzman, E. A. and Miles, M. B. (1995) *Computer Programs for Qualitative Data Analysis: A Software Sourcebook.* Thousand Oaks, CA: Sage.

Willig, C. (2001) Introducing qualitative research in psychology: Adventures in theory and method. *Qualitative Research*, 2.

Wolcott, H. F. (1994) *Transforming Qualitative Data: Description, Analysis, and Interpretation.* Thousand Oaks, CA: Sage.

Wooffitt, R. (2005) *Conversation Analysis and Discourse Analysis: A Comparative and Critical Introduction.* London and Thousand Oaks, CA: Sage.

Woolf, N. (2014a) Analytic strategies and analytic tactics. In Friese, S. and Ringmayr, T. (eds.), *ATLAS.ti User Conference 2013: Fostering Dialog on Qualitative Methods.* Berlin: University Press, Technical University Berlin.

Woolf, N. and Silver, C. (2014b) *How to use ATLAS.ti Powerfully: Translating Analytic Tactics in Qualitative Data Analysis.* Santa Barbara, CA: Sage.

Index

Tables and Figures are indicated by page numbers in bold print.

auto-coding 50, **87**, 90, 92, 100, 281, 297–8
  and searching 146
  of structures 316–17
automation and conduct of qualitative analysis
    336–7
axial coding 164, 236

back-ups 109
Bazeley, P. 58
Berg, B. 166
Bernard, H.R. and Ryan, G.W. 26
bibliographies 13, 126, 127
Boolean operators 50, 56, 320–1
Boolsen, M.W. 12
breaking data down 206
broad-brush coding 50, 54, 163, 206, 210
Bryant, A. and Charmaz, K. 29
Bryman, A. 32
Bryman, A. and Burgess, R.G. 16
Buzan, T. 258

CAQDAS (Computer Assisted Qualitative Data
    AnalysiS)
  activities and tools **45**
  bringing researcher close to data 335
  choice of packages 21–2, 108–9, 338
  choice of tools 59
  common tasks supported **9–10**
  general software resources **76–8**
  history of 20–1, 337
  Networking Project 76, 333, 334
  planning use of 333–4
  scepticism 335
  see also ATLAS.ti; HyperRESEARCH;
      MAXQDA; QDA Miner; Qualrus;
      TRANSANA
case studies 289–**90**
case study examples 16, 37–44, **39**, **40**, **41**
  three approaches 37
  see also Coca-Cola Commercials (case study);
      Financial Downturn (case study); Young
      People's Perceptions (case study)
case-based codes 281, 298–9
categories 17, 26, 28, 29, 68, 161
Charmaz, K. 29, 238
charts 326
checking work 315
Chicago School 28
choosing software 21–2, 22, 108–9, 338
cluster groupings 152, 195, 329
CMap 259
Cmap Tools 78
co-occurrences 320
Coca-Cola Commercials (case study) 44
  audiovisual data 44
    annotations 143–4
    direct coding **178**

Coca-Cola Commercials (case study) *cont.*
    snapshot coding **179**
    transcription **175**, 176
  charts 326–**7**
  coding **177**
  coding schemes 208, **223**, **225**
  exploring data 51, **145–6**
  inductive coding 165
  interrogating data 58, 307–8, 312–**13**
  mapping and linking concepts **270**
  multimedia data 97–8
  notes 245
  organising data 53, **289**
  processes and interpretations **250**
  processes for theory-building inductive
      analysis **39**, **40**, **41**
  project set-up and data preparation **122**
  reflection 56
  retrieval 189, 198–**9**
  testing theories 307–8
  writing 244–5
code-based and non-code-based analysis 16, 17,
    18–19
codes/coding 10, 15, 17, 18–19, 52, 158–82, 234
  abductive (combined) coding 170–5
    theory-informed **173–4**
  aim 180
  and analysis 19
  and annotations 49
  audiovisual data 136, 175–80
    direct coding 177–80
    indirect coding 175–7
  auto-coding 50, **87**, 90, 92, 100, 281, 297–8
    and searching 146
    of structures 316–17
  axial coding 164, 236
  bases for coding 180–1
  broad-brush coding 50, 54, 163, 206, 210
  case-based codes 281, 298–9
  and categories 28
  co-occurrences 320
  code frequency 193–4
  codes as collection devices **129**
  coding frames 140
  coding queries 320–1
  colouring 207, 318, 326
  comparisons 192–3, 235
  deductive coding 166–70, 206, 207
    computer- and human-driven 167
    question-based coding 168–70
    software tasks 168
    theoretical coding 168
  deductive/inductive approaches 18, 52, 54,
      160, 161
  defining relationships between 262
  definition of qualitative coding 158
  descriptive codes 166